The Age of Lone Wolf Terrorism

Mark S. Hamm and Ramón Spaaij

Columbia University Press
New York

Columbia University Press
Publishers Since 1893
New York   Chichester, West Sussex
cup.columbia.edu
Copyright © 2017 Columbia University Press
All rights reserved

Library of Congress Cataloging-in-Publication Data
Names: Hamm, Mark S., author. | Spaaij, R. F. J. (Ramón F. J.), author.
Title: The age of lone wolf terrorism / Mark S. Hamm and Ramón Spaaij.
Description: New York: Columbia University Press, [2017] | Series: Studies in
transgression | Includes bibliographical references and index.
Identifiers: LCCN 2016050672| ISBN 9780231181747 (cloth: alk. paper) |
ISBN 9780231543774 (pbk.)
Subjects: LCSH: Terrorists—Psychology. | Radicalization. | Terrorism—Prevention.
Classification: LCC HV6431.H3456 2017 | DDC 363.325—dc23
LC record available at https://lccn.loc.gov/2016050672

Columbia University Press books are printed on permanent and durable acid-free paper.
Printed in the United States of America

Cover design: Faceout Studio

Contents

Foreword

Simon Cottee

The Age of Lone Wolf Terrorism—a massive study of lone-actor terrorism in the United States—is the product of years of patient and dogged empirical investigation. It is also the culmination of a lot of hard thinking about the interior world and entanglements of that most quintessentially American iteration of contemporary terrorism: the atomized and anomic loner who kills for political purposes. Just what is it about these individuals that so captivates the authors of this book? Hamm and Spaaij, for their part, offer few clues; they are far too interested in their subject matter to indulge in any emoting about their own subjectivity. Nonetheless, it is not hard to intuit the rudiments of an answer to this question: lone actor terrorists present a conundrum, an endlessly fascinating perplexity. They were not born terrorists, and there was nothing inevitable about their trajectory toward terrorism. So how did they become transformed, or transform themselves, into terrorists? This remains an underexplored and dimly understood question, even in the field of terrorism studies, where the focus is almost exclusively on *collective* political violence. The enduring merit of *The Age of Lone Wolf Terrorism* is that it provides an empirically robust and theoretically nuanced framework for addressing how ordinary individuals can become the agents of extraordinary violence and destruction.

A common complaint leveled at scholarly work on terrorism is that it lacks a firm grounding in empirical research on actual terrorists and terrorist groups. "The study of terrorism," Martha Crenshaw wrote in 2000, "still lacks the foundation of extensive primary data based on interviews and life histories of individuals engaged in terrorism." There is some justice to the complaint. But it is not one that can reasonably be targeted at *The Age of Lone Wolf Terrorism*. Quite the contrary: drawing on an extensive database of all known cases of lone wolf terrorism in the U.S. between 1940 and mid-2016 (123 cases in total), *The Age of Lone Wolf Terrorism* provides a model for empirically driven research on terrorism, using rich case-studies, first-hand interviews with lone wolf terrorists ("Today," the authors dryly comment, "it may be easier for a convict to escape from an American prison than it is for a criminologist to enter one") and other ethnographic documents, to illustrate and support broader theorization about the social and psychological processes involved in lone actor terrorism.

There is a minor cottage industry of research on definitional issues related to terrorism. Hamm and Spaaij, thankfully, do not engage in any tortuous semantic exercises; they define lone wolf terrorism, commonsensically enough, as "political violence perpetrated by individuals who act alone; who do not belong to an organized terrorist group or network; who act without the direct influence of a leader or hierarchy; and whose tactics and methods are directed by the individual without any direct outside command or direction."

What will you learn about lone wolves from reading this book? You will learn, variously:

- that since 9/11 high-velocity firearms have displaced bombs as the favored weaponry of lone wolves;
- that over the same period the target of lone wolf attacks has switched from civilians to law enforcement and military personnel;
- that a third of lone wolves, as if reading from a Quentin Tarantino movie script, reference and copy the example of earlier lone wolves;
- that lone wolves are becoming younger (the average age of the pre-9/11 lone wolf at the time of their attack was 38, compared to 31 for their post-9/11 counterparts);
- that, typically, lone wolves are white, unemployed, single men from an urban area and with a prior criminal rap-sheet;

- that lone wolf terrorism is largely male: there have been no women lone wolf terrorists in the U.S. since 1993, and only five out of the pre-9/11 sample were women;
- that lone wolf terrorism and cloudless mental health don't tend to go together: approximately 40 percent of the lone wolves in Hamm and Spaaij's database suffered from mental illness;
- that lone wolves are motivated by a combination of personal and political grievances;
- that lone wolves are "enabled" by others, in terms of both ideological inspiration and direct unwitting assistance;
- that an active engagement with, and immersion in, a "warrior subculture" is a crucial element in the moral career of becoming a lone wolf terrorist;
- that lone wolves nearly always broadcast their intent to commit terrorism; and
- that acts of lone wolf terrorism are often catalyzed by a "triggering event."

The last five data points form the basis of what Hamm and Spaaij call "the radicalization model of lone wolf terrorism," according to which lone wolf terrorism is the culmination of a cumulative "process of human change and transformation." Although this suggests a certain neatness to the radicalization process, Hamm and Spaaij make it clear that their model isn't necessarily linear, insisting that the distinct and fateful phases they identify in the life-histories of lone actor terrorists—grievances, affinity with an extremist group and enablers, behavioral cuing of intent to do harm, and triggering events—vary in the order in which they materialize.

"He had learned the worst lesson that life can teach," writes the narrator of Philip Roth's *American Pastoral*, "that it makes no sense." *American Pastoral* is a murder mystery in which the focal point of contention is not the who, but the why. The book's central protagonist, Seymour Levov, is a successful businessman whose sixteen-year-old daughter Meredith ("Merry") blows up a post office to protest the Vietnam War, killing a bystander. All Seymour can think about is why Merry did it. She was an adored only child who grew up in a privileged and decent family in the idyllic hamlet of Old Rimrock, New Jersey. Seymour is desperate to locate "the wound" that caused Merry's violence. But there was no wound, and as the novel progresses, what Seymour learns is that his daughter is "unknowable," and that "there are no reasons," that "reasons are in books." I have a great deal of sympathy for this position. Yet Hamm and Spaaij give it a good run for its money, showing that however tangled and complex the lives of lone actor terrorists are, there are commonalties of experience across scores of cases. Perhaps terrorists are, at some level, knowable after all.

In a recent article on the "stagnation in terrorism research," Marc Sageman lamented that after a decade of sustained research on terrorism, "we are no closer to answering the simple question of 'What leads a person to turn to political violence?'" *The Age of Lone Wolf Terrorism* presents a strong case for revising this judgment.

THE AGE OF LONE WOLF TERRORISM

Introduction

The Age of Lone Wolf Terrorism

Today the United States and its Western allies face two evolving terrorist threats inextricably linked by the social and political dangers of the post-9/11 era. The first is a domestic threat posed by lone wolf terrorists. As a political matter, *the age of lone wolf terrorism* can be traced to August 15, 2011, when President Barack Obama announced that a lone wolf terrorist strike in the United States is more likely than a major coordinated effort like the 9/11 attacks. Speaking several weeks after thirty-two-year-old Anders Breivik killed seventy-seven people in back-to-back terrorist attacks in Norway, the president observed, "The risk that we're especially concerned over right now, is the lone wolf terrorist, somebody with a single weapon being able to carry out wide-scale massacres of the sort that we saw in Norway recently."[1]

In addition to the Norway massacre, a number of high-profile attacks that have occurred in the United States since 2009 have also shaped the government's reaction to lone wolf terrorism. Representing diverse points on the political spectrum, these attacks include the shooting of six police officers by a white supremacist in Pittsburgh, Pennsylvania; a fatal drive-by shooting by an Islamic militant at an Army recruiting center in Little Rock, Arkansas; the murder of a security guard by an eighty-nine-year-old neo-Nazi at the Washington, DC, Holocaust Museum; and the mass shooting at Fort Hood, Texas, by an al-Qaeda sympathizer. Other attacks tied to a single individual include the shooting of an Arizona congresswoman and her supporters in Tucson; the shooting rampage at a Sikh temple in Oak Creek, Wisconsin; two firearm attacks against Los Angeles police; the shooting at a Jewish community center in suburban Kansas City, Missouri; and the mass murders at an African American church in Charleston, South Carolina, at military facilities in Chattanooga, Tennessee, at an Oregon community college, at a movie theater in Louisiana, and at a Planned Parenthood clinic in Colorado. In all, these attacks left more than 170 innocent people killed or wounded, some grievously. Essentially, lone wolf attacks represent an undefined threat to national security because they are seemingly impossible to predict or gather intelligence on.

The second evolving threat is well defined, though equally difficult to predict. It is the threat posed by the Islamic State of Iraq and Syria (ISIS; also known as Islamic State, or ISIL), which began as an insurgency against the Western-backed Free Syrian Army battling the brutal military government of President Bashar al-Assad in Syria's civil war, but has since spilled over into Iraq. Condemning ISIS in the strongest of terms, President Obama said they have "rampaged across cities and villages, killing innocent, unarmed civilians in cowardly acts of violence. . . . They have murdered Muslims—both Sunni and Shia—by the thousands. They target Christians and religious minorities, driving them from their homes, murdering them when they can for no other reason than they practice a different religion."[2]

In the summer of 2014 Western intelligence agencies began sounding an alarm about the group's global ambitions to attack targets in Europe and the United States. On August 25, General Martin Dempsey, the chairman of the Joint Chiefs of Staff, declared that ISIS posed an "immediate threat" to the West because thousands of Europeans along with an undetermined number of Americans had joined the group, and with the passports to travel freely, they could carry the fight to their home countries, including the United States.[3] Central to this international threat was again the lone wolf terrorist. On the eve of the thirteenth anniversary of 9/11, New York City Police Commissioner Bill Bratton told reporters that compared to attacks by al-Qaeda, "ISIS would be much more into the inspiration of the lone wolf. . . . They're very sophisticated in their capabilities through their videos, through their social media, through their magazines."[4] The same day, FBI director James Comey also cast the ISIS threat in terms of homegrown lone wolf terrorists. "These are people who are never directed by al-Qaeda or any of its progeny, but are able to be inspired and trained by the material they find on the Internet," Comey said. "They can get everything they need while in their pajamas in their basement, and then emerge to engage in jihad here in the United States."[5] Senator Dianne Feinstein, chair of the Senate Intelligence Committee, told CNN, "One of the problems is that the Internet, as well as certain Muslim extremists, are really firing up this lone wolf phenomenon."[6] Armed with court-approved surveillance technology, FBI analysts intensified their efforts to monitor the activities of Americans who had expressed extremist views in online forums in an attempt to chart the radicalization of potential lone wolf terrorists. It was an instant failure.

The first ISIS-inspired lone wolf attack in America came on September 26, 2014, when thirty-year-old Alton Nolen beheaded a co-worker at a food processing plant in Oklahoma. A prison convert to Islam whose digital footprint involved ISIS propaganda, Nolen was stopped from beheading a second victim when a co-worker shot him with a rifle.

In late September an ISIS spokesman released a rambling forty-two-minute audio statement urging sympathizers to target police and military officers in countries that support the American-led bombing campaign in Iraq. The spokesman advised killing "from your place, wherever you may be. Do not ask for anyone's advice and do not seek anyone's verdict. If you are not able to find an IED or a bullet . . . smash his head with a rock, or slaughter him with a knife, or run him over with your car, or throw him down from a high place, or choke him, or poison him. If you are unable to do so, burn his home, car or business."[7]

Lone wolf attacks continued apace. On October 18, twenty-five-year-old Martin Couture-Rouleau ran over two soldiers with his car near Montreal, killing one and injuring the other before police shot and killed him. Couture-Rouleau had been under surveillance by Canadian authorities who feared that he had jihadist ambitions and seized his passport when he tried to travel to Turkey. Less than twenty-four hours later, thirty-two-year-old Michael Zehaf-Bibau assassinated a sentry with one shot from a Winchester rifle on Canada's National War Memorial in Ottawa before charging into the Canadian Parliament where he was killed by police. Zehaf-Bibau's photograph was tweeted from an ISIS account just five minutes after authorities identified him as the gunman.

On October 24, thirty-two-year-old Muslim convert Zale Thompson attacked four rookie New York City police officers with an eighteen-inch hatchet on a busy street in Queens, slashing one in the head and another in the arm, before the uninjured police shot and killed him. In a comment posted on a pro-ISIS video several weeks earlier, Thompson had described jihad as "a justifiable response to the oppression of the Zionists and the Crusaders."

ISIS's explicit call for Western supporters to carry out "lone wolf" attacks in their home countries became a core part of the group's propaganda over the next two years. Then came the massacre in Orlando, Florida. On June 12, 2016, twenty-nine-year-old Omar Mateen stormed a gay nightclub, wielding an assault rifle and a pistol, and carried out the worst terrorist attack since 9/11, killing forty-nine people and wounding another fifty-three. Before he was killed in a police shootout, Mateen shouted to his victims, "It's time to end the bombing in Syria," and then called 911 to proclaim allegiance to ISIS.[8]

For years, counterterrorism experts had issued warnings of such an attack by recognizing a blurring of distinctions between homegrown terrorism and terrorism inspired by ISIS. Lone wolf terrorism and the ISIS-inspired attacks in the United States and Canada, said Senator Feinstein in 2014, were "one big problem."[9] FBI official Michael Steinbach used a more trenchant metaphor (drawn from a method for creating computer viruses) when he warned Congress in 2015 that the ultimate danger to national security was from a new *blended threat* that combined homegrown extremism and the radicalization of Americans with the potential for becoming foreign fighters for ISIS.[10] Director of National Intelligence James Clapper agreed with this assessment in early 2016 by describing ISIS as America's "number one terrorist threat" and warned that homegrown lone wolf attacks were the most likely to be planned.[11] The House Homeland Security Committee simultaneously released a report identifying seventy-five ISIS-linked terrorist plots against the West between 2014 and 2016 and indicating that 83 percent of the plots had been waged by lone wolves or returning foreign fighters.[12] Putting a finer point on the threat assessment, terrorism expert Peter Bergen observed that "the real threat from ISIS, it has become more and more clear, isn't likely to be Americans trained abroad by the group but rather those inspired by it—once again, the lone-wolf threat."[13] Following the Orlando massacre, CIA director John Brennan gave a grim assessment of the prospect for more attacks and noted that ISIS continued to use propaganda to inspire what he termed "lone wolf" attacks like Omar Mateen's.[14]

By 2016, as ISIS gained footholds in twelve countries from the Middle East to North Africa and its recruits killed more than 1,300 civilians outside of Iraq and Syria—including the notorious attacks in Paris, San Bernardino, and Brussels—the FBI estimated that there were 250 Americans in Syria with suspected ties to ISIS or other terrorist networks.[15] Yet the United States faces an exceptional challenge in creating successful prevention and intervention strategies for this problem. Whereas well-developed European jihadist pipelines have channeled some six thousand Western fighters through southern Turkey to Syria, in the United States there appears to be no organized means for assisting radicalized Americans to travel to Syria. Instead, they make their way to the roiling conflict of the Middle East independently, embarking on the road to terrorism as loners.[16]

What, then, can be done about the new blended threat of terrorism? Answering this question requires, first and foremost, an in-depth, evidence-based understanding of the evolution of lone wolf terrorism, the radicalization of lone wolves, and the sociopolitical contexts within which the phenomenon is situated. This book aims to provide such insight. In so doing, it seeks to offer meaningful steps toward prevention by providing new ways of thinking about and responding to lone wolf terrorism. This demands a clear definition of the phenomenon, and one that distinguishes how lone wolf terrorism differs from other types of terrorism.

A precise definition of lone wolf terrorism is imperative, especially because the term is often misused or used imprecisely. Here "lone wolf terrorism" refers to terrorist actions carried out by lone individuals, as opposed to those carried out on the part of terrorist organizations or state bodies. The element of terrorism highlighted in this distinction—namely, the subject who commits terroristic violence (an individual)—follows in the tradition of researchers who define the lone wolf as "a person who acts on his or her own without orders from—or even connections to—an organization."[17] Under this formulation, a lone wolf is not one who conspires with others in an attempt to commit terrorism. The lone wolf is solitary by nature and prefers to act totally alone, although his or her radicalization to action may be spurred by violent media images, incendiary books, manifestos, and fatwas. Like most researchers, we define radicalization as the process by which individuals adopt extreme views, including beliefs that violent measures need to be taken for political or religious purposes.

While acting independently, the lone wolf is nevertheless a political creature who is not pursuing purely egocentric goals.[18] Thus assassins like Sirhan Sirhan, who in his diary wrote that he hated 1968 presidential candidate Robert Kennedy because of his support for Israel, qualifies as a lone wolf terrorist, while John Hinckley, who wrote that his primary motive for shooting President Ronald Reagan in 1981 was to impress the actress Jodie Foster, does not. In contrast to Sirhan, who had a larger political aim that transcended the immediate target of his violence, Hinckley was what the eminent terrorism scholar Bruce Hoffman would call a "lunatic assassin"—one whose motive is more often "intrinsically idiosyncratic, completely egocentric and deeply personal."[19] By contrast, the lone wolf terrorist is typically someone who acts out of a strong ideological or religious conviction, carefully plans their actions, and may successfully hide their intentions from others.

There is no professional consensus on the definition of lone wolf terrorism, and some scholars reject the term altogether. For example, Jonathan White, author of *Terrorism: An Introduction*, argues that the term has little practical value. "Some Lone Wolves are better viewed as true believing extremists who go off the deep end," he observes. "The term glorifies their actions and should not be used."[20] White is not alone in his critique. The veteran terrorism researcher Brian Jenkins also argues that "lone wolf terrorism" is "a romanticizing term that suggests a cunning and deadly perpetrator" when that is not always the case.[21] To avoid this perceived glorification, researchers often refer to the phenomenon with such pseudo-scientific buzzwords as "lone-actor terrorism," "solo actor terrorism," "single-actor terrorism," "lone rat terrorism" (the term preferred by FBI Director Comey), "solitary terrorism," "freelance terrorism," "self-starter terrorism," "idiosyncratic terrorism," "lone avenger terrorism," "lone wolf actor terrorism," or the pointless "lone wolf pack terrorism."

Yet even if the term "lone wolf terrorism" does glamorize the loner, there is no evidence that this has impeded problem-solving capabilities in the area. The term is generally accepted as valid by law enforcement and intelligence officials, politicians, journalists, and even a president of the United States. It was FBI administrators of the Reagan era, in fact, who coined the term. And it is indeed a useful analytical tool because it draws attention to the uniqueness of this specific type of ideologically motivated violence, setting it apart from common crime and the closely related hate crime. Whereas "hate crime" (or "bias crime") refers to a range of both violent and nonviolent offenses that are committed due to the perpetrator's prejudice against a particular group represented by the victim, terrorism is a violent act intended exclusively to coerce a government or a civilian population in the furtherance of political or social objectives.[22] While the lone wolf's ideological motivation partially explains why this figure has received hyperbolic attention in academic circles, it is the very status of the "loner" that makes this terrorist unique, poorly understood, and, most importantly, unpredictable in his or her selection of targets for violence. Due to their lack of terrorist training and supporting manpower, lone wolves usually avoid hard targets (such as well fortified government buildings) in favor of simpler attacks against undefended soft targets (such as public gatherings). These characteristics distinguish terrorism committed by unaffiliated individuals from that perpetrated by broader radical movements. Far more than a figure of speech, then, "lone wolf terrorism" is an epistemological recognition of the methods, validity, and scope of this particular form of political violence.

Within the literature, there is also a curious lack of consensus on what actually constitutes a terrorist who acts alone. Some experts use an expansive definition of lone wolf terrorism in terms of both motives and the number of perpetrators involved. Jeffrey Simon, author of *Lone Wolf Terrorism*, defines the crime as the use of violence against the government, society, business, or the military by an individual acting alone "or with minimal support from one or two other people" in support of political, social or financial goals. This definition includes what Simon calls the "criminal lone wolf" or "those who perpetrate their violence for purely personal or financial gain."[23] Such a wide-open definition would include small groups of opportunistic criminals lacking a political motive for their violence. Under this definition, for example, violence committed by bank robbery gangs and drug crews would be considered acts of lone wolf terrorism.

Other researchers avoid defining lone wolf terrorism and focus instead on the classification of terrorists. Paul Gill takes this approach in his book *Lone-Actor Terrorism* by considering three categories: individual terrorists who train alone and select their own targets; individuals who received training from terrorist organizations and were given targets for an attack; and couples who may have radicalized each other, but who received no external direction.[24] Similarly, other experts, such as Christopher Hewitt, have defined a terrorist group as consisting of at least four people; anything less is considered a lone wolf operation. In this definition, couples and trios are also counted as lone wolf terrorists.[25]

What these previous studies teach us, then, is that research on lone wolf terrorism is contentious and dynamic. Nowhere is the evolving nature of this research more apparent than in the authoritative work of Bruce Hoffman. In 1998, Hoffman declared that "to qualify as terrorism, violence must be perpetrated by some organizational entity with at least some conspiratorial structure and identifiable chain of command beyond a single individual acting on his or her own."[26] Five years later, Hoffman moderated his view by explicitly recognizing that terrorism can take place in the absence of such an organization, noting that lone individuals with no connection with or formal ties to established or identifiable terrorist organizations were rising up to engage in political violence.[27] Hoffman affirmed this position in the aftermath of Omar Mateen's lone wolf attack in Orlando by noting that "this was clearly an act of terrorism."[28]

As we see it, two essential issues are troubling the waters of research on this matter. One relates to the number of individuals involved in a terrorist attack. Arguably, if two or three people carry out an act of terrorism, then it is no longer a "lone" act committed by an "unaffiliated" individual since there were multiple perpetrators who were at least affiliated with one another. The other issue relates to violent radicalization. In cases of lone wolf terrorism, an aggrieved individual typically becomes radicalized within his or her own attainable means, such as violent media imagery, online sermons and political screeds, or personal veneration of terrorists who came before.[29] Small terrorist groups (including couples or trios) have a different kind of dynamic whereby radicalization occurs with the conspiratorial aid of other group members.[30]

It is around these issues that we differ from previous researchers. According to our conceptualization, a lone wolf terrorist does not conspire with anyone in their attempt to commit political violence. There is no second party, no third party or more. The lone wolf acts totally alone. Yet, as Hoffman warns about the loners, they "can be just as bloody-minded" as terrorist groups.[31] And herein lays the challenge of preventing lone wolf terrorism.

Some experts contend that the perceived threat posed by homegrown extremists is an overreaction to a rather minor problem, all things considered. From this point of view, programs to prevent lone wolf terrorism are seen as an enormous waste of time and money. Other critics claim that prevention programs are bound to fail because there is no clear profile of an individual who becomes a lone wolf and no clear pathway to the radicalization that leads to terrorism. And still other critics argue that prevention programs target only people who are critical of U.S. foreign policy. "That says nothing about whether someone is going to be committing unlawful activity," argues one critic, adding that prevention programs are "built on a false premise" that terrorism is predictable. "Mathematically, it's just not so."[32]

We argue just the opposite in this book: that violent radicalization is a social process involving behavior that *can* be observed, comprehended, and modeled in a clearly understandable diagram. Thus, insofar as the behavioral patterns can be detected by family members, friends, and other associates, a lone wolf attack may be preventable. In this book we provide evidence that lone wolf attacks have, in fact, been stopped by the interventions of family members and ordinary citizens. This finding is significant because it calls into question the taken-for-granted nature of a sociological dynamic known as the "bystander effect," which holds that individuals do not intervene to help others due to their own apathy.

The major aim of our research is to develop, test, and verify such an explanation of lone wolf terrorism. The work is organized around the radicalization model, providing a central thread of the research that we return to time and again. There are five aspects of the model, and each is examined in detail. They include the tendency of lone wolf terrorists to mix personal vendettas with political grievances (chapter 4); their affinity with extremist groups and/or online sympathizers (chapter 4); the influence of enablers, those who inspire terrorism by example (chapter 5); the deliberate broadcasting of terrorist intent through spoken and written communication (chapter 6); and triggering events, or catalysts, for terrorism (chapter 7). The model is then summarized in chapter 8, which explicates the interconnections among each aspect of radicalization and identifies similarities with the pre-attack behaviors of group-based terrorists, school shooters, and assassins. This comparative approach allows for a use of information on other types of violence to better understand lone wolf terrorists.

Our primary contribution to the literature is this radicalization model, which applies to all political motives—be they jihadist, white supremacist, or other forms of anti-government extremism. While we offer "thick descriptions" of examples to demonstrate the model, three exceptional cases of jihadist and white racist terrorism during the Obama years are extensively mined for deeper insights into radicalization. Chief among these insights concerns the process of identity transformation whereby alienated young men turn into armed warriors.

The empirical basis for the book is a study of American lone wolf terrorism we conducted for the National Institute of Justice between 2012 and 2015.[33] Our research involved the creation of an extensive database of all known cases of lone wolf terrorism (as we define it) in the United States between 1940 and mid-2016, when this book went into production.[34] Ranging from "Mad Bomber" George Metesky who terrorized New York City from World War II through the Cold War years, to the political assassins of the turbulent 1960s and 1970s, to the Unabomber, anti-abortion extremists, and white supremacists of the 1980s and 1990s, to the jihadists and neo-Patriots of the 2000s and beyond, this database is the largest and most comprehensive ever created on lone wolf terrorism. It contains evidence regarding the radicalization of such infamous figures as James Earl Ray, Sirhan Sirhan, Mark Essex, Joseph Paul Franklin, Lynnette "Squeaky" Fromme, Theodore Kaczynski, Eric Rudolph, Nidal Hasan, Jared Loughner, Wade Page, Dylann Roof, and Omar Mateen. The butcher's bill for their terrorism involves hundreds of murders and injuries caused by bombings and mass shootings. More than that, lone wolf terrorists have been able to turn the tides of history. Witness as a prime example the ineffable losses from the American body politic of Martin Luther King Jr., and Robert F. Kennedy—both killed in their prime by lone gunmen.

The database is complemented by a comparative analysis distinguishing lone wolf terrorists from individuals who undergo radicalization in either a large terrorist organization or a small terrorist cell, thereby pinpointing the precise differences and similarities between loners and group actors (including duos or trios). This allows for a comparison of lone wolves to several outstanding examples of domestic terrorism recently carried out by couples, including the Tsarneav brothers, perpetrators of the deadly Boston Marathon bombing of 2013, and the husband and wife couple who perpetrated the ISIS-inspired terrorist attack in San Bernardino in late 2015. If the radicalization model identifies a way for preventing lone wolf terrorism, perhaps it can be used to prevent terrorism waged by couples or small groups.

This book also has a theory-informed case study component based on interviews and correspondence with FBI agents, intelligence analysts, police, and five lone wolf terrorists in prison, including a young jihadist who attempted to commit the first suicide bombing in America and America's original returning foreign fighter from the Middle East. This may be the most unique feature of the work. Since 9/11, a thousand new books have been added to the terrorism literature each year. An average of four new books on terrorism is published each day; one book appears every six hours. Still, it is estimated that only 1 percent of these works have included direct contact with terrorists.[35] This book is part of the 1 percent.

This book also presents a new history of the crime of lone wolf terrorism. Interpreting past events, it seeks to explain how those events shaped the behaviors of people living at the time. Lone wolf terrorists of today, as will be seen, differ dramatically from those of the 1960s and 1970s in terms of political motives, technologies of radicalization, advanced weaponry, the means of ambushing police and military officers, and the sheer carnage they inflict, which often involves violence against women as a precursor crime. To get at the root causes of these new tendencies, we present abundant case study material showing how sociopolitical factors influence lone wolf terror, along with an overarching narrative describing the lived reality of lone wolf violence as it exists today. Thoughtful deliberations about events and details are essential for providing the historical specificity needed to flesh out the evolving nature of this mounting form of political violence. Put another way, we must describe the trees to explain the forest.

Coming full circle to the blended threat of terrorism toward the end of the book, we apply the radicalization model to an FBI sting operation involving a Muslim extremist who was prevented from joining ISIS in Syria. In other words, the radicalization model explains domestic lone wolf terrorism in the same way that it explains lone wolves who have the potential for becoming foreign fighters.

FBI sting operations comprise a major approach to preventing lone wolf terrorism in the United States. The last two chapters of the book are dedicated entirely to the sting policy, detailing who is likely to be targeted in stings, the tactics used by FBI agents to lure suspects into stings, and the ethics of arresting and prosecuting individuals who are incapable of committing terrorism without the government's assistance in providing the necessary weapons, money, and transportation to carry out a terrorist attack on American soil—all done in the name of countering violent radicalization. In no uncertain terms, the FBI's sting program is the nation's leading preemptive counterterrorism strategy against lone wolf terrorism. It is also the most controversial. Yet it has achieved some successes.

Understanding this success may be vital to national security. Doing so begins with recognizing commonalities among lone wolf terrorists. Who are the lone wolves? Do they come from similar backgrounds? Do they walk the same pathways to radicalization? Are they psychopathic "nut cases" or do they embrace fully formed ideological beliefs? Are the two mutually exclusive? And, what drives them to murder and maim for a cause they are willing to die for?

CHAPTER 1

Identifying Commonalities Among Lone Wolf Terrorists

T
o say that lone wolf terrorism is a neglected field of research is an understatement. The Congressional Research Service lists a total of 1,649 published reports on the general topic of terrorism. Only ten of them address the problem of lone wolf terrorism, and each concentrates on the lone wolf provision of the United States Foreign Intelligence Surveillance Act (FISA).[1] Wholly absent is research on factors associated with the radicalization of individuals who become lone wolves. There are no publicly available FBI reports dealing specifically with lone wolf terrorism, and (prior to our research in 2015) none by the Department of Justice (DOJ) or the Department of Homeland Security (DHS)—despite the fact that a 2009 DHS report concluded that "lone wolves and small terrorist cells embracing violent rightwing extremist ideology is [sic] the most dangerous domestic terrorism threat in the United States."[2] The research void is doubly worrisome given that lone wolves are extremely difficult to detect and defend against.[3] Moreover, the impact of existing counterterrorism measures on lone wolf terrorism remains unknown at a point in history when not only do lone wolf attacks appear to be increasing, but the lone wolf is changing the dynamics of international terrorism.[4]

Due to this lack of research, a new generation of police and intelligence officials will find that they are ill-prepared to meet the challenges of lone wolf terrorism in the future. Their college textbooks offer only scant information on the subject, typically providing case studies based almost entirely on press reports. Jonathan White's *Terrorism: An Introduction*—the most widely used university text on terrorism today—contains only three brief cases of lone wolf terrorism, all perpetrated by white supremacists.

Empirical studies of lone wolf terrorism are equally scarce, and the reason for this lack of analysis has become the subject of debate among terrorism scholars. A common explanation is that terrorism has historically been an organized crime; consequently, researchers have focused on group dynamics (such as charismatic leadership, top-down recruitment, in-group solidarity) to explain individual pathways to terrorism. A related explanation is that most scholars who study terrorism are concerned with risk factors at the level of societies, not of the individual, so it is hardly surprising that few researchers have studied lone wolf terrorists.

Three studies dominate the small body of empirically based international research on lone wolf terrorism. While these studies (and related literature on lone wolves and radicalization) offer a guidepost for future research, they are also subject to varying definitions of the crime and rely on various units of measurement, making comparisons between the studies problematic. Yet these obstacles do not preclude the identification of several commonalities among the lone wolves. As the following review illustrates, these commonalities both validate and contest some key assumptions of the broader terrorism literature.

The Hewitt Study

The earliest analysis is Christopher Hewitt's survey of three thousand terrorist incidents drawn from FBI annual terrorism reports, journalistic accounts, and previous research. Out of those incidents, Hewitt identified thirty cases of lone wolf terrorism in the United States between 1955 and 1999. Perpetrators were classified as rightwing racists, Islamic extremists, black militants, or anti-abortionists. While these cases represented only 2 percent of those arrested for terrorism offenses during the period in question, they accounted for 15 percent of all terrorist fatalities. Implying cross-cultural variations, Hewitt argued that lone wolf terrorism is predominantly a U.S. phenomenon. "American terrorism differs from terrorism in other countries," he wrote, "in that a significant portion of terrorist attacks have been carried out by unaffiliated individuals rather than members of organized groups."[5]

Hewitt explained the comparatively high incidence of lone wolf terrorism in the United States in terms of the strategy of leaderless resistance, adopted by American rightwing extremists and anti-abortion activists in response to a federal law enforcement crackdown on domestic terrorists during the 1980s. Leaderless resistance is based on the idea that a terrorist group, no matter how secret or well organized, simply cannot evade law enforcement; hence, terrorism is more readily accomplished by individual actors rather than a group.[6] A decade after the radical Right's move to leaderless resistance, FBI agents in San Diego, California, opened an investigation into the criminal activities of a self-proclaimed white supremacist named Alex Curtis. The investigation was dubbed "Operation Lone Wolf" due to Curtis's encouragement of other white supremacists to follow what Curtis referred to as "lone wolf" activism.[7] Thus was born the term *lone wolf terrorism*.

Hewitt found that lone wolf terrorism in America increased dramatically in the decades before 9/11. His statistics showed that only 7 percent of terrorist victims were killed by lone wolves between 1955 and 1977, but from 1978 to 1999 the proportion rose to 26 percent. "If the Oklahoma City bombing is included," Hewitt wrote, "a *majority* of deaths after 1978, but before September 11, resulted from terrorism by unaffiliated individuals."[8]

Though prescient, Hewitt's analysis raises two methodological concerns. The first relates to his definition of lone wolf terrorism. As discussed in the introduction, Hewitt defined a terrorist group as consisting of at least four people; therefore, in addition to individuals, couples and trios were also counted as lone wolf terrorists. Such a methodology can potentially inflate the incidence of lone wolf terrorism.[9] The second issue involves the units of analysis employed in the study. While Hewitt argued that a "significant portion" of terrorist attacks in the United States are carried out by lone wolves, he arrived at this conclusion by examining the number of victims killed in the attacks. Conflating the number of attacks with the number of fatalities can also obscure the incidence of lone wolf terrorism.

The Spaaij Study

A tighter conceptualization is offered by Ramón Spaaij in a series of reports on lone wolf terrorism in a global context.[10] Spaaij defines lone wolf terrorism as political violence perpetrated by individuals who act alone; who do not belong to an organized terrorist group or network; who act without the direct influence of a leader or hierarchy; and whose tactics and methods are conceived and directed by the individual without any direct outside command or direction. The purpose of such a narrow definition is to distinguish lone wolf terrorism from terrorist activities carried out by large terrorist networks, small terrorist groups, or states.

Under this definition, attacks committed by couples or trios do not qualify as lone wolf terrorism (therefore Spaaij's definition is not entirely compatible with Hewitt's). This effectively excludes some terrorist attacks that are often attributed to lone wolves, including the Oklahoma City bombing. Even though the attack was perpetrated by an individual, Timothy McVeigh, it is well-documented that his accomplice, Terry Nichols, played a role in building the bomb that killed 168 people, including 19 children, and wounding more for than 500 others.[11] Likewise, John Wilkes Booth would be excluded since historians are unanimous in their conclusion that Booth's 1865 assassination of President Abraham Lincoln was part of a larger conspiracy to revive the Confederate cause.[12]

The case of Lee Harvey Oswald is less clear cut. Both the Warren Commission (President's Commission on the Assassination of President Kennedy) and FBI Director J. Edgar Hoover concluded that Oswald acted alone in the slaying of John F. Kennedy. Oswald does share some signal characteristics of the lone wolf terrorist, yet aspects of the case cast doubt on his classification as such. Namely, the destruction of critical evidence concerning the Kennedy assassination by FBI agents in Dallas, as well as the refusal by the CIA to release files on Oswald's September 1963 visit to the Cuban and Soviet embassies in Mexico City—including evidence of a potential motive for the assassination—make it impossible to know the full truth, especially in ascertaining whether Oswald had been encouraged by foreign interests to kill JFK. For these reasons, Oswald cannot be considered a lone wolf terrorist.[13]

Also excluded by the definition—because they lack an overt political motive—are acts of violence committed out of personal grief or in pursuit of personal vengeance, financial profit, or fame, thereby eliminating from consideration school shootings like those at Columbine, Sandy Hook, and Virginia Tech.[14]

Based on his narrow definition, Spaaij analyzed the RAND-MIPT Terrorism Knowledge Base and the Global Terrorism Database (GTD) and identified forty cases of lone wolf terrorism in the United States between 1940 and 2010. Cases are corroborated through media and security reports, and chronologies and encyclopedias of terrorism. Spaaij also used the databases to identify forty-eight cases of lone wolf terrorism in Europe, Canada, and Australia between 1968 and 2010.

Last, drawing on media reports, writings and statements of perpetrators, police and court documents, and relevant literature, Spaaij employs a case study approach to analyze the micro-dynamics of lone wolf terrorism in five cases selected on the basis of (1) the number of fatalities and injuries, (2) the time span (ranging from a single attack to a prolonged terrorist campaign), and (3) the geographical location of the attacks. One case is drawn from each of the following countries: Austria, Israel, The Netherlands, the United Kingdom, and the United States (Unabomber Theodore Kaczynski). The analysis concentrates on four aspects of the lone wolf phenomenon: motivations, social-psychological circumstances, processes of radicalization, and interactions between lone wolves and their environment.

Spaaij identified 198 lone wolf attacks in the United States and the other nations combined, claiming 123 lives and injuring hundreds more in bombings and firearms attacks. Lone wolf terrorism killed on average 0.62 people per attack, as compared to 1.6 deaths per attack for all types of terrorism. Spaaij's study indicates that lone wolf terrorism is more prevalent in the United States than in other Western nations and, like Hewitt, Spaaij explains this variation by the relative popularity of the leaderless resistance strategy among American rightwing and anti-abortion activists. (The popularity of this strategy will be discussed later in the chapter.) A secondary analysis of Spaaij's research suggests, however, that lone wolf attacks are more common and more deadly than terrorist group attacks in the United States (controlling for the 9/11 attacks by al-Qaeda).[15]

Also consistent with Hewitt, Spaaij's data shows that American lone wolf terrorism has increased markedly over the past two decades, but it has increased markedly in other Western nations as well. Between the 1970s and 2000s, the total number of lone wolf attacks in the United States rose by 45 percent (from twenty-two to thirty-two attacks) and by a spectacular 412 percent (from eight to forty-one attacks) in the other countries.[16]

Yet it is the qualitative portion of Spaaij's work on the case studies that offers insight into the process of radicalization, or how individuals adopt extreme views, including beliefs that violent measures need to be taken for political or religious purposes. While there is no standard profile of the lone wolf, Spaaij concludes that radicalization "tends to result from a combination of individual processes, interpersonal relations and socio-political and cultural circumstances."[17] Such a view is consistent with research showing that there is no single "conveyer belt" to radicalization. Instead, radicalization is a process involving a complex interaction of multiple pathways, including personal victimization, political grievances, and the influence of radical group dynamics.[18] In this respect, Spaaij offers five insights.

First, Spaaij found a combination of personal and political motives at work in lone wolf terrorism. That is, lone wolves tend to create their own ideologies that combine personal vendettas with broader political or religious grievances.[19] Though important, this finding also highlights the difficulties of assigning clear-cut motives for the terrorist attacks. Kaczynski's political views, for example, reflected elements of anarchism and Luddism, which were intricately linked to both his personal resentment over perceived social rejection by organized society and frustration over his inability to establish a relationship with a woman. Such a worldview does not fit neatly into any of the commonly accepted categories of terrorist ideology such as right-wing racists, Islamic extremists, Black militants, or anti-abortionists.

Second, while previous research shows that terrorists do not suffer from any identifiable mental illness, the five cases examined by Spaaij indicate that lone wolves are likely to suffer from some form of psychological disturbance.[20] Those disturbances included anxiety attacks and depression for all five lone wolves, two of whom also suffered from schizophrenia. This finding is consistent with other recent studies of lone wolf terrorism.[21] Yet the lone wolves were not, to put it crudely, "crazy people." Consistent with other research in the area, Spaaij concluded that the nature of the lone wolves' psychological disorder typically did not cause lone wolf terrorists to become cognitively disorganized, and in most cases they did not fully lose contact with reality.[22]

Third, lone wolves are inclined to suffer from social ineptitude: To varying degrees, they are loners with few friends and prefer to act alone.

Fourth, even though lone wolves are by definition unaffiliated with a terrorist organization, they may identify or sympathize with extremist groups and may have been members of such groups in the past. (In their manifestos, both Kaczynski and Anders Breivik claimed to have been former members of extremist organizations.) These organizations provide "ideologies of validation" for lone wolves and function as communities of belief by transferring personal frustrations onto the transgressive "other." Accordingly, the extremist organizations play a vital role in the psychological mechanism of externalization as well as in the formation of ideological belonging.[23]

Fifth, and most important in terms of prevention, lone wolf terrorism does not take place in a social vacuum.[24] This is crucial to identifying processes of radicalization for individuals who become lone wolves. Spaaij's case studies reveal that radicalization can manifest itself in an activist stance involving the public expression of one's political beliefs and a hyperactive search for both physical and verbal or written confrontation with adversaries. While lone wolves may physically isolate themselves from society, at the same time they communicate with others through spoken and written statements. In other words, lone wolves tend to *broadcast their intent* to commit terrorism. A classic example is the "Unabomber Manifesto"—a 35,000-word essay written on a manual typewriter by Kaczynski at his log cabin deep in the Montana wilderness ("in order to get our message before the public, we've had to kill people," reads one line) and sent to the *New York Times* and the *Washington Post* with a warning that his terror would continue until the Manifesto was published, leading to Kaczynski's arrest and ending his seventeen-year bombing campaign.

Kaczynski is not the only case in point. The tendency to distribute ideas, manifestos, and overt threats extends to American lone wolves not covered in Spaaij's research. In 2009, anti-abortion activist Scott Roeder posted a column entitled "Tiller Watch" on the Internet, decrying the activities of Wichita, Kansas, abortion doctor George Tiller. Shortly thereafter, Roeder murdered Tiller while the doctor was serving as an usher at his church.[25] James von Brunn, the Holocaust Museum shooter, ran an anti-Semitic website, had his own user page on Wikipedia, and wrote a self-published book, *Kill the Best Gentiles*, which praises Adolf Hitler.[26] Prior to his 1999 Midwestern shooting spree (killing two and wounding ten), white supremacist Benjamin Smith was questioned by police in Bloomington, Indiana, for passing out hate-filled fliers against Jews, blacks, and Asians and was interviewed for a story about race relations on Indiana University's television broadcasting station.[27] Before he shot U.S. Congresswoman Gabrielle Giffords in Tucson, Jared Loughner displayed his contempt for government in numerous online postings. Loughner derided

Giffords as a "fake" to classmates and even confronted the congresswoman at a prior public meeting.[28]

It is commonly assumed that lone wolves have a critical advantage in avoiding detection before and after their attacks because most of them do not communicate with others regarding their intentions. As former DHS Secretary Janet Napolitano once noted, lone wolf terrorist attacks are "the most challenging" from a law enforcement perspective, "because by definition they're not conspiring. They're not using the phones, the computer networks . . . they're not talking with others."[29] On the contrary, it appears that they are doing precisely that.[30] Research in this area has profound implications for the prediction and prevention of lone wolf terrorism.

The Pantucci Study

Raffaello Pantucci's typology of lone wolf terrorists does not include a conventional dataset nor does it offer the rich case study material offered by Spaaij.[31] What it does provide is a novel way of thinking about radicalization. Pantucci focuses exclusively on individuals who deploy Islamist justifications for their terrorist acts in Europe and North America. Pantucci defines lone wolf terrorists as "individuals who, while appearing to carry out their actions alone and without any physical outside instigation, in fact demonstrate some level of contact with operational extremists."[32] Most importantly, this includes contact with organized extremists through the Internet. Pantucci argues that lone wolves are thereby persuaded by justifications for violence found in the narrative of world events expounded by al-Qaeda and its offshoots and that "personal issues" underlie their receptivity to such a narrative. "In other words," Pantucci concludes, "they may be troubled individuals who seek solace in the extremist ideology—an ideology that while for the most part remains self-taught, also appears to be reinforced through online contact with extremists."[33] This is similar to Jarret Brachman's notion of the "jihobbyist"—an individual who gathers with others in online chat rooms to share files and discuss their support for real-world extremists, including members of al-Qaeda and its affiliates.[34] Similarly, Marc Sageman has described the terrorist threat in terms of a "leaderless jihad," whereby the Internet has enabled a new generation of terrorist wannabes, or just "a bunch of guys"—friends, roommates, or classmates—to undergo the process of radicalization together.[35]

Pantucci identifies three cases of lone wolf terrorism that illustrate this profile, including that of Nidal Hasan, the U.S. Army psychiatrist who perpetrated the Fort Hood massacre. Reports indicate that Hasan had been psychologically traumatized by the stories of soldiers returning from battle in Iraq and Afghanistan, leading him to believe that American Muslims should not be sent to fight Muslims in foreign lands. Hasan had recently received his own deployment orders for Afghanistan, however, and this served as a *triggering event* for his attack on Fort Hood. Hasan also engaged in e-mail correspondence with Anwar al-Awlaki (1971–2011), the Yemen-based radical cleric who was then known for spreading al-Qaeda's ideology over the Internet. Consistent with Brian Jenkins's observation that lone operators sometimes reach out to others for moral reinforcement, it appears that al-Awlaki was an *enabler* of Hasan's act of lone wolf terrorism.[36] Even though al-Awlaki had nothing to do with planning and executing the attack, without him there possibly would have been no mass shooting at Fort Hood.

Pantucci's research is significant because it demonstrates that leaderless resistance—the impetus for the high prevalence of lone wolf terrorism in the United States—should not be viewed as a strategy unique to the American radical right. Indeed, in early 2010 Al-Qaeda in the Arabian Peninsula's (APAQ's) English-language online magazine, *Inspire*, acknowledged the organization's strategic shift to "individual terrorism jihad" (clandestine jihadi operations carried out by a single individual or small cells) by encouraging American Muslims to "fight jihad on U.S. soil," rather than attempting to travel overseas for training. The article celebrated the merits of mass murder and praised the Fort Hood shooter Nidal Hasan. Spaaij's research shows that the number of international lone wolf terrorist attacks inspired by radical Islam appears to be on the rise, certainly in response to this call by al-Qaeda ideologues for individual jihad. Jenkins's work likewise shows that two-thirds of the homegrown al-Qaeda-inspired terrorist plots in the United States since 9/11 have involved a single individual.

Fort Hood opened a new chapter in American terrorism, prompting Bruce Hoffman to further moderate his view on the organizational requirement of terrorism. In an interview with *Time*, Hoffman reacted to the Fort Hood shooting by saying that "this new strategy of al-Qaeda is to empower and motivate individuals to commit acts of violence completely outside any terrorist chain of command. . . . The nature of terrorism is changing and Major Hasan may be an example of that."[37] Other experts weighed in on the Fort Hood shooting, fueling debate over definitions within the terrorism studies community. Citing a former high-ranking intelligence officer who called Hasan's massacre an act of terrorism, Jonathan White countered with the opinion of government officials who referred to the shooting as the act of a mentally deranged soldier. "Even the country victimized by murder," White concluded, "seemed unable to decide on a definition of terrorism."[38] At the same time, though, the role of mental illness did assume a central role in the public conversation about lone wolf terrorism. Testifying before the Senate Homeland Security Committee in the aftermath of Fort Hood, Brian Jenkins was asked whether Nidal Hasan was a terrorist or a deeply troubled man. "The two descriptions are not mutually exclusive," Jenkins replied. "Terrorism is not an activity that attracts the well-adjusted."[39]

Such a national debate on mental illness and domestic terrorism suggests the need for a new way of looking at lone wolf terrorism. Building on previous studies and examining a host of relevant external and internal factors associated with individual pathways to violent radicalization, it is possible to create a more nuanced portrait of lone wolf terrorism. While drawing on multiple methodologies, such a study must concentrate on the relationship between radicalization processes and counterterrorism strategies to answer the central research question: How can law enforcement and intelligence communities deal with the threat of lone wolf terrorism and the challenge of identifying, targeting, and arresting people acting on their own?

CHAPTER 2

Old Wine in New Skin

Reimagining Lone Wolf Terrorism

O ur goals in this book include producing an easily accessible database on lone wolf terrorism in America and presenting a number of case studies that elucidate the lone wolf phenomenon. The objective of our study has been to validate a series of evidence-based commonalities regarding external and internal factors associated with pathways to radicalization for lone wolves and to compare the radicalization processes between lone wolves and members of terrorist groups. Again, we define *radicalization* as the process by which individuals adopt extreme views, including beliefs that violent measures need to be taken for political or religious purposes.

The American Lone Wolf Terrorism Database

The American Lone Wolf Terrorism Database that we created (hereafter referred to simply as the database) is publicly available through the National Archive of Criminal Justice Data (NACJD). It has been used for analytical purposes by the counterterrorism divisions of several large police departments, civil rights groups, journalists, and other terrorism researchers. To be included in the database, the case had to conform to the definition of lone wolf terrorism used by Ramón Spaaij in his international study—namely, that it is political violence perpetrated by individuals who act alone; who do not belong to an organized terrorist group or network; who act without the direct influence of a leader or hierarchy; and whose tactics and methods are directed by the individual without any direct outside command or direction.[1] Put simply, we define the lone wolf terrorist as someone who acts totally alone in the commission of political violence without the aid of a second party or more, although he or she may be influenced by outside sources, including books, propaganda, and media coverage of terrorists who have preceded them.

We discovered that between 1940 and mid-2016, 123 cases fit this definition; these represent all known cases of American lone wolf terrorism (as we define it) for the period.[2] A list of the 123 cases appears in the appendix, where cases are organized by case number, year of attack/plot, name of terrorist, terrorist event, and source for identifying the case.

Information on the 123 cases was gathered from an extensive review of previous research, biographies and memoirs of lone wolf terrorists, media sources, government reports, and most importantly, court documents, including criminal complaints, trial transcripts, supporting affidavits and letters, and medical and psychiatric evaluations.

As expected, information on the 123 cases was not evenly distributed. For some of the more well-known individuals—such as James Earl Ray, Theodore Kaczynski, Eric Rudolph, and Nidal Hasan—data was easily attainable through multiple sources. Fourteen books have been written about James Earl Ray alone, including two memoirs by Ray himself. The Unabomber has been the subject of eleven books. And more than 250 media articles, two government reports, and three scholarly works have appeared on Nidal Hasan. For others, such as the long-forgotten racist serial killer Joseph Christopher, the evidence was limited to a handful of contemporaneous media reports.

The database catalogues the 123 cases across 21 different variables, generating 2,583 original data points. It is the largest and most extensive database ever created on lone wolf terrorism. The database begins with a case number for the lone wolf, the individual's name (including years living), and the year he or she was active. After this basic information, the following twenty variables are addressed:

Attacks/Plots
Fatalities/Injuries
Weapons Used

Age at Time of Attack/Plot
Race/Ethnicity
Prior Criminal History
Personal/Political Grievance
Military History
Employment Status at Time of Attack/Plot
Mental Health Problems
Affinity with Extremist Groups
Marital Status
Broadcasting Intent to Commit Terrorism
Enabler of Terrorism
Locus of Radicalization
Triggering Event
Capture/Arrest
Popular Culture Influence
Influence on Popular Culture
Source

Several of these variables require further explanation. To begin with, prior research has generally ignored both lone wolf plots (as opposed to executed attacks) and information on capture and arrest. However, one study that examined eighty-six group and lone wolf terrorist plots between 1999 and 2009 found that lone wolves were more likely than group terrorists to be involved in a foiled plot.[3] Foiled plots are crucial to assessing counterterrorism responses because they are by definition terrorist "failures" and law enforcement "successes." Likewise, information on the capture/arrest of lone wolf terrorists can be used to identify the extent to which there are shared strategies in successful investigations.

Neither has previous research paid much attention to the locus (or place) of radicalization for lone wolves, even though the military, prisons, and the Internet have been a source of concern for their radicalizing potential since the first waves of terrorist attacks against the West following 9/11. Studying the locus of radicalization (or the breeding ground of extremist ideas) can determine if lone wolves are truly "self-radicalized" as many analysts suggest. The self-radicalization of lone wolf terrorists—to the extent that it exists—is critical because it is a phenomenon that lies beyond the reach of law enforcement's post-9/11 preventative strategy. The threat was identified by the National Security Preparedness Group in a report issued on the tenth anniversary of 9/11. "It is simply impossible to know the inner thinking of every at-risk person," wrote the group. "Thus, self-radicalization poses a serious emerging threat in the U.S."[4]

Also overlooked in previous research have been the criminal histories of lone wolf terrorists. Yet, such information is central to understanding the role criminality plays in the radicalization process. For example, two years before his attempted assassination of President Richard Nixon with a hijacked commercial airliner on February 22, 1974, Sam Byck was taken into custody and questioned by Secret Service agents in his hometown of Philadelphia after making a remark about killing Nixon in a barroom conversation. Byck was deemed harmless and released. In 1973, Byck was arrested outside the White House for protesting without a permit and again questioned by the Secret Service; again he was considered harmless and released.[5] Prior to her 1993 assassination attempt against abortion doctor George Tiller in Wichita, Kansas, Shelley Shannon was arrested more than a dozen times for trespassing against abortion clinics.[6] And nearly thirty years before he attacked the United States Holocaust Museum in 2009, James von Brunn tried to take the Federal Reserve Board hostage at gunpoint and was sentenced to prison for the attempt.[7]

Admittedly, there is a slight overlap between what we call an "affinity with an extremist group" and an "enabler" of terrorism. An *enabler* refers to a specific individual who either directly, albeit unwittingly, assisted the lone wolf's attack or indirectly inspired a lone wolf through their actions, speeches, books, Internet postings, or fatwas. An *affinity* with an extremist group is a more vicarious experience involving sympathy with distinct groups such the Ku Klux Klan, al-Qaeda, or ISIS. Affinity with extremist groups is a variable that corresponds to research showing that lone wolf terrorists are likely to be socially isolated but connected in some ways to "wider pressure groups."[8]

Finally, terrorism studies typically overlook the influence of media and popular culture. Media and popular cultural influences can, however, contribute to modus operandi by providing the lone wolf with a source of information for attack planning, ideology, and terrorist tactics. For instance, in stalking Martin Luther King from Dr. King's Atlanta home to Memphis, Tennessee, on the basis of newspaper and television reports, James Earl Ray arrived in Memphis on April 2, 1968. At the time, he did not know where King was staying, but on the morning of April 4, when Ray bought a copy of the *Memphis Commercial Appeal* featuring a page-one photograph of King standing in front of room 306 at the Lorraine Motel, the assassin had the intelligence he needed. When King opened the door of room 306 and stepped onto the balcony at 5:55 P.M., Ray killed him with one shot from a rifle.[9] It was that simple: The attack was predicated entirely on media sources.

Likewise, Al-Qaeda in the Arabian Peninsula's (AQAP's) *Inspire* article "Make a Bomb in the Kitchen of Your Mom" has been linked to four bombing plots by domestic lone wolf terrorists in the United States since 2011. (British intelligence eventually hacked the article and swapped out its recipes for bombs with one for cupcakes.) Subsequently, in late 2014 *Inspire* published a how-to manual for bombing airplanes, specifically designed for the lone wolf terrorist. ISIS has also published a detailed "secret agent" training manual, which is distributed on the Internet and designed to provide prospective ISIS supporters in Western nations with ways to disguise themselves and their motives when trying to plan and carry out lone wolf attacks.[10] Such propaganda is not solely intended for the lone wolf, of course. "Make a Bomb in the Kitchen of Your Mom" also served as a blueprint for the deadly explosives made by the Tsarnaev brothers in the Boston Marathon bombing.[11] Evidence indicates that prior to their attack on San Bernardino, Syed Rizwan Farook and his wife, Tashfeen Malik, dabbled online looking at jihadist propaganda, including *Inspire*. Immediately before the rampage, Malik went on Facebook to pledge loyalty to the leader of ISIS.[12] In terms of media and cultural influences, then, there may be important similarities in the radicalization of lone wolf terrorists and terrorists who belong to small groups.

The lone wolf may also influence popular culture through his or her violence. That is, terrorists are sometimes able to create a feedback loop via media representations: Terrorists commit acts of violence; those acts are depicted in literature, film, and music; and then others come along to imitate the media depictions in real life. A classic example is the assassination of civil rights leader Medgar Evers by white supremacist Byron de la Beckwith in Jackson, Mississippi, on the night of June 12, 1963. The assassination inspired author Eudora Welty's 1963 short story "Where is the Voice Coming From?," one the first attempts at giving voice to the deep hatred of Southern white supremacy. The Evers assassination was also the subject of Nina Simone's landmark 1964 civil rights anthem, "Mississippi Goddam," and Bob Dylan's "Only a Pawn in Their Game," which Dylan played at Martin Luther King's "I Have a Dream" speech before an audience of 250,000 on the steps of the Lincoln Memorial in Washington, DC, on August 28, 1963—the defining moment of the American civil rights movement.

Two Hollywood films recount events surrounding Byron de la Beckwith's act of lone wolf terrorism. The 1996 movie *Ghosts of Mississippi* tells the story of the Evers assassination with James Woods portraying Beckwith in an Academy Award-nominated performance. The other film is *Mississippi Burning* (1988), which stars Gene Hackman in a depiction of the FBI's 1964 investigation into the murder of three civil rights workers in Philadelphia, Mississippi. In the latter film, a local unemployed racist named Larry Shoemake was recruited to play the role of a pallbearer for one of the civil rights workers, a role that Shoemake later described in a suicide letter as his "contribution" to Southern history. Eight years after acting in *Mississippi Burning*—on the afternoon of April 12, 1996—Shoemake completed the feedback loop by arming himself with an assault rifle and twenty thousand rounds of ammunition before going on a shooting rampage in a black neighborhood of Jackson, Mississippi, leaving nine dead and wounded, mostly women and children. Jackson was the city where Beckwith had assassinated Medgar Evers thirty-three years earlier.[13]

This exercise in cultural criminology matters primarily for investigative reasons. During police inquiries into the 2002 Washington beltway sniper shootings, for example, absent any solid leads, investigators searched the Internet for information on movies, rap music, and literature, including criminology literature on gangs and terrorism, looking for any bit of information to help them solve the crimes.[14] Our database offers a prism for understanding this investigative potential in cases of lone wolf terrorism during the twenty-first century.

Using the Database

The database has three principal uses. First, it can help determine trends in lone wolf terrorism over time. An assessment of cases in the database provides an empirical baseline for answering the all-important question: Is American lone wolf terrorism on the rise? Second, the database enables us to explore changes in modus operandi among lone wolf terrorists, including their choice of weaponry, the frequency of copycat attacks, and the diversity of lone wolf terrorism, including variations in target selection, tactics, and the frequency of repeat attacks. This allows for an exploration of such key questions as how tactics and targets shift over time, and once new tactics are initiated, where and when they spread. Last, the database allows us to tease out evidence on the social backgrounds of the lone wolf terrorists, their motives, and most importantly, their radicalization.

How can law enforcement and intelligence communities deal with the threat of lone wolf terrorism and the challenge to identify and arrest people acting on their own? One goal of this book is to answer that question. Doing so requires an understanding of *how* lone wolf attacks are formulated and thus a rigorous analysis of the radicalization process. As discussed in chapter 1, the international literature points to a set of commonalities among lone wolves: They often combine *personal and political grievances*; they tend to suffer from *psychological problems*; and they are inclined to have an *affinity with an extremist group*. Their radicalization does not occur in a social vacuum. Instead, they often *broadcast their intent to commit terrorism*; they may be *enabled* by others; and their violence may be preceded by a *triggering event*. Our objective is to quantitatively test the validity of these commonalities through an analysis of all the cases in the database. Further validity testing is offered through qualitative research using case studies and direct contact with lone wolf terrorists. Along the way, the research situates the commonalities within the framework of those social institutions where radicalization took place and the role criminality played in the process of terrorist development, as well as surveying law enforcement efforts to detect and prevent the occurrence of lone wolf terrorism.

The database is also used as a starting point for identifying what, if any, factors distinguish lone wolves from those who undergo radicalization in either a large terrorist organization or a small terrorist group. This requires, first, a comparison of the database analyses with studies that provide databases and/or case studies of large terrorist organizations. In making these comparisons, we rely primarily on several milestone studies, including Marc Sageman's investigation of 172 Salafi jihadists involved in terrorist activities in the 1990s and early 2000s, some of whom were members of al-Qaeda;[15] Edwin Bakker's research on 242 European jihadists;[16] and four studies of domestic terrorist groups in the United States involving some 130 group actors.[17] Second, the database can be compared to studies and reportage on small terrorist cells like the Tsarnaev brothers in the Boston Marathon bombing, the ISIS-inspired couple in San Bernardino, the Washington

Beltway snipers, or the Oklahoma City bombers. Moreover, these comparisons suggest that it may be useful to think of terrorist actors along a continuum ranging from lone individuals to small terrorists groups to large terrorists organizations. Accordingly, we can begin to identify precisely how lone wolves deviate from small and large terrorist groups and why this matters from analytical and practical viewpoints.[18]

The Paradigmatic Case Studies

In chapters 9, 10, and 12, three special cases of lone wolf terrorism are selected from the database, with two focusing on post-9/11 attacks waged by jihadists and one by a rightwing extremist.[19] Individuals motivated by these ideologies currently pose the greatest terrorist threat to the United States, and that threat is the essential selection criterion for the three cases.

While more than fifty cases of lone wolf terrorism during the post-9/11 era fall into these categories, we have culled our three cases from these using the method of paradigmatic case study selection, an under-used strategy that holds great promise for terrorism research. Paradigmatic cases are carefully selected examples extracted from a larger phenomenon.[20] As applied to terrorism research, the process of isolating pivotal cases from a large database is a deliberate research tactic that can reveal key elements of the terrorism phenomenon.

The paradigmatic cases of lone wolf terrorism selected for this research demonstrated comparable modus operandi and were marked by contentious political views. Drawing from the toxic wells of both Middle Eastern politics and American anti-liberalism, the selected lone wolf terrorists engaged those ideologies in service of a particular criminal transgression: mass murder. Each case is historically significant because it functioned as a model for a *strain* of future terrorist attacks that had similar cultural contours. Here we rely on the insights of the French sociologist Michel Wieviorka who argues that paradigmatic terrorism cases are distinguished by their unity with an historical synthesis.[21]

For example, Palestinian émigré Sirhan Sirhan's 1968 assassination of Robert Kennedy was the first major incident of political violence in the United States stemming from the Arab-Israeli conflict in the Middle East. In terms of political grievance, there is a historical through-line from Sirhan to the pre-9/11 lone wolf terrorists Hussein Kholya, an Iranian extremist who hijacked a commercial flight from Texas to Mexico in 1983; to Pakistani Mir Kansi, who assassinated two CIA employees outside agency headquarters in 1993; to Palestinian Rashid Baz, who machine-gunned fifteen Jewish boys on the Brooklyn Bridge in 1994; and to Palestinian Ali Kamal, who shot seven tourists on the observation deck of the Empire State Building in 1997. This is what Wieviorka means by saying that paradigmatic cases have *unity with an historical synthesis.*

On the domestic side of the equation, James Earl Ray is an unparalleled figure in America's race tragedy of the pre-9/11 era. Ray's assassination of Martin Luther King directly inspired lone wolf terrorist Joseph Paul Franklin, the only racially motivated serial killer ever pursued by the FBI, in connection with the killing and wounding of twenty-three people between 1977 and 1980. Other cases in this strain include Neal Long's private race war in Dayton, Ohio, between 1971 and 1975, in which he killed an estimated twenty-five black men; Joseph Christopher's 1980 killing spree in Buffalo, New York, which left twelve African American men dead, some beheaded; Frank Spisak's 1982 self-declared race war in Cleveland, Ohio, where he killed and wounded four African American men and a man he assumed was Jewish; Leroy Moody's 1989 Southern mail-bombing spree, which injured or killed forty-one African Americans and a federal judge; white supremacist Benjamin Smith's 1999 Midwestern shooting spree, which left twelve black and Asian victims dead or wounded; Buford Furrow's shooting rampage at a Los Angeles Jewish Community Center in 1999, which left six Jewish and Asian victims; and Richard Baumhammers's killing and wounding of six Jews and Asian immigrants in Pittsburgh in 2000. James Earl Ray was the sociopolitical model for this deadly trail of racist violence.

Contrast these cases to that of Floyd Simpson, a self-described Christian segregationist who in 1963 murdered a civil rights worker in rural Alabama over a dispute about what Jesus looked like; or to that of the eccentric idealist Norman Mayer, who in 1982 overtook the Washington Monument and threatened to blow it up with a thousand pounds of TNT unless President Reagan initiated a national dialogue on the threat of nuclear weapons; or to that of the neo-Nazi Jonathan Haynes, who killed a plastic surgeon in 1993 and a hair colorist in 1987, believing that plastic surgeons and hair stylists where guilty of defiling Aryan beauty. Simpson, Mayer, and Haynes have had no influence on subsequent lone wolf terrorists, and their identities have been largely consigned to the dustbin of history. By contrast, James Earl Ray and Sirhan Sirhan are household names, and theirs are paradigmatic cases of lone wolf terrorism in the pre-9/11 era. The point is this: Not all terrorists are (equally) worthy of a case study. Or to use terrorism scholar Michael Kenney's more formal observation, knowledge of "dark learning" is not randomly distributed among illicit actors.[22]

Thus, it is paradigmatic cases and/or other cases within the historical strain that are most useful in research, since they represent the terrorist phenomenon at hand. Each paradigmatic case presented in our work also demonstrates a notable level of tradecraft, although the skills were not as developed as those in members of large terrorist organizations, which often have elaborate training camps, terrorist manuals, and organizational resiliencies. Even so, each paradigmatic case represents the defining criminological trait that makes terrorism tragic and dangerous—stealth, the ability to attack with surprise.

Sources for the paradigmatic cases include previous research, media reports, legal documents, law enforcement and government reports, and writings and statements of the lone wolves. Unlike previous research, ours includes interviews and mail correspondence with the terrorists. Their cases are examined through the lens of life-course criminology, which allows us to focus on the sequence of individual "turning points" leading to terrorism and to consider the extent to which those turning points are common among lone wolves.[23] At the same time, this theoretical approach leads to a greater understanding of the lone wolf terrorist in that it helps us better imagine the texture of their lives, their criminal thinking styles, and the personal and political circumstances that set them on a pathway to violent extremism.

Throughout the book, in discussing dozens of cases drawn from the database, we offer what anthropologists call "thick descriptions" (detailed accounts explicating patterns of cultural and social relations) even as we extensively mine the paradigmatic cases of the post-9/11 era for insights into radicalization, which go far beyond information available in the secondary sources used to construct the database. As stated earlier, our chief concern is with understanding an identity transformation that turns alienated young men into armed warriors, and to this end our paradigmatic cases include the jihadist Carlos Bledsoe and the white supremacist Richard Poplawski, both of whom were assassins who killed with stealth, and Sami Hassoun, the target of one of the FBI's most intensive lone wolf sting investigations of the post-9/11 era, who attempted to kill with stealth using a bomb given to him by FBI agents.

In the way of all good ethnography (and all good art), these cases allow us to take a hot-button issue and boil it down to the human beings at its center. These are the human beings at the center of our story about the age of lone wolf terrorism: Carlos Bledsoe, Richard Poplawski, and Sami Hassoun.

Interviewing Terrorist Inmates

All three were incarcerated in maximum security prisons, a setting that offers a unique opportunity for studying terrorists for a variety of reasons. To begin with, that is where many terrorists are. According to the most recent count, an estimated one hundred thousand terrorists are locked up in prisons around the world.[24] In the United States, there were 362 federal prisoners serving sentences on terrorism-related charges at the end of 2011. Most (269 inmates, including dozens of al-Qaeda members) were involved in international terrorism, and another 93 inmates were imprisoned for domestic terrorism.[25]

Given the heightened state of security in the United States since 9/11, however, gaining access to these terrorist inmates for research purposes is remarkably difficult. In fact, today it may be easier for a convict to escape from an American prison than it is for a criminologist to enter one. A researcher does not simply call the warden of a maximum security prison and ask to speak with a terrorist inmate. These prisoners live under conditions of hyper-incarceration. In order to be interviewed, inmates must first be vetted by the Bureau of Prisons, the FBI, and the Department of Homeland Security, with advice from the CIA when foreign nationals are involved. Then written permissions must be obtained from inmates, their lawyers, and institutional review boards. This tortuous research process is why so few academics even try to make contact with terrorists.

Yet compared to other high-risk ethnographic situations for studying terrorism—and none are more dangerous than conflict zones like Iraq and Syria—U.S. prisons are controlled and relatively safe environments for both the researcher and the terrorist. Once sentenced to prison, terrorists have time to rest, read, and reflect upon their past. Researchers can benefit from this contemplative state and engage in detailed dialogue with terrorists, seeking answers to such vital turning point questions as: What makes a young person adopt extremist views? How does the Internet affect that transformation? What triggers an extremist to turn violent? And what kind of signals does someone give off before turning violent?[26]

CHAPTER 3

The American Lone Wolf Terrorist

Trends, Modus Operandi, and Background Factors

Trends in lone wolf terrorism are difficult to ascertain, in part due to differing definitions of the crime and variations in data sources, the number of cases examined, units of measurement, and the time period involved. At least two recent studies conclude that American lone wolf terrorism is increasing.[1] In making this claim, the authors rely on Spaaij's research which measures trends in terms of number of attacks and deaths per incident between 1968 and 2010. While Spaaij found that the number of attacks is increasing, he also discovered that "there is no evidence that the overall lethality of lone wolf terrorism is on the rise."[2] Another study focuses solely on fatal attacks committed by lone rightwing extremists between 1990 and 2010 and finds that "there have been significantly more loner attacks that have occurred after September 11th compared with before." The authors conclude, "We do not know why this has been the case."[3] Taken together, then, these few studies paint a rather murky picture.

Adding to the confusion, some researchers contend that neither the number of lone wolf attacks nor the number of fatalities is an effective way to measure trends. Jeffrey Simon, for instance, argues: "In terrorism, it is the type of incident and its impact upon society and government that counts."[4]

Our analysis takes these complexities into account. As in the Spaaij study, the primary unit of analysis here is the lethality of lone wolf attacks.

Lethality represents the combined number of fatalities and injuries committed by each lone wolf terrorist under study. The database includes 39 lone wolf terrorists between 1940 and 2000 and 69 lone wolves between 2001 and mid-2016, for a total of 108 cases (excluding 15 sting operations).[5] By comparing the pre-9/11 cases with the post-9/11 cases across the full spectrum of twenty-one variables, we attempt to discover why lone wolf terrorism has trended the way it has.

Lethality

From 1940 through 2000, the 39 lone wolf terrorists of the pre-9/11 era committed 173 attacks, claiming 100 lives and injuring another 305. An array of firearms and homemade bombs were used in the attacks. Roughly 60 percent of the lone wolves committed a single attack, and 40 percent committed multiple attacks, including such prolific lone terrorists as Unabomber Theodore Kaczynski, who committed 16 bombings over a 17-year period, the racist serial killer Joseph Paul Franklin, who was responsible for an estimated 23 attacks over 4 years, and Muharem Kurbegovic, the so-called "Alphabet Bomber" (due to his letters to the media designating a letter of the alphabet for each attack), who launched 10 attacks in 2 years.

From 2001 through mid-2016, the 69 lone wolves of the post-9/11 era committed 147 attacks, killing 156 people and injuring 184. These attacks involved not only firearms and bombs but also small aircraft, biological weapons, knives, and construction equipment. In short, lone wolves have expanded their arsenal of weaponry in the post-9/11 era. While the multiple-attack lone wolves were prominent in the pre-9/11 era, the single-attack lone wolf has risen to prominence since then and include such lone mass-murderers as Nidal Hasan, who killed 13 and injured 30 in the Fort Hood shooting of 2009; Jared Loughner, who killed 6 and wounded 13 in the Tucson massacre of 2011; Wade Page, who killed 6 and wounded 4 in a 2012 shooting rampage at a Sikh temple in Oak Creek, Wisconsin; Dylann Roof, who killed 9 and wounded 1 in the 2015 shooting at the Emanuel African Methodist Episcopal Church in Charleston, South Carolina; and Omar Mateen, who killed 49 and wounded 53 at a gay nightclub in Orlando, Florida in 2016.

Trends in lethality are displayed in figure 3.1. A relatively stable pattern emerges in the data over time. Between 1940 and 1958, on average there

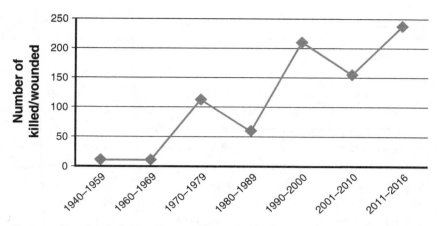

Figure 3.1 Trends in lethality of lone wolf terrorism in the United States, 1940–mid-2016

were .02 people killed or wounded per lone wolf attack. For the decade 1960–1969, the number killed or wounded per attack was 2.2. For 1970–1979, the figure was 2.3; for 1980–1989, it was 1.8; and for 1990–2000, the figure rose to 4.8—an increase due to the unusually large number of victims (182) who were wounded in attacks during the period. Of these 182 victims, 110 were injured in a single attack: Eric Rudolph's bombing of the Atlanta Olympic Games in 1996. While the number killed or wounded for 2001–2010 normalized at 2.4, between 2011 and mid-2016 it increased to 8.3. This upsurge was also due to the lethality of a particular case: Of the 235 victims for 2011–2016, 102 of them were killed or wounded by Omar Mateen in Orlando.

Figure 3.1 indicates that during the first five-and-a-half years of the 2010s, the lethality of American lone wolf terrorism rose to an all-time high. Of the period's 235 victims, 98 percent of them were killed or wounded by firearms.

The Social Impact of Lone Wolf Terrorism

The preceding numbers are superficial representations of the true threat posed by lone wolf terrorists in the United States. Simon is right when he argues that it is the *impact* of terrorism on society and government that counts.[6] In this regard, lone wolves tend to see themselves as historical figures, and indeed, they have undeniably changed American history through their violence. Several examples from the database make this crucial point.

When Byron de la Beckwith assassinated black civil rights leader Medger Evers in Jackson, Mississippi, on June 12, 1963, not only did he set the cause of civil rights in Mississippi back a decade or more, but he also created popular support for the emergence of the Ku Klux Klan in southern counties of the state where the Klan had historically failed to gain a foothold; this, in turn, created a support system for the 1964 murders of civil rights workers James Chaney, Andrew Goodman, and Mickey Schwerner in Philadelphia, Mississippi. Similarly, Sirhan Sirhan's 1968 assassination of presidential candidate Robert Kennedy in Los Angeles cut down a prominent American statesman in the midst of what was a transformative period for Kennedy, demoralizing the political base of the civil rights movement and foreclosing a range of future options for addressing issues such as Vietnam, rural poverty, and racism. And when Martin Luther King died at the hands of James Earl Ray in Memphis on April 4, 1968, part of the nation's conscience died with him. News of King's assassination sparked riots in more than one hundred American cities. Houses were set on fire, businesses were looted, complete neighborhoods were destroyed, and black militants fought gun battles with police. Dozens were killed in the disturbances; thousands were injured and arrested.

The influence of lone wolf terrorists has reached far beyond the body politic. The cultural landscape of New York City's avant-garde underwent a profound change after uber-feminist Valerie Solanas (author of the *SCUM [Society for Cutting Up Men] Manifesto*, which encouraged women to "overthrow the government and eliminate the money system") shot pop icon Andy Warhol in 1968.[7] Moments after the faded California flowerchild Lynette "Squeaky" Fromme tried to assassinate President Gerald Ford in 1975, Secret Service agents placed her in a police cruiser where a photographer captured an image of Fromme that became popular around the world as a testament to end of 1960s idealism. The attempt on Ford's life also reignited national interest in gun control legislation, which had begun to take hold after the King and Kennedy assassinations of 1968.[8]

Have lone wolf terrorists changed the course of America history since 9/11? It is too early to tell. For now, we can point to changes that appear to be more subtle. The collective effects of the Tucson, Fort Hood, Oak Creek, Charleston, and Orlando mass shootings—combined with public outcry following the Aurora and Sandy Hook massacres—have animated a national discussion on gun control, mental health, and the civil limits of political discourse. The shootings have also created a backlash as gun advocates aggressively pushed state legislatures to pass a raft of new "license-to-carry" laws based on the argument that more guns in society make us safer.[9] In addition, lone wolf attacks have led to important but little-known security improvements. Joseph Stack's 2010 suicide airplane attack on the Austin, Texas, IRS building led to more than $38 million in security upgrades at IRS offices nationally. Likewise, Paul Ciancia's 2013 shooting at the Los Angeles International Airport reignited post-9/11 debate over the effectiveness of airport security and led to suggestions for arming Transportation Services Administration (TSA) officers. Perhaps the most poignant change occurred only days after white supremacist Dylann Roof's rampage at the African American church in Charleston, when a contentious public symbol of South Carolina's past, the Confederate battle flag, was removed from the state capitol grounds.

A New Target: Law Enforcement and the Military

A relatively newer trend in terrorism involves acts waged by jihadists influenced by al-Qaeda and its offshoots, a phenomenon linked to the remarkable rise of organized Islamist terrorism worldwide over the past two decades. Consistent with this trend, lone jihadists in the United States since 9/11 differ from lone Middle Eastern extremists of the pre-9/11 era. In the years before 9/11, Middle Eastern loners killed or wounded 22 victims in 5 attacks, or 4.4 people per attack. Since 9/11, lone Islamists (including ISIS supporters) have killed or wounded 179 in 16 attacks, or 11.1 per attack. This trend belies Marc Sageman's 2008 prediction that "Islamist terrorist attacks in the United States are unlikely because the al Qaeda ideologies do not resonate with the personal experience of American Muslims."[10] They clearly do.

There has also been an important change in the targets of terrorism. Like Sirhan Sirhan and James Earl Ray, lone wolves of the post-9/11 era have continued to target political leaders, the most notable cases being Jared Loughner's 2011 shooting of U.S. Representative Gabrielle Giffords and her supporters at a town hall meeting in Tucson and Oscar Ortega-Hernandez's attempt on the life of President Obama and his family in

2011. But in large part, lone wolves have increasingly targeted uniformed police and military personnel.

A total of 12 law enforcement officers were killed or wounded by lone wolf terrorists in the 60 years preceding 9/11. This figure quadrupled in the first 16 years following 9/11, when the number of law enforcement personnel killed or wounded by lone wolves rose to 50. A majority of the attacks occurred between 2009 through 2015—the years coinciding with the Obama presidency.

These attacks began with white supremacist Richard Poplawski's killing and wounding of six Pittsburgh policemen in 2009. A paroxysm of lone wolf violence against police followed the Poplawski incident. They included:

- Christopher Monfort's 2009 police ambush in Seattle, Washington, which killed one officer and wounded another;
- Joshua Cartwright's killing of two Florida policemen in 2009;
- James von Brunn's 2009 firefight with security officers inside the Washington Holocaust Museum, which killed one;
- Byron Williams's shootout with the California Highway Patrol in 2010, which wounded two officers;
- Wade Page's shooting of a police officer eight times during his 2012 rampage at the Sikh temple in Oak Creek;
- Thomas Caffall's 2012 police shootout in College Station, Texas, which left five officers killed or wounded;
- Christopher Dorner's attacks against the Los Angeles Police Department in 2013, which killed and wounded four officers, a police captain's daughter, and her fiancé;
- Paul Ciancia's shooting at the Los Angeles International Airport in 2013, which killed and wounded three TSA officers;
- Eric Frein's 2014 attack on Pennsylvania State Police, which killed one officer and wounded another;
- Zale Thompson's 2014 hatchet attack against New York City police, which injured three;
- Shannon Miles's 2015 killing of an officer in Houston, Texas;
- Robert Dear's killing and wounding of six officers at a Planned Parenthood clinic in Colorado Springs in late 2015.

Before 9/11, lone wolf attacks against police were motivated by black power, the Palestinian question, and abortion. Since 9/11, attacks on law enforcement have emanated primarily from anti-government extremism and white supremacy anger over the election of the nation's first African American president. The paradigmatic case here is Richard Poplawski.

Not a single member of the United States military was targeted by lone wolf terrorists prior to 9/11. Even during the most turbulent period of protest against the Vietnam War, lone wolves did not attack military personnel. Since 9/11, lone wolves have killed or wounded fifty members of the military. Lone wolves have also attacked military bases or have been arrested in thwarted attacks against military installations. All of these terrorist events were bracketed by the years 2009 to 2015. In every case, they were conducted by al-Qaeda or ISIS sympathizers angered over U.S. foreign policy.

The first such case is Carlos Bledsoe's drive-by shooting at the Army recruiting center in Little Rock, Arkansas, on June 1, 2009, which killed one soldier and injured another. Subsequent attacks included:

- Nidal Hasan's attack at Fort Hood, which killed thirteen soldiers and wounded thirty others in what was then the deadliest terrorist attack against the United States since 9/11;
- Naser Jason Abdo's attempted bombing at Fort Hood in 2011;
- Yonathan Melaku's shooting spree at military facilities in Washington, D.C., in 2010 and an attempted bombing of Arlington National Cemetery in 2011;
- Khalid Aldawsari's 2010 attempted bombing of the homes of three former U.S. soldiers who were stationed at Iraq's Abu Ghraib prison and the Dallas home of former President George W. Bush;
- Mohammad Abdulazeez's 2015 attack on armed forces recruiting centers in Chattanooga, Tennessee, which killed and wounded six unarmed soldiers.

In each of these cases, lone jihadists waged terrorist attacks with identical targets, ideological motives, and religious inspiration. The paradigmatic case is Carlos Bledsoe.

These findings contradict other recent studies of lone wolf terrorism in America, especially research based on the Global Terrorism Database (GTD), a product of the National Consortium for the Study of Terrorism and Responses to Terrorism (START) Center at the University of

Maryland. START's analysis of lone wolf terrorism in the United States between 1992 and 2010 suggests that "the targets of lone actors tended to be private citizens and abortion facilities." The START researchers claim that there was not a single case of lone-actor terrorism in the United States in 2009.[11] Yet 2009 was the year of military and police attacks by Bledsoe, Hasan, Poplawski, Cartwright, von Brunn, and Monfort, as well as a Massachusetts killing spree by neo-Nazi Keith Luke, who also raped a black woman, attempted to commit mass murder at a synagogue, and then engaged in a police shootout. All told, twenty-one police and military officers were killed in these 2009 attacks and thirty-four were wounded. Another three civilians were killed or wounded by Luke. Ignoring these attacks not only misrepresents the threat of lone wolf terrorism in the United States, but also disregards the motives behind this new incarnation of the American lone wolf terrorist—namely, anti-government and white supremacist rage over the presidency of Barack Obama and Islamist discontent over the wars in Iraq and Afghanistan.

How can this discrepancy be explained? START claims that its GTD is the "most comprehensive unclassified data base on terrorist events in the world"—yet it fails to include the historic case of Nidal Hasan. According to START researchers, this is a technical error: Hasan and the other 2009 cases either did not exist in the GTD or they were incorrectly coded and therefore excluded from the analysis.[12] Remarkably, however, a simple Google search of "lone wolf terrorism in America 2009" yields information on nearly all of the missing START cases.[13]

Weaponry

Equally important to changes in modus operandi is the lone wolf's choice of weaponry. Prior to 9/11, a total of 234 victims were killed or wounded in bombings perpetrated by American lone wolf terrorists—a phenomenon similar to the bombing campaigns of terrorist organizations around the world during much of that period. In 1971 and 1972 alone, the FBI reported more than 2,500 domestic terrorism bombings, nearly five a day; yet there were few casualties.[14]

Since 9/11, there have been only six victims of lone wolf bombings in the United States (although there have been several foiled plots), all carried out in the Midwest over a five-month period in 2002 by anti-government extremist Luke Helder.[15] This decline may reflect the stringent government controls on the purchase of bomb-making materials enacted in the aftermath of the Oklahoma City bombing. Consistent with the relaxation of U.S. gun laws since the early 2000s, the lone wolf's preferred weaponry is now a staggering range of high-velocity firearms. Not only has the lethality of firearm weaponry increased by an order of magnitude, but lone wolf attacks have also become more personal.

The single greatest act of lone wolf terrorism against law enforcement before 9/11 was Mark Essex's 1972–1973 attack on the New Orleans police. From a sniper's perch, Essex used a .44 Magnum rifle to kill five policemen and wound five more. In contrast, Richard Poplawski used an AK-47 assault rifle, a shotgun, and two handguns to shoot the six Pittsburgh policemen from close range inside his mother's home. Poplawski was so close to his victims that he could read their name badges. The United States Marshals Lone Wolf Terrorism Task Force refers to this method of killing as *corralling*; it was also used by (among others) Nidal Hasan, Robert Dear, and Dylann Roof, as well as Omar Mateen, who killed his victims inside the packed "comfort zone" of a gay nightclub. "This means their targets, like sheep, will not have any guard up and be paying little attention," said a task force member.[16]

Among the forty-two post-9/11 lone wolf terrorists who committed their attacks with firearms, 50 percent of them used multiple weapons, 32 percent used only handguns, and 14 percent used only assault rifles. The most frequently used gun was the 9mm Glock semi-automatic pistol. The lightweight but durable and relatively inexpensive 9mm Glock has therefore assumed a major role in the gun culture of American lone wolf terrorism. The renowned political historian Richard Hofstadter popularized the phrase "gun culture" when writing about increased gun violence in the United States in 1970 and noted that a certain mystique or "celebrity" is often attached to particular firearms.[17] The celebrity firearm has a long tradition in the American terrorist underground. The Ruger .223-caliber assault rifle is an example. The gun was used in the notorious 1984 slaying of a black Arkansas state trooper by a member of the revolutionary white supremacist group known as the Covenant, the Sword, and the Arm of the Lord. The same type of weapon was used in a string of 1994 bank robberies by the Midwestern terrorist group called the Aryan Republican Army. Among the guns confiscated from Timothy McVeigh after he blew up the Oklahoma City federal building was a Ruger .223-caliber assault rifle and a

.45-caliber Glock pistol.[18] In his manifesto, Anders Breivik claimed that he was profoundly influenced by McVeigh; that is why Breivik used a Ruger .233-caliber assault rifle and a 9mm Glock in his deadly corralling of victims at the Norwegian youth camp.[19] There is some evidence, then, that group-based terrorists and lone wolf terrorists share a common gun subculture that extends beyond U.S. borders.

The examples of lone wolves using advanced firearm weaponry are overwhelming. Christopher Dorner used a 9mm Glock, an AR-15 assault rifle, and a silencer-equipped Remington sniper's rifle against his victims in Los Angeles. Five victims were ambushed at close range as they sat inside their cars. At Fort Hood, Nidal Hasan used a FN Five-seven semi-automatic pistol which he had fitted with two laser sights, one red and one green, to fire on 400 unarmed soldiers inside the Soldier Readiness Processing Center as they were being deployed to Afghanistan. In his ambushing of Texas police, Thomas Caffall stood at his front door and fired dozens of rounds from a Vz 58 Tactical Support rifle, a Mosin-Nagant M91/30 rifle with a bayonet, and a .40-caliber Glock pistol belonging to a slain policeman. For backup, Caffall possessed a Soviet Red Army carbine and a Czech assault rifle.

This access to and use of devastating firepower has helped to make lone wolf terrorism a more personal affair. In the ultimate political assassination of the pre-9/11 era, James Earl Ray took a sniper's position across the street from the Lorraine Motel and fired one shot from a Remington 30.6-caliber rifle into Dr. King's jaw. The most notable assassination attempt since 9/11 has been Jared Loughner's attack on Gabrielle Giffords at the Tucson town hall meeting. Using a 9mm Glock with an extended clip, Loughner walked straight up to Giffords and shot her point-blank in the forehead before spraying the crowd with gunfire—leaving eighteen more victims, including a nine-year-old girl who died instantly. This is a fundamentally different form of lone wolf terrorism—more personal and more carnal than anything seen before.

Innovation in Lone Wolf Terrorism

A few lone wolves have used more creative weaponry to carry out their attacks. For example, over a two-month period in 2013, Jason Woodring, a thirty-seven-year-old anarchist and methamphetamine addict, used a hacksaw, bolt cutters, gasoline, and a tractor with a winch to down two electrical power lines and destroy a high-voltage switching station in rural Arkansas. Although no one was killed or wounded, some ten thousand customers lost power for several hours and the damage to electrical power stations was estimated at $3 million. Notable about Woodring's attack is his targeting of certain crucial components of the power grid. Upon police questioning, Woodring admitted that it took him a month to remove bolts from one electrical tower base since he took just a few bolts at a time (this may be where the meth proved useful). Woodring said that it took him thirty minutes to saw through the live power line connectors, allowing power lines to fall across a railroad track, which then created a dangerous situation for the next oncoming train.[20] Woodring's monkey-wrenching may represent a new era of terrorism tactics, one that parallels the unsolved April 2013 sniper attack on seventeen giant transformers that funnel power to California's Silicon Valley. The attack raised fears that the country's power grid is vulnerable to terrorism and led to closed-door, high-level meetings in Congress and the White House. There is also an international correlate. In Europe, terrorist organizations have been linked to some 2,500 attacks on transmission lines or towers from 1996 to 2006.[21] Woodring is the first American lone wolf terrorist to adopt this tactic, which represents a genuine innovation.

Copycat Attacks

One unexpected finding in our analysis of the database is evidence of a copycat phenomenon in a third of the cases. A partial motive for Sam Byck's 1974 assassination attempt against President Nixon was the inspiration he gained from news coverage of Mark Essex's police killings in New Orleans a year earlier. Sara Jane Moore's 1975 attempted assassination of President Gerald Ford in San Francisco came less than three weeks after Lynette Fromme's attempt on Ford's life in Sacramento.

Similarly, by examining the elaborate network of anti-abortion activists in America, we can connect the dots between violent abortion clinic attacks by Shelley Shannon (1992–1993), Michael Griffin (1993), Paul Hill (1994), John Salvi (1994), and James Kopp (1998). In a comparable situation, neo-Nazi Bufford Furrow began planning his August 10, 1999, attack on the Los Angeles Jewish Community Center on the Fourth of July, 1999, the same day that white supremacist Benjamin Smith ended his Midwestern killing spree by committing suicide after a high-speed police chase, while white racist Richard Baumhammers's April 28, 2000, Pittsburgh killing spree may have been retaliation against black racist Ronald Taylor's widely publicized killing spree in nearby Wilkinsburg, Pennsylvania, two months earlier.

Copycat attacks have continued into the post-9/11 era. Examples begin with Shelley Shannon's 1993 gun wounding of Wichita abortion doctor George Tiller. Sixteen years later, on May 31, 2009, Tiller was shot through the eye and killed by anti-abortion extremist Scott Roeder. (Roeder was romantically attracted to Shannon and had visited her numerous times while she was in prison for the Tiller shooting.) The following day, Carlos Bledsoe attacked the Little Rock Army recruiting center, and then Bledsoe became the model for Nidal Hasan's copycat attack on Fort Hood five months later. Hasan, in turn, inspired Naser Jason Abdo's attempted bombing at Fort Hood in 2011, as well as playing a key role in the radicalization of Orlando shooter Omar Mateen. News coverage of Hosam Smadi's plot to bomb a Dallas skyscraper in 2009 motivated Khalid Aldawsari to research the feasibility of carrying a backpack bomb into a Dallas nightclub in 2011. While Smadi was a controlled FBI sting operation, Aldawsari was not, a fact that suggests that the FBI's actions in the Smadi case may have been the catalyst for an attempted act of real terrorism by Aldawsari.

Criminologists view the "copycat effect" in terms of a tendency—largely among young males with prior criminal records, severe mental health problems, or histories of violence—to be inspired by sensational publicity surrounding violent murders.[22] The constant media coverage of these events gives those with preexisting violent tendencies a chance to enjoy their "fifteen minutes of fame" as Andy Warhol put it, through the act of imitation. The effect of the media is indirect, in the sense that media coverage gives people who are already violent the idea of how to commit violence, rather than directly influencing a large number of criminals. Criminals are often obsessed with the shock value of their actions, and those with a violent tendency will most likely exercise that tendency.

But the lone wolf terrorists in our database display a different profile. Of the twelve lone wolf copycats identified in the preceding paragraphs, only three were young. A third were middle aged or older, including Byck (age 44), Moore (age 45), Hill (age 40) and Roeder (age 51). Although most had a criminal record, only two had histories of violence (Furrow and Baumhammers). Several had been arrested numerous times for protesting their causes (Byck and especially James Kopp, who was arrested dozens of times for his anti-abortion actions). And only three had mental illnesses (Furrow, Baumhammers, and Roeder).

What distinguishes the lone wolf copycats from traditional criminal copycats is motive: Rather than (merely) seeking fame, the lone wolf terrorists imitated other lone wolves to make a political point. Sam Byck, for instance, may have been content with carrying on his nonviolent protests outside the Nixon White House were it not for a widely circulated January 1973 newspaper article about the Essex attack on New Orleans police, including the detail that Essex had scrawled *"Kill Pig Nixon!"* on his apartment wall. For Byck, Essex demonstrated that one person dedicated to political violence could capture the media's attention. A similar phenomenon is apparent in the case of James Kopp and the other anti-abortionist protesters who were intensely committed to their cause. Rather than seeking fame only for themselves, the lone wolves were committed to bringing attention to their causes.

Herein lies a difference between lone wolf terrorists and mass murderers. Anthropologist Elliott Leyton has argued that while multiple murderers see themselves as "soldiers on a mission," as "unjustly maltreated heroes wreaking vengeance on their oppressors," their protest is "not on behalf of others"; instead, they murder in order to "relieve a burning grudge engendered by their failed ambition."[23] Although, as will be seen, this argument has relevance to lone wolf terrorism, too, it fails to fully acknowledge the ways in which lone wolf terrorists are shaped and motivated by ideology and how these processes are influenced by those who have gone before and by extremist groups or movements with whom they identify.[24]

By turning political causes into violent action, lone wolf terrorists become role models for others who are sympathetic to those causes, inviting what European scholars call "bandwagon attacks."[25] Like nearly every other aspect of lone wolf terrorism, the Internet and social media have greatly influenced this phenomenon. The prison memoirs of Shelley Shannon and Eric Rudolph are currently featured on the anti-abortion Army of God website, which influenced lone wolf Paul Evans's 2007 attempted bombing of an abortion clinic in Austin, Texas. Evans's own writings, such as his essay on "Methodical Terrorism," are now also featured on the Army of God site. Carlos Bledsoe and Nidal Hasan have been praised in the pages of *Inspire* magazine, which, in turn, influenced Antonio Martinez and other jihadists targeted in the FBI stings, while Richard Poplawski and the "martyred" Benjamin Smith are routinely feted on *Stormfront* and other white supremacy websites, inspiring bandwagon attacks by the likes of Kevin Harpham, who in 2011 tried to attack a Martin Luther King Day celebration with a pipe bomb containing rat poison.

Hoaxes and Aborted Attacks

In addition to the 173 attacks recorded in the pre-9/11 era, lone wolves were also responsible for at least 34 threats or aborted attacks (not recorded in the overall attack count).[26] Included was white supremacist Leroy Moody's mailed death threats to a dozen federal judges in 1989 and the Alphabet Bomber's mock biological attacks against Congress and the United States Supreme Court in 1974.

Due to technological advances, the post-9/11 era has seen a greater number of threats and aborted attacks, some causing serious disruptions of public life. (Hoaxes and aborted attacks were also excluded in the attack count for post-9/11.) In a copycat of the 2001 anthrax attacks waged by the government scientist Bruce Ivins, anti-abortion extremist Clayton Waagner mailed 554 letters to abortion clinics across the United States in 2001, each containing white flour and an anthrax threat. His letters disrupted clinic operations and caused hundreds of abortion clinics to be temporarily shut down. Likewise, from a Denver jail cell inmate Marc Ramsey singlehandedly brought John McCain's 2008 Republican presidential campaign to a temporary standstill as a result of a mailed anthrax hoax, again a copycat of the Ivins attack. Later that year, FBI agents removed a cache of radioactive materials from the Maine home of neo-Nazi James Cummings in what represented the first attempt to build a dirty bomb in the United States (another innovation in lone wolf terrorism). Cummings had purchased the radioactive materials over the Internet and planned to detonate his bomb at the presidential inauguration of Barack Obama, but the attack was aborted when Cummings's wife murdered him.

Background Factors

Who are the American lone wolf terrorists? Have there been any significant changes in their backgrounds over time? What factors, if any, distinguish lone wolf terrorists from organized terrorists? Our best answers to these questions, based on the research, are below.

Age and Education

Edwin Bakker's study of 242 European jihadists indicates that Western Islamist groups are comprised of single males aged 22 to 24 who have some university education.[27] In his analysis of 172 global Salafi Jihadists (predominantly male) Marc Sageman found that the average age for joining the jihad was 26 years old. These "neo-jihadists" were well educated, with over 60 percent having some college experience.[28] Organized domestic terrorists in the United States have historically been approximately 27 years of age, yet most of them lacked education beyond high school.[29]

There is a significant age difference between American lone wolf terrorists and organized terrorists. The average age of pre-9/11 lone wolves at the time of their attack/plot was 38, more than ten years older than the average member of a terrorist group. The average age of post-9/11 lone wolves at the time of their attack/plot was 31 years old. The age differences may reflect differences in the radicalization process: Organized terrorists are typically radicalized in networks of common believers and are thus subject to peer-group pressure to adopt militant views, while the process of radicalization for lone wolves is more individualized and may thereby result in their taking longer to embrace views that make terrorism possible. The other point to be made is that while lone wolf terrorists are consistently older than organized terrorists, they are becoming younger. Before 9/11, teenagers did not commit lone wolf terrorism. This has changed. Included among the post-9/11 cases is fifteen-year-old al-Qaeda sympathizer Charles Bishop who committed a suicide airplane attack on the Bank of America in Tampa, Florida, in 2002; seventeen-year-old neo-Nazi Derek Shrout who attempted to bomb an Alabama high school in 2013; neo-Nazi Jacob Robida, eighteen, who killed and wounded 6 in a cross-country shooting spree in 2006; and eighteen-year-old ISIS sympathizer Faisal Mohammad who wounded four college students in a knife attack at the University of California, Merced, in 2015.

American lone wolf terrorists also tend to be less educated than those who join international jihadist organizations.[30] Less than one-third of the pre-9/11 lone wolf terrorists were university educated. One notable exception was the Unabomber, Theodore Kaczynski, who graduated from Harvard at the age of twenty and earned a Ph.D. in mathematics from the University of Michigan before going on to become the youngest professor ever hired at the University of California, Berkeley. He had an IQ of 167.[31] About one-third of the post-9/11 lone wolves were educated in universities. Nidal Hasan and Bruce Ivins both held graduate degrees, while James von Brunn was a member of Mensa, the society for certified geniuses. Overall, though, educational levels have been relatively low for lone wolf terrorists. Whereas 60 percent of Sageman's neo-jihadists were university educated, fewer than half as many American lone wolves had attained this level of education. The reason for these differences may be found in socioeconomic factors.

Race, Class, Marital Status, and Criminal History

The pre-9/11 lone wolves were predominantly white, urban, unemployed, single males with a prior criminal record. This sketch is virtually identical for the post-9/11 cases. A majority of them were single (80 percent) white males (64 percent) who lived in urban areas (70 percent). Most were unemployed (73 percent) and had a criminal background (60 percent).

These findings are consistent with research showing that rightwing loners in the United States are more likely than terrorist group members to be unmarried.[32] The findings are also in line with Bakker's research on European jihadists—mainly second-generation Muslim male migrants from North Africa—which shows that most were from the lower classes, fewer than half were married, and about a quarter of them had a criminal record.[33]

Once again, however, the American lone wolves differ from the Salafi jihadists in Sageman's research, the majority of whom were married with children and had committed only petty crimes in the past.[34] In terms of employment, at the time of joining the jihad, 75 percent were either professionals in scientific occupations or public servants, including policemen, civil service employees, and university students.[35] (Even so, Sageman noted: "Just before they joined the jihad, the prospective mujahedin were socially and spiritually alienated and probably in some form of distress."[36]) Robert Pape's pioneering study of 462 Islamic suicide bombers also indicates that only 17 percent of the terrorists were unemployed or from the lower classes.[37]

One explanation for these class differences, as well as educational differences, is that nationalistic movements—such as American white supremacy movements—have tended to produce terrorists from the lower classes, while religious terrorists like al-Qaeda members come from all classes.[38] Moreover, pathways to radicalization develop differently for different causes.[39] American white supremacy groups can have a religious foundation, as is the case in obscure death cults like Christian Identity and the Phineas Priesthood, yet only one lone wolf terrorist committed his attacks for such a religious ideal (neo-Nazi Benjamin Smith, who also had an upper-class background). In other words, religion plays a minor role in lone acts of terrorism committed by white supremacists. Since a number of the American lone wolves have demonstrated an affinity with white supremacy groups, and since most white supremacists come from lower class backgrounds, this may explain the comparative class differences between lone wolves and organized jihadists.

Military Experience

Sageman and Bakker did not examine the military backgrounds of organized Islamists. Yet military experience plays a crucial role in distinguishing American lone wolf terrorists over time. More than half of the pre-9/11 lone wolves had served in the military, some in combat roles during World War II, Korea, and Vietnam. Less than a quarter (24 percent) of the post-9/11 lone wolves had served in the military, however, and only two had combat experience: one in Vietnam and the other in World War II (eighty-nine-year-old James von Brunn, who was a decorated combat veteran). None of the post-9/11 lone wolves had served in the Iraq and Afghanistan wars.

In this way, American lone wolf terrorists of the post-9/11 era resemble U.S. rightwing domestic terrorist groups during the early 1980s. The most dangerous terrorist organizations of that period—the Order (responsible for assassinations, armored truck robberies, and bombings across the American West) and the Covenant, the Sword, and the Arm of the Lord—were comprised of men who had come of age in the crucible of Vietnam, yet none had made a personal appearance on the battlefield.[40] Adopting a "New War" mentality against immigration, drugs, crime, and farm foreclosures, the traditions of what scholar James William Gibson calls "a warrior's solo pursuit of battle glory" merged with the killing capacity of new firearm technology. Assault weapons, gun ranges, and "action-adventure" movies like *Rambo* became the cultural rage while paramilitary groups also thrived and provided another outlet for the militants' warrior dreams.[41] During the 1990s, this warrior subculture produced two of the twentieth century's most ruthless terrorists: Timothy McVeigh and Eric Rudolph.[42]

Analogous sociological shifts are afoot in post-9/11 America. After years of dormancy, the radical Right has experienced a revival brought about by the Obama presidency, rising unemployment, and the contentious debate over immigration. Revivalist views also play a key role in the global jihad movement, given that religious terrorism stems from the belief that the world has fallen into a morass of greed and moral depravity. As the wars in Iraq, Afghanistan, and Syria galvanized young Muslims worldwide to join the fight against the West, homegrown radicals actively sought involvement with al-Qaeda and ISIS by networking with one another over the Internet.[43] Meanwhile, the United States continued to operate the most permissive system of firearms regulation in the Western world, providing the lethal means for a new generation of domestic radicals to act out their warrior dreams.

Gender

Scholars of the Salafi Jihad, including Bakker and Sageman, conclude that women play a nebulous role in the movement.[44] Historically, this has not necessarily been the case for lone wolf terrorists. Five of the pre-9/11 lone wolves were women, and all of them were assassins. Along with Shelley Shannon, Sara Jane Moore, Lynette Fromme, and Valerie Solanas, they included a forty-two-year-old African American woman named Izola Curry who attacked Martin Luther King with a penknife at a Harlem book signing in 1958, believing that King had become a member of the Communist Party. It nearly cost King his life. He memorialized the attack in his "I've Been to the Mountaintop Speech" of April 3, 1968, the evening before he was slain by James Earl Ray. "The X-rays revealed that the tip of the blade was on the edge of my aorta, the main artery," said King in the speech. "And once that's punctured, you're gone, drowned in your own blood—that's the end of you."[45]

Women are capable of becoming lone wolf terrorists in the same way that men are. Yet there is also a difference between lone wolves of the two eras. There have been no female lone wolf terrorists in the post-9/11 period. In fact, there have been no female lone wolf terrorists in the United States since 1993.[46]

The gendered nature of lone wolf terrorism is often noted, but rarely treated in a satisfactory manner. Jeffrey Simon posits that a number of factors contribute to the predominance of men in the world of lone wolf terrorism. First and foremost, he argues, women are more risk-averse than men, and they value human interactions and connections more than men.[47] The present analysis provides a more sociological interpretation by linking lone wolf terrorism to engagement with a warrior subculture that fuses violence and politics with masculinity. This subcultural script provides a model for problem-solving: It sensitizes (and socializes) the lone wolf to the cause and to the belief that a violent attack is both necessary and a transformative experience. We will also show, later in the book, that for some of the most lethal lone wolf terrorists, interpersonal conflicts with women can act as a triggering event for their terrorist campaigns.

Mental Health

Finally, lone wolf terrorism has an important mental health component. Several of the lone wolves in our database had been committed to psychiatric hospitals and subsequently released prior to their attacks. In contrast, Sageman's and Bakker's researches show that members of large jihadist groups do not display any psychological pathology.[48] Neither is there any indication that small-group terrorists have psychological problems. The Boston Marathon bombers, the San Bernardino shooters, the Washington Beltway snipers, and the Oklahoma City bombers—none of these terrorists was diagnosed with a mental illness.

In comparison, fully half of the pre-9/11 lone wolves suffered from a documented mental illness.[49] Nine of the thirty-nine (23 percent) were diagnosed as either schizophrenic or bipolar. Seven (18 percent) were diagnosed as manic depressives, and another four (10 percent) were known to be delusional. While the overall figure was lower for the post-9/11 cases, the number of unknown diagnoses was higher. Among those whose mental health could not be determined was an important clutch of mass shooters: Wade Page, Nidal Hasan, James von Brunn, and Omar Mateen.

In all, 42 percent of the post-9/11 lone wolves suffered from a diagnosed mental illness (twenty-nine out of sixty-nine cases). Thirteen of them

(19 percent) were diagnosed as either schizophrenic or bipolar. Twelve (17 percent) were diagnosed as delusional, autistic, intellectually disabled, or as having an unclassified mental illness.

These figures must be placed in their proper context. The National Institute of Mental Health estimates that 18.1 percent of U.S. adults suffer from mental illness.[50] The figure is much higher for criminals. An estimated 56 percent of prisoners in the United States have a mental health problem according to a 2006 National Institute of Justice report.[51] And as reported earlier, 60 percent of American lone wolf terrorists have a criminal background. In general, lone wolves may be considered a small subset of the U.S. criminal population. Many of the lone wolves were assassins. Another National Institute of Justice report indicates that 43 percent of lone assassins in the United States since 1949 have evidenced some form of mental illness.[52] Hewitt's research shows that the rate of mental illness is considerably higher among lone wolves as compared to terrorist group members.[53] A study comparing 119 lone wolf terrorists with a matched sample of group-based terrorists shows that the odds of a lone wolf terrorist having a mental illness is 13.49 times higher than the odds of a group actor having a mental illness.[54] Another study of lone wolf terrorists in the European Union between 2000 and 2015 found that 35 percent of the perpetrators reportedly suffered from some kind of mental disorder.[55] Our research shows that the rate of mental illness among American lone wolf terrorists is roughly 40 percent. This figure is therefore consistent both with other research on lone wolf terrorists and with broader studies of criminals and assassins.

Something must also be said about cause and effect. Let us be clear about this: Mental illness does not cause lone wolf terrorism. Indeed, most of the lone wolves since 1940 (56 percent) have not been mentally ill, or at least there has been no evidence of mental illness among the majority. The U.S. Census for 1940 exceeded 131 million. Using National Institute of Mental Health figures, we can estimate that roughly 26 million Americans may have lived with mental illness in the year 1940. Exactly one of them was a lone wolf terrorist. The census for 1970 exceeded 203 million, with an estimated 40 million who were mentally ill. Not a single one of them committed an act of lone wolf terrorism in 1970. Skip ahead to 2010, when the U.S. population exceeded 308 million, with an estimated 60 million who experienced mental illness: only three were lone wolf terrorists. The chance of getting hit by lightning is estimated at 1 in 700,000. The chance of a mentally ill person committing lone wolf terrorism is somewhere in the neighborhood of 1 in 20 million.

Mental illness does not cause lone wolf terrorism. Something else is needed—namely, engagement with a warrior subculture. This has proven to be a transformative experience in the violent radicalization of both Islamist and anti-government groups. In order to commit terrorism, an extremist must first dehumanize his victim and then raise himself to the position of moral superiority. Internalizing these psychological preconditions, extremists begin to think of themselves as soldiers.[56] This is why, for example, Said and Cherif Kouachi wore military outfits when they attacked the Paris office of *Charlie Hebdo* with assault rifles in 2015. It is why Anders Breivik wore a police costume with a riot helmet, a holstered pistol, combat boots with spurs, and a badge reading "Muliculti Traitor Hunting Permit" when he exploded a car bomb in Oslo's government district and then assassinated young people at the summer camp in Norway. It is why Christopher Dorner dressed like a commando, clad in camouflage from head to toe, when he attacked Los Angeles police with assault rifles. And it is why, during the Orlando massacre, Omar Mateen described himself to a police negotiator as an "Islamic soldier." They all self-identified as soldiers even though they came from different cultures, spoke different languages, and held various ideological beliefs. The U.S. Marshals Task Force on Lone Wolf Terrorism finds that many lone wolves tend to be "incapable of identifying people as humans" and see them instead "as tangible targets to achieve their specific goals. The lone wolf attacks involve detailed and calculated planning, full on target type identification and almost a military precision for the follow-through. It is almost sanitary."[57]

Yet the issue of mental illness does raise compelling questions about radicalization. First, are mentally ill lone wolves more lethal than those who are not afflicted with the illness? It appears not. Of the 340 victims killed or wounded by lone wolf terrorists between 2001 and mid-2016, less than a third (30 percent) were attacked by loners with a known mental illness. Such a finding appears to support the work of terrorism scholars who criticize the assumption that radicalization is rooted in pathology.[58]

Where, then, does mental illness fit in the radicalization process? When in their individual life trajectories do mental health problems first arise for lone wolves, before they genuinely radicalize, or when they are fully radicalized and already committed to violent action? Evidence suggests that certain stressors occurring because of terrorist activity may result in psychological disturbance in terrorists.[59] Three of the jihadists in Bakker's study, for example, underwent severe depression after their arrests.[60] In other words, involvement in terrorism may activate an underlying mental illness.

At the end of the day, however, answers to these questions will likely be different for each mentally ill lone wolf terrorist, and therefore the questions are best addressed through qualitative case study research. Suffice it to say that in the opinion of American courts, most lone wolf terrorists were able to plan and implement their attacks in an "effective" way. That is, mental health problems did not incapacitate their mission; rather, it is likely that they shaped and fueled their sense of righteousness and the dehumanization of the "other."

Summary: The Meaning of Lone Wolf Terrorism

The wolf is one of nature's most fearsome creatures. Wolves are social animals that travel in nuclear families, hunting in mated pairs with their offspring. Packs are led by an alpha wolf who routinely leads attacks on an omega wolf, the lowest animal in the pack. "This unfortunate individual often becomes the pack scapegoat," notes one authority, "suffering so much physical and mental stress that it may leave the pack."[61] The omega wolf abandons the pack at a young age and, failing to catch sufficient prey and without pack protection and the socialization it was instinctively bred for, dies early.

A tragic figure of natural selection, nature's lone wolf is more than a convenient metaphor for individuals who undertake acts of terrorism outside of a command structure. Lone wolf terrorists act to advance ideological beliefs of an extremist movement, but they typically never have personal contact with the movement they identify with, and they devise terrorist tactics and methods solely on their own. The lone wolf terrorist suffers alienation and stress and often dies early. More than one-third (25) of the post-9/11 American lone wolf terrorists are deceased—most dying before the age of forty in suicides or police shootouts.

While there is no standard profile of the American lone wolf terrorist, the evidence shows that most are single white males from urban areas who are unemployed and have a criminal record. Compared to members of large terrorist organizations, lone wolves are older, less educated, and more prone to mental illness. When compared to those who join the global jihad, domestic lone wolves are more likely to be unmoored from society, making them unlikely candidates for recruitment into terrorist organizations. Taken together, the findings imply that lone wolf terrorism is caused by relative deprivation. In their isolation, lone individuals feel deprived of what they perceive as the goods and social status to which they are entitled and form grievances against the government or a population group whom they hold responsible for their unemployment and for discrimination and injustices perpetrated against them. Their violence is a deviant adaptation to this gap between limited means and the goal of social respectability. In this way, the predominantly single, white, and unemployed lone wolves experience what sociologist Michael Kimmel terms an "aggrieved entitlement." They feel that "their" country and sense of self are being taken away from them by women, immigrants, people of color, GLBT individuals, and others.[62] Within society, probably no one is more alienated than the lone wolf terrorist, as revolutionary theorists have suggested for years. In his seminal *Minimanual of the Urban Guerrilla*, Brazilian Marxist Carlos Marighella noted that the main vulnerability of a guerilla cell is the danger of extreme isolation among its members.[63] Before going underground to avoid arrest by the FBI, 1960s firebrand Abbie Hoffman sought advice from the Weather Underground. When Hoffman said that he planned to go on the run alone, a Weatherman advised him: "Alone is very tough. None of our people make it alone."[64]

Terrorism scholars traditionally invoke alienation theory to explain how people who have no effective voice in society are recruited into terrorist organizations where they are encouraged by leaders to displace aggression onto out-groups, as they become socialized to see terrorist groups as legitimate and out-group members as evil.[65] The desire for belonging in a social network of extremists offers individuals a group identity and motivates them to take action against out-groups. This is the essence of large-group radicalization. Small-group radicalization relies on a different dynamic wherein a dominant figure exerts control over a subordinate figure. Prior to the Boston Marathon bombing, for instance, and in keeping with an ethnic tradition among Muslim Chechens where the eldest brother rules over all siblings, Tamerlan Tsarnaev had a profound influence on his younger brother Dzhokhar, turning him from a "sweet, weightless cloud" into a terrorist.[66] But what happens when there is no such interpersonal power dynamic? What happens when there is no social network to support recruitment into a large terrorist organization and no charismatic leader to provide indoctrination and empower the radicalization process? Do individuals become actors in their own radicalization, or are they influenced by brainwashing campaigns of radical movements stressing such global issues as war, capitalism, and consumerism, or both?

What remains to be understood about the lone wolf terrorist is whether radicalization resulting from alienation leads to an identity crisis related to issues of "damaged masculinity," as some research suggests, which in turn forms an ideological motive for social change through violence.[67] It is to these crucial issues of radicalization that we now turn.

CHAPTER 4

The Roots of Radicalization

A logical place to begin a study of radicalization is with a question rarely asked in terrorism research: *Where* does radicalization occur? It is often assumed that lone wolves "self-radicalize," but that is unsubstantiated by our database evidence.[1] Lone wolves do not operate in isolation, and their radicalization can be traced to various social networks. Often they are radicalized in more than one network. Identifying the locus (or place) of radicalization is important because it draws attention to the social institutions or means by which an individual embarks on the pathway to extremism. Without radicalization there would be no terrorism. The loci of radicalization for both the pre- and post-9/11 eras are presented in figures 4.1 and 4.2.

As figure 4.1 shows, the most common locus of radicalization in the pre-9/11 era was an extremist group to which the lone wolves once belonged but had since abandoned (26 percent of the total). Examples include mail-bomber Leroy Moody's previous membership in the John Birch Society; mass shooter Benjamin Smith's prior involvement with the racist World Church of the Creator; and anti-abortionist extremists Shelley Shannon, Michael Griffin, Paul Hill, John Salvi, and James Kopp who were all formerly affiliated with the amorphous anti-abortion movement known as the Army of God.

The post-9/11 era has seen a decline in this respect. Figure 4.2 indicates that only 10 percent of the lone wolves were primarily radicalized in

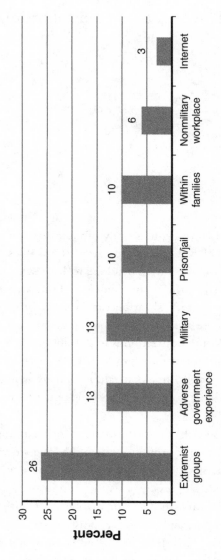

Figure 4.1 Pre-9/11 loci of radicalization

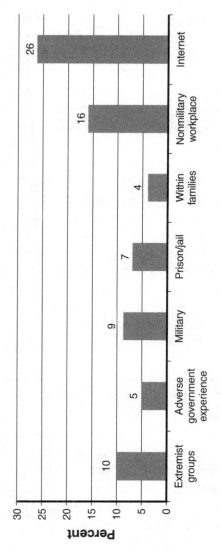

Figure 4.2 Post-9/11 loci of radicalization

extremist groups. They include James Lee, who was radicalized on the fringes of the environmental movement and later took three hostages in an armed takeover of the Discovery Channel headquarters in Washington, DC, in 2010; and would-be assassin Casey Brezik, who was radicalized during protests surrounding the Toronto G20 summit in 2010.

The military is a somewhat more stable locus of radicalization over time. During the pre-9/11 era, 13 percent of the lone wolves were radicalized either fully or in part by their military experiences. Floyd Simpson, who assassinated civil rights crusader William Moore in rural Alabama in 1963, was radicalized during his combat experiences in World War II and Korea and later through his affiliation with the United Klans of America.[2] Similarly, Byron de la Beckwith was radicalized in the Marine Corps during his World War II battles with the Japanese and later through the racist Mississippi Citizens Council.[3] The New Orleans police sniper Mark Essex was radicalized by the racism he encountered as a Vietnam-era Navy officer and later through his involvement with the Black Panthers.[4] Eric Rudolph's radicalization can also be traced to the military. While attending Airborne School at Fort Benning, Georgia, around 1987, Rudolph was allegedly lied to by an Army recruiter about his assignment to the Ranger Indoctrination Program, a necessary prerequisite for Rudolph's hoped-for transfer to Special Forces. Instead, Rudolph was posted to a regular infantry unit at Fort Campbell, Kentucky. This created a degree of personal anger for Rudolph that would later be matched with his political grievances.[5]

During the post-9/11 era, 9 percent of the lone wolves were radicalized in the military. They include Nidal Hasan, Naser Jason Abdo, and Marine Corps reservist Yonathan Melaku.

Before 9/11, about 10 percent of the lone wolves were radicalized in prison or jail. Among them was James Earl Ray, who became loosely affiliated with a prison chapter of the Ku Klux Klan while imprisoned at the Missouri State Penitentiary at Jefferson City in 1964. It was there that Ray grew obsessed with the civil rights work of Martin Luther King and a prison rumor that the White Knights of the Mississippi Klan were willing to pay a $100,000 bounty for King's head.[6]

After 9/11, 7 percent of the lone wolves were radicalized behind bars. They include the Pennsylvania police killer Eric Frein, Alton Nolen, who committed the beheading in Oklahoma, and black militant Ali Brown, who assassinated three white men in Seattle in 2014.

About 10 percent of the pre-9/11 lone wolves were radicalized within their families. They include most notably the racist serial killer Joseph Paul Franklin. Raised by bigoted parents in the American South during the civil rights era, Franklin's grandparents on his mother's side were supporters of the Nazis during World War II. Born James Clayton Vaughn Jr., in Mobile, Alabama, in 1950, he later changed his name to Joseph Paul Franklin in honor of the Nazi Paul Joseph Goebbels and Benjamin Franklin. Joseph Paul Franklin later joined both the racist National States Rights Party and the Ku Klux Klan, but then left both groups because he found them not violent enough.[7]

Terrorism scholar Jerrold Post argues that ideology is often transmitted from generation to generation and that traditions of violent radicalization are passed on in this manner.[8] But that may not explain American lone wolf terrorists of the twenty-first century: after 9/11, the number of lone wolves radicalized within their families fell to 4 percent. Post also makes the point that there are real psychological differences between those terrorists who carry on the work of their parents, and those who are trying to destroy the world of their parents. A range of European revolutionary groups have set foot on the latter path in completely rejecting their past, leading one scholar to describe them as "children without fathers."[9] This phenomenon may partially explain changes in the loci of radicalization for American lone wolf terrorists—they have become children without families.

For post-9/11 lone wolves, traditional loci of radicalization have been replaced by informal social networks, the civilian workplace, and mass media.

Prior to 9/11, only 6 percent of the era's lone wolves were radicalized through nonmilitary workplace experiences or friendship networks. The figure rose to 16 percent in the post-9/11 era.

Not surprisingly, given the technology of the time, only one lone wolf of the pre-9/11 era was radicalized over the Internet. After 9/11 the figure rose from 3 percent to 26 percent. Similarly, not a single lone wolf was radicalized via cable television or radio prior to 9/11. Following 9/11, 9 percent of the lone wolves were radicalized through these venues. Interestingly, these increases were evidenced primarily in relation to lone wolves of the radical Right. Contrary to conventional belief, Islamic extremists in the database were *not* primarily radicalized through the Internet. For them, radicalization stemmed mainly from experiences in the military or within friendship networks. The Internet served as a secondary locus of radicalization. Two important cases exemplify this distinction.

The primary locus of radicalization for the Fort Hood shooter, Nidal Hasan, was the military. As an Army psychologist at the Walter Reed Medical Center in Bethesda, Maryland, Hasan became sensitized to the realities of war through therapy sessions with vets returning from Iraq and Afghanistan, which also made him fear his own deployment to Afghanistan. To fellow soldiers at Walter Reed, Hasan proclaimed that suicide bombing against Americans was justified; the soldiers distanced themselves from him as a result. Once stationed at Fort Hood, Hasan endured harassment from other soldiers because of his Muslim faith—he was called a "camel jockey," and his car was vandalized—and he became exasperated in an attempt to find a legal resolution to the discrimination. It was also at Fort Hood that Hasan received weapons training and thereby gained the basic skills required for the subsequent shooting. Hasan simultaneously searched al-Qaeda websites for Islamic justifications to oppose the war and sent sixteen e-mail messages to Anwar al-Awlaki in Yemen. The cleric ignored all but two of the messages, however, and offered no encouragement to Hasan for the idea of killing fellow soldiers. On balance, then, the military was Hasan's primary locus of radicalization while the Internet was a secondary locus.[10]

Wade Page, the Sikh temple shooter, also began his radicalization in the Army. While stationed at Fort Bragg, North Carolina, in 1995, Page met infantrymen with white supremacy leanings who introduced him to the movement's literature. In this way, Page became familiar with National Alliance founder William Pierce's racist and anti-Semitic 1978 novel *The Turner Diaries*, which became an obsession for Page and set him on the pathway to a warrior subculture. The murder that same year of a black couple in Fayetteville by two members of Fort Bragg's Eighty-Second Airborne Division revealed the presence of a neo-Nazi skinhead movement among soldiers at the base. Page was among them. He referred to non-whites as "dirt people" and had the white supremacist slogan "14 Words" tattooed on his shoulder (the words are "We must secure the existence of our people and a future for white children"). Page once told the criminologist Pete Simi, "If you don't go into the military as a racist, you definitely leave as one." Upon his discharge, Page drifted into the white power music scene of Southern California, where he played bass guitar in two skinhead bands known as End Apathy and Definite Hate, respectively. Like many white power musicians, Page adhered to the belief that music encouraged cultural diversity within the white power movement and provided a venue for group identity. Around 2011, approximately a year before the Sikh temple massacre, Page became a "fully patched" member of the Northern Hammerskins, the Midwest faction of the Hammerskin Nation (a white supremacist group) and tattooed himself with the logo HFFH (for "Hammerskins Forever, Forever Hammerskins"). Page eventually cut his ties with the group but continued his radicalization through social media and became a frequent poster on white supremacy websites, where he once wrote about "doing something," not just talking about it on the Internet, representing the first instance in which Page's radicalization assumed violent intentions. Page also became an avid fan of Radio White, a California online radio program catering to racists. The white power music community and racist Internet websites were Page's primary loci of radicalization, while the military served as his secondary locus.[11]

Personal and Political Grievances

An essential finding of previous research is that lone wolf terrorists tend to combine personal frustrations with wider political agendas, as Jessica Stern observed in 2003, writing that "Lone wolves often come up with their own ideologies that combine personal vendettas with religious or political grievances."[12] Perhaps more than any other factor, it is this combination of personal and political grievances that distinguishes lone wolves from members of large terrorist organizations, where individual grievances are less important than the social-psychological processes of an entire group. Historically, terrorism scholars have therefore focused on a group dynamic wherein members share common personal grievances leading to the adoption of a common ideology. In explaining this group dynamic among the Salafi jihadists, Sageman goes into detail about how the jihadists' personal experiences with cultural and geographic dislocation after leaving their home countries became a manifestation of what they collectively saw as a war on Islam:

> They were isolated when they moved away from their families and friends and became particularly lonely and emotionally alienated in

this new individualistic environment. The lack of spiritualism in a utilitarian culture was keenly felt. Underemployed and discriminated against by the local society, they felt a personal sense of grievance and humiliation. They sought a cause that would give them emotional relief, social community, spiritual comfort, and a cause for self-sacrifice. . . . They joined the global jihad, which gave them both a cause and comrades.[13]

Personal grievances also appear to be less important than ideology for terrorists who join small groups, although it is impossible to be positive about this due to a lack of systematic research. For example, from what is known about the FBI's investigation of the San Bernardino attack, Syed Rizwan Farook and Tashfeen Malik were inspired by foreign terrorist organizations, including ISIS and the Nusra Front, the al-Qaeda affiliate in Syria, yet there is no indication that they were directed by these groups. Instead, their attack arose from interpersonal dynamics. The couple began e-mailing each other about jihad and martyrdom in 2013, before they met in person and before the emergence of ISIS in Syria. They were married in 2014 and spent the next year preparing for the attack, including taking target practice and making plans to take care of their child and Farook's mother. While the FBI investigation locates the attackers' motive in jihadist ideology, the investigation is silent about the couple's personal grievances, to the extent that such grievances existed in the first place. Neither had a criminal record, and both were college educated. Farook was gainfully employed as a government food inspector, and coworkers recalled that he had "no obvious grudges." Malik came from a landowning family in Pakistan with political influence, and she had recently hosted a baby shower for her daughter. There is, then, little evidence of the group alienation witnessed among the Salafi jihadists in Sageman's study.

Compared to organized jihadists (both large and small scale), lone wolf terrorists are more idiosyncratic in belief and behavior. They combine various political causes with any number of highly personal vendettas in complex and extremely individualized ways, thereby challenging traditional academic attempts at ascribing to terrorism such ideal-typical motives as "Islamic extremism" and "jihad," "rightwing racism," or "black militancy." Lone wolf terrorists are more complicated than that. Sometimes politics is the dominant theme of their radicalization; other times, politics is a submerged theme. The same seesaw applies to personal grievances.

Personal and political grievances matter because they go to the crucial question of motive. The hypothesis that lone wolves combine personal and political grievances is the first commonality of radicalization tested in this study. To validate the commonality, there must be evidence of both a personal and political grievance for any given case. For the pre-9/11 lone wolves, evidence of both themes was found in 80 percent of the cases (30 of the 39 cases). The following cases illustrate the basic point that both themes play a role in the radicalization process.

The Empire State Building Attack

Ali Abu Kamal, a sixty-nine-year-old Palestinian from Gaza, was a well-respected English professor, a tutor, and an accomplished translator who lived with his family in relative affluence.[14] Yet following his retirement, Kamal lost some $500,000 in bad business deals and relocated by himself to the United States, arriving in New York City on Christmas Eve, 1996. On January 11, 1997, he checked into a motel near Miami, Florida, and using that address as his legal residence, purchased a .380-caliber Beretta semi-automatic pistol. Kamal was a Muslim but he was not religious (he had once been kidnapped by Hamas and beaten for smoking hashish and drinking alcohol) and upon his return to New York, Kamal squandered the last of his money on liquor and prostitutes.

Shortly after 5 P.M. on February 23, Kamal stood in a crowd of sightseers on the observation deck of the Empire State Building. Suddenly, Kamal pulled the Beretta from his coat and shouted, *"Are you from Egypt?"* before opening fire at the crowd, killing one person and wounding six others, including two children. Kamal then took his own life with a gunshot to the head.

New York police found a pair of identical letters, one in English and one in Arabic, in a pouch around Kamal's neck. The letters were a diatribe against Zionists and the "Big Three"—the United States, France, and Britain—for their mistreatment of Palestinians. "My restless aspiration is to murder as many of them as possible," he wrote, "and I have decided to do that by striking at their own den in New York." While the letters provided evidence of political motive, Kamal's widow offered another explanation, saying that the shooting was motivated by financial ruin. Kamal's letter named two business partners who Kamal claimed had swindled him out of a fortune. "My husband is not a terrorist," his widow said. "He was just hopeless." However, in 2007, ten years after the attack, Kamal's daughter told the press that she was "tired of lying" about her father's motive and indicated that Kamal's hidden diary stated that he had wanted to punish the United States for supporting Israel. She claimed that her mother's 1997 account was a cover story fabricated by the Palestinian Authority to maintain the peace agreement with Israel, yet that explanation discounts the full content of Kamal's letter found at the Empire State Building. But more to the point of lone wolf terrorism, Kamal's attack was motivated by some combination of personal and political grievances.

The Cleveland Race War

Frank Spisak was the son of a racist Cleveland factory worker who had moved his family out of the city because too many blacks had moved into their neighborhood.[15] In 1976, twenty-five-year-old Spisak suffered a serious head injury in a car accident. A year later, he started dressing as a woman and changed his name to "Frankie Ann" Spisak. He received treatment from the Gender Dysphoria clinic at Cleveland Metropolitan Hospital, was treated by a psychologist, and started taking female hormones in preparation for gender reassignment surgery. After being fired from a factory job of five years for showing up as a female, Spisak wandered the back streets of Cleveland dressed as an old woman and carrying a .22-caliber pistol in a hollowed-out copy of *Mein Kampf*. In 1979, "Frankie Ann" completely gave way to "Nazi Frank," and Spisak began to accumulate Third Reich memorabilia and constantly played taped speeches by Hitler and Rudolph Hess. He was also stockpiling weapons and ammunition.

Everything came to a head on February 1, 1982, when Spisak spotted a fifty-seven-year-old African American minister in the stall next to his in a men's restroom at the Cleveland State University library. Spisak propositioned the minister for sex, the minister declined, and Spisak pulled his .22-caliber pistol, stuck the nose through a hole in the stall, aimed at the minister's torso, and squeezed the trigger until there were no more bullets. Thus began Spisak's race war, or what Spisak called his "search and destroy" missions on behalf of the American neo-Nazi movement to "exterminate as many niggers and Jews as possible."

Four months later Spisak shot a fifty-five-year-old black factory worker seven times on a train platform; the man survived, however. That August, Spisak entered a CSU women's room armed with his .22 and accosted a female employee who shoved Spisak aside and ran down the hallway as Spisak fired at her but missed. Three weeks later, Spisak shot and killed CSU's fifty-year-old maintenance supervisor, believing that the supervisor was Jewish. Three days later, Spisak shot and killed a seventeen-year-old black male student at a bus stop near the CSU campus.

A week after this killing, Spisak got drunk and fired his gun out of the window of his house. For this he was arrested, but was allowed to post bond. After an anonymous phone call suggested to police that they reexamine the gun seized from Spisak's house, they were able to match the weapon used in the killings and the one Spisak had when he was arrested.

Again there is evidence of both personal and political grievances. Spisak admitted to the murders and displayed his motive by autographing his trademark swastika t-shirt for the detectives who arrested him. During his trial, Spisak grew a Hitler-style mustache, gave a Nazi salute to the jury as he entered the courtroom, and proudly carried his copy of *Mein Kampf*. He was convicted of the murders and sentenced to death on August 10, 1983. At his sentencing, Spisak blamed the shootings on his hatred of homosexuals, African Americans, Jews, and mental illness, which he claimed was related to confusion about his sexual identity. Spisak further claimed that he was under orders from God and that Jews were to blame for his sexual identity problems because they had seized control of his mind. His lawyers argued that Spisak was severely mentally ill with bipolar disorder and conflicted over his sexuality.

Spisak was executed at the Southern Ohio Correctional Facility, Lucasville, on February 17, 2011. He set the Ohio record for the longest time on death row, at more than twenty-seven years, where he lived as a woman.

The Milk and Moscone Assassinations

Dan White had high hopes upon his 1978 election to the San Francisco Board of Supervisors.[16] At thirty-two, White was a Vietnam veteran, a former police officer, and a rising star in the local Republican Party. But once in office, he failed to do much of anything except speak out against the city's burgeoning gay community and a proposed treatment program for disturbed teenagers in his district. White's efforts to stop the program were initially supported by fellow supervisor Harvey Milk, a prominent gay rights activist. Yet when Milk withdrew his support, White felt betrayed and infuriated with Milk. White resigned from the Board of Supervisors, citing dissatisfaction with corruption in San Francisco politics, and fell into a deep depression worsened by mounting financial pressures and marital difficulties. "I don't even like myself," he admitted to his wife. Growing irritable and unable to sleep, White comforted himself with a diet of junk food.

Because of his financial problems, however, White petitioned San Francisco's liberal mayor, George Moscone, for reinstatement to his job. At the urging of Milk and others who were troubled by White's conservative voting record on the board, the Mayor ultimately refused. It was here—at the crossroads of personal vendetta and political grievance—that White decided to assassinate Milk and Moscone.

On November 27, White went to City Hall with the intention of killing not only Milk and Moscone, but also the liberal California Assembly Speaker Willie Brown (future mayor of San Francisco) and Supervisor Carol Ruth Silver. White entered the building through a ground-level window to avoid a metal detector at the front door (which would have detected the gun he was carrying and the ten extra bullets he had wrapped in a handkerchief). After entering Moscone's office, White pleaded to be reinstated to his job, but Moscone refused. White then killed Moscone by shooting him four times with a .38-caliber revolver, twice in the head. White then ran across City Hall to the supervisor's area and entered his former office where he re-chambered four of the extra bullets. Then he called for Milk and enticed him to enter the office where White shot him five times, the final two shots with the gun barrel touching Milk's skull.

Incidentally, the assassinations brought national attention to then-board president Dianne Feinstein, who became mayor of San Francisco and then U.S. senator for California. As chair of the Senate Intelligence Committee in 2008, Feinstein presided over passage of the nation's preemptive foreign policy to battle lone wolf terrorism—the Lone Wolf amendment to the Foreign Intelligence Surveillance Act, or FISA.

Dan White was sentenced to seven years for manslaughter. At Soledad prison, he became a jogging partner with Sirhan Sirhan. White was released from prison in 1984. On October 21, 1985, he committed suicide by carbon monoxide poisoning inside his garage.

These cases are representative of personal and political grievances among lone wolf terrorists of the pre-9/11 era. For lone wolf terrorists of the post-9/11 era, evidence of both personal and political grievances was found in 55 of the 69 cases, again representing 80 percent of the cases and indicating that the commonality is a signature of radicalization among lone wolf terrorists. Two cases highlight the combination of personal and political grievances.

The Knoxville Unitarian Church Shooting

At 10:18 on the Sunday morning of July 27, 2008, fifty-eight-year-old Jim David Adkisson walked into the Tennessee Valley Unitarian Church in Knoxville, Tennessee, carrying a guitar case and wearing a fanny pack containing seventy-four shotgun shells.[17] Some two hundred people were watching a youth performance of *Annie Jr.* when Adkisson pulled a 12-guage Remington shotgun from the guitar case and began firing. An usher moved in front of the gunman to protect the congregation but Adkisson shot him in the face. The killing and wounding went on until Adkisson was wrestled to the floor by five men. Police responded within three minutes of the first 911 call and took Adkisson away in handcuffs. In a matter of seconds, Adkissson had killed two, bloodied six, and traumatized dozens more for years to come.

Upon questioning, Adkisson freely admitted that he hated liberals, blacks, and gays. Akkisson told police that he targeted the church because of its liberal teachings and his belief that all liberals should be killed because they were ruining the country, adding that Democrats had tied "his nation's hands" in the war on terrorism and that they had destroyed America with the aid of major media outlets. In a four-page manifesto mailed to the media and posted online before the attack, Adkisson stated that because he could not kill leaders of the liberal movement, he would target the "foot soldiers" who had voted them into office. "This was a hate crime," Adkisson later admitted to the criminologist Lo Presser. "This was a political protest. This was a symbolic killing. . . . I thought I'd do something good for this country." Adkisson intended to kill as many people as he could until police got to him.

Adkisson's manifesto also cited as a motive his inability to find a job due to age discrimination. Ten years unemployed and five times divorced at the time of his shooting, Adkisson was alienated and suffered from depression. He said that "this whole thing could have been avoided" if he had a woman in his life. Adkisson had physically abused one of his former wives, however, and another former wife was a member of the Knoxville Unitarian church, further suggesting a personal motive for the massacre.

Adkisson did not act in isolation. "If you want to know what I think," he told Presser, "just listen to Rush Limbaugh." In his manifesto, Adkisson stated that his list of wished-for targets for killing could be found in several books written by popular conservative commentators, including Bernard Goldberg's *100 People Who Are Screwing Up America*, *Liberalism Is a Mental Disease* by radio personality Michael Savage, *Let Freedom Ring* by Fox News host Sean Hannity, and *The O'Reilly Factor* by Bill O'Reilly of Fox News.

Adkisson told police that he had been planning the attack for about a week. He said the shooting was a "political protest," but it was triggered by personal loss related to his inability to find "an honest decent job" and medications for depression. Adkisson recalled: "I was fixing to lose everything. I was fixing to go live under a bridge. I'm not gonna live under no man's bridge."

On February 9, 2009, Adkisson was sentenced to life in prison.

The Austin IRS Attack

On the morning of February 18, 2010, fifty-three-year-old Joseph Stack set fire to his two-story house in Austin, Texas, and then drove to a hanger he rented at Georgetown Municipal Airport, some twenty miles away.[18] He boarded his single-engine Piper Dakota airplane and took off around 9:45 A.M. As Stack became airborne, he radioed to the control tower operator, "Thanks for your help. Have a great day." Ten minutes later Stack's plane descended and collided at full speed into Echelon I, a building housing 190 employees of the Internal Revenue Service, resulting in a huge fireball and explosion, killing Stack and an IRS manager and injuring 13 others.

Stack was a software engineer whose political grievances were intricately linked to a long-running personal feud with the IRS. Back in 1994, while living in California, Stack had failed to file a state tax return on a dying software business, and in 1999 his wife filed Chapter 11 Bankruptcy, citing

IRS liabilities totaling over a quarter million dollars. Another of Stack's software companies was shut down in 2004 for non-payment of state taxes, which resulted from an IRS ruling eliminating a tax break for software consultants. Over the next six years, Stack spent thousands of dollars trying to get government officials to listen to his concerns. When his pleas failed, Stack's rage against the IRS broadened into hatred against President George W. Bush, government bank bailouts, and the Federal Aviation Administration. On the morning of the attack, Stack posted his grievances in a lengthy suicide note on his company website. The note expressed outrage not only at the IRS, but also against unions, drug and health care insurance companies, the Catholic Church, and government reactions to 9/11. The suicide note ended: "I saw it written once that the definition of insanity is repeating the same process over and over and expecting the outcome to suddenly be different. I am finally ready to stop this insanity. *Well, Mr. Big Brother IRS man, let's try something different; take my pound of flesh and sleep well.*"

Stack wrote that his attack "has been coming for a long time." Stack divorced his first wife in 2004, just as his business crumbled and he faced growing conflict with the IRS. He remarried and moved to Austin in 2005, but his tax problems continued and his marriage deteriorated. By 2010 his marital difficulties and animus toward the federal government had become insoluble. During the second week of February, Stack received notice of a forthcoming audit by the IRS. That was the triggering event for Stack. After receiving the notice, Stack replaced the seats of his two-man Piper Dakota aircraft with extra fuel drums in preparation for an act of lone wolf terrorism. On the night of February 17, Stack's wife took her daughter to a hotel to get away from Stack because he had become impossible to live with. The next morning, Stack burned down their house and launched his suicide attack on the IRS.

The Complexity of Lone Wolf Motives

While these examples provide insight into the commonality of personal and political grievances among lone wolf terrorists, they also reveal the complexity of defining their motives. Politically, the post-9/11 cases were both motivated by violent anti-government extremism. Personally, they were motivated by a range of factors, including age and legal discrimination, alienation, depression, financial problems, marital discord, and perceived legal injustices. Similar complexities are evidenced in 80 percent of all cases of lone wolf terrorism—a figure that indicates that, unlike for members of large and small terrorist groups, there is no overarching clarity of causation or purpose that can be attributed to the phenomenon of lone wolf terrorism. The term "anti-government extremist" is oversimplified shorthand for the motives of Adkisson and Stack. What ties these cases together is raw emotion: For both men, the intensity of their anger at the government dramatically set them apart from others. Therefore, the full import of motive can be best understood on a case-by-case basis.

Affinity with Extremist Groups

Affinity implies that lone wolf terrorists have sympathy with extremist groups and that their beliefs are in accord with a clearly defined organizational entity. Even Theodore Kaczynski, the most iconoclastic lone wolf terrorist of all, had an affinity with radical environmental groups of the American West during the late 1970s.[19] The database shows that 63 percent of the pre-9/11 lone wolves had an affinity with an extremist organization. As might be expected, these groups reflected the social contentions of the times: Southern segregationist organizations borne of the civil rights era, Palestinian movements, small neo-Nazi outfits, and for anti-abortionists, the Army of God.

A major finding of this research is that the affinity with extremist organizations among lone wolf terrorists is declining. Only 48 percent of the post-9/11 lone wolves had an affinity with such organizations. In other words, in most cases lone wolves did *not* show an affinity with extremist groups. In cases where an affinity was found, the groups reflected the contentions of a post-9/11 America—al-Qaeda, Tea Party Patriots, the neo-Nazi National Alliance, and after 2013, ISIS. At the same time, the overall finding implies that lone wolves are seeking ideological direction through venues other than organizations—namely, via networks of anonymous online activists. The shift from an affinity with extremist *groups* to an affinity with anonymous *online sympathizers* is one of the most important transformations in the history of lone wolf terrorism because it has expanded the base of support for leaderless resistance. The shift can be seen by comparing the next two cases.

After earning his degree from Cumberland Law School in Birmingham, Alabama, in 1996, thirty-two-year-old Richard Baumhammers traveled to Riga, Latvia, where he acquired citizenship and set out to regain ownership of properties lost by his family of Latvian émigrés during the Soviet occupation.[20] In 1997, Baumhammers made legal claims on the property under Latvia's denationalization policy, but the claims were denied because Baumhammers had filed the paperwork too late. Baumhammers talked to acquaintances about getting a job with a prestigious accounting firm or teaching law at a Latvian university, yet nothing came of it. A loner by nature, Baumhammers made few friends in Latvia, spoke only a few words of the language, and found no intimacy beyond the companionship of prostitutes.

Upon his return to the United States in the spring of 1999, Baumhammers moved into his parents' home in the affluent Pittsburgh suburb of Mount Lebanon. Supported by a $4,000 monthly allowance from his wealthy father, Baumhammers did not need to work. With sufficient time on his hands and still interested in exploiting the market economy of the former Soviet bloc, Baumhammers established an Internet website called the "Free Market Party" with Baumhammers listed as chairman of the board. The site championed the rights of European Americans, claiming that they were outnumbered by minorities and immigrants and thus deprived of what was lawfully theirs. Stirring the pot of discontent even more, Baumhammers began reading racist literature and came to view Timothy McVeigh and Adolf Hitler as his role models. Accordingly, he stepped up his goal of recruiting others into a new far-right political movement to help him fight against the onslaught of non-white immigration to America. Baumhammers met with the national leader of the John Birch Society and sought his assistance in setting up a party but was rebuffed when the leader determined that Baumhammers was "a nut." Failing to recruit any members to his cause, Baumhammers closed his website.

Concurrently with these events, on April 30, 1999, Baumhammers walked into a sporting goods store in Washington, Pennsylvania, and bought a Smith & Wesson .357-caliber semi-automatic pistol for $528. Nine days later, Baumhammers voluntarily checked himself into a psychiatric hospital and was diagnosed with delusional disorder. Baumhammers had long history of mental illness. In 1993, he had been hospitalized by his parents after displaying extreme paranoia. Since then, Baumhammers had seen eight psychiatrists and four clinical psychologists and had been put on sixteen different medications. A court-appointed psychiatrist would later determine that Baumhammers suffered from paranoid schizophrenia.

Upon his release from psychiatric care, Baumhammers returned to his parents' home where he began using America Online to download treatises on lone wolf terrorism posted by the veteran California racist Tom Metzger on his White Aryan Resistance (WAR) website. The WAR website openly advocated random lone wolf terrorist attacks against minorities as a form of leaderless resistance. In effect, Baumhammers became the first American lone wolf terrorist to be radicalized by the Internet.

WAR offered Baumhammers something he could not find on his own: people who were sympathetic to his racist views. WAR became the platform for his involvement with other extremist groups as well. Baumhammers joined an e-mail list for the skinhead band Aggressive Force, whose songs celebrated racial warfare. The band's record label, *Panzerfaust* (named after the Nazi armored tank command of World War II), championed the "lone wolf political activist." Baumhammers downloaded video clips and writings about William Pierce, leader of the National Alliance and author of *The Turner Diaries*. He also registered as a user at the neo-Nazi web server Stormfront and made more than a thousand visits to the site. Also at Stormfront, Baumhammers logged on to the White Singles page and contacted a woman from the World Church of the Creator who was associated with Matthew Hale, the self-styled "Pontifex Maximus" of the racist and anti-Semitic group. In July 1999, a former Church adherent, Benjamin Smith, went on a Midwestern killing rampage against Asians, African Americans, and Jews.

These influences came into full relief on March 1, 2000, when news reports indicated that a black racist in Wilkinsburg, Pennsylvania, named Ronald Taylor, had gone on a killing spree that left three white people dead and two wounded at a McDonalds restaurant. This became the triggering event for Richard Baumhammers to commit a reverse copycat attack. He would retaliate by killing only minorities.

At 1:30 P.M. on April 28, 2000, Baumhammers walked to the home of his next door neighbor, a sixty-three-year-old Jewish woman who had been friends with Baumhammers's parents for years, and fatally shot her six times with his Smith & Wesson before setting fire to the house. Baumhammers then drove his Jeep Cherokee to the Beth El Congregation and fired into the synagogue windows. Exiting his vehicle, he spray-painted two red swastikas and "Jew" on the building. From there, Baumhammers drove to an Indian grocery store where he shot and killed an Indian customer and then shot the Indian store manager in the neck, paralyzing him. Baumhammers next drove to the Ahavath Achim Congregation where he scattered gunfire against the synagogue windows. Then he drove to a Chinese restaurant where he shot and killed the Chinese manager and a Vietnamese cook. From there, Baumhammers drove to a Korean karate school, where he shot and killed an African American man before fleeing in his Jeep. Fifteen minutes later, Baumhammers was captured by police.

Two days after Baumhammers was charged in the shootings, Tom Metzger's website hailed the killings. "Mr. Richard Baumhammers, a white man from Mt. Lebanon in Pennsylvania, recently decided to deliver Aryan justice in a down home way," Metzger wrote.

On September 6, 2001, when sentencing Baumhammers to five death sentences for his crimes, the presiding judge told Baumhammers that he had been "coaxed and coached by the mongers of venom and violence," adding that Baumhammers had "acted as Benjamin Smith did in a 'lone wolf' attack against minorities. This is what the Internet has spawned. This is the new terrorism in America . . . human time bombs with their fuses set across the information super highway. . . . This is the true insanity of our times." These were not empty words. In 2011, the same judge presided over the trial of Richard Poplawski, who had murdered three Pittsburgh police officers in 2009 and who was similarly radicalized online as a registered user of Stormfront and other social media sites.

The "Jew Tube" Alternative

On the afternoon of January 21, 2009, twenty-one-year-old Keith Luke knocked on the door of an apartment in Brockton, Massachusetts, looking for a twenty-year-old Cape Verdean woman who had recently spurned his romantic advances at a local gym.[21] When the woman's twenty-two-year-old sister answered the door, Luke barged in, brandishing a gun and threw her to the floor. He reached into his backpack and grabbed a set of handcuffs, which he used to bind the woman's wrists, and then he raped her. As he did so, Luke told the woman to wipe some methamphetamine from his mouth and then pulled out a syringe and tried to plunge it into her arm. Suddenly, the younger sister walked into the apartment. Luke got up, grabbed his 9mm Glock, and shot her three times in the back as she tried to run away, killing her. Luke returned to the older sister and shot her seven times from head to toe through a stuffed teddy bear she was clutching. Yet she managed to escape from the apartment and ran to the street where two men came to her rescue. One was white and the other black. Luke appeared on the sidewalk and fired on the black rescuer, but missed before driving off in his van. A few blocks away, Luke happened upon an elderly Cape Verdean homeless man, whom he knew from the neighborhood. Luke stepped out of the van and fired two shots, killing him. Luke then drove toward the Temple Beth Emunah synagogue intent on killing as many Jews as he could as they left a bingo game. An eyewitness to the street killing provided police with Luke's license plate number and a description of his vehicle. Brockton police spotted Luke's van as it headed toward the synagogue. When they tried to pull Luke over, he fired on officers, and they pursued the van in a high-speed chase until it crashed into two vehicles, leading to Luke's capture and ending his plans for mass murder at the synagogue.

Keith Luke was a hulking, 250-pound neo-Nazi skinhead. Luke told police that he opposed the "Zionist occupation" of Palestine and admitted that his plan was to "kill as many Jews, blacks, and Hispanics as humanly possible" before killing himself. Luke said that he was angry about black men raping and killing white women on a "genocidal scale" and that the "Jew-controlled media" had done nothing to report it. Inside Luke's backpack, police found two hundred rounds of ammunition along with another rape kit containing handcuffs, blindfolds, and a gag—all purchased with his mother's credit card. When he appeared for his arraignment the next day, Luke had managed to carve a fresh swastika into his forehead. Luke had a history of mental illness and had been in psychiatric care for three years prior to his rampage. He was diagnosed as suffering from paranoid schizophrenia.

Luke had no known affinity for any extremist group, neo-Nazi or otherwise. In fact, he had no friends and spent most of his time alone. He lived with his mother and had held a job for only one day of his life. But Luke did have an affinity with online sympathizers, none of whom he knew outside of cyberspace. Some researchers challenge the assumption that the Internet promotes radicalization without face-to-face contact with another person, arguing that the emotional appeal to personal identity and group solidarity are more significant than online activity.[22] Luke puts the lie to that test: He developed his beliefs solely by reading Internet postings on Passmate, a neo-Nazi website designed by a fifty-something American racist named Rick Price as an alternative to YouTube, which Price referred to as "Jew Tube" due to its policy of banning racist and anti-Semitic content.[23] Passmate glorified lone wolf killers and featured a video tribute to Benjamin Smith, suggesting a copycat angle in the Luke case. While Price was an enabler for Luke's terrorism, the real source of his radicalization was the anonymous online supporters of the racist Passmate community.

Luke was sentenced to life in prison in 2013 and committed suicide by strangulation in his cell the following year.

The difference between these two cases is subtle but crucial. Richard Baumhammers drew inspiration from several well-established racist and anti-Semitic organizations. In particular, WAR and the World Church of the Creator (WCOTC) were membership organizations headed by prominent leaders of the far Right. Several of their followers had achieved notoriety for committing racially motivated murders. Taken together, these traits created organizational identities for WAR and the WCOTC. Baumhammers's affinity for those group identities played a major role in his radicalization.

Luke had no such affinity. Passmate was an obscure crowdsourcing platform for distributing racist content. It was not a "group" in the sense that it had no membership roll, no organizational identity, and no leader; Price was simply a webmaster. Nor did Passmate have any historical connection to racist violence. Luke's radicalization occurred independently of any formal group influence. A 2009 DHS report on lone wolf terrorists made a related warning about them: "White supremacist lone wolves pose the most significant domestic terrorist threat because of their low profile and autonomy—separate from any formalized group—which hampers warning efforts."[24] A statement attributed to Dylann Roof, the twenty-one-year-old gunman in the Charleston massacre of 2015, made the same point in a manifesto posted on his own website just hours before the shooting. Complaining about the absence of membership organizations in the modern white supremacy movement, Roof wrote: "We have no skinheads, no real KKK, no one doing anything but talking on the Internet. Well, someone has to have the bravery to take it to the real world and I guess that has to be me."[25] Like Keith Luke, Roof was radicalized entirely via the Internet. In Roof's case, the source was the Council of Conservative Citizens website, which displayed bogus crime statistics showing that "hundreds" of black on white murders were being ignored by the media. In April 2015, a CCC poster advised "White Crackers" to buy "a handgun for self-protection, and a shotgun for protecting your home." Days later, Roof bought the .45-caliber Glock pistol he would use in Charleston.[26]

As the 2009 DHS report acknowledges, these differences have obvious implications for preventing lone wolf terrorism. Certain preventative actions can be taken against groups that promote leaderless resistance, yet such actions are unavailable and ineffective for communities of unidentified online sympathizers who support the leaderless resistance strategy. WAR is a prime example of the former. Following the 1988 murder of an Ethiopian immigrant named Mulegeta Seraw by three skinheads affiliated with WAR, the group was sued in civil court by attorney Morris Dees on behalf of the Southern Poverty Law Center. Dees argued that WAR influenced Seraw's killers by encouraging them to commit violence. Dees won the lawsuit, thereby bankrupting Tom Metzger and WAR.[27] No such actions have ever been tried against independent enablers like Rick Price.

CHAPTER 5

The Enablers

Enabling plays a complex role in the radicalization process. Lone wolf terrorists are enabled either *directly* by people who unwittingly assist in planning attacks or *indirectly* by people who provide inspiration for terrorism. Whereas affinity for extremist groups or with online sympathizers is a vicarious experience best understood in terms of an ideological validation generated and transmitted by others, an enabler is best understood at a personal level as someone who either performs tasks that facilitate an attack or someone who indirectly encourages terrorism by example. Because they inspire by previous example, indirect enablers can include figures no longer living. Seventy years after his death, Adolf Hitler continues to inspire acts of lone wolf terrorism around the world.[1] The role of enablers is demonstrated in the following examples.

Direct and Indirect Enablers

A pre-9/11 example of direct enabling is exemplified in the case of Leroy Moody. A virulent racist and skilled conman, fifty-five-year-old Moody committed murder and attempted murder and made threats against judges and court personnel across the American South in 1989.[2] Moody's attacks were meant to terrorize the National Association for the Advancement of Colored People (NAACP), instill widespread fear for public safety, and instigate the disruption of constitutional government. His initial attack came on August 21, 1989 when staff at the NAACP office in Atlanta opened a package sent by Moody containing a tear-gas explosive. The resulting blast injured forty African American men, women, and children. Moody then meticulously built four mail-bombs. On December 16, near Birmingham, Alabama, Moody's first mail-bomb killed federal Judge Robert Vance of the Eleventh Circuit Court of Appeals and gravely wounded Vance's wife. A second bomb was defused by staff at the court's offices in Atlanta. On December 18, a third bomb killed Savannah, Georgia, civil rights attorney Robert Robinsons, who had represented the NAACP on a school desegregation case. Moody's fourth bomb was rendered safe after being sent to the NAACP office in Jacksonville, Florida. Moody also sent threatening letters to twenty judges of the Eleventh Circuit Court and NAACP offices in Atlanta and Birmingham.

Moody had two direct enablers. The first was a man named Ted Banks, Moody's former cellmate at the Atlanta Federal Penitentiary, where Moody had served time in the 1970s for attempted murder and possession of a bomb. During the planning stages for Moody's 1989 bombings, Banks performed welding on several lengths of pipe for Moody and provided his former cellmate with a tear-gas canister. Unbeknownst to Banks, Moody used the pipe to construct his mail-bombs, and he used the tear-gas canister in his attack on the Atlanta NAACP. The second enabler was Moody's wife, Susan McBride Moody who suffered from physical and emotional abuse at the hands of her husband. Susan unquestioningly performed whatever tasks Moody gave her during his bombing spree, including the procuring of bomb-making material and a typewriter used in his letters to the media. Yet like Ted Banks, she was unaware of the larger purpose of her actions. Neither Banks nor Susan Moody was prosecuted in connection with the bombings.

Indirect enabling is demonstrated in the pre-9/11 case of Eric Rudolph.[3] After his bombing of the 1996 Olympic Games in Atlanta, Rudolph sent letters to the media claiming credit in the name of the Army of God, followed by what FBI agents called "the Waco code"—the numbers 4-1-9-9-3, referring to the date of the disastrous FBI raid on the Branch Davidian compound in Waco, Texas (April 19, 1993), which caused the deaths of seventy-six Davidians, including a number of women and children. On April 19, 1995, two years later, to the very day, Timothy McVeigh bombed the Oklahoma City Federal Building in revenge for the Waco raid, believing that orders to attack the Davidians were issued from the building. Among the books later found at Rudolph's residence was the recently published *"All-American Monster": The Unauthorized Biography of Timothy McVeigh.*[4]

Within the American radical Right, the selection of a calendar date as an ideological justification for violence is based on a scene in William Pierce's 1978 novel, *The Turner Diaries*, which is generally considered the Bible of the radical Right. Two pages of the book were found in McVeigh's getaway car after the Oklahoma City bombing. In the novel, a fictitious group known as "The Order" (later adopted by the real terrorist group, the Order) declares a given date as the "Day of the Rope." On that day, somebody from the news media must be hanged, preferably a Jew. Yet for McVeigh the penultimate scene of the *Diaries* involved the Order's directions for constructing a bomb to be employed against FBI headquarters using "a little under 5,000 pounds of ammonium nitrate fertilizer. Sensitized with oil and tightly confined, it makes an effective blasting agent . . . able to punch through two levels of re-enforced concrete flooring while producing an open air blast wave powerful enough to blow the façade of a massive and strongly constructed building"[5]

For extremists enraged by the Waco tragedy, April 19 became the Day of the Rope, and bombing became the preferred terrorist tactic against state authority. Accordingly, through his example in Oklahoma City, Timothy McVeigh indirectly enabled the radicalization of Eric Rudolph even though Rudolph never crossed paths with McVeigh.

During the pre-9/11 era, 57 percent of the lone wolf terrorists in the database were enabled by others. In the post-9/11 era, the figure rose to 70 percent. These figures indicate another signature of radicalization. For the post-9/11 lone wolves, nearly all of the enabling was indirect.

Among jihadists of the post-9/11 years, the most frequent (indirect) enablers were Osama bin Laden and Anwar al-Awlaki. These charismatic leaders of the global Salafi Jihad inspired the Florida suicide airplane attack by Charles Bishop in 2002; Carlos Bledsoe's 2009 drive-by shooting at the Little Rock Army recruiting center; Yonathan Melaku's attacks on military facilities in the Washington, DC, area in 2010 and 2011; Khalid Aldawsari's 2010 attempted bombing of the homes of three former soldiers stationed at Abu Ghraib and the Dallas home of former President George W. Bush; Oscar Ortega-Hernandez's 2011 attempted assassination of President

Obama and the first family; Muhammad Abdulazeez's attack on the Chattanooga military recruiting offices in 2015; and Omar Mateen's mass murder at the Orlando gay nightclub.

For anti-government extremists of the post-9/11 period, the most frequent enablers were McVeigh, Pierce, and Alex Jones, conservative radio host, documentary filmmaker, writer and Internet personality described by the Southern Poverty Law Center as "the most prolific conspiracy theorist in contemporary America."[6]

Stochastic Terrorism

Indirect enabling often takes the form of *stochastic terrorism,* or the use of mass media to provoke random acts of ideologically motivated violence that are statistically predictable but individually unpredictable. Imagine an archer who shoots one hundred arrows at a target and hits the bull's eye only once. The bull's eye shot is statistically unpredictable, yet it is statistically predicable that a certain number of the arrows will strike somewhere on the target. The archer does not have to be skilled at archery. He simply needs to keep slinging arrows at the target and eventually one will hit the mark. In this analogy, the stochastic terrorist is the archer who sends out incendiary messages to thousands if not millions of people who consume the messages. The bull's eye is the one consumer who uses the messages to justify violent action. Stochastic terrorism is the method of international recruitment used by ISIS, which has brought an unprecedented sophistication to it through cosmopolitan use of social media, an extensive digital infrastructure provided by multilingual supporters from around the world, and gruesome beheading videos.

A stochastic terrorist indirectly enables the expression of violence through persuasive communication techniques, but he or she has no way of knowing exactly who will pick up on the messages and commit the violence. When emergent lone wolves are the consumers of these messages, there is roughly a 50 percent chance that the loner will have either a criminal background or a mental illness, or both. What often matters most in stochastic terrorism is the emotional intensity of the messaging and the way it is socially constructed or interpreted by the consumer, not the intentions of the messenger. In other words, the messenger does not have to actively promote violence for violence to occur. The next two cases shine a light on the phenomenon of stochastic terrorism in the post-9/11 era, one involving a radical right-wing cause and the other a radical left-wing cause.

The California Shootout

Shortly after midnight on July 18, 2010, two California Highway Patrol officers on Interstate 580 in Oakland attempted to stop a speeding pickup weaving through traffic.[7] The driver, forty-five-year-old Byron Williams, stopped his truck in the middle of the freeway rather than pull to the road-side. As the officers approached on foot, they spotted firearms inside the truck and saw Williams grab a pistol, a 9mm Glock. Williams suddenly opened fire at the officers, who retreated to their squad car and returned shots. After lodging a barrage of bullets from the Glock, Williams started firing rounds from a .308-caliber rifle until he ran out of ammunition. The shootout lasted twenty minutes. In the end, the two officers were wounded, and Williams lay face-down on the pavement with five bullet wounds in areas of his body not covered by his bulletproof vest. Oakland police later announced that Williams was stopped in route to the San Francisco offices of the American Civil Liberties Union (ACLU) and the Tides Foundation, where he planned to commit mass murder.

Byron Williams was a career criminal with convictions for assault, property destruction, and hit-and-run and drunk driving. Since 2001, he had been imprisoned twice for bank robbery. Facing life in prison as a three-strike offender when he was pulled over on the Oakland freeway, Williams was determined not to return to prison and his shootout was likely an attempt at suicide by cop. Williams had allegedly quit drinking years before but his mother found "18 or 20 beer bottles" in the home on the day of the attack.

Politically, Williams was an anti-government zealot with a profound hatred for President Obama, which was based upon a conspiracy theory. According to Williams, Obama had deliberately caused the April 2010 Deepwater Horizon oil spill off the coast of Louisiana to financially benefit liberal elites. At a personal level, Williams was alienated in a profound way. As a parolee, he had been unable to find employment because of his felony record. His mother recalled that Williams spent most of his time at home researching online information about the "shadow government" and watching Fox News, and she noted that her son was upset by "the way Congress was railroading through all these left-wing agenda items." In response, Williams later told investigators, he wanted to "start a revolution by traveling to San Francisco and killing people of importance at the Tides Foundation and the ACLU."

Williams targeted Tides because he believed that American billionaire philanthropist George Soros was controlling the Tides Foundation and using it "for all kinds of nefarious activities," including making a financial killing on Wall Street by betting on the Deepwater Horizon disaster. In a press interview, Williams cited Fox News commentator Glenn Beck as the primary source for his information on the liberal conspiracy to benefit from the oil spill.

On his Fox News program, which drew 2 to 3 million viewers each night, Beck had famously called President Obama a racist with a "deep-seated hatred for white people" and compared him to Adolf Hitler. Beck had attacked the Tides Foundation twenty-nine times in the eighteen months preceding the California shootout. Two of Beck's tirades came the week prior to Williams's attack. Williams also explored representations of the Horizon disaster as a "false flag" operation on the Alex Jones websites Infowars.com and PrisonPlanet.com. Williams's radicalization was therefore indirectly enabled by the conspiracy theories spouted by Glenn Beck and Alex Jones. Indeed, those theories were the very essence of Williams's motive. Yet, Beck and Jones have dismissed any responsibility for the influence of their theories on lone wolves like Williams, as well as Richard Poplawski, who also engaged with their ideas.

In 2014, Williams was sentenced to life imprisonment and taken to San Quentin.

The Family Research Council Attack

At 11 A.M. on August 15, 2012, twenty-eight-year-old Floyd Corkins entered the Washington, DC, headquarters of the Family Research Council, a conservative Christian lobbying group, and told a receptionist that he was interviewing for an internship.[8] After approaching an unarmed security guard and being asked for identification, Corkins said: "I don't like your politics." He grabbed a 9mm semi-automatic pistol from his backpack and fired three shots at the guard, striking him once in the arm. The guard rushed Corkins and with others wrestled the gun away from him and pinned him to the floor. A 911 call was made and within minutes police arrived along with FBI agents and hauled the shooter away.

Floyd Corkins had no criminal history and had purchased his firearm only days before the shooting, which may explain why it took Corkins three shots to hit an unarmed guard standing directly in front of him.

Upon questioning by the FBI, Corkins said he was a gay rights activist and that he had intended to commit mass murder at the Family Research Council (FRC). When agents searched his backpack, they found a box of 9mm ammunition and fifteen sandwiches from a Chick-fil-A restaurant. Corkins said that he was a volunteer at a local LGBT community center. When asked how he chose his target, Corkins replied: "Southern Poverty Law, lists . . . uh . . . anti-gay groups. I found them online."

The FRC was known for promoting traditional family values and lobbying against LGBT rights, such as same sex marriage. In a 2010 issue of its online magazine, *Intelligence Report*, the liberal-leaning Southern Poverty Law Center had described the FRC as an anti-gay hate group, claiming that the FRC had been a "font of anti-gay propaganda throughout history," and featured a "Hate Map" giving the exact location of FRC headquarters in Washington. This was the report read by Corkins, which indirectly enabled his radicalization.

The fast-food chain Chic-fil-A became the focus of controversy in June 2012, when its CEO made a series of public comments opposing same-sex marriage. This followed reports that Chic-fil-A's charitable arm, the S. Truett Cathy WinShape Foundation, had made millions in donations to political organizations that oppose LGBT rights. Gay rights activists called for protests and boycotts of the chain. Corkins's attack was apiece with this gay rights protest, and the fifteen Chic-fil-A sandwiches were symbolic of his commitment to the cause. Corkins intended to smear the sandwiches in the faces of his victims as they lay dying to make a statement about gay rights opponents.

Following Corkins's arrest, President Obama issued a condemnation of the attack and a joint statement was distributed by twenty-five LGBT groups further condemning Corkins's actions. The FRC called the shooting "an act of domestic terrorism" and criticized the Southern Poverty Law Center for being "reckless" in labeling organizations as hate groups. The

Southern Poverty Law Center responded by calling the FRC's accusation "outrageous."

Corkins pled guilty to terrorism charges in January 2013 and was sentenced to twenty-five years in prison, where he was diagnosed with an unspecified mental illness.

Enablers come in all shapes and sizes. After killing three white people and wounding two others in Wilkinsburg, Pennsylvania, on the morning of March 1, 2000, the self-described "black separatist" Ronald Taylor reportedly told arresting officers that he did it for Adolf Hitler and Timothy McVeigh and predicted that "the United Snakes of America will burn in hell."[9] Enablers are unpredictable in the strange world of lone wolf terrorism. Sometimes they can even stop an attack, as demonstrated in the following narrative.

The Maine Dirty Bomb Plot

On the morning of December 9, 2008, Amber Cummings, thirty-one, sat down to breakfast with her nine-year-old daughter at their home in Belfast, Maine.[10] But things were not idyllic. Amber got up from the table and went to her bedroom, where she put a gun in her mouth and considered killing herself. Instead, she decided that she needed to kill her husband, thirty-nine-year-old James Cummings, to protect their daughter. Amber wrapped her hand around the Colt .45-caliber revolver, walked into her husband's bedroom, and fired two bullets into his head while he slept, then fled with her daughter to a neighbor's home and called police.

Authorities began a homicide investigation, which quickly turned into something more when Amber told police that James had frequently spoken about "dirty bombs" as he mixed chemicals in the kitchen sink, adding that he had become "very upset" when Barack Obama was elected president. In no uncertain terms, Cummings had told Amber that he wanted to assassinate Obama with the dirty bomb he was making. Amber did not call police about this. Instead, she directly enabled James by allowing him to experiment uninterrupted for more than a month with radioactive bomb-making ingredients inside their home.

The FBI entered the case as part of a larger threat assessment on President-elect Obama prior to his inauguration on January 20, 2009. Agents spent days searching the Cummings home and removed a supply of radioactive materials, radiological dispersal device components, and literature on how to make a dirty bomb. It was determined that Cummings had purchased these components online from a U.S. chemical company. For the FBI, the Cummings case was a matter of great urgency because it represented the first attempt to build a dirty bomb on American soil.

James Cummings was a fervent neo-Nazi who had subjected his wife to mental, physical, and sexual cruelty during their decade-long marriage. According to Amber, Cummings began to collect materials for his dirty bomb in the wake of the 2008 presidential election, and he planned to assemble and detonate the explosives at Obama's inauguration. "He talked a lot about killing the president," said Amber. "I worried about it every day."

Cummings grew up in California and lived in Texas before moving to Maine in 2007. He did not need to work because he was supported by a multimillion dollar trust fund established by his father, a prominent California developer, who had also been murdered a decade earlier. Cummings had blown through most of his inheritance, however, and was involved in a six-year lawsuit against trustees who, he claimed, had mismanaged his money. Because of the experience, Cummings "hated people," recalled Amber. An acquaintance described Cummings as an angry and controlling person who was verbally abusive to his wife. Cummings talked incessantly to this person about his love of guns and his fascination with Hitler. Cummings had a collection of rare Nazi memorabilia around the house, including a prominently displayed swastika flag, and he occasionally dressed in full Nazi regalia. Among his possessions investigators also found an application for membership in the National Socialist Movement. But most importantly, as it turns out, Cummings was obsessed with watching child pornography on the Internet and had instructed Amber to conduct online chats to lure young girls to Maine. This led to an "escalating sense of doom" for Amber, who worried that Cummings was becoming sexually preoccupied with their daughter, and this in turn led her to murder Cummings. Although she was initially a direct enabler of lone wolf terrorism, by killing her husband Amber Cummings may have singlehandedly prevented the assassination of an American president—something even the FBI could not do.

The Cummings case was ruled a justifiable homicide, and Amber Cummings spent no time in jail. Underlying this narrative is another crucial aspect of the radicalization process: Cummings freely confided his terrorist intent to his wife Amber. Cummings is not the only lone wolf terrorist to broadcast his violent intentions. In the next chapter, we turn our attention to broadcasting intent as a key aspect of lone wolf terrorism, one that holds considerable potential for the prevention of lone wolf attacks.

CHAPTER 6

Broadcasting Intent

The Key to Preventing Lone Wolf Terrorism

roadcasting intent is also referred to by some investigators as "seep-age" or "signaling." The terms are synonymous. While lone wolves may physically isolate themselves from society, at the same time they communicate with others through threatening statements, letters, manifestos, and videotaped proclamations, which are similar to the martyrdom videos uploaded to the Internet by members of al-Qaeda and ISIS. Broadcasting intent can explicitly refer to an upcoming attack or it can imply that an attack is imminent. Broadcasting may occur in the weeks, days, hours, and even minutes before an attack. Broadcasting intent is crucial to understanding the process of radicalization for lone wolf terrorists.

Broadcasting intent infers that radicalization manifests itself in an activist stance involving the public expression of one's grievances, as well as an intense search for both physical *and* verbal or written confrontation with adversaries. Broadcasting intent is based on terrorists' need for becoming renowned for their causes. "The desire for renown," writes terrorism scholar Louise Richardson, "speaks to the desire to redress the perceived sense of humiliation at the hands of the enemy and is linked to the conviction most terrorists have that they are acting morally and on behalf of others."[1] The U.S. Marshals Lone Wolf Terrorism Task Force likewise notes: "We find that the deaths of others are not the motive [for lone wolves], but the catalyst to achievement of their mission or goal to force society in general to see the world from their perspective."[2]

Focusing on this immediate objective of radicalization among lone wolves, rather than on their underlying grievances, may sharpen our ability to see the imminent dangers posed by lone wolf terrorism. Broadcasting intent is about *how* radicalization is displayed, not about who is radicalized or why. In this way, broadcasting intent can be viewed as the most important commonality from the standpoint of prevention: If lone wolves typically announce their intentions to commit violence beforehand, then presumably steps can be taken to stop them.

Broadcasting intent is pervasive among lone wolf terrorists. In the Maine dirty bomb plot, for instance, James Cummings told his wife Amber about his plan to assassinate President Obama at his inauguration with a radioactive device, which, in turn, provided the FBI with valuable information about the case. Similarly, it was the publication of the anonymous "Unabomber Manifesto" that led David Kaczynski to suspect that his brother, Theodore, was the Unabomber. David's notifying authorities and providing the FBI with details about Kaczynski's whereabouts led directly to his capture.

Evidence of broadcasting intent among lone wolves can be found in every decade since the 1940s. In the pre-9/11 era, evidence of broadcasting appears in 84 percent of the cases in the database. They include some of the most pivotal cases in the history of lone wolf terrorism.

The "Mad Bomber" of New York City

Over a sixteen-year period (1940–1956), George Metesky placed thirty-three meticulously assembled pipe bombs, of which twenty-two exploded, in highly populated areas of New York City, including the Consolidated Edison Building, Grand Central Terminal, Radio City Music Hall, the New York Public Library, Macy's Department Store, the Empire State Building, and numerous movie theaters.[3] Bombs were also left in subways, phone booths, storage lockers, public restrooms, and—Metesky's signature—within the upholstery of movie theater seats. Metesky injured fifteen people in the attacks.

George Metesky's personal grievance was against his former employer, the Consolidated Edison utility company and was the result of an unsettled workman's compensation claim that left Metesky suffering from tuberculosis. Metesky harbored a profound hatred for Con Ed's attorney and three co-workers who allegedly perjured themselves during

Metesky's workman's compensation hearing. Over the years his rage became more political as he generalized his grievance to the New York Police Department and other New York institutions that had failed to grant him justice. Metesky was thirty-seven years old at the time of his first bombing; fifty-three at the time of his last. He was single and lived with his two unmarried sisters in Waterbury, Connecticut, a sixty-mile drive from New York. He suffered from undiagnosed paranoid schizophrenia.

In 1951, Metesky began placing anonymous phone calls to the buildings where he had planted the bombs. He also began writing unsigned letters to newspapers warning of his next attack. Metesky was, in fact, a prolific broadcaster of intent. Over the years, he sent more than one hundred letters and postcards to reporters, police precincts, private citizens, Con Ed, and the Workman's Compensation Board. Metesky even wrote to President Franklin D. Roosevelt prior to America's entry into World War II. The letters not only provided advance warnings that could have limited death and injury among New Yorkers, but also maximized publicity for Metesky's cause. Each communication was written in penciled block letters. Typical of his missives was the one sent to the *New York Herald Tribune* on October 22, 1951:

BOMBS WILL CONTINUE UNTIL THE CONSOLIDATED EDISON COMPANY IS BROUGHT TO JUSTICE FOR THEIR DASTARDLY ACTS AGAINST ME. I HAVE EXHAUSTED ALL OTHER MEANS. I INTEND WITH BOMBS TO CAUSE OTHERS TO CRY OUT FOR JUSTICE FOR ME.[4]

Hundreds of law enforcement officers became involved in what was known in New York as the "Mad Bomber" case. Led by the New York Police Department's seventy-six-member Bomb Investigation Unit (BIU), investigators operated on the obvious assumption that the bomber was a former Con Ed employee with a grudge against the company. The BIU checked and double-checked the company's personnel files of disgruntled or terminated employees, but to no avail. At the end of 1956, NYPD Commissioner Stephen Patrick Kennedy declared that the Mad Bomber case involved the "greatest manhunt in the history of the Police Department." Handwriting analysts, fingerprint experts, bomb technicians, and linguists joined the investigation, along with forensic specialists from the FBI crime lab in Washington. Portions of the bomber's letters were reprinted in the daily newspapers, and citizens were asked if they could recognize their peculiarities of language. Dr. James Brussel, a criminologist and psychiatrist for the New York State Commission for Mental Hygiene, was assigned to the case and developed a forensic portrait of the bomber, representing the first case of criminal profiling in law enforcement history. Among his conclusions, Brussel put forth the theory that the bomber was a "loner" with no friends, little interest in women, unmarried, and probably living with an older female relative. Given the meticulous care that went into the construction of the bombs, Brussel speculated that the bomber would be careful in how he presented himself to others. When he was arrested, said Brussel, the bomber would likely be wearing a neatly buttoned double-breasted suit.

The *New York Times* published Brussel's profile on Christmas Day 1956 under the banner headline "16-Year Search for a Madman." The following day, the profile was published in the *New York Journal American*, along with an open letter to the bomber urging him to give up and surrender to police. Metesky could not contain himself. He immediately replied to the editors, writing that he would not surrender until he could "BRING THE CON EDISON TO JUSTICE." Later in the letter Metesky wrote:

MY DAYS ON EARTH ARE NUMBERED—MOST OF MY ADULT LIFE HAS BEEN SPENT IN BED—MY ONE CONSOLATION IS—THAT I CAN STRIKE BACK—EVEN FROM MY GRAVE—FOR THE DASTARDLY ACTS AGAINST ME.[5]

This broadcasting of intent led directly to Metesky's capture. It came not through superlative police work, but through citizen cooperation. A Con Ed clerk named Alice Kelly had read the Christmas Day profile and Metesky's response to it, and she began scouring the company's worker's compensation files for employees with a serious health problem, something investigators had failed to do. On January 18, 1957, while searching the final batch of claims, Kelly found a file marked in red with the words "injustice" and "permanent disability"—words that had been printed in the profile. The marked file was for one George Metesky, an employee from 1929 to 1931, who had been injured in a plant accident in Waterbury on September 5, 1931. Several letters in Metesky's file used phrases also similar to the profile, including the term "dastardly acts." Police were notified that afternoon.

Around midnight on January 21, 1957, four NYPD detectives accompanied by Waterbury police knocked on Metesky's door and were let in by one of the sisters. Moments later, Metesky walked out of his bedroom wearing polished brown shoes, a brown sweater, a red necktie—and a double-breasted blue suit, buttoned neatly.

The main lesson of the Mad Bomber case is that an ordinary citizen may be well placed to pick up on the broadcasting of intent by a lone wolf terrorist and can therefore do something about it. The lesson has echoed down through the decades. Fifty-seven years after Alice Kelly identified George Metesky, NYPD Commissioner Bill Bratton convened a high-level security summit at One Police Plaza to coordinate international police efforts to combat lone wolf terrorism. Two weeks earlier, the ISIS-inspired lone wolf Zale Thompson had picked up a hatchet and attacked four policemen in Queens. Bratton pointed out that people who knew Thompson said that he had grown increasingly distant and agitated in the days before the attack. "There's oftentimes a dramatic change in behavior, appearance; oftentimes it may be more subtle, but very seldom does [terrorism] just happen. There are usually warning signs," Bratton said. The commissioner went on to remark that "it's vital to build trust with communities, so people feel comfortable reporting their suspicions and concerns."[6] The value of that advice is demonstrated in the next case.

The Attempted Assassination of President John F. Kennedy

Richard Pavlick was a seventy-three-year-old retired postal worker from Belmont, New Hampshire, with no wife and a prior criminal record for attempted assault with a deadly weapon.[7] He was well known in the Belmont community for making angry political rants, often over trivial matters. At one public meeting, Pavlick bitterly complained that the meeting hall's American flag was not being displayed properly. In other tirades Pavlick condemned the pope and the Catholic Church. Following John F. Kennedy's November 8, 1960, defeat of Richard Nixon in one of the closest presidential elections of the twentieth century, Pavlick turned his hostility toward the president-elect, the first Catholic to win the nation's highest office. Pavlick openly criticized JFK's wealthy father, Joseph P. Kennedy, claiming that the elder Kennedy had bought the election.

So angry was Pavlick that he turned his property over to a local youth camp, loaded his meager belongings into his 1950 Buick, and set out to assassinate the newly elected president. Pavlick began stalking Kennedy, presumably following Kennedy's movements in news reports. First Pavlick visited the Kennedy compound at Hyannis Port, Massachusetts, where he photographed the property and observed the compound's security. Pavlick then stalked JFK to Palm Beach, Florida, where the Kennedys maintained a vacation home. During his drive south, Pavlick stopped along the way to mail postcards to someone he was familiar with through his former workplace: the Belmont postmaster, thirty-four-year-old Thomas Murphy.

On Sunday morning December 11, 1960, as Kennedy was preparing to leave for mass at St. Edward Church in Palm Beach, Pavlick waited in his Buick near the Kennedy home. In the truck was a cache of dynamite. Pavlick's plan was to crash the car into Kennedy's vehicle, thereby causing a fatal explosion. It would be, in today's parlance, a suicide bombing. However, Pavlick changed his mind after seeing Kennedy with his wife, Jacqueline, and the couple's two small children.

The postcards to Belmont Postmaster Thomas Murphy continued. Pavlick could not contain himself. Murphy found one of the postcards to be unusually boastful. Pavlick wrote that the town of Belmont would hear from him soon "in a big way." The card was postmarked Palm Beach, Florida. Curious, Murphy checked the other cards mailed by Pavlick and noticed that the postmarked dates coincided with visits by JFK to those communities, which, in turn, led Murphy to call the Belmont police with his concern for Kennedy's safety. Belmont police contacted the Secret Service, who immediately opened an investigation on Pavlick. After interviewing locals, agents learned of Pavlick's previous public outbursts and that he had recently purchased dynamite.

Back in Palm Beach, Pavlick was still working on his plan to assassinate Kennedy. This time he would attack JFK in church. Pavlick went to St. Edward Church and surveyed its interior. But before he could launch an attack, Pavlick's broadcasting of intent caught up with him. Based on the tip provided by Murphy, the Secret Service had informed the Palm Beach police to be on the lookout for Pavlick's automobile. On December 15, a Palm Beach police officer spotted Pavlick's Buick crossing the Flagler Memorial Bridge. Reinforcements were called in, and officers surrounded the vehicle (which still contained ten sticks of dynamite) and arrested Pavlick. After he was taken into custody, Pavlick told officers, "Kennedy money bought the White House and the presidency. I had the crazy idea I wanted to stop Kennedy from being president."

Once again, the thread that unraveled a case of lone wolf terrorism was pulled by a common citizen, in this instance, the lowly government bureaucrat Thomas Murphy.

Thomas Murphy, Alice Kelly, David Kaczynski, and Amber Cummings are overlooked figures in the history of lone wolf terrorism—they are certainly more obscure than the terrorists they helped to stop—but they may be its unsung heroes. As such, they challenge a social dynamic known as the "bystander effect," which attempts to explain why people do not intervene when they know violence is about to occur. Murphy and the others refused to be apathetic bystanders. In the current counterterrorism vernacular, they saw something and said something. More often than not, however, when lone wolves broadcast their intent to commit terrorism, others fail to heed the warnings. Acts of lone wolf terrorism escalated during the 1970s, providing numerous examples in which warning signs were ignored.

The New Orleans Police Sniper

The reason for Mark Essex's military discharge did not bode well.[8] On February 10, 1971, after a two-year Navy hitch that included a court martial for assault and AWOL charges, officials cashiered the twenty-one-year-old black seaman for "reasons of unsuitably due to character disorder."[9] For his part, Essex claimed that he was subjected to ceaseless racial abuse during his service, and after repeated unsuccessful attempts to "work within the system," his personal frustrations took on the militant mood of the prevailing Black Power movement.

Following his discharge, Essex spent time with other black radicals in San Francisco before moving to New York where he spent three months with the Harlem chapter of the Black Panther Party. There he met Bernice Jones, one of the Panthers' primary organizers in New York and an articulate critic of black poverty and police brutality. Jones was presently at the center of FBI Director J. Edgar Hoover's secret war against the New York Black Panthers (as part of the FBI's COINTELPRO, or counterintelligence program) and at the periphery a Panther "subcell" known as the

Black Liberation Army, which was responsible for the May 1971 assassination of two New York police officers and the critical wounding of two more.[10] Bernice Jones would have a profound effect on Essex, enabling the single greatest ambush of policemen in American history.

Essex left New York and went home to Emporia, Kansas, where he had a string of jobs, but lost them all because of his attitude towards whites. Since a former Navy buddy lived in New Orleans, Essex relocated there in August 1972, where he rented a small apartment and continued his radicalization through reading Black Panther newspapers, the Nation of Islam's *Muhammad Speaks*, and *Black Rage*, a popular paperback published in 1968 by black psychiatrists William H. Grier and Price M. Cobbs. Essex covered his apartment walls with Black Nationalist slogans written in graffiti, including the phrase *"Kill Pig Nixon and All His Running Dogs!"*

The triggering event for Essex occurred on November 16, 1972, when two black students were killed during a standoff with police at Southern University in Baton Rouge. Several weeks later, Essex mailed a letter to New Orleans television station WWL clearly broadcasting his intent to commit terrorism. The letter read: *"Africa greets you . . . on Dec. 31, 1972 apprx. 11 p.m., the downtown New Orleans Police Department will be attacked. Reason—many, but the death of the two innocent brothers will be avenged. And many others."*[11] The letter was signed "Mata" (the Swahili word for "hunter's bow"). Essex could not contain himself. Several days later, he wrote to his parents in Emporia saying, "I have now decided that the white man is my enemy. I will fight to gain my manhood or die trying."[12] The attack would happen just as Essex described it, yet neither the WWL staff who had received his letter or Essex's parents would take the threat seriously—despite the fact that Essex was specific as to the date, time, and place of the attack.

Essex held true to his word. At approximately 11 P.M. on December 31, 1972, he hid in a parking lot across from the New Orleans central lockup and fired at a group of policemen with a .44-Magnum rifle, killing one officer and wounding another. Leaving a trail of firecrackers behind for diversion, Essex fled to an abandoned building and from there he shot a policeman in the back (he would later die) and wounded another. Essex then disappeared, only to return a week later with a vengeance.

On the morning of January 7, 1973, Essex shot a local grocer he suspected of aiding police and then jacked a car and drove to the Howard Johnson Motor Lodge on Loyola Avenue, where he shot and killed a doctor and his wife and then set fire to their room. Essex shot his way into other rooms and set eight more fires, creating a diversion. Along the way, he shot and killed two hotel managers and established a sniper's perch on the upper floors. Over the next eleven hours, more than six hundred fire-fighters and law enforcement personnel were called to the scene. Essex continued his sniper attack, killing two uniformed policemen and the police department's deputy superintendent Louis J. Sirgo. He wounded numerous others and opened fire on the nearby Charity Hospital. Meanwhile, black youth cheered the sniper with shouts of "Right On!" and "Off the Pigs!"

Essex was eventually killed by police; an autopsy revealed more than two hundred wounds to his body. In all, Essex shot nineteen people, including ten police officers. Five of them were killed outright. All but one was white. Over the next two months, black militants in New York and Washington, DC, were involved in ten different incidents of police shootings, prompting the *New York Times* to ask: "Are there really organized cells of blacks dedicated to the ambush of urban patrolmen? Or if nothing that extensive, are there a handful of 'guerrilla' assassins moving from city to city and getting help from friends along the way?"[13]

Through his example Essex would enable another sniper years later. When the Howard Johnson Motor Lodge shooting was covered live by television station WWL the entire day, twelve-year-old John Allen sat transfixed in front of the television at his grandmother's home in Baton Rouge. He would never forget it. After converting to the Nation of Islam years later, he changed his name to John Allen Muhammad. In 2002, Muhammad became the Beltway Sniper, who along with Lee Malvo, killed ten and wounded three others in a terrorist spree that paralyzed Washington, DC, and surrounding counties for weeks.

The Attempted Assassination of President Gerald R. Ford

Lynette "Squeaky" Fromme received widespread media attention as a member of the Charles Manson Family during the late 1960s and early 1970s.[14] Fromme was never implicated in the infamous Tate-Labianca murders of 1969, however, and she had no record of violent crime. Yet due to her reputation as a Manson follower, Fromme was well known to California law enforcement. In 1974, five years after the Tate-Labianca murders, the California state attorney general released a report entitled *Terrorism in California*. The report predicted that "the Manson Clan" could become involved in a terrorist plot to free Manson from prison. In reference to Fromme and former Family member Sandra Good, the report warned that "two former members of the Manson Clan are now living in Sacramento."[15]

Fromme's political grievance was based on her commitment to environmental values espoused by the Manson family. At the height of his influence—fueled as it was by psychedelic drugs and sexual orgies with Fromme, Sandra Good, and others—Charles Manson adopted the syncretic belief that the Beatles and the Book of Revelation spoke directly to him about the revolutionary imperatives of ecology. The biblical source stated, "Then from the smoke came the locusts"—or *beetles*—"they were told not to harm the grass of the earth or any green growth or any tree, but only those of mankind who have not the seal of God upon their foreheads."[16]

At a personal level, Fromme never severed her emotional ties with Manson and was committed to gaining his freedom after he was imprisoned for the Tate-LaBianca slayings. Crucial to her cause was an event that had occurred several years earlier. Back on August 4, 1970, early in Manson's murder trial, President Nixon commented at a press conference that Manson was "guilty, directly or indirectly, of eight murders without reason."[17] Manson had yet to be convicted of any crimes, however, and Fromme would never forget Nixon's statement because it revealed the naked injustices rendered unto Manson.

By early 1975, the family had disintegrated. Manson was in Folsom Prison. Fromme and Sandra Good had moved to Sacramento to be near him. And President Gerald Ford had pardoned Nixon for crimes linked to Watergate. By then, twenty-seven-year-old Squeaky Fromme was a radical environmentalist and a pagan ascetic who was seen around Sacramento wearing a red robe meant to signify a new religious order that would pray for Manson's release from prison. Fromme still blamed Nixon for the wrongful conviction of Manson in the Tate-LaBianca murders, and she blamed Ford for both pardoning Nixon and continuing his policies of environmental ruin. Because of this, Fromme began contemplating an assassination attempt against President Ford. She did not intend to kill Ford, but in attempting to assassinate him, Fromme hoped to create an opportunity for promoting her cause. Once arrested and prosecuted for the assassination attempt, Fromme reasoned that Manson would be called as a witness for the defense, thereby providing him with the forum he needed to gain his pardon and save the world.

Fromme broadcasted her intent to family members in prison, neighbors, former teachers, and reporters. In July 1974, Fromme was seen recruiting students to her cause on the campus of Sacramento State University. Beginning in early 1975, she appeared at news bureaus around Sacramento, complaining about Manson's raw deal and Ford's failures on environmentalism. She called newspapers and television stations in San Francisco and Los Angeles, railing against Ford and impending ecological calamities. Fromme could not contain herself. She met with a Denver journalist sympathetic to her environmental goals. A German magazine published a profile on Fromme, in which she held up a photo of President Ford and said, *"He will have to pay for what he's doing!"*[18] She wrote a letter to the editors of *Ms. Magazine*, criticizing women who used their bodies to sell animal-based cosmetics. Some reports placed her in Hollywood, where she tried to warn Led Zeppelin guitarist Jimmy Page of "bad energy" surrounding him.

In the summer of 1975, Fromme mailed a letter to the California State Assembly Criminal Justice Committee; threatening to "release thoughts that will destroy you" (she signed it "C. Manson") (206). Fromme told a neighbor that she was planning something "bigger than the Tate killing" (207). In late August, Fromme visited a Sacramento TV station to protest logging in the Redwood National Forest. A reporter declined to air her concerns, saying that he was working on a bigger story. He had just learned that President Ford was planning a visit to Sacramento on September 5. That is how Fromme learned of the Ford visit to Sacramento, triggering her assassination attempt. The plot was spontaneously formulated, with little planning.

Many had witnessed Fromme's broadcasting of intent, but not one person reacted. Most importantly, her broadcasting was ignored by criminal justice authorities, even though the California attorney general had warned that Fromme could become involved in a terrorist plot to free Manson from prison. Fromme's broadcasting was also ignored by a legion of reporters, friends, prisoners, acquaintances, and students at Sacramento State.

So on the morning of September 5, 1975, as President Ford shook hands with well-wishers during a walk through Capitol Park on his way to the California statehouse for a meeting with Governor Jerry Brown, Fromme emerged from the crowd in her red ceremonial gown with a World War I-era Colt .45 automatic pistol (the gun had not been fired in years), and pointed it at the president's stomach. A Secret Service agent restrained Fromme, wrestled her to the ground, and took the gun away as Fromme managed a small grin and said, "The gun didn't go off" (264). Because Fromme did not intend to shoot Ford, there was no bullet in the gun's firing chamber nor did Fromme know how to chamber a bullet into the weapon. Her sole intent was to seek renown for her dual grievances over the imprisonment of Charles Manson and environmental destruction.

Fromme was sentenced to life imprisonment for the attempted assassination of President Ford. She was released in 2009 after serving thirty-four years.

The Ultimate Lone Wolf Terrorist

The decisive factor in Joseph Paul Franklin's radicalization was not the racist traditions of his family, the biographies he read as a boy on Civil War guerrilla leader William Quantrill and bank robbers Jesse James and John Dillinger, or the copy of Hitler's *Mein Kamp* he stole from a public library when he was fifteen.[19] Instead, it was a bicycle accident at the age of seven that severely impaired his eyesight. A prison psychologist would later theorize that over time Franklin developed expert marksmanship with firearms as a means of compensating for this handicap. His skill with guns, combined with a childhood marked by constant and brutal beatings from both parents, led to Franklin's murderous rages as an adult. Along the way he had several enablers within the racist Right, none more important than Jerry Ray, brother of James Earl Ray. In essence, the racially bigoted killing spree of Joseph Paul Franklin was a copycat of the Martin Luther King assassination.

Franklin began broadcasting his intent long before he killed anyone. And he did so with deliberate exhibitionism. On September 18, 1970, Franklin—then an obscure twenty-year-old racist from Mobile, Alabama—was photographed in a Nazi uniform outside the Nixon White House while protesting a state visit by Israeli Prime Minister Golda Meir. Over the next several years he was involved in other racial protests and was arrested for assault and battery and carrying concealed weapons. In 1976, Franklin sent a letter to President Jimmy Carter, threatening to kill him for his pro–civil rights views. There is no contemporaneous evidence, however, of Secret Service attempts to connect the photograph of Franklin at the Golda Meir protest, his criminal record, and his assassination threat against President Carter. No Secret Service threat assessment was ever done on Franklin. Essentially, he was ignored.

Franklin's terrorist campaign began on August 7, 1977. Over the next four years he would commit sixteen bank robberies, two bombings (one on a synagogue), six aggravated assaults, the gunshot wounding of five people, including civil rights leader Vernon Jordan, and the murder of an estimated twenty others, including a mentally disabled child. Because he intended nothing less than to start an American race war, Franklin targeted "mixed-race" couples and Jews. Among his victims was *Hustler* publisher Larry Flynt. On March 6, 1978, in Lawrenceville, Georgia, in retaliation for a *Hustler* article showing interracial sex, Franklin fired one shot from a .44-caliber rifle into Flynt's abdomen, leaving him paralyzed from the waist down. Franklin's preferred method of killing was the sniper rifle. Although blind in his right eye from the childhood accident and nearsighted in the other, Franklin was an extraordinary marksman. Most of his victims died instantly.

Franklin killed in multiple jurisdictions using multiple weapons, numerous aliases, and various disguises (including wearing cowboy outfits, blackening his face with charcoal, and wearing Afro wigs), all of which made it difficult for police to identify him. Although Franklin committed his sniping in broad daylight or on well-lit streets, witnesses were rare. Nor could police determine a motive for the shootings.

But in 1978, on a visit home to Alabama, Franklin admitted to his sister that he had embarked upon his cross-country killing spree a year earlier. Had she simply reported this to police, it is possible that Franklin would have been apprehended early in his campaign. But hers was not the only missed opportunity. Prior to killing two black men as they jogged with two white women in Salt Lake City, Utah, on August 20, 1980, Franklin told a prostitute that he hated blacks, but the police would learn about this statement only after Franklin's capture. And hours before shooting Vernon Jordan in the back after seeing him with a white woman at a Marriott hotel in Fort Wayne, Indiana, on the night of May 29, 1980, Franklin told a complete stranger that he hated African Americans. That, too, went unreported at the time.

Neither was the Franklin investigation conducted with anything approaching competency by the various police agencies in jurisdictions where the attacks occurred. Twice in early 1980—prior to his most prolific period of killing—Franklin was arrested and jailed for traffic violations and carrying concealed weapons. Both times he was released. Following the Salt Lake City murders, police developed a composite sketch of Franklin based on a witness description. After Franklin murdered two black adolescents in Cincinnati on June 8, 1980, a prostitute came forward in response to a $50,000 reward. Although she did not know his name, police were able to get Franklin's automobile license plate number from the motel where he had taken her. She was also able to tell police that Franklin had a bald eagle tattoo on his arm. All of these tips—the car license plate number, the composite sketch, and a description of the tattoo—were entered into the FBI database and an arrest warrant was issued for the unnamed suspect.

A major break came on September 25, 1980, when police were arresting an armed robbery suspect at a motel in Florence, Kentucky. As the suspect was being taken into custody, another motel guest complained to officers about all the noise. Unsatisfied with their response, the guest called the Florence police dispatcher four times but was repeatedly told to calm down and go about his business. The guest could not contain himself. After the fifth call, the dispatcher became apprehensive and called the motel manager to get a make on the guest's car. A background check showed a match on the vehicle used in the Cincinnati murders. Franklin was arrested at the motel and locked up in the Florence jail. But before police could interview him, Franklin escaped.

For some nine years, then, Joseph Paul Franklin had broadcasted his intent. He had been in police custody three times, but either escaped or was freed without questioning. These developments reveal an astonishing series of missed opportunities to capture Franklin.

Finally, FBI agents learned that Franklin had resorted to selling blood to survive after a man matching Franklin's description was seen at a blood bank in Birmingham, Alabama, and alerts were sent to blood banks across the South. Franklin was captured at a blood bank in Lakeland, Florida, on October 28, 1980, after a nurse recognized the bald eagle tattoo on his arm.

Not only did the missed opportunities cost the lives of many victims, but they helped to create a personality cult around Franklin. In 1982, after being convicted of several murders, Franklin was incarcerated at the U.S. Penitentiary in Marion, Illinois, where a gang of black convicts attacked Franklin and stabbed him fifteen times in the neck and abdomen, leaving him at the brink of death. Surviving the assault, he went on to give interviews to *60 Minutes*, *TV Guide*, and *People* magazine. In 1989, William Pierce dedicated *Hunter*, the sequel to Pierce's hugely popular *The Turner Diaries*, to Franklin in honor of Franklin's shooting of the pornographer Larry Flynt. *Hunter*'s fictional protagonist is the lone wolf terrorist whose murders of interracial couples set an example for other whites to carry out spontaneous acts of assassination without the assistance of a leader or an organization. With Pierce's dedication in *Hunter*, Joseph Paul Franklin became universally known as the ultimate lone wolf terrorist. Franklin's name is listed in nearly every encyclopedia on serial killers and terrorists. He was eventually convicted and sentenced to twelve different life terms plus the death penalty. Today he is glorified on white supremacy websites as a lone wolf killer who took it upon himself to do "God's will."

Franklin was executed by the Missouri Department of Corrections on November 20, 2013. But that did not end his legacy.

Another fan of *Hunter* was the former Klansman Frazier Glenn Miller, who exchanged correspondence with Franklin during his long years of incarceration. In the run up to Franklin's execution, Miller, whose star in the radical Right had faded long ago and who was now suffering from an incurable illness, became his loudest and most loyal advocate, arguing in a neo-Nazi website posting that Franklin was "the bravest, therefore the greatest White Nationalist hero America has ever produced." On April 13, 2014—on what would have been Joseph Paul Franklin's sixty-fourth birthday—Miller entered the Jewish Community Center in Overland Park, Kansas, armed with an assault rifle. Shouting "Heil Hitler!" he opened fire on a lunchroom crowd, killing two elderly people and a teenager.

It was the first act of lone wolf terrorism in America that year. Even though lone wolves act alone, they do not live in a social vacuum. Among lone wolf terrorists, there exists something akin to an institutional memory.

The Atlanta Bombing

In terms of sheer body count, Eric Rudolph is the most prolific American lone wolf terrorist as of this writing.[20] In four separate bombing attacks between 1996 and 1998, Rudolph mortally wounded 3 people and injured another 117. Rudolph was driven by a complex set of overlapping motives. While he was undoubtedly a racist and anti-government fanatic whose personal grievance stemmed from his failed attempt to join the Army's elite Special Forces, the essence of his political grievance was anti-abortion absolutism. "The murder of 3.5 million children every year will not be tolerated," he wrote to the media following his bombing of an Alabama abortion clinic (122). Because Rudolph believed that violence was necessary to stop abortion, he justified killing law enforcement officers who defended abortion rights. According to Rudolph's statement to the court, his purpose in bombing the Atlanta Olympic Games in 1996 "was to confound [and] anger and embarrass the Washington government in the eyes of the world for its abominable sanctioning of abortion on demand." Rudolph was also angered by the "homosexual agenda," which he considered an "assault on the integrity of American society"—hence his bombing of a gay and lesbian nightclub in Atlanta (290). Yet this trail of bloodshed might have been avoided had Rudolph's broadcasting of terrorist intent been taken seriously. He broadcasted his intent not to friends or the media, but directly to police.

The 1996 Summer Olympic Games began on July 19 with the lighting of the Olympics torch by Muhamad Ali. It took place a little more than one year after the Oklahoma City bombing, so security was at a heightened state of readiness, with some 30,000 local, state, and federal agents and private security guards assigned to protect the games, which were expected to draw a crowd of 85,000 spectators each day. Tactical units, bomb technicians, rescue squads, and other specialists were on hand to provide around-the-clock security.

Yet shortly after midnight on July 27, thirty-year-old Eric Rudolph managed to slip past hundreds of security officers and enter the twenty-one-acre Centennial Park adjacent to the Olympics Stadium. An estimated 50,000 people were in Centennial Park, designated the "town square" of the Olympics, dancing at a free concert, drinking, and visiting in the late summer night.

Rudolph carried a heavy green military backpack containing a pipe bomb. He sat down on a park bench near an NBC-TV sound and video tower. Rudolph placed the backpack under the bench and walked away. Moments later, a drunken teenager spotted the backpack and began tugging at it and tipped it over. He considered stealing the backpack but found it too heavy to carry so he left it behind. Richard Jewell, a thirty-three-year-old private security guard, was next to see the backpack. Suspicious, he called a nearby guard from the Georgia Bureau of Investigation who in turn radioed bomb technicians and asked them to come to area. Jewell then evacuated people from the area to make room for the bomb techs, an act that would ultimately save many people from injury or death.

What happened next is a profound example of the preventative possibility of terrorist broadcasting.

At roughly 12:30 A.M., Rudolph went to a phone booth and dialed 911. After making sure that the operator could understand him, Rudolph began to deliver a warning that there was a bomb in Centennial Park. Yet the operator hung up on Rudolph before he could finish his statement.

Rudolph could not contain himself. Assuming that the call had been traced, Rudolph went looking for another phone booth and located one at a Days Inn a block away. His second 911 call was made at 12:58 A.M. "*There is a bomb in Centennial Park,*" said Rudolph. "*You have 30 minutes. We defy your . . . ,*"[21] but the operator cut him off again.

The 911 operator first attempted to call the Atlanta Police Department Command Center (ACC), but she got a busy signal. After several minutes, the operator was able to get a police dispatcher on the line and the following exchange ensued.[22]

"You know the address to Centennial Park?" asked the operator.

"Girl, don't ask me to lie to you," joked the dispatcher.

"I tried to call ACC, but ain't nobody answering the phone. And I just got this man telling me about there's a bomb set to go off in 30 minutes in Centennial Park," said the operator before explaining that she had tried to get the computerized communications system to recognize Centennial Park, but was unsuccessful when she typed it in.

"Oh Lord, child. One minute, one minute. . . . Centennial Park. You put it in and it won't go in?" asked the dispatcher.

"No, unless I'm spelling Centennial wrong. . . . How are we spelling Centennial?" asked the operator.

"C–E–N–T–E–N–N–I. . . . How do *you* spell Centennial?" asked the dispatcher.

"I'm spelling it right. It ain't taking . . ." said the operator.

"Wait a minute. That's the regular Olympics Stadium, right?" asked the dispatcher.

After several more minutes the operator located a street address for Centennial Park and entered it into the system, which alerted the Atlanta Police Department to Rudolph's bomb threat. Unfortunately, however, there was no direct line of communication set up between the Atlanta Police Department and the command center at Centennial Park. Due to this abject failure in local police communications, officers on the ground at Centennial Park never got the warning.

Rudolph's motive for the warning calls was anything but altruistic. By broadcasting his intent to bomb Centennial Park, Rudolph assumed that police would clear the area of citizens, leaving only police in direct proximity of the blast zone. Rudolph's aim was to kill as many police officers as possible.

In Centennial Park, the bomb's timing device was ticking toward ignition inside the backpack as two technicians knelt over it looking for booby traps. Finding none, an officer inspected the contents of the backpack with a flashlight. He saw wires, a plastic container, and the metal end of a pipe. The technicians quickly moved away and called the bomb disposal unit. But it was too late.

At 1:18 A.M., the timing device triggered the explosion, sending thousands of white hot chunks of pipe and nails through the air and into the crowd, killing a woman and injuring 110 others, some grievously. A cameraman racing to the scene collapsed and died of a heart attack.

In another display of gross incompetence, once FBI agents entered the bombing investigation, they designated Richard Jewell, the private security guard who had reported the backpack and cleared the area, as a possible suspect based on a "lone bomber" criminal profile.[23] Jewell then became the subject of intense media coverage and was ridiculed as the "Unabubba." Meanwhile, Rudolph was free to maim and murder. Six months later, Rudolph set off a similar bomb outside an abortion clinic in the Atlanta suburb of Sandy Springs. An hour later, he detonated a second bomb next to a dumpster where he knew police and first responders would gather. In all, six were injured, including two federal agents. On February 21, 1997, Rudolph bombed a gay and lesbian nightclub in midtown Atlanta, although no one was injured. While inspecting the area, an officer found a second bomb hidden near the front entrance, which was rendered safe by a robot. Almost a year later, Rudolph used a model airplane controller to detonate a bomb outside an abortion clinic in Birmingham, Alabama, killing an off-duty policeman and critically injuring a nurse.

Following the Birmingham bombing, a witness saw a long-haired man leaving the abortion clinic in a Nissan pickup, seemingly unconcerned about the chaos behind him. The witness wrote down the vehicle's license plate number, which police traced to Eric Rudolph. Yet Rudolph had escaped into the vast Appalachian wilderness where he would spend the next five years surviving on previously stored food, wild game, acorns, salamanders and pilfered vegetables. In October 1998, he was named as a suspect in the four Atlanta bombings and the FBI offered a $1 million reward for information leading to his capture. Federal, state, and local law enforcement search teams scoured the wilderness while locals turned Rudolph into a cultural icon. A country song was written about him, "Run, Rudolph Run." His image appeared on a popular t-shirt, women admitted to having erotic dreams about the fugitive, and he became the subject of widespread Internet traffic. Among those influenced by the postings was David Copeland, one of Britain's most prolific lone wolf terrorists, who later confessed that he had been inspired by Rudolph's attack on the Olympics.[24] The age of the Internet "entrepreneur of violence" had begun.

Rudolph was arrested without incident behind a Save-A-Lot store in Murphy, North Carolina, at 4 A.M. on May 31, 2003 by a rookie police officer. He appeared to be well fed. In 2005, Rudolph was sentenced to four consecutive life terms and taken to the Federal Supermax at Florence, Colorado. Richard Jewell was cleared of wrongdoing and publicly thanked by Georgia Governor Sonny Perdue in 2006 for saving the lives of those at the Olympics. He died the following year.

But a potentially different scenario might have unfolded had Rudolph's broadcasting of intent been taken seriously. His first warning call of July 27, 1996, was made at about 12:30 A.M. Some forty-eight minutes would transpire before the timing device detonated his pipe bomb, allowing sufficient time for Richard Jewell and responding police to clear the park. Had the 911 operator not ignored Rudolph's initial warning, she might have attempted to alert the Centennial Park command center, had there also been a direct line of communication between the Atlanta Police Department and Centennial Park to begin with. Still, a competent 911 operator might have then traced the location of the phone booth where Rudolph made his warning call. According to Rudolph, the phone booth was a ten-minute walk from the park bench where he had placed the bomb. The location of the phone booth might have been radioed to street patrols and the area could have been cordoned off and searched for a lone male suspect, perhaps retreating quickly. That may have led to Rudolph's capture. If so, none of the other bombings would have occurred.

Such a disaster in police communications would play a central role in the event that came to define the age of lone wolf terrorism. Nine minutes after Anders Breivik bombed the Justice Department in Oslo, Norway on the afternoon of July 22, 2011, a pedestrian named Andreas Olsen phoned a police hotline and said that he had earlier observed a man in the area wearing a crash helmet and police uniform and walking with a pistol in his hand before getting into a civilian van. Sensing that there was "something strange" about him, Olsen had recorded the license plate number and make of the vehicle in his cellphone and he gave this important information to the police operator. Yet the message would not be read by a police supervisor for another half hour, giving Breivik the time he needed to flee Oslo for the youth summer camp where he would kill the majority of his victims.[25] The Norway massacre did not result from bystander apathy, then, but from the failure of law enforcement to heed the warning of a bystander.

The broadcasting of intent extended into the post-9/11 era. Among the post-9/11 lone wolves in our database, 76 percent broadcasted their intent, often more than once. Broadcasting intent is therefore another signature commonality in the radicalization of lone wolf terrorists. Yet there is a major difference in more recent cases due to advances in technology that have created new forms of broadcasting, including e-mails, text messages, Facebook postings, podcasts, Skypes, and YouTube videos. Nevertheless, for all the rapidity and potential anonymity of communication through these media, each broadcast of a lone wolf attack made through any of these means still presented opportunities for prevention. Two cases are noteworthy.

The Attempted Assassination of the Obama Family

Oscar Ortega-Hernandez was a walking contradiction. He was a single, unemployed Hispanic jihadist who claimed to be a born-again Christian. He lived in Idaho Falls, Idaho, which was known during the American 1980s and 1990s as a hotbed of anti-government extremism.[26] In 2009, nineteen-year-old Ortega-Hernandez began exhibiting erratic behavior and adopted a wide range of bizarre beliefs. He was a "grievance collector," who embraced conspiracy theories regarding government control of

Americans through GPS chips, fluoride, and aspartame (a sugar substitute). Along with these odd beliefs, Ortega-Hernandez became critical of the United States for the wars in Iraq and Afghanistan and grew sympathetic to the cause of al-Qaeda, even though he had little apparent knowledge of the Salafi Jihad. In 2010, Ortega-Hernandez's ranting to friends and family became more threatening. He described himself as a "cold-hearted warrior" and declared, "It's time for Armageddon."[27] Ortega-Hernandez became obsessed with President Barack Obama and believed that Obama was oppressing citizens in numerous ways, including by his continuing criminalization of marijuana.

As his anger for the federal government increased, he began target practicing with an assault rifle at a desolate crater on federal land. He tattooed himself with religious symbols, including the word "Israel" on his neck and rosary beads and hands clasped in prayer on his chest, to match his apocalyptic worldview. He also slipped into a depression and adopted the paranoid belief that the government was out to get him and that the president was involved in the conspiracy. To family he called Obama "the devil" and "the anti-Christ." To others, Ortega-Hernandez declared that he was "on a mission from God to take out Obama."[28]

In September 2011, Ortega-Hernandez met a film studies student in the gym at Idaho State University and the two planned to make a video of Ortega-Hernandez that they would send to Oprah Winfrey in an attempt to get on the Oprah Channel. They later went to the university's broadcasting studio and recorded a tedious forty-five-minute video featuring Ortega-Hernandez dressed in all black, wearing a crucifix and reading unctuously from a battered notebook: "You see Oprah, there is still so much more that God needs me to express to the world. It's not just a coincidence that I look like Jesus. I'm the modern day Jesus Christ that you have all been waiting for."[29] Ortega-Hernandez accused the United States of "fighting or should I say bullying other countries for their oil. Our freedom is at stake."[30] The video was received at Oprah Channel headquarters, where it was filed, until a copy was handed over to the Secret Service after Ortega-Hernandez became the subject of a nationwide manhunt.

Ortega-Hernandez could not contain himself. In early October, he made two more videos at the home of a friend, in which he praised Osama bin Laden for having the courage to stand up to the United States and called for revolution against the federal government. Ortega-Hernandez stated that he "needed to kill" President Obama and that he "will not stop until it's done."[31] His broadcasting of intent was explicit. Yet the videos remained a secret between Ortega-Hernandez and his friend. After making the videos, Ortega-Hernandez loaded up his black 1998 Honda Accord and disappeared. Family and friends in Idaho Falls heard nothing from him for weeks, nor did they report him missing to local police. He had become a lone wolf.

At 8:50 P.M. on Friday, November 11, 2011, Ortega-Hernandez stopped his Honda Accord in the middle of the road at Seventeenth Street and Constitution Avenue NW in Washington, DC, some 750 feet from the White House. With the passenger-side window of his car lowered, Ortega-Hernandez grabbed a Romanian-made Cugir semi-automatic assault rifle equipped with a telescopic sight and aimed it straight at the White House. He fired nine shots, several striking the Truman balcony only feet away from where a Secret Service agent was stationed. Five bullets hit the executive mansion between the second and third floors, the living quarters of the first family. Ortega-Hernandez sped away, driving erratically in a westerly direction. Moments later he lost control of his car and crashed it into the on-ramp of the Theodore Roosevelt Memorial Bridge. After failing to restart the car, he fled on foot, across the bridge, over the Potomac River and into Virginia.

President Obama was not at the White House when the shootings occurred. He and First Lady Michelle Obama were in San Diego, preparing for a trip to Hawaii. Inside the White House, though, were the Obama's youngest daughter, Sasha, and Michelle's mother, Marian Robinson. Malia Obama was out with friends and expected back at any minute.

Inside the Honda, investigators found Ortega-Hernandez's assault rifle, ammunition, and nine spent shell casings. The car had Idaho license plates and was registered to Ortega-Hernandez, giving police their first lead. Secret Service agents distributed photos of their suspect at several places where they learned he had been in recent weeks, including a Hampton Inn outside Indiana, Pennsylvania. But they did not need to go so far afield. The day after the attack, police in Arlington County, Virginia, responded to a call about a man behaving oddly in a local park. They questioned Ortega-Hernandez but had no idea that he was a suspect in a shooting, so they let him go. Two days later, on November 14, Ortega-Hernandez was caught on a surveillance camera inside an empty hopper car on a freight train near Shenandoah Junction, West Virginia. The following day, he was identified by a surveillance camera standing outside a car wash in Greensburg, Pennsylvania, trying to hitch a ride. On November 16, Ortega-Hernandez returned to the Hampton Inn in Indiana, Pennsylvania. When employees recognized him from the Secret Service photo, they called the state police, who arrested Ortega-Hernandez without incident on November 17. In 2014 he was sentenced to twenty-five years in federal prison.

News reports said that President Obama was "extremely upset" when he returned home after the attack on his family. A *Washington Post* investigation later revealed that the Secret Service fumbled its response to the shooting (agents initially thought the gunfire came from a street gang); this led to a congressional hearing, the resignation of Secret Service Director Julia Pierson, and agency changes to its personnel and procedures surrounding White House security—all of which might have been avoided had bystanders acted on the broadcasting of terrorist intent by Oscar Ortega-Hernandez.

Finally, along the continuum between stopping lone wolf terrorism by acting on the broadcasting of intent and ignoring the broadcasting altogether is an area of "near misses"—those lone wolf terrorists who barely got away. No case demonstrates this better than Paul Ciancia's.

The Los Angeles International Airport Shooting

Paul Ciancia was a single, twenty-three-year-old unemployed white motorcycle mechanic, who had recently moved from New Jersey to the Sun Valley neighborhood of Los Angeles, where he shared an apartment with several roommates.[32] Probably through his interest in conspiracy theory websites (although no digital footprint exists to confirm it), Ciancia developed an obsession with the Transportation Services Administration (TSA), the federal agency responsible for airport security. Ciancia's grievance against the TSA grew from his belief in a conspiracy theory about the New World Order, which claims that global elites are plotting to form a socialist "one-world government" that will crush American freedoms. Although the term is traditionally linked to the Patriot Movement of the 1990s, it had been recently updated and popularized by the Internet conspiracy theorist Alex Jones. Police would later find a one-page manifesto among Ciancia's belongings stating that he "wanted to instill fear" in the "traitorous minds" of TSA agents because they were "pigs." The note mentioned "fiat currency," also a catchphrase of the neo-Patriots, denoting economic dominance by the New World Order. Ciancia defined himself as a "pissed off patriot," who was upset at former DHS Secretary Janet Napolitano. (DHS is charged with administering the TSA.) Ciancia's manifesto called Napolitano a "bull dyke" and contained the phrase "FU Janet Napolitano." Such language is also consistent with rightwing homophobes of the neo-Patriot movement who allege that TSA agents engage in hand searches that are really intended to sexually grope travelers at American airports.

Sometime in 2013, Ciancia began to experience unidentified problems in his personal life. In late October, he asked a roommate for a ride to the Los Angeles International Airport so that he could fly home to Pennsville, New Jersey, claiming that his father was ill. Yet Ciancia's father was not ill, and Ciancia changed his mind about going to the airport. Ciancia then began to speak with his roommates about committing suicide.

Ciancia's subsequent broadcasting of intent came fast and furious but still he could not contain himself. On the morning of November 1, 2013, Ciancia rushed into a roommate's bedroom and demanded a ride to the airport immediately, again claiming that he needed to fly home to New Jersey. This time they did set out for LAX. That morning Ciancia also sent text messages to his brother in Pennsville. One said that Ciancia was about to kill himself. The brother wrote back, but Ciancia did not reply. Alarmed, the brother texted his father, who sent several text messages to Ciancia, but again there was no reply. Ciancia's father then called the Pennsville police, who in turn called the Los Angeles Police Department with a request to issue a missing person's report on Ciancia, given that his family had not heard from Ciancia after repeated attempts to make contact. The call came into the LAPD switchboard at 10:06 A.M. LAPD officers arrived at Ciancia's apartment six minutes later and were told by another roommate that Ciancia was not home but had been there earlier in the morning. Because the police had confirmation of Ciancia's whereabouts, they could not file the missing person's report, so they left.

Ciancia was dropped off at LAX around 9:15 A.M. At 9:20, he entered Terminal 3 wearing dark clothing over a bulletproof vest and carrying a duffle bag containing a Smith & Wesson .223 semi-automatic rifle along with five 30-round magazines, hundreds of additional rounds of ammunition enclosed in boxes, and his manifesto. Given Ciancia's text messages, he was likely on a mission to commit suicide by cop.

Walking up to a TSA checkpoint, Ciancia pulled the weapon from his bag and ambushed an unarmed TSA officer, shooting him in the chest at point-blank range. Ciancia went up an escalator but returned to the checkpoint and shot the TSA officer again, after seeing him move, leaving the officer bleeding to death. Ciancia then moved to the TSA screening area, where he continued firing, passed the checkpoint, and moved farther into a secure area of the terminal where he shot two TSA agents and a male bystander. Ciancia began walking down the terminal's concourse, repeatedly asking people if they were TSA officers and then moving on without shooting when they said no. Reaching the end of the terminal, he entered a food court, where airport police cornered him, shot him four times, including once in the face, and arrested him. In all, he had killed one TSA officer and wounded two more, in addition to injuring four civilians.

The LAPD officers had arrived at Ciancia's apartment a mere forty-five minutes after he left for the airport. Essentially, the rampage was nearly averted through a police response to the broadcasting of intent.

The Radicalization Controversy and the "Known Wolf" of Orlando

Despite years of research, the exact nature of radicalization to terrorism is not completely understood. Although researchers have developed numerous theories and models to explain radicalization, rarely have these been empirically tested. Further complicating matters, while researchers conceptualize radicalization as occurring in different phases, they use different terminologies to describe the phases based upon their own academic orientations. At the most basic level, however, most researchers agree that radicalization is a dynamic process involving behavioral change in an individual.

Brian Jenkins defines radicalization as "the process of adopting for oneself or inculcating in others a commitment not only to a system of [radical] beliefs, but to their imposition on the rest of society."[33] This act of imposing one's radical beliefs on society is consistent with the phase of radicalization we have termed the broadcasting of terrorist intent. Lone wolves consider their radical beliefs to be truth in the absolute sense, thereby negating any attempt at questioning the beliefs, critical thinking, or dissent. They are *true believers*, Eric Hoffer's classic term used to describe the social psychological process of fanaticism.[34] As Randy Borum argues, such absolutist thinking gives to the terrorist a moral authority for framing an "us versus them" mentality as a way of distinguishing between good and evil.[35] This, too, squares with our concept of broadcasting intent: The lone wolf terrorist tends to communicate absolutist beliefs to others. In identifying phases of the radicalization process, other researchers have concentrated on the distinctions between phases. John Horgan notes, "A critical implication of these distinctions is the recognition that each of them may contain unique, or phase-specific, implications for counterterrorism."[36] Here again we see a similarity with the broadcasting of intent for lone wolf terrorists: This specific phase of their radicalization has obvious implications for counterterrorism. If lone wolf terrorists announce their violent intentions beforehand, then steps can be taken to stop them.

Yet some researchers have cautioned against viewing radicalization as a phased process that starts with grievances and ends with violence, noting that it is notoriously difficult to predict violent behavior of any sort.[37] Other researchers further this argument by contending that indicators of violent radicalization displayed by behavioral changes in individuals are simply signs of normal human behavior and that there is little need to study the processes of radicalization. Most notably, the National Counterterrorism Center (NCC) takes the position that indicators of radicalization—such as isolating oneself and obsessing about violent videos and guns—reflect behaviors seen in all people.[38] For the NCC, the goal of counterterrorism is to "actively and aggressively counter the range of ideologies violent extremists employ to radicalize and recruit individuals by challenging justifications for violence and by actively promoting the unifying and inclusive vision of our American ideals."[39]

Thus, the concern for the NCC is not with understanding what motivates people to adopt extremist views, what their grievances are, or how they display behavioral indicators of radicalization, but with reasserting American ideals as they are conceived by power elites in Washington. The NCC's assumption that indicators of radicalization reflect common human behaviors is based entirely on the agency's analysis of individuals radicalized into large terrorist organizations. The hypothesis is unsupported in cases of lone wolf terrorism. The facts speak for themselves.

From 1940 to 2015—as this chapter has shown—lone wolf terrorists have openly broadcasted their intentions to bomb public places, kill innocent citizens and police officers, and assassinate politicians. They have sent menacing letters and videos to the media, specifying the exact nature of their forthcoming attacks. They have proclaimed their violent intentions to friends, family members, co-workers, students, prisoners, total strangers, and even to law enforcement. Clearly, these indicators of violent radicalization do not reflect behaviors seen in all people. Indeed, the Orlando gunman Omar Mateen had a long history of broadcasting his intent to commit terrorism. As our concluding narrative suggests, there were opportunities to use his broadcasting in ways that may have prevented the greatest act of terrorism in the United States since 9/11.

After the terrorist attacks of September 11, 2001, Omar Mateen, then fourteen years old and living with his Afghan Muslim parents in Port St. Lucie, Florida, celebrated the attacks at school and boasted that his uncle was Osama bin Laden, sparking conflict with other students.[40] This behavioral indicator of violent extremism would not be a random occurrence in the short life of Omar Mateen. After graduating from high school in 2003, Mateen enrolled at a local community college, where he majored in criminal justice technology and earned his degree in 2006. That October, Mateen was hired by the Florida Department of Corrections, but then around the time of the Virginia Tech massacre in April 2007, Mateen's suggestion to guards that he might bring a gun onto the prison yard at the Martin Correctional Institution led to his immediate dismissal from the job.[41] After his applications to two police departments were rejected, Mateen was hired as a private security guard for the Wackenhut Corporation. Upon passing firing range tests with near-perfect scores, Mateen was issued a .38-caliber Smith & Wesson revolver and assigned to guard the St. Lucie County courthouse, located on Florida's eastern seaboard.[42] Over the next few years, Mateen's marriage fell apart after he repeatedly battered his wife. During their brief marriage, Mateen also made derogatory statements about homosexuals. Co-workers began to express concerns to supervisors about Mateen's threatening behavior at work, but nothing was done about it. "He talked about killing people all the time," said a co-worker.[43]

Following an argument at the courthouse with a deputy sheriff about the Boston Marathon bombers in October 2013, Mateen claimed that he had family connections to Tamerlan and Dzhokhar Tsarnaev. Mateen further told the deputy that he was connected to both al-Qaeda and Hezbollah and said he hoped that the FBI would raid his apartment so that he could become a martyr. He then launched into a diatribe against women and Jews and followed it up by praising the Fort Hood shooter Nidal Hasan.[44] The county sheriff was called to the scene, whereupon Mateen grew even more agitated and warned the sheriff that he could have al-Qaeda kill the deputy and his family. The sheriff reported Mateen to the FBI, which opened an investigation of him. After placing Mateen on the Terrorism Watch List, FBI agents followed Mateen and monitored his cell phone conversations, digital traffic, and financial records. Agents interviewed Mateen twice about his possible connections to terrorism and began a sting operation involving an undercover informant.[45]

The informant was dispatched to the courthouse (the FBI did not alert Mateen's employer to their investigation), where he began discussions with Mateen that were intended to encourage his participation in a plot to commit terrorism against the United States. Either because Mateen was too shrewd to accept the proposition, recognizing the informant for what he was based upon his own criminal justice training, or because he may have become angry that he was being manipulated in this way, Mateen declined the informant's offer. As the county sheriff later recalled, the FBI attempted to "lure Omar into some kind of act and Omar did not bite."[46] The FBI's attempt to entrap Mateen into agreeing to carry out a terrorist attack raises the important question of whether the bureau played a role in enabling Mateen's mass murder at the Orlando nightclub in 2016.

Meanwhile, Wackenhut (now rebranded as G4S) conducted a mental health rescreening of their employee. Mateen was given a clean bill of health by G4S and cleared by the FBI from suspicion of posing a possible terrorist threat. Subsequently, he continued his guard duties but was reassigned to a security booth at a resort community.[47] In March, 2014, the FBI removed Mateen from the Terrorism Watch List.

Two months later, however, Mateen was again questioned by the FBI, this time about his connection to Moner Abu-Salha, a twenty-two-year-old Palestinian American from Vero Beach, Florida, who on May 25 became the first American suicide bomber in Syria. Prior to his attack, Abu-Salha had released a video saying he was inspired by the radical cleric Anwar al-Awlaki. During this second investigation of Mateen, the FBI received a call from a man named Mohammad Malik, a longtime friend of Mateen's and a member of the same mosque where Mateen and Abu-Salha prayed. Malik told investigators about a conversation he recently had with Mateen, wherein Mateen confided that he had been listening to al-Awlaki's Internet sermons.[48] Yet, again, Mateen was cleared by the FBI after agents determined that he did not pose a terrorist threat. Moreover, this decision was unaffected by the tip concerning Mateen's potential online radicalization by Anwar al-Awlaki. Following the Orlando attack, though, FBI director Comey would concede that the intelligence community was "highly confident that this killer [Mateen] was radicalized in part by the Internet."[49]

Mateen began making visits to the Pulse, the gay dance club in Orlando where he would commit his rampage, and his second wife came to fear that Mateen was going to attack the club. She pleaded with him not to do anything violent, but she failed to report her suspicions to the police.[50] Mateen lifted weights, took steroids, searched online for jihadist propaganda including ISIS beheading videos, and continued his violent outbursts at work, telling a co-worker at one point that he was "going to kill a bunch of people." The co-worker reported Mateen to his supervisor, but once more the warning was ignored.[51] A woman who regularly encountered Mateen in his booth at the resort would later say that he "acted like a straight-up predator."[52]

Around May 15, 2016, Mateen tried to buy military-grade body armor and more than one thousand rounds of ammunition from Lotus Gun Works in Jensen Beach, Florida (near St. Lucie County), yet was turned away by an observant clerk, who became concerned about the questions Mateen was asking. During his encounter with the clerk, Mateen paused to make a phone call and spoke in a "foreign language." The clerk alerted the FBI about this "very suspicious" person, but since no purchase was made and the gun store had no name for the person, no credit card information, and only a grainy surveillance video of him, the FBI was "unable to conduct any meaningful follow up," as a spokesman later said.[53] After the Orlando attack, Comey declared that the FBI was committed to "going back to look hard at our own work to see if there is something we should have done differently."[54] In our opinion, this is one scenario worthy of consideration.

The gun store incident marked a crucial turning point in the FBI's investigation of Mateen. Understood in retrospect, the FBI did have the means and opportunity to conduct a meaningful follow up of the incident. By this time, Mateen was a potential "known wolf"—a term FBI analysts use to denote a person who passes an investigation and then becomes a terrorist. Even though Mateen had been removed from the Terrorism Watch List, records from the investigations of Mateen in 2013 and 2014 were still on file at the FBI office in Orlando. After being alerted to the incident at

Lotus Gun Works, agents could have searched files of recent terrorism investigations in eastern Florida involving men who spoke a foreign language and thereby produced a photo lineup that might have been shown to the Lotus clerk to see if he could pick out the "very suspicious" person. Mateen's photo would have been in the lineup, and it might have been identified by the clerk. If so, agents could have brought Mateen in for questioning, which could possibly lead to his (re)placement on the Terrorism Watch List and further FBI scrutiny, including physical surveillance of him. These investigative procedures may have prevented Mateen's ensuing act of lone wolf terrorism. Given the dire warnings then coming from ISIS, it is also surprising that such preventative measures were not taken.

On May 22, 2016, the ISIS spokesman Tweeted an audio recording calling for a new round of attacks against the United States and Europe and urging followers to carry out attacks against military and civilian targets during the Muslim holy month of Ramadan, which was to begin in early June.[55] Between June 4 and June 9, Mateen entered the St. Lucie Shooting Center gun shop on two occasions and bought ammunition magazines and the weapons he would use in the massacre—a Remington-made Sig Sauer .223-caliber assault rifle with a collapsible stock and a 9mm Glock, easily passing the background check both times, despite his earlier placement on the Terrorism Watch List. No laws were broken, however, since persons formerly on the Terrorism Watch List are allowed to buy firearms in the United States. This so-called "terror gap" in federal gun laws would later be cited by the U. S. Senate as a primary cause of the terrorist attack on Orlando.[56]

Mateen walked into the Pulse nightclub around midnight, Saturday, June 11. He paid his cover charge at the door and was given a wristband allowing him to move past security going in and out. Then he left the Pulse for two hours. At 2 A.M. on June 12, Mateen returned to the club with a shaved head and wearing his khaki security officer's uniform, thereby generating a sense of deference among the club patrons yet also creating a social distance to avoid drawing attention to his concealed weapons and multiple rounds of ammunition.[57] (A similar tactic was used by Anders Breivik who wore a policeman's outfit in the Norway massacre.) At 2:02 A.M., Mateen posted on Facebook his allegiance to ISIS, expressed his solidarity with the suicide bomber Moner Abu-Salha, and demanded that the United States stop bombing ISIS territory. "You kill innocent women and children by doing us [sic] airstrikes," he wrote. "Now taste the Islamic state vengeance."[58]

Mateen unfolded the assault rifle, inserted an ammunition clip, and began moving methodically around the club, mowing people down in cold blood. He used the Glock to shoot people corralled inside locked bathroom stalls. Not only had Mateen broadcasted his intent to commit terrorism, but as the rampage unfolded, he broadcasted his performance of terrorism. At 2:35 A.M., Mateen called 911 and pledged his allegiance to ISIS leader Abu Bakr al-Baghdadi and referred to the Tsarnaev brothers as his "homeboys."[59] Over the next hour, Mateen spoke by phone three times to a hostage negotiator, identifying himself as an "Islamic soldier" and demanding an end to the U.S. bombing in Syria and Iraq. Mateen warned that there was a car bomb outside the club, adding that he had a suicide vest of the kind "used in France" by ISIS followers.[60] As Mateen stood on the floor slicked with blood, the dead and wounded piled over one another, he used his phone to search "Pulse Orlando" and "Shooting" and texted his wife to ask if he was seen on the news. Mateen then called an Orlando television news station saying, "I'm the shooter. It's me. I am the shooter. I did it for ISIS."[61] His final Facebook postings railed against "the filthy ways of the west" and concluded: "May Allah accept me."[62] Just after 5 A.M., a SWAT team stormed the nightclub and killed Mateen in a gun battle.

Mateen's broadcasting of terrorist intent to police officers at the St. Lucie County courthouse, which prompted an FBI sting investigation, combined with hostile statements he made to his wives and co-workers and his suspicious demeanor at the first gun store do not reflect behaviors seen in all people. The tendency to announce intentions prior to an attack seems to be a behavioral trait pertinent yet not unique to lone wolf terrorists. School shootings show a similar pattern of the shooter's broadcasting threats and advertising impending crimes, which are intended to increase the attention of an audience. "School shooters rarely seek anonymity," one authoritative study found.[63] Neither does the lone wolf terrorist.

Yet the broadcasting of terrorist intent does not necessarily mean that an individual will commit terrorism. For that to occur, there is typically a catalyst, or a triggering event, a subject we turn to next.

CHAPTER 7

Triggering Events

The last component of the radicalization process is a triggering event—the ultimate catalyst for lone wolf terrorism. Triggering events may be personal or political or some combination of the two. Understanding these events may also tell us something about planning for an attack. Triggering events are sometimes "sharp" or immediate, in which case the attack may be instantaneous with little or no planning involved, as was seen in Lynette Fromme's assassination attempt against President Ford. Other times events accumulate over time—evolving through a series of "escalation thresholds"—until the loner psychologically snaps under the pressure, triggering the act of terrorism. Joseph Stack's radicalization seems to have advanced through numerous escalation thresholds ("This has been coming for a long time," he wrote) until his suicide attack was triggered by news of an IRS audit. In these cases, planning often runs in parallel with the final stages of the loner's meltdown.

Triggering events are another commonality among lone wolf terrorists. Triggering events were present in 84 percent of the pre-9/11 cases and in 71 percent of the post-9/11 cases in our database. In addition, a new phenomenon emerged after 9/11 regarding the underlying basis for the triggering events—a noteworthy connection between lone wolf attacks and the abuse of women, which we will discuss later in the chapter. Like other aspects of terrorist action, these transformations are best understood by example. First is a pre-9/11 case of a sharp triggering event.

The Bull Camp Incident

Claude Dallas was a throwback to another time and place.[1] Living rough in the Idaho wilderness, the thirty-one-year-old mountain man supported himself by hunting wild horses and trapping game. As one who routinely violated game laws by killing animals out of season (misdemeanor violations in Idaho), Dallas lived by the informal "subsistence law," which holds that a person should be able to kill an animal when they are hungry, regardless of the season. Dallas also harbored a bitter personal hatred of law enforcement stemming from a 1973 arrest for failing to report for military induction. FBI agents had yanked the young buckaroo from his horse and escorted him by car back to his home state of Ohio, locking him up in various jails along the way, only to have the charges dismissed before going to trial. "He'd changed," remarked a friend upon Dallas's return to Idaho. "He came back more savvy, more wary. He had felt the heat of authority and he didn't enjoy it" (92).

Dallas's treatment in FBI custody was his first locus of radicalization. The other was tied to the Sagebrush Rebellion that swept across western America during the 1970s and 1980s. Sagebrush Rebels attempted to influence environmental affairs by pressuring government officials to roll back grazing and mineral extraction policies on public lands. Not insignificantly, the rebellion occurred in conjunction with the decline of the American cowboy as a cultural icon. Throughout the West, federal agents found themselves insulted, locked off federal land, and periodically confronted by cowboys brandishing firearms. Because Claude Dallas lived off public land and was often in conflict with these federal agents, he became personally caught up in the Sagebrush zeitgeist. Dallas's biographer described the United States government at the time as "a Goliath hampering the lone wolf's freedom."[2]

Over the years Dallas experienced several run-ins with federal and state game wardens, and to an acquaintance he once broadcasted his intent to shoot an agent from the Bureau of Land Management. During a subsequent discussion about purchasing a rifle, Dallas told a friend that the weapon could be used to "shoot a BLM man" (110). A Nevada game warden who once attempted to search Dallas's makeshift camp came away from the experience with an impression that Dallas should be taken "special care of" and approached with caution (119).

Dallas's radicalization was enabled by a local bar owner and conspiracy theorist named George Nielson. Nielson would later destroy crime scene evidence at Dallas's request, drive him to a drop-off point in the desert, and then lie to law enforcement about where it was. The lead investigator on the case would describe Dallas as a "romantic paranoid" who had read too many cowboy novels and paramilitary manuals. "I think that between reading [Western novelist] Louis L'Amour and listening to George Nielson's bullshit," he remarked, "that's what led Claude up to Bull Camp" (149).

Bull Camp was situated down a stone canyon in the desolate reaches of southern Idaho. When Claude Dallas awoke at the campsite on the morning of January 5, 1981, he had no intention of killing anyone. Soon, however, two Idaho Department of Fish and Game wardens appeared at the camp and asked Dallas about some bobcat hides hanging inside his tent. Dallas asked to see a search warrant, and the lead warden replied that he did not have one nor did he need one to investigate a poaching violation. Dallas argued that the tent was his home and that the warden had no right to enter without a warrant. The warden said to Dallas: "You can go easy or you can go hard," meaning that Dallas could either cooperate or leave the camp by force.[3] That threat instantly triggered a double homicide.

Dallas saw the warden reach for his sidearm so Dallas drew his .357-magnum revolver and shot the warden. He turned his gun on the other warden and shot him too. Dallas then used a rifle to shoot both wardens execution style, once each in the head. A visitor to the camp witnessed these events and asked Dallas why he had shot the wardens. "I swore I'd never be arrested again," replied Dallas, referring to his 1973 arrest by the FBI.[4]

Dallas dumped the body of one warden in the river next to Bull Camp and hauled the other one up the mountain on his mule and hid it in a coyote's den. With the help of George Nielson, Dallas then escaped. With a $20,000 reward on his head, Dallas eluded capture for nearly sixteen months, trapping, hunting, and taking advantage of his growing renown among Idahoans as a folk hero of the mythical frontier. People gave him food and money; they sheltered him, loaned him their trucks, and celebrated his deed until an informant's tip led police to a trailer in northern Nevada where Dallas was arrested on April 18, 1982, after being wounded in a shootout with an FBI SWAT team. Dallas was convicted on two counts of manslaughter in October 1982 and sentenced to thirty years. But the legend had just begun.

On Easter Sunday 1986, Dallas escaped from the Idaho State Correctional Institution near Kuna by simply walking out the front door of the prison with a group of visitors. He was on the run for almost a year, fueling his legend as a renaissance man of the West. In 1987, Dallas was captured outside a convenience store in Riverside, California. Following his 1987 trial, Dallas did time in federal prisons in Nebraska, New Mexico, and Kansas. He completed his final weeks back in an Idaho prison and was released in 2005 after serving twenty-two years.

While interesting, the Claude Dallas case had no discernable influence on the history of lone wolf terrorism, and today it is largely forgotten. That is not true, however, for another pre-9/11 case in which terrorism resulted from a sharp triggering event.

The Assassination of Senator Robert F. Kennedy

Sirhan Sirhan was born into a Christian Arab family of Jordanian descent in the British-ruled Old City of Jerusalem on March 19, 1944.[5] The Old City would become his locus of radicalization. When he was a child, Sirhan's family was forced from their home by the fighting between Arabs and Jews over control of the Old City. During the conflict, Sirhan witnessed horrifying acts of violence. He saw the disembowelment of a man by a bomb. He saw a group of Arabs blown apart while waiting for a bus. And most traumatically, he saw his brother crushed to death by a Zionist military truck swerving to avoid sniper fire. These experiences established Sirhan's personal grievance.

When he was twelve years old, Sirhan's family immigrated to the United States, first to New York and then to Los Angeles, where Sirhan attended school and community college. He supported himself with odd jobs, including a stint as a stable boy at the Santa Anita racetrack. He developed no affinity with any pro-Palestinian organization, nor did he come under the influence of an enabler. An ultimate loner, Sirhan had no romantic relationships. Instead, he busied himself with an independent study of religion, joining Baptist and Seventh-day Adventist churches, and then in 1966, he joined the occult organization Ancient Mystical Order of the Rose Cross, commonly known as the Rosicrucians, a philosophical secret society dedicated to uncovering ancient truths of the past.

Sirhan was by this time a fervent advocate of the Palestinian cause. In early 1968, Sirhan heard of a *New York Times* report indicating that U.S. Senator Robert F. Kennedy promised to sell fifty Phantom jet bombers to

Israel if elected president. This became Sirhan's political grievance. He would kill Kennedy to prevent him from fulfilling his pledge to support Israel.

In preparation for the assassination, Sirhan began taking target practice with a .22-caliber Iver-Johnson cadet revolver he had acquired back on August 10, 1965. Sometime around May 5, 1968, Sirhan broadcasted his intent by telling his garbage collector that he wanted to shoot Kennedy. But it would take something immediate to trigger the attack.

According to Sirhan, he had no intention of murdering Senator Kennedy when he awoke on the morning of June 4, 1968. But later that day, Sirhan saw an advertisement for a "Miracle March for Israel" parade on Wilshire Boulevard to celebrate the one-year anniversary of the Israeli victory over the Arabs in the Six-Day War of June 1967. Experiencing what he called "a burning feeling inside," Sirhan drove down to the parade, only to find that he had misread the advertisement: The celebration was scheduled for the next night, June 5.[6]

Sirhan aimlessly walked down Wilshire Boulevard until he found a storefront campaign party for a U.S. senatorial candidate from California. Sirhan entered the party where he overheard a conversation about a larger party for presidential candidate Robert Kennedy going on down the street at the Ambassador Hotel.

Sirhan went to the Ambassador Hotel at 3400 Wilshire Boulevard, where he proceeded to down four Tom Collins cocktails. Around midnight, Sirhan returned to his car and attempted to drive home. But finding himself too intoxicated to drive, Sirhan re-parked the vehicle. He grabbed his .22 caliber revolver from the glove box and went back to the Ambassador.

Bobby Kennedy was on the platform in the Ambassador ballroom giving a speech celebrating his victory in the 1968 California presidential primary. All smiles, Kennedy left the podium to cheers of "We Want Bobby! We Want Bobby!" and walked into a kitchen pantry accompanied by his bodyguards. Sirhan followed close behind.

As Kennedy reached to shake the hand of a supporter, Sirhan emptied all eight chambers from his gun. Kennedy was hit three times, once in the head and twice in the back. The bodyguards pummeled Sirhan to the floor and wrestled the gun away. Kennedy died twenty-six hours later. Five of his supporters were also wounded in the attack.

Sirhan would later talk about his assassination of Bobby Kennedy. Of the "Miracle March for Israel" parade that brought him to Wilshire Boulevard on the night of June 4, he said: "That was the catalyst that triggered me on that night. In addition, there was the consumption of liquor."[7]

Polls indicated that Robert F. Kennedy had a real chance of becoming president in 1968, and historians have since debated what kind of president he might have been.[8] Many argue that RFK would have confronted the problems of poverty and discrimination and may have tried to end the killing in Vietnam. Yet these same historians have typically overlooked Kennedy's stance on another important social problem at the time—one that ultimately caused his own death and would, in the years to come, play a central role in the dynamics of lone wolf terrorism.

Back on May 27, 1968—seven years after the slaying of his brother John and less than two months after the killing of Martin Luther King—RFK stood on the steps of the Douglas County Courthouse in Roseburg, Oregon, preparing to address a crowd of 1,500 locals during his campaign swing through the state. The senator's "face was grim as he took the microphone," wrote a reporter from the *New York Times*, and then he launched into an impassioned plea for federal gun control legislation. Kennedy was heckled and booed by people holding signs reading: "Protect Your Rights to Keep and Bear Arms." Kennedy challenged them, ignoring local sentiment and political consequences, by shouting: "With all the violence and murder and killings we've had in the United States, I think you will agree that we must keep firearms from people who have no business with guns or rifles. To put guns in the hands of people who are mentally insane, does that make sense? I just ask you."[9] Bobby Kennedy lost the Oregon primary on May 28 and left the state for California, where he was murdered by Sirhan Sirhan.

Nearly fifty years later, Roseburg, Oregon, became the center of another debate over gun control after a twenty-six-year-old lone wolf terrorist named Christopher Harper-Mercer killed nine people and wounded nine others at Roseburg's Umpqua Community College. The gunman suffered from a mental illness, Asperger's Disorder, and had amassed fourteen firearms, all purchased legally.

When we examine the cases in our database, lone wolves of the post-9/11 era appear to be similar to those of the pre-9/11 period. Some experienced sharp triggering events with no attack planning and others evidenced an evolving series of triggering events accompanied by substantial planning. If there is anything that distinguishes triggering events for lone wolf terrorists of the post-9/11 era, it is their conflict with women—something that was briefly touched upon in the earlier cases of Joseph Stack, Keith Luke, Jim David Adkisson, and James Cummings. Nothing of the kind can be found before 9/11. The terrorism of such essential pre-9/11 figures as George Metesky, James Earl Ray, Sirhan Sirhan, Joseph Paul Franklin, Leroy Moody, and Eric Rudolph was triggered either by legal or administrative rulings unfavorable to these terrorists or by news reports about their victims. Victims were targeted by virtue of opportunities associated with their routine activities. The factors that made them suitable targets for terrorism were situation specific. That is, the victims were attacked as they went about their routine activities of gathering in public places, opening the mail, or walking the streets. Women, per se, played no role in the events that triggered the terrorism.

But the triggering events for some of the most lethal post-9/11 lone wolf terrorists show that interpersonal conflicts between male loners and women matter a great deal. Three critical cases highlight this development. These cases share a striking similarity with those of other recent terrorists whose political violence began with attacks against their girlfriends and wives. Before Tamerlan Tsarnaev carried out the Boston Marathon bombing, he was arrested for assaulting his girlfriend. Prior to his ISIS-inspired lone wolf attack on a coffee shop in Sydney, Australia, in late 2014—which left two hostages and the gunman dead and four others injured—Man Haron Monis had been charged as an accessory to the murder of his ex-wife. He also faced more than forty charges of sexual and indecent assault while working as a self-proclaimed spiritual healer. Prior to his ISIS-inspired attack on the gay nightclub in Orlando, Omar Mateen routinely battered his wife, confiscated her paychecks, and kept her as a virtual captive inside their home. These cases show that the home can serve as the training ground for future attacks, with terrorists rehearsing and perfecting violence against their families first.[10] The cases also mirror domestic violence research showing that the triggering event for most male brutality is the "dangerous exit"—that point when women announce their intention to leave an abusive relationship.[11] Other lone wolf terrorists have explicitly broadcasted their intent to murder women. Most notably, in his manifesto Anders Breivik proclaimed that the evils of "cultural Marxism" could be traced to "touchy feely" men who bow to a radical feminist agenda. Breivik devoted a chapter of his manifesto to "Killing Women on the Field of Battle" and exhorted male readers: "You must therefore embrace and familiarize yourself with the concept of killing women, even very attractive women."[12] Of the seventy-seven victims killed by Breivik, thirty were females, mostly teenagers shot in the head.

The Florida Police Killings

Around 9:30 A.M. on April 25, 2009, twenty-eight-year-old Joshua Cartwright got into an argument with his wife, Elizabeth, because he could not find a tube of Clearasil in the bathroom of their apartment in Fort Walton Beach, Florida.[13] Over the next half hour, Cartwright repeatedly bashed Elizabeth in the face, threw her around, and yanked her by the hair. He took away her cell phones and guns when she tried to defend herself. Elizabeth eventually escaped from the apartment and drove herself to a hospital where she was treated for abrasions. Deputies from the Okaloosa County Sheriff's Department arrived, and Elizabeth informed them that her husband had domestic violence charges pending against him from a similar incident in 2008. She stated that Cartwright had not attended mandatory counseling sessions and that he had multiple firearms and knives in their apartment. Elizabeth informed deputies of the make and model of Cartwright's truck and said that he had plans to meet friends at a local gun range that morning.

At 12:50 P.M., two deputies wearing bullet proof vests arrived at the gun range and confronted Cartwright in the parking lot. Cartwright carried a rifle, a shotgun, and two pistols, including a Ruger 9mm strapped to his thigh in a tactical holster. When the deputies attempted to arrest Cartwright on the domestic violence charge, he resisted. A deputy fired on Cartwright with a Taser gun, causing him to fall to the ground. Five seconds later Cartwright came up shooting his Ruger, and the deputies fired back in a hail of deadly force. Cartwright struck one officer five times and hit the other officer twice, once in the head, and then fled in his pickup. The two officers were soon airlifted to Pensacola, where they died.

Cartwright was headed for neighboring Walton County when a deputy spotted him and began a high-speed pursuit as Cartwright opened fire from his moving vehicle. At a key intersection, police erected a roadblock and put down three sets of spike strips on the pavement. At 1:10 P.M., Cartwright approached the intersection appearing "calm as a cucumber" as a deputy recalled. Cartwright veered around two of the spike strips, but when attempting to avoid the third, he nearly ran over a deputy who shot multiple rounds at Cartwright. Another officer ran his vehicle into Cartwright's truck after its tires were punctured by the spikes, causing the truck to flip over several times until it smashed into a patrol car and landed on its roof. Cartwright came out in a voracious fit of violence, blistering some sixty rounds at the deputies in thirty seconds.

In all, Cartwright was shot seventeen times and suffered numerous injuries when he wrecked his truck. Ultimately, he died from a self-inflicted gunshot wound to the head.

Joshua Cartwright was also an Obama hater. According to the Florida police investigation, Cartwright was known to be not only an angry husband who had repeatedly threatened and abused his wife, but also "severely disturbed" that Obama had been elected president, as well as suspicious that the United States government was conspiring against him. "There was something more than a domestic situation involved here," concluded the Okaloosa County Sheriff.[14]

Cartwright was a member of the National Guard and a former bouncer at a Fort Walton Beach bar, where he had the reputation of being a notorious bully with a penchant for carrying a flashlight with a sharp attachment that he used on customers who got out of line. Cartwright was also interested in militias but he had no affinity with any extremist group. He had no enabler, nor did he broadcast his intent to commit violence. His police shooting was instantaneous, triggered entirely by the deputies' attempt to arrest Cartwright because of his personal conflict with a woman. Perhaps equally important, Cartwright had been laid-off from his job at a Staples store the day before the rampage.

The Seattle Shooting

Despite the way he described himself to others, Naveed Haq was not a true jihadist.[15] Any political grievances he harbored about Middle Eastern affairs were subordinate to his personal demons caused by chronic unemployment, mental illness, and misogyny. Haq was a Pakistani American, the son of an engineer and prominent Muslim leader in the Seattle, Washington, area who founded the state's first Islamic Center. During high school, Haq was seen as a "calm and collected guy," according to one source, but he began having problems while attending dentistry school at the University of Pennsylvania in the mid-1990s.[16]

In 1996, Haq was diagnosed with bipolar disorder and placed on powerful psychiatric medications, including lithium and Depakote. After dropping out of dentistry school, Haq returned home and completed a degree in electrical engineering at Washington State University. Upon graduation, however, Haq was incapable of holding down a job and spent most of his time sleeping or flirting with girls on the Internet. Haq had few friends and no steady relationships until he entered into an arranged marriage on a trip with his parents to Pakistan in 2001. Disliking the woman because she was overweight, Haq returned home alone, where he disavowed Islam and converted to Christianity thinking that church would be a better place to meet women, all for naught. Haq bounced from one menial job to the next and was unemployed for months on end. "He got fired quite a bit," said a former roommate. "Or quit. People didn't like him on the job."[17]

Over a five-month period in 2006, Haq, then thirty years old, passed through four discernible escalation thresholds during which he fashioned a plan to kill all the women he could, particularly Jewish women.

First, in March 2006 Haq was arrested at a Seattle-area mall for lewd conduct after standing on a fountain near a Macy's department store and harassing young women at a nearby cosmetics counter. When a teenage girl walked by, Haq unzipped his pants and flashed his penis at her. Police determined that Haq was under the influence of methamphetamine at the time. When an officer asked Haq why he had exposed himself to the girl, he replied, "It's hard to meet women."[18]

Haq's personal problems reached a turning point with the lewd-conduct arrest, an event that deeply embarrassed his family. It also coincided with the bloodiest point of the Iraq War, which Haq followed in the news. In response, he began making offhand anti-Semitic remarks to the only friend he had. Wick Renner was Haq's former college roommate, and in May the two began sharing a government-subsidized apartment in Everett, Washington. It is through Renner's eyes that Haq's escalation thresholds can be understood.

When Haq moved into the apartment, not only was he facing a court date and possible jail time for lewd conduct, but he was unemployed, on food stamps, living out of a duffle bag, driving a battered wreck, and battling manic depression. To cope with his demons, he was taking lithium and methamphetamine. And he had no woman, something he wanted more than anything else. Renner witnessed Haq's torment over his failure with women. "He was hung up on girls," recalled Renner. "It really bothered him. He would get really upset. Almost crying. He thought it was because of his baldness and his size [Haq was 5'5" and 160 pounds]. Sometimes he would get real loud and say, 'I've got a lot to offer; why won't women give me a chance?'"[19]

He continued his online flirting with women, but all of his advances were spurned. To Renner, Haq complained that Muslim women were "frigid," and he thought that sexual repression "was the reason so many Middle Easterners are so angry." On June 7, Haq had an ominous confrontation with two women after a car crash. Haq accused the female driver of lying about what happened, began yelling at her, and followed her across the street into a store. Another time, Haq brought a prostitute back to the apartment and disappeared into the bathroom with her for half an hour. "Afterwards, he felt kind of disgusted and embarrassed," said Renner. "He said the condom kept falling off." Yet another time, when Renner and Haq were watching a Seattle Mariners baseball game on TV, the camera panned over a girl in the crowd. Thinking she was the teenage girl who had identified Haq to police as the man who flashed his penis at her in the mall, Haq shouted, "That looks like the woman witness. I'd like to rip her head off and shit down her throat."

The second escalation threshold befell Haq while he was in the depths of his despair over women. Sometime in June, Renner and Haq went to the movies and saw *United 93*, Hollywood's version of the plane crash in Shankesville, Pennsylvania, on 9/11. Of particular interest to Haq was a scene in the movie where a terrorist grabs a stewardess, places a knife to her throat, and forces his way into the cockpit. "The movie mesmerized him," Renner recalled. After the movie, "he was just running red lights, not paying attention." This pivotal scene would play a crucial role in Haq's act of lone wolf terrorism.

Haq's third escalation threshold emerged from the Israel–Hezbollah War of 2006. On July 12, Israeli Defense Forces began a thirty-four-day aerial bombardment of Lebanon, hammering Hezbollah strongholds and civilian infrastructure with cluster bombs. Televised images of the bombing showed neighborhoods in ruin and civilians killed and wounded. Haq watched it all but felt that the media was downplaying the extent of Israeli atrocities. Fox News was the worst, Haq told Renner, because "it was owned by the Jews."[20]

Amidst these events, on July 21, Haq went to two different gun stores and bought two semi-automatic firearms—a Smith & Wesson .45-caliber revolver and another .40-caliber handgun. Though legally barred from purchasing firearms because of his mental illness (not to mention his possession of a controlled substance at the mall following his lewd-conduct arrest), Haq was able to buy these guns by simply lying on a questionnaire. He paid for the weapons by selling food stamps and was informed that he could pick up his guns after the mandatory five-day waiting period.

Three days later, on July 24, Renner and Haq had their last conversation. Renner wanted to talk about a job prospect for Haq, but all Haq wanted to talk about was the war in Lebanon. He believed that Israel was running out of cluster bombs and that the United States was giving them more. Haq said that he had read about it on the Internet.

The final escalation threshold for Haq occurred on July 27, the day that he was scheduled to appear in court on the lewd conduct charge. Haq was indignant about the charge and denied his action, claiming that he had only been urinating in the fountain mall when the girl walked by. As Haq was preparing for the hearing that morning, hoping to be cleared of wrongdoing and vindicated in the eyes of his family, his lawyer called and told Haq that the hearing was postponed.

That was the ultimate catalyst for Haq. Being denied his day in court was a tragic disappointment for him, and a very personal injustice. As fate would have it, the waiting period for Haq's purchase of two high-velocity firearms expired the same day, July 27, allowing Haq to pick up his weapons from the gun stores, along with several boxes of ammunition. Haq then went searching on his laptop for someone to kill. The political novice that he was, Haq began by Googling the words "something Jewish." What came back was the Jewish Federation of Greater Seattle, established in 1928 to serve the religious and cultural needs of the city's Jewish community. Their website showed that most staff members were women. The next day, Naveed Haq became a lone wolf terrorist of the most vicious kind.

Around 4 P.M. on July 28, Haq entered the lobby of the Jewish Federation building and hid behind a potted plant until he spotted a fourteen-year-old girl walking alone through the lobby. Imitating the scene in *United 93*, Haq grabbed the girl and put a gun to her back. Then he forced the girl to use the intercom so they could be buzzed into the federation's offices on the second floor. "I'm doing this for a statement," Haq said as he followed the girl up the steps.[21] Upon entering the offices, Haq asked the receptionist about speaking with a manager, as the girl walked to the bathroom and locked herself inside. An employee picked up the phone to dial 911, but before she could, Haq shot her in the knee.

"I'm a Muslim American," shouted Haq, "I'm angry at Israel!" And then the carnage began. Haq walked down the hallway, shooting into office after office as he passed by. Haq shot three women in the abdomen. He shot a fifty-eight-year-old woman in the chest, and then once in the head, killing her. Other women jumped out the second-story windows. Haq tried to shoot a woman who was five months pregnant in the abdomen, but the bullet hit her raised arm. Lying on the floor and bleeding, she dialed 911 on her cellphone as Haq screamed, "Now you're the hostage and I don't give a fuck if I kill you or your baby!" Haq said he was a Muslim and the shooting was his personal statement against Jews and the Bush administration for starting the Iraq War, adding that he was doing this to get Jews out of Lebanon. Haq said that he wanted to talk to CNN. He was handed the cellphone and told the police operator, "These are Jews and I'm tired of getting pushed around and our people getting pushed around by the situation in the Middle East."[22] Haq demanded that the United States immediately withdraw its military forces from Iraq.

Minutes later, Haq simply quit. He calmed down and told the operator he would surrender to police. Haq walked out of the building with his hands on his head at 4:15 P.M.

Five of the women were taken to a hospital, where three were listed in critical condition. One had a bullet lodged in her spine and would never walk again.

On January 13, 2010, Haq was sentenced to life in prison.

Because of its significance to the contemporary history of American lone wolf terrorism, the final case demands a comprehensive examination.

The Tucson Massacre

The post–World War II automobile boom created untold opportunities for small businessmen across America.[23] Among them was World War I veteran Akiba Hornstein, the son of a Lithuanian rabbi, born in 1900. In 1949,

Hornstein opened El Campo Tire, a combined gas and tire station on the rural southeast side of Tucson, Arizona. To avoid anti-Semitism, Hornstein changed his name to Giffords—a name he had somehow acquired as a child growing up in New York—but continued to raise his family in the Jewish tradition. During the 1950s, "Giff" Giffords became a minor celebrity in Tucson due to his self-produced El Campo television commercials featuring pithy homilies about leading a better life. Giff retired in 1959 and turned El Campo over to his son, Spencer Giffords, a graduate of Mexico City College, who in 1964 wed University of Arizona student Gloria Spencer. As the tire business expanded to a second store and then a third, the Giffords began a family. Their first child, Melissa, was born in 1968. Gabrielle Dee was born on June 8, 1970. She was nicknamed "Gabby" and would become known by that name to all who knew her.

As a child, Gabby rode horses in the desert, joined the Girl Scouts, acted in musical theater, and excelled at school. Later she rode motorcycles and helped out her father by changing tires at El Campo. Yet her true gift was in the area of interpersonal relations. Remembering Gabrielle Giffords as a student at University High School in the late 1980s, a former teacher remarked, "We called her 'Gabby,' and not because it was short for her name. She was pretty much a social animal. She was the type of person you would expect to grow up to become a newspaper reporter or something."[24]

Gabby Giffords was a daughter of privilege, given to great hopes of making a difference in the world. In 1993, she earned a Bachelor of Arts degree in sociology and Latin American history from Scripps College in California. Giffords then became a fellow at Harvard's John F. Kennedy School of Government where she met Robert Reich, the Clinton-era secretary of labor, who would became her lifelong friend and mentor. Giffords spent a year as a Fulbright Scholar in Chihuahua, Mexico, before receiving a master's degree in regional planning from Cornell University in 1996, concentrating on Mexican-American relations. She then went to work as an economic development specialist at Price Waterhouse in New York City; but a few months into the job, Giffords quit and returned to Tucson where she took over the reins of El Campo Tire from her ailing father. By now, Spencer Giffords had expanded El Campo to twelve locations with one hundred employees and $10 million in annual revenues. Like her grandfather, Gabby began a series of El Campo television commercials, featuring her trademark "buck stretcher" deals, and became a recognized personality in southeastern Arizona.

"I think I can change this industry," said the twenty-six-year-old CEO to a local reporter in 1996. "I think there's great potential for independent tire dealers." Drawing on her extensive experiences, Gabby planned to expand El Campo to international markets. "I'm in it for the long haul," she declared. "I'd like to turn it over to my kid someday."[25]

But that was not to be. Citing difficulties of local businesses in the competition against large multinationals, Giffords sold El Campo to Goodyear Tire in 2000. The Giffords family made a fortune in the deal, and part of it was used to launch Gabby's political career as a conservative Democrat in a conservative state. The strategy was wildly successful.

Giffords was elected to the Arizona House of Representatives in 2001 and served until 2003. After visiting Israel for the first time in 2001, Giffords publicly identified herself solely with the Judaism of her father and joined Congregation Chaverim, a Tucson Reform synagogue. Giffords was then elected to the Arizona State Senate in 2004. At thirty-four years old, she became the youngest woman to ever hold that seat. She served in it until 2005, when she resigned to run for the seat vacated by retiring Democratic Congressman Jim Kolby.

Giffords launched her candidacy for the United States Congress on January 24, 2006. She instantly showed a flair for attracting attention. Her campaign featured photos of Giffords on a motorcycle and with her fiancé, the Discovery astronaut Mark Kelly. Attractive, bright, and a gifted public speaker, Giffords seized the national spotlight and earned endorsements from such Democratic heavyweights as Bill Clinton, Senator Tom Daschle, and Robert Reich. On September 12, Giffords easily won her party's nomination in the primary election.

Her Republican opponent in the general election was an ultraconservative former state senator named Randy Graf, known for his "get tough" position on immigration and illegal aliens—hot button issues among residents in towns along Interstate 19 south of Tucson. Graf, though, was a single-issue candidate with little popular appeal and the national GOP pulled their financial support, effectively conceding the election to Giffords. When Giffords won the race on November 7, her victory was hailed in the media as evidence that Americans were willing to move in the direction of comprehensive immigration reform.

Wearing a red dress and smiling brightly, Giffords was sworn in on January 3, 2007, making her Arizona's first Jewish congresswoman. In her inaugural speech on the floor of the House of Representatives, Giffords called for a comprehensive immigration reform package, including up-to-date technology to secure the U.S.-Mexican border, more border patrol agents, tough employer sanctions for businesses that knowingly hire illegal immigrants, and a guest-worker program. In her first month in office, Giffords was awarded a seat on the powerful Armed Services Committee and traveled to the Iraq war zone; she voted in favor of increasing federal funding for embryonic stem-cell research, raising the minimum wage, and endorsing the 9/11 Commission recommendations. Her ambition continued to draw notice from the media, especially National Public Radio, whose reporters shadowed Giffords throughout her freshman year.

Giffords returned to Arizona nearly every weekend, making 340 appearances in her district during 2007. On August 25, Giffords hosted a Congress on Your Corner event at a Tucson mall, where she kicked things off by speaking to the Girl Scouts of Southern Arizona. Following her formal remarks, Giffords opened the floor to questions.

A pale teenage boy with a mop of curly hair stepped forward and asked the nonsensical question: "What is government if words have no meaning?"[26] After pausing for a moment, Giffords responded in Spanish and moved on with the meeting. Later, the teenager complained to a friend that Giffords had not sufficiently answered his question and that he was "aggravated" about the way Giffords had treated him.

Thus began Jared Loughner's obsession with Gabrielle Giffords. Days later, Loughner received a form letter from Giffords's office thanking him for attending the Congress on Your Corner event. Loughner put the letter together with an envelope containing some handwritten notes and placed them in a bedroom safe.

Three years later, Loughner would retrieve that envelope from the safe and scrawl on its front, "*Die bitch*" and "*Assassination plans have been made.*"[27]

The Assassin

An only child born in Tucson to Randy and Amy Loughner in 1988, Jared Lee Loughner spent his youth playing saxophone in the school band, writing short stories, making passing grades, and hanging around the alternative music scene. Loughner had no radical political beliefs as a teenager, but when he was in the tenth grade, Loughner experienced what one friend called "a mental downfall" following his breakup with a girlfriend. That would be it for romantic relationships; he never had another.

Loughner began acting strangely and drifted into a drug-oriented life-style, binge-drinking vodka and experimenting with marijuana, halluci-nogenic mushrooms, and other drugs, including *Salvia divinorum*—also known as "Diviner's Sage," a psychoactive plant grown in the desolate forest regions around Oaxaca, Mexico, which in some users can mimic psychosis. Concomitantly, Loughner developed an interest in esoteric the-ories about "conscious dreaming" and language development. His grades fell, and Loughner dropped out of high school in 2006 after completing his ju-nior year. Six months later, he was in trouble with the law. In October 2007, Loughner was cited for possession of drug paraphernalia, and a year later he was arrested for defacing a street sign. He tried to enlist in the Army in 2008 but was rejected that December after admitting to drug use on his application.

But then he cleaned up his act. According to a friend, Bryce Tierney, who knew Loughner from junior high school onward, in late 2008 Loughner quit partying "completely." Committed to a healthier lifestyle, Loughner abstained from everything and started working out, dropping ten pounds in the process. And that is when his real problems began, around the age of twenty. After Loughner gave up drugs and drinking, said Tierney, "his theories got worse. He was just off the wall."[28]

Loughner's first locus of radicalization was the Internet, where he found videos on lucid dreaming, mind control, and anti-government conspir-acy theories. Around 2008 Loughner became interested in the online films *Zeitgeist: The Movie* (2007), an Alex Jones production warning that the United States was about to be merged with Canada and Mexico, and *Loose Change* (2005/2009), a Jones-supported contribution to the 9/11 Truth movement, an Internet phenomenon. Alex Jones became Loughner's enabler.

For legions of his Internet followers—including some of the most vio-lent lone wolf terrorists of the post-9/11 era—Jones's appeal was based on his ability to stretch the boundaries of credulity while retaining just enough factual evidence to make him dangerous. Jones accused the United States government of complicity in the Oklahoma City bombing, of orchestrat-ing the 9/11 attacks, and of filming fake moon landings. Jones argued that government and big business had colluded to create a New World Order through manufactured economic crises, sophisticated surveillance technology, and inside-job terrorist attacks ("false flag" operations) that deliberately fueled public hysteria. It was through his disturbed interpretation of these kinds of conspiracy theories that Loughner came to begrudge Representative Giffords for her political views.

A second locus of radicalization for Loughner was Pima Community College, where he attended classes from 2008 to 2010. Loughner ultimately grew resentful of the school due to perceived injustices, which further increased his fanaticism.

Loughner cobbled together a political grievance based on anti-government rage, conspiratorial beliefs about 9/11 popularized by both right- and leftwing polemicists, and condemnation of the Federal Reserve System promoted by some Tea Party groups. In effect his grievance was solidly cast in what Richard Hofstadter termed the *paranoid style* of American politics. As Hofstadter argued, economic panaceas have exerted a traditional fascination for the American Right, leading to a vast literature on gold, silver, paper currency, and the Federal Reserve system.[29] Within this milieu, politicians like Gabrielle Giffords were seen as agents of a dreadful tyranny, manipulating the economy and turning Americans into slaves. A friend remembered that Loughner developed "a hate for government and just how everything was systematic. . . . He thought government controlled people too much."[30]

As he adopted these extreme beliefs, Loughner's feelings for Giffords turned from dislike to violent hatred. These intense emotions became the basis for Loughner's integration of personal and political grievances. Loughner's hatred was partly due to his encounter with Giffords at the 2007 event. It was also partly due to Giffords's immigration reforms, her endorsement of the 9/11 Commission report, and her perceived neglect of language development in schools. "It wasn't a day-in, day-out thing," recalled Bryce Tierney, "but once in a while, if Giffords did something that was ridiculous or passed some stupid law or did something stupid, he related that to people."[31] And it was partly due to the simple fact that Giffords was the most accessible politician against whom Loughner could vent his hostility. Ultimately, though, Loughner was a misogynist. He believed that women should not hold positions of power and to Tierney and others he derided Giffords as a "fake" or as "stupid and unintelligent."[32] He would later call her a bitch.

Yet Loughner's views on treasonous government agents were rooted in something far more dangerous than personal vengeance and a general climate of political paranoia: They were rooted in profound mental illness. That—combined with Loughner's unrestricted access to high-velocity firearms and ammunition—became the primary cause of the Tucson massacre.

The Tea Party Troubles

In April 2008, Giffords spent four days in Afghanistan and Pakistan and returned to Congress where she called for a phased withdrawal of troops from Iraq and a greater emphasis on Afghanistan, a position that put Giffords on the cusp of public opinion about the wars and further elevated her national stature. In October 2008, Robert Reich was quoted in an *Arizona Republic* article as saying, "I wouldn't be surprised if Gabby's the first or second female president of the United States. She's of that caliber."[33] In November 2008, Giffords won reelection to Congress, handily defeating her Republican opponent with 55 percent of the vote. "There's too much partisan bickering in the House of Representatives," observed Giffords in her victory speech, before outlining her views on health care, solar energy, and support for the troops.[34]

Giffords continued working on immigration reform, turning her attention to the criminal matters of drug trafficking and violence between Arizona and Mexico. On April 8, 2009, she invited sixty federal, state, and local law enforcement officers to Tucson for a summit in order to address cartel violence in northern Mexico and its spillover into the United States. Flanked by the Southwest's leading police officials, Giffords announced in a press conference that Mexico's drug wars had caused an estimated seven thousand deaths in the past year. She called on Congress to approve funding for additional law enforcement equipment and personnel for border security.

But then the "partisan bickering" turned ugly. And with it, the threat of gun violence became a recurrent feature of Giffords's public life. In August 2009, someone dropped a handgun on the floor during a raucous debate over healthcare at a Congress on Your Corner event in Douglas, Arizona, prompting calls to police by Giffords's staff. On April 23, 2010, an angry call came into the office of Representative Raul Grijalva, a veteran Tucson Democrat whose congressional district sits immediately to the west of Giffords's. A young male voice came on the line, brimming with fury over immigration. The caller announced that he was going to "come down there and blow the brains out" of Grijalva and his staff.[35]

A month earlier, in the early morning hours of March 25, 2010, after the national healthcare bill passed with Giffords's support, someone hopped a gated fence to gain access to Giffords's district office and fired a pellet gun into the glass-paneled front door and side window. A visibly shaken Giffords appeared on MSNBC the next morning. "You look at these examples around the country, which really try to incite people and inflame emotions, then chances are they're going to have a couple of people, extremes on both sides, frankly," Giffords said without finishing her thought.[36] The vandalism was preceded by calls to her office that were "more nasty and rude" than anything before, according to Giffords's staff. Tea Party supporters—"hundreds and hundreds of protestors shouting some pretty disparaging comments," as Giffords said in her MSNBC interview—had begun appearing outside the office with placards reading, "Gabby, You're Gone."[37]

In the 2010 midterm election, Giffords faced off against Republican candidate Jesse Kelly (no relation to Mark Kelly), a thirty-year-old gun-toting Tea Party candidate whose campaign ads featured a picture of the 6-foot-8 former Marine holding an assault rifle along with the slogan "Send a Warrior to Congress." He was a ruthless opponent. Kelly dismissed Giffords's immigration reforms as a "failure," opposed the Obama healthcare plan, charged that Social Security was a "giant Ponzi scheme," and received endorsements from organizations considered extremist and racist by civil rights groups. On June 12, 2010, Kelly organized a campaign fundraiser at a local gun range, urging supporters to "Get on Target in November/Help remove Gabrielle Giffords from office/Shoot a fully automatic M16 with Jesse Kelly." Giffords managed to squeak out a narrow victory and was sworn in for her third term on January 4, 2011.

During the Tea Party troubles, Giffords professed to be unconcerned about her own safety and did not travel with security, even as the intimidation seemed to worry her staff. To Mark Kelly, however, she would tell a different story. "Gabby was troubled by the hostile political rhetoric," he recalled, "and we were both worried that the angry discourse might even descend into violence."[38] Giffords carried on, appearing at hundreds of public events and continuing her efforts to protect Arizona's borders by steering through Congress a $600 million border security bill. When a respected Cochise County rancher named Rob Krentz was shot and killed on his ranch by a drug smuggler, Giffords reached across the aisle and joined Arizona Republican Senator John McCain in calling for assistance from the White House, leading to President Obama's decision to deploy 1,200 National Guard troops to protect the Arizona-Mexico border. In her statement from Tucson, Giffords announced that "more boots on the ground means a safer and more secure border. Washington heard our message."[39]

But her enemies had not retreated. The Krentz murder touched a local nerve and demands were made throughout Giffords's district to seal the border and kill any Mexican who tried to cross. "Gringo," a poster on the *Tucson Weekly* website, summarized the issue: "And Gabrielle Giffords slithers in to steal the limelight. . . . We all knew it was going to come to something like this [the Krentz murder] and it won't be long before more blood is spilled."[40]

Missed Opportunities

Meanwhile, Loughner was broadcasting his intent to commit terrorism. And he did so with flagrant exhibitionism. Everything Loughner did from this point on—including the Tucson shooting—was intended to attract attention to himself. Between 2009 and 2010, he displayed his contempt for government in numerous Facebook and Myspace postings along with several YouTube videos. In one video Loughner is seen burning an American flag. In another he parrots popular themes of the American radical Right and even gives his own definition of terrorism. And in still another Loughner describes inventing a new U.S. currency and complains about the illiteracy rate among people living in Giffords's congressional district. A witness would later tell authorities that Loughner was seen at the Pima Community College library watching Giffords's speeches online and yelling at the computer screen.

From February through October 2010, Loughner had five contacts with Pima Community College police for classroom disruptions; his teachers also complained to the administration about his bizarre behavior. In his first run-in with campus police, Loughner was questioned for carrying a knife and making statements about strapping bombs to babies. He also made comments about terrorism in one of his classes, and a classmate later said she worried that Loughner might commit a school shooting.

On September 23, 2010, after Loughner threw a tantrum in class over a grade and was ordered by police to leave campus, he uploaded a video to YouTube titled, "Pima Community College School—Genocide/Scam-Free Education-Broken United States Constitution." In the video, Loughner walks alone on the campus at night saying that the college is a torture chamber and illegal under the Constitution.

As Loughner's virtual obsessions expanded, his real world diminished. His language became more dissociative and his exhibitionism more manic. As friends fell away, Loughner asserted power over fellow students and total strangers by confronting them with weird statements, just as he had with Giffords back in 2007, only now more menacing. "He would do it because he thought people were below him and he knew they wouldn't know what he was talking about," said Bryce Tierney.[41] This sense of superiority was crucial for Loughner. Two longstanding psychological preconditions for mass killing are the dehumanization of victims and the symbolic elevation of the executioner to a position of moral sanctity.[42] Loughner had an abundance of both. These tendencies were exacerbated by Loughner's descent into madness and his acquisition of a semi-automatic firearm capable of firing thirty bullets in a matter of seconds—and allowing Loughner to achieve a feeling of omnipotence.

The slide began in early 2010 when Loughner was fired from his job at a store in the Tucson Mall, leaving him dependent on small amounts of cash from his parents, with whom he continued to live. Loughner's father recalled that his son "was just never the same" after losing his job at the mall.[43] On September 29, 2010, six days after Loughner posted his YouTube video criticizing Pima Community College, Loughner's parents were called to a meeting with college officials who urged them to have their son evaluated, warning that he had become a danger to himself and others, but they never followed up. Failing to produce a mental health evaluation, Loughner was suspended from the college on October 4. By then, Loughner was claiming that he spent most of his waking hours in a dream world that he had learned to control—a state of mind that not only matches some forms of mental illness, but also the hallucinatory effects of *Salvia divinorum*.

On November 30, 2010, Loughner entered a Sportsman's Warehouse and, after immediately passing the required background check, bought a Glock Model 19 9mm handgun with an extended clip and one box of Winchester bullets. He took target practice in the desert and carried the gun wherever he went, claiming that police were out to get him. Around this time, Loughner underwent a dramatic physical change. He shaved his head, tattooed two bullets on his arm, and began dressing in camouflage fatigues. He spouted hatred for the government to anyone who would listen and texted messages termed "nihilistic . . . the belief in nothing."[44] On December 6, he pulled from his safe the 2007 "thank you" letter from Giffords's office along with the envelope and inscribed on it *"Die bitch"* and *"Assassination plans have been made."* Beside it, he wrote *"Giffords."*[45]

Loughner continued his exhibitionism on social media. His Myspace page now displayed a photo of the Glock lying across a United States history book bearing an image of the White House. In one Myspace update, Loughner complained about how Congress was spending "illegal money" and how he could not trust the police anymore. In another, he referred to suicide. On December 8, Loughner wrote about strange dreams he was having. "There are important figures in my dreams that accomplished political aspirations: Hitler, Hillary Clinton and Giffords to name a few," he wrote.[46] On December 20, he activated his cap lock to emphasize the point: "I HAVE THIS HUGE GOAL AT THE END OF MY LIFE: 165 rounds fired in a minute!"[47] On December 30, Loughner posted his penultimate message: "Dear Reader . . . I'm searching. Today! With every concern, *my shot is now ready for aim*. The hunt, a mighty thought of mine."[48] His broadcasting of intent could not have been more explicit.

The Triggering Event

By the early days of January 2011, as Gabrielle Giffords was beginning her third term in Congress, Loughner had alienated most of his friends and was showing extremely angry behavior at home. His father was so concerned that he took away Loughner's shotgun and disabled his car to prevent him from leaving the house at night.

On Wednesday, January 5, Giffords's staff announced that the congresswoman would host her premier Congress on Your Corner event of 2011 on the morning of January 8 at the Casas Adobes shopping center on the northeast side of town. The announcement was sent via an automated "robo-call" to the homes of some twenty thousand constituents in Giffords's district, including the home of Jared Loughner.

That was the triggering event for Loughner. Loughner lived within walking distance of Casas Adobes, in his own neighborhood where he would feel comfortable, and the woman he hated most would be there within a matter of days. *"I'll see you on National T.v.!"* he wrote to "friends" on Myspace. *"This is a foreshadow . . . why doesn't anyone talk to me?"*[49]

Yet despite what Loughner had written on the envelope inside his safe, "assassination plans" had not been made. He needed more ammunition to commit the shooting, but bullets were not the first thing on his mind. First was the need for exhibitionism.

At 11:35 P.M. on January 7—roughly ten hours before he began his rampage—Loughner went to a Walgreens on Ina Road and dropped off a roll of 35mm film to be developed. The photos, shot in a mirror, show Loughner posing with the Glock against his crotch and bare buttocks while wearing a bright red women's G-string.

Earlier that day, a writer for Jon Stewart's *Daily Show* had e-mailed Giffords about a state representative who said that his goal was to try to keep news about Arizona off the *Daily Show*. "My poor state!" Giffords replied. "The nut jobs have stolen it away from the good people of Arizona."[50]

The Attack

At 12:29 A.M. on Saturday, January 8, Loughner checked into the Motel 6 on Ina Road. At 2:00 A.M., he phoned Bryce Tierney. Like the rest of his friends, Tierney wanted nothing to do with Loughner, so he did not pick up. "Hey man, it's Jared," recorded the voicemail. "Me and you had good times. Peace out. Later."[51] Nineteen minutes after that, Loughner returned to the Walgreens and retrieved the developed photographs.

At 4:12 A.M., Loughner logged on to Myspace for the last time, posting: "Goodbye friends. Please don't be mad at me. The literacy rate is below 5%. I haven't talked to one person who is literate. I want to make it out alive. The longest war in the history of the United States. Goodbye. I'm saddened with the current currency and job employment. I had a bully at school. Thank you. P.S.—plead the fifth!"[52]

At 7:04 A.M., Loughner entered the Walmart at Foothills Mall and tried to buy a box of 9mm ammunition but was turned away by an observant clerk because of his erratic behavior. Loughner then went to another

Walmart in the nearby town of Marana where he successfully bought the ammo, no questions asked. Investigators would later claim that no "red lights" went off before the Tucson shooting, but at 7:30 A.M. Loughner ran a red light near I-10 and was stopped by a Fish and Game warden. The officer made the curious observation that Loughner was "calm but nervous."[53] Because Loughner had no outstanding warrants, the officer told Loughner that he would not be getting a ticket, whereupon Loughner broke down crying and drove away.

Around 8 A.M., Loughner returned home and removed a black bag from his car. His father confronted him, and Loughner ran into the desert carrying the bag. At 9:41, a cab driver picked up Loughner from a nearby Circle K store.

At 10 A.M., as some two dozen Giffords constituents were gathering in front of the Safeway supermarket at Casas Adobes, Loughner appeared in the crowd wearing a black hoodie and looking like a "fringe character" as one witness recalled. He approached a Giffords volunteer and asked to speak with the congresswoman. He was politely told to sign in and wait his turn. The sign-in clipboard was handed to Loughner at 10:10, just as Giffords stepped before the audience and began speaking with sixty-three-year-old federal judge John Roll, who was there to lend his support after attending Saturday mass. No security guards were present. Suddenly, someone shouted "*Gun!*" as Loughner moved toward Giffords with the Glock outstretched in his right hand. He shot Giffords once above the left eyebrow, sending the bullet through her brain, and then turned on the crowd, shooting eighteen people and killing six, including Judge Roll and a nine-year-old girl. Loughner was tackled by three bystanders after his gun jammed while he was trying to reload another magazine. Arrested by police minutes later, he said, "I plead the Fifth."[54]

Aftermath

In his first press conference on the rampage, Pima County Sheriff Clarence Dupnik blamed the prevailing political climate because it was adding fuel to the "vitriol" that caused the attack, saying that Arizona had become "the mecca for prejudice and bigotry."[55] When asked by reporters after the shooting if his daughter had any enemies, Spencer Giffords replied, "Yeah—the whole Tea Party."[56] Asked if the Tea Party was responsible, Raul Grijalva told the *Nation*: "When you stoke these flames, and you go to public meetings and you scream at the elected officials, you threaten them—you make us expendable, you make us part of the cannon fodder."[57]

Reporting on the massacre quickly turned to the website of former Alaska governor Sarah Palin, whose political action committee had displayed a gun's cross hairs over a "target list" of Democratic lawmakers Palin wanted to see unseated in the last midterm elections. The image had disturbed Giffords when it was originally posted the previous March. "We're on Sarah Palin's target list," Giffords had warned in her MSNBC interview. "But the thing is the way that she has it depicted has the cross hairs of a gun sight over our district. When people do that, they've got to realize there are consequences to that."[58]

International media discussed the divisive political climate in the United States and the Palin map in particular. The French newspaper *Le Monde* said that the Tucson attack seemed to confirm "an alarming premonition that has been gaining momentum for a long time: that the verbal and symbolic violence that the most radical right-wing opponents have used in their clash with the Obama administration would at some point lead to tragic physical violence." Numerous foreign dignitaries also commented on the shooting, including British Prime Minister David Cameron, Spanish Prime Minister Jose Luis Rodriguez Zapatero, and Cuba's Fidel Castro.

On January 10, 2011, the booking photo of a wild-eyed, shaven-headed Jared Loughner was released to the media and published on front pages of newspapers around the world. The *Washington Post* described him as "smirking and creepy, with hollow eyes ablaze," while the *New York Times* called the picture "intense and arresting. It invited you to look and study, and wonder."

Based on two evaluations conducted at the U.S. Medical Center for Federal Prisoners in Springfield, Missouri, Loughner was later diagnosed with undifferentiated schizophrenia. In psychiatric evaluations and conversations with his lawyers, Loughner maintained that he had succeeded in killing Giffords and did not accept the fact that she survived his assassination. He was eventually sentenced to life in prison.

On January 12, 2011, as Giffords fought for her life in the intensive care unit at the University of Arizona's Medical Center, she was visited by President Obama. As he was leaving the hospital room, Obama and Mark Kelly saw Giffords open her eyes for the first time since the shooting five days earlier. Obama then went to a memorial service at McKale Center on the University of Arizona campus where he delivered what some historians consider to be the most powerful speech of his presidency.

"I have come here tonight as an American who, like all Americans, kneels to pray with you today and will stand by you tomorrow," he began. After quoting from the Book of Psalms, Obama summarized the events of the previous Saturday, remarking that Giffords and the other victims had been shot while "gathered outside a supermarket to exercise their right to peaceful assembly and free speech." Six times over, he spoke of the six lives lost, ending with nine-year-old Christina-Taylor Green, born on September 11, 2001. "I hope you jump in rain puddles," said the President with an eloquence rarely seen in modern politics. Riffing on a verse from the Book of Job, Obama said that "terrible things happen for reasons that defy human understanding." Then he said something intended to push the issues of gun control and mental illness to the top of America's national security agenda:

> For the truth is that none of us can know exactly what triggered this vicious attack, what thoughts lurked in the inner recesses of a violent man's mind. . . . [But] already we have seen a national conversation commence, not only about the motivations behind these killings, but about everything from the merits of gun safety laws to the adequacy of our mental health system. And much—much of this process—of debating what might be done to prevent such tragedies in the future is an essential ingredient in our exercise of self-government.[59]

On January 22, 2012, Gabby Giffords announced her retirement from Congress in order to concentrate on recovering from her wounds, but promised to return to public service in the future.

On February 26, 2015, at the seaside docks in Mobile, Alabama, the Navy launched the first gun-free warship in American military history. The ship was christened the *USS Gabrielle Giffords*.

At the Tucson memorial service, President Obama identified a key aspect of this research when he remarked: "None of us can know exactly what triggered this vicious attack." Yet armed with 20/20 hindsight, we do know what triggered the attack: It was the seemingly harmless robocall from Giffords's staff to Loughner that provided him with the exact date, time, and place for his rampage. The robocall, which allowed Loughner to fuse motive with opportunity, created the situational condition necessary for terrorism. Just as James Earl Ray stalked Martin Luther King to the Lorraine Motel through a Memphis newspaper article, Loughner stalked Gabrielle Giffords to Casas Adobes through an automated phone message. But things should never have gotten this far because there were many chances to prevent the shooting. Loughner broadcasted his violent intentions to numerous people before the attack. He threatened to commit mass murder on Myspace and mentioned Giffords by name; he displayed his contempt for government in YouTube videos and openly ridiculed Giffords to friends; he fetishized his 9mm Glock by posting a photo of the gun online and presented himself to friends as an armed warrior; and through his troubled and disruptive behavior, he aroused the suspicions of his parents, fellow students, and community college officials. Loughner was a walking timebomb. Hours before the shooting, he called a friend and bid his final farewell and then turned to Myspace and wrote: "Goodbye friends." Apparently, however, no one cared enough to act on these dire warnings. *"I'll see you on National T.v.!"* Loughner announced on Myspace shortly after receiving the robocall. *"This is a foreshadow . . . "* And then, in a desperate plea for online sympathy, he asked, *"Why doesn't anyone talk to me?"*

The answer is obvious. By this point Loughner's behavior had become so strange and unpredictable that his friends were ignoring him. The real question is why didn't Loughner's friends talk to one another about Loughner? Put another way, why didn't the bystanders communicate among themselves? This is what distinguishes Loughner's attack from cases of lone wolf terrorism that were prevented. In those cases, bystanders freely talked to one another, confirming their suspicions about a possible attack, and then they called police and lives were saved in the process. This lack of communication among bystanders marks the final, tragic lesson of the Tucson massacre. Yet perhaps it can also serve as a lesson for developing a coherent approach to stopping future acts of lone wolf terrorism, a subject we turn to next.

CHAPTER 8

The Radicalization Model
of Lone Wolf Terrorism

The results of our investigation into commonalities among American lone wolf terrorists, based on our analysis of cases in the database, are summarized in table 8.1. It shows that in 80 percent of both pre- and post-9/11 cases, lone wolf terrorism involves a combination of personal and political grievances. This is a signature trademark of the lone wolf's radicalization. Unlike members of a terrorist group who share collective grievances, lone wolves integrate various ideologies with highly personal vendettas. The end result is the same, however. For both lone wolves and organized terrorists, violence is considered the only alternative to an unjust system.

One of Spaaij's essential findings is that lone wolf terrorists draw on beliefs and ideologies of validation generated and transmitted by extremist movements.[1] This facet of radicalization was measured by the lone wolf's affinity with an extremist group. The characteristic was present in 63 percent of the pre-9/11 cases, but it was found in only 48 percent of the post-9/11 cases.

Another component of radicalization is the influence of an enabler. The commonality was confirmed in 57 percent of the pre-9/11 cases and in 70 percent of the post-9/11 cases. Such a finding is supported by research on lone wolf terrorism in other parts of the world. For example, prior to his killing of twenty-nine Palestinian worshippers and the wounding of 120 others at the Cave of the Patriarchs near Hebron in 1994, Jewish ex-

TABLE 8.1
Commonalities among lone wolf terrorists

Variable	% of Pre-9/11 Cases	% of Post-9/11 Cases
Personal/political grievances	80	80
Affinity with extremist group	63	48
Enabler	57	70
Broadcasting intent	84	70
Triggering event	84	73

tremist Baruch Goldstein is believed to have received tacit approval for the massacre from a group of Orthodox rabbis.[2] Anders Breivik had two distinct categories of enablers. On an ideological level, he was enabled by the Americans Robert Spencer, founder of the Jihad Watch website, and Pam Geller, who ran the blog *Atlas Shrugs*, as well as by British political theorist Bat Ye'or, author of *Eurabia: The Euro-Arab Axis*, which foretells the transformation of Europe into a cultural and political appendage of the Arab/Muslim world. On an operational level, Breivik learned his terrorist tactics from a study of the IRA, the Basque terrorist group ETA, al-Qaeda, and Timothy McVeigh.[3]

The radicalization of Salafi jihadists, which sprang from "an enabling interpretation" of global affairs related to the perceived war on Islam, sheds further light on lone-wolf radicalization in that deification of heroes and martyrs is also a central feature.[4] Acclaimed terrorism researcher Ariel Merari made a similar observation in his study of Palestinian would-be suicide bombers belonging to Hamas and al-Fatah. Most of the bombers "have heroes they admire and want to resemble," wrote Merari. "These can be fictional figures from movies or literature, admired family members, historical personalities, or current public figures."[5] All of the heroes represented Islamists associated with collective memory and bravery in war.

Research on assassins has comparable findings. Nearly 80 percent of all U.S. assassins read literature on assassination, emulated assassins, visited assassination sites, and/or watched movies or television shows or listened to music about assassinations.[6] School shooters also tend to have model heroes. A study of twenty-eight school shootings in Europe and North America between 1999 and 2011 found that a majority of them was influenced by Eric Harris and Dylan Klebold, the Columbine shooters, and that their shared admiration for the two gave subsequent school shooters an imagined sense of community.[7]

Likewise, lone wolves rely on indirect enablers who inspire by example, the most important of whom—Osama bin Laden, Anwar al-Awlaki, William Pierce, Timothy McVeigh, and Alex Jones—are representatives of warrior subcultures.

Specific media and cultural influences have an enabling effect across all categories of terrorism, be it terrorism committed by large groups, small groups, or loners. Umar Farouk Abdulmutallab, the "underwear bomber" who attempted to bring down a U.S. jetliner bound for Detroit on Christmas Day, 2009, was introduced to violent jihad through hours of online listening to Anwar al-Awlaki's sophisticated lectures on the Salafi Jihad. It was al-Awlaki who recruited the young Nigerian into the bombing plot organized by Al-Qaeda in the Arabian Peninsula (AQAP) and arranged for the filming of his martyrdom video. Tamerlan Tsarnaev was also introduced to jihadist ideology through al-Awlaki's YouTube lectures, and in turn persuaded his younger brother, Dzhokhar, that jihad was their calling. When it came time for the construction of their pressure-cooker bombs to be placed at the finish line of the Boston Marathon, the brothers turned to step-by-step instructions found in al-Awlaki's *Inspire* magazine (the article "Make a Bomb in the Kitchen of Your Mom"). It was also through *Inspire* and al-Awlaki's online sermons that Syed Rizwan Farook was introduced to the idea of committing a jihadist attack against America, which he would later share with his wife, Tashfeen Malik, and neighbor Enrique Marquez, who supplied the couple with assault rifles for the San Bernardino attack. The list of lone wolf terrorists indirectly enabled by al-Awlaki's online sermons includes such important figures as Carlos Bledsoe, Nidal Hasan, Mohammad Abdulazeez and Omar Mateen. Indeed, Peter Bergen found that "of the 330 Americans charged with or convicted of involvement in jihadist terrorist activity since the 9/11 attacks, more than 80 were found to have Awlaki's writings or sermons in their possession or cited him as an influence, and a further 7 had corresponded with him or traveled to Yemen to meet him."[8]

Previous research also has something to say about the role of direct enablers. Veterans of wars in Afghanistan and Bosnia (former *mujahideen*) who later relocated to the West have played a crucial role in spreading extreme religious views in Muslim diasporic communities, espousing radical rhetoric, and providing paramilitary training.[9] In such cases, direct enablers play a role in creating *situational factors* that make it possible for potential lone wolves to combine the motive, means, and opportunity necessary for a terrorist attack.[10] "From our perspective," write psychologists Clark Mc-Cauley and Sophia Moskalenko, "the most dangerous indicator of potential for lone wolf terrorism is the combination of radical opinion with means and opportunity for radical action."[11]

The means and opportunity for "radical action" are also relevant for understanding not only why the United States leads the world in lone wolf terrorism, but also why lone wolf attacks in the United States tend to kill more people than attacks by lone wolves in other countries.[12] It is because in America it is relatively easy for disaffected individuals to acquire high-powered firearms and ammunition. Terrorists seem to understand this. In a YouTube video calling for lone wolf attacks against the United States, al-Qaeda spokesman Adam Gadahn once proclaimed: "America is absolutely awash with easily obtainable firearms. You can go down to a gun show at the local convention center and come away with a fully automatic assault rifle, without a background check, and most likely without having to show identification. So what are you waiting for?"[13] Even people on the FBI's Terrorism Watch List can freely purchase handguns or assault rifles, as did Omar Mateen, the rationale being that prohibiting possession of guns does not stop terrorist suspects from illegally acquiring them.[14] Likewise, commercial gun manufacturers have come to design and market their products explicitly for single individuals, rather than for the military as has historically been the case, thereby creating the "private army of one" as gun historian Pamela Hagg notes.[15] Simultaneously, U.S. gun sales have shifted from rural purchasers of hunting rifles to urban buyers of combat firearms.[16] Criminologists have long argued for the need to focus not only on motives, but also on the situational factors leading to criminal violence.[17]

The broadcasting of terrorist intent was verified in 84 percent of the pre-9/11 cases and in 70 percent of the post-9/11 cases. This is also consistent with international research on lone wolf terrorism. An outstanding example is Yigal Amir, the Jewish extremist who assassinated Israeli Prime Minister Yitzhak Rabin in 1995. In the lead-up to the assassination, Amir brazenly announced to friends and family members that Rabin needed to die for his support of the peace process and even made such pronouncements at public gatherings.[18] Anders Breivik labored for nearly two years on his 1,500-page manifesto entitled *2083: A European Declaration of Independence*, which called for the eradication of all traces of Islamic culture from Europe. Breivik dealt in depth with such foreboding issues as bomb building, the infiltration of "the youth camp connected to the largest political party" in Norway, and "putting on disguises" such as a police uniform so that he could move around with weapons unchallenged. During his "writing" period (much of the manifesto was cut and pasted material from the Internet), Breivik also amassed some eight thousand e-mail addresses of avowed rightwing extremists and keyed them into his laptop. Ninety minutes before the Oslo bombing, Breivik attached his manifesto and hit the send button.[19]

While broadcasting intent apparently never happens in large terrorist groups like al-Qaeda or ISIS, Merari found that most Palestinian suicide bombers talked to family members about suicide prior to their foiled attacks.[20] Other researchers have applied "signaling theory" to suicide bombing, arguing that risk factors for suicide bombing are found in pre-attack signals, like threatening to kill others, which are "difficult to fake."[21] And while broadcasting intent would seemingly never happen within small terrorist groups either, the research says otherwise. Upon his return to Massachusetts from Dagestan in 2011, Tamerlan Tsarnaev was interviewed three times by FBI agents concerning his suspected ties to jihadist organizations. A year later, he twice spoke out in his local mosque against the imam and was once asked to leave the building after disrupting services. His brother, Dzhokhar, subsequently told two college roommates that he knew how to make a bomb, adding that there were "some things in the Koran worth dying for." His pronouncements were not random. On April 9, 2013, Dzhokhar posted a video on social media about the carnage in Syria, which ended with the line: "Syria is calling. We will answer."[22] Six days later, they bombed the Boston Marathon.

These findings are also relevant to assassination research, which shows that 39 percent of assassins either talked with others about assassination or wrote to known assassins prior to their attacks.[23] Equally important, as noted in chapter 6, broadcasting intent is consistent with research on school shootings. An influential 2002 Secret Service/U.S. Department of Education study analyzed the pre-attack behavior of forty-one school shooters between 1974 and 2000 and found that other students usually knew a shooting was to occur—but did not alert an adult. More than 80 percent of the shooters had confided their intentions to others, and more than half told at least two people. The most significant pre-attack confessions involved direct and specific threats.[24]

On balance, broadcasting intent is a trademark of lone wolf terrorists, and, as an observable phenomenon, it can help to (at least) give insight into lone wolf terrorism and possibly lead to action to prevent its occurrence.

The final commonality is a triggering event, the ultimate catalyst for terrorism. The commonality was present in 84 percent of the pre-9/11 cases and in 73 percent of the post-9/11 cases. Here again there is corroborating evidence in the international literature on lone wolf terrorism. Anders Breivik first distributed his manifesto to conservative Norwegian political figures in 2010 and anticipated receiving positive comments from them. None came. This rejection of his manifesto was the triggering event for Breivik's decision to independently take his online campaign to the next level and to acquire the bomb-making components, firearms, and fake police uniform he would use in the attacks.[25] Evidence also exists on triggering events among lone jihadists abroad. On December 11, 2010, a twenty-eight-year-old Iraqi-born Swedish citizen named Taimour Abdulwahab al-Abdaly blew himself up with a pipe bomb and wounded two others in an attempt to kill Christmas shoppers in Stockholm. Moments before the blast, al-Abdaly sent an e-mail to Swedish police and the media vowing revenge in the name of Islam on Sweden for its participation in the Afghanistan war and further indicated that he had been incited to violent action by cartoons published by a Swedish artist depicting the prophet Muhammad in an unflattering light.[26]

In terms of triggering events, we also see many parallels with large terrorist organizations. European and Middle Eastern terrorists have told their life stories to numerous researchers over the years, documenting specific events that served as catalysts for political violence. Michael Baumann, a founding member of Germany's leftist Movement 2 June, recalled that it was the unprovoked killing by the German police of a student demonstrator that turned him into a terrorist. Members of the Finucane family (named after Patrick Finucane, a Belfast solicitor murdered in 1989 by loyalist paramilitaries acting in collusion with the British government) have described how they were radicalized by the experience of being driven from their homes by Protestant mobs during the height of the Troubles in Northern Ireland.[27] An important catalyst for Islamic radicalization in general and terrorist attacks in particular is Western foreign policy. Osama bin Laden once said that he began thinking about attacking the West following the

American-supported Israeli assault on Lebanon in 1982.[28] Most female suicide bombers in Iraq are thought to have had family members who were killed by American-led military forces or by state forces in the country.[29] Global media coverage of the humiliation suffered by Muslim detainees at the U.S.-operated prisons at Abu Ghraib and Guantanamo has been cited as the catalyst for al-Qaeda and Taliban suicide bombings across Afghanistan.[30] One radicalization framework identifies triggering events as part of the immediate situation that challenges a radical group. Triggering events are conceived as "single events, or a series of events happening in close succession, that trigger within the group the conviction that acts of violence and terrorism by a group are necessary. The triggering event is the 'last straw' beyond which the only recourse is violence."[31]

Small terrorist groups are also motivated to action by triggering events. The FBI's armed assault on the Branch Davidians at Waco was the catalyst for Timothy McVeigh and Terry Nichols's bombing of the Oklahoma City Federal Building.[32] On a more personal level, the catalyst for the Washington Beltway sniper attacks was an experience John Allen Muhammad had while serving in the U.S. military during the Persian Gulf War. Muhammad was wrongfully accused of igniting a grenade in a tent full of soldiers and was brutalized during his interrogation with military intelligence. The experience left Muhammad with a bitter hatred for his country and, combined with a later family dispute, prompted him to copycat the Mark Essex New Orleans police sniping by recruiting and training the teenaged Lee Malvo to fire an assault rifle from a car trunk—the method used in each of the Beltway sniper attacks.[33] Relatedly, though on a more cognitive level, an overwhelming 98 percent of school shooters suffered a loss or failure they perceived as serious prior to their attacks, a trauma that set their anger in motion.[34]

Overall, these data indicate that the commonalities in radicalization for lone wolf terrorists have identifiable correlates in research on terrorist groups (large and small), assassins, and school shooters, which in turn suggests that there is something to learn about lone wolf terrorism from other types of violent criminality. Likewise, research on these other forms of violence may benefit from understanding the commonalities of lone wolf terrorism. The only variable that could not be identified as a commonality is the one that relates to an affinity with an extremist group in the post-9/11 era. This feature of radicalization has changed over time and is no longer as important as it once was. Why has this change occurred?

The Rise of Online Sympathizers

Rightwing loners of the pre-9/11 period—racists like Floyd Simpson, Byron de la Beckwith, and Leroy Moody—took encouragement from civil rights era groups like the Ku Klux Klan, the American Nazi Party, and the John Birch Society. Lone wolves from the Left—such as Mark Essex, Sam Byck, and the Alphabet Bomber—drew inspiration from the Black Panthers, the Symbionese Liberation Army, and the Weather Underground. Middle Eastern lone wolves from Sirhan Sirhan to Ali Kamal were sympathetic to Palestinian liberation movements. And nearly every lone wolf who took up the anti-abortion cause was inspired by the durable Army of God. In many instances, lone wolf terrorists were "failed joiners" of these extremist movements.

These sorts of affinities still exist among lone wolf terrorists. Nearly half of the lone wolves in the post-9/11 era—including such figures as Nidal Hasan, Mohammad Abdulazeez, and Omar Mateen—demonstrated an affinity with extremist organizations ranging from al-Qaeda and ISIS to various neo-Nazi groups. But those affinities are an exception to the rule that lone wolf terrorists are becoming increasingly more independent. This should come as no surprise since lone wolf terrorists are iconoclastic by nature.

At the root of this change is technology.[35] With the advent of Internet chat rooms, conspiracy theory websites, Facebook, Twitter, and Instagram, stochastic terrorists like Anwar al-Awlaki and Alex Jones have been able to connect scattered people worried about everything from American foreign policy and drone strikes to a one-government world and a pending imposition of martial law and tell them that they do not worry in isolation, that they are no longer failed-joiners but part of a community protected by and isolated in one of the most primitive forms of social organization— the tribe. The affinity with extremist groups has therefore been replaced by an *affinity with online sympathizers*.

Online sympathizers are important to the lone wolf terrorist because they provide personal and ideological support to individuals while simultaneously allowing them to operate anonymously within their chosen community. As such, online sympathizers broaden the base of support for the strategy of leaderless resistance, often to worldwide audiences as demonstrated by ISIS. The Internet and social media make it possible for an individual to become radicalized in the solitude of his or her bedroom through linking and interacting with virtual "friends," electronically exchanging militant propaganda, and even acquiring technical know-how for committing acts of terrorism through online manuals. As Sageman remarks, "The Internet has dramatically transformed the structure and dynamic of the evolving threat of . . . terrorism by changing the nature of terrorists' interaction."[36] Or as the U.S. Marshals Task Force on Lone Wolf Terrorism puts it: "We see tell-tale signs quite often that lone wolves who are literate or computer and Internet savvy will seek reinforcement for their own ideologies and innuendos of their ultimate solutions."[37] In this way, incipient lone wolves become "Net Nazis" or "Cyber Jihadists" who are known to other extremists only by their online identities. The more they increase their involvement with online sympathizers, the more they isolate themselves from people in their real-world communities, which, in turn, makes it easier for them to change identity and live outside of ordinary social arrangements, thereby fueling the radicalization process even more. Put simply, living their social lives online can increase their engagement with radicalism.

This new development in lone wolf terrorism is incorporated into the radicalization model presented below. Yet the model also includes affinity with extremist groups. Even though this aspect of radicalization may be declining, it was still present in 48 percent of the post-9/11 cases. The overarching point is this: Virtually all lone wolves have an affinity with some person, community, or group, be it online or in the real world. This is a significant finding because it contests the policy assumption that lone wolf terrorists do not communicate with others or follow in the violent tradition of others. They clearly do.

The Radicalization Model of Lone Wolf Terrorism

The Radicalization Model of Lone Wolf Terrorism (figure 8.1) is unique in the field of terrorism studies for a number of reasons. First, it is the only known radicalization model dedicated exclusively to lone wolf terrorism.[38] Second, it is inclusive of all lone wolf motives and ideologies; many models

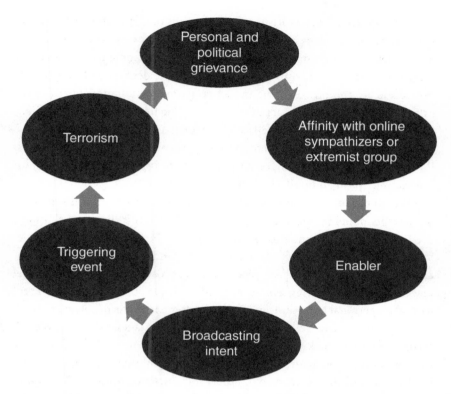

Figure 8.1 The radicalization model of lone wolf terrorism

concentrate only on the radicalization of Islamists.[39] Third, while radicalization models typically map pathways to extremism, not all extremism
ends in terrorism.[40] Radicalization theorist Peter Neumann views this
distinction in terms of *cognitive radicalization*, emphasizing extremist beliefs,
and *behavioral radicalization*, emphasizing violence.[41] Our model represents
the latter: The cases used to construct our radicalization model all ended
in terrorism or attempted terrorism. Fourth, and relatedly, radicalization
models are usually intuited by analysts through literature reviews, or they
are based on theories of radicalization. While figure 8.1 is deduced from
previous research, each component of the model has been empirically verified through an analysis of all 106 cases of lone wolf terrorism in our database. Although our model is simple, it is not simplistic.[42]

The model suggests that violent radicalization is a process by which an
individual progresses through an interest in personal and political causes

to accepting the use of terrorism as a valid means of furthering those causes. Radicalization involves a transformation from one stage to another. It is not sudden. That is, individuals do not "snap" and become radical. Rather, they move toward terrorism, although certain incidents (like losing a job) can accelerate the process. The model contains five components of radicalization precipitating the act of terrorism. (The final arrow in the model, looping terrorism to another phase of personal and political grievances, is intended to recognize the potential for copycat attacks.) The model shows that radicalization is not the result of a single factor but a combination of interacting "push and pull" factors.

Like other radicalization models, this one is not necessarily linear: It is not a stage model in which an individual must progress through each succeeding phase to become a lone wolf terrorist.[43] For instance, it is possible for an individual to first encounter an enabler and then be introduced to a community of online sympathizers. Likewise, broadcasting intent may take place both prior to a triggering event and after. Or, it is possible for one to formulate personal and political grievances after encountering enablers and/or sympathizers. Moreover, an individual can skip stages and move toward terrorism rather quickly. Indicative of this phenomenon, none of the facets of radicalization achieved 100 percent empirical verification, as should be the case with any instance of credible social science research. The point is that figure 8.1 should be thought of as a heuristic device that can be used to identify indicators of radicalization, rather than as a lock-step sequential model. Once these indicators are witnessed by others—friends, family members, co-workers, students, civic leaders, police, and retail gun store clerks—they can lead to intervention.

Capturing Lone Wolf Terrorists

One way to appreciate the practical significance of the radicalization model is by looking at its implications for capturing lone wolf terrorists. First, a review of background factors is necessary. Among the pre-9/11 lone wolves in our database, 27 percent were captured at the crime scene. Some were arrested without incident, and others were captured after resisting arrest.

Another nine of the lone wolves from the pre-9/11 era (23 percent) were either killed by law enforcement, or they committed suicide at the crime scene. Identifying commonalities among these lone wolves has obvious implications for public safety. As a group, these pre-9/11 lone wolves were extremely violent. All told, the nine lone wolves killed or wounded sixty-four people, including twelve police officers. Their political grievances were all over the board, ranging from Black Power and anti-government extremism to neo-Nazism and anti-abortion absolutism. They were ethnically diverse, and they ranged in age from twenty to sixty-nine years of age. They were mostly single unemployed males with a criminal record. They all broadcasted their intent to commit terrorism, and their violence was in each case precipitated by a triggering event.

A distinguishing trait of the pre-9/11 lone wolf terrorists was their ability to elude capture, due in large part to their formidable criminal skills and ability to operate under the radar of law enforcement for extended periods of time. More than a third of them (38 percent) evaded law enforcement for months, years, and even decades. They included Joseph Paul Franklin, the Unabomber, and Eric Rudolph. These three lone wolves avoided capture for a combined total of twenty-eight years. There is much to learn from these earlier cases about evasive criminal techniques, terrorist tradecraft, and the international lengths lone wolves are willing to go to avoid arrest, traits rarely seen in other types of criminality. Consider the case of James Earl Ray.

The search for Martin Luther King's assassin was the largest manhunt in American history at the time. It involved 3,500 agents from J. Edgar Hoover's FBI, assisted by the Royal Canadian Mounted Police and New Scotland Yard. The assassin's capture resulted from the interweaving of physical, circumstantial, and anecdotal evidence. At first, the assassin's identity was unknown. It would take agents two weeks to figure this out. Fingerprints from the rifle found at the Memphis murder scene (the assassin had dropped his rifle outside the rooming house where the lethal shot was fired) were tied to prints found on an abandoned car in Atlanta. The car was traced to a work order for the vehicle performed in Los Angeles, which led investigators to the address of an LA apartment and phone records from it. Those records indicated that numerous calls had been placed to the LA presidential campaign headquarters of the racist Alabama governor George Wallace and thus pointed to a motive for the King assassination, as if one were needed. Calls had also been made to a local dance school. The dance school records showed that the suspect had once attended a local bartending school. At the bartending school agents found a graduation photo bearing the suspect's image.

Positively identifying the suspect in the photo as James Earl Ray took FBI agents less than an hour, yet by that time Ray was in Toronto, Canada. From there he flew to London using a passport in the name of "Ramon Sneyd." In London, Ray ran out of money and committed an armed robbery to fund his next trip: to Rhodesia via Belgium, where he planned to become a mercenary for the cause of white supremacy. By then, an alert had been issued to British airlines to be on the lookout for "Ramon Sneyd." On June 8, 1968, two months after assassinating Dr. King, Ray was arrested without incident at Heathrow Airport while awaiting a flight to Brussels.[44]

Equally instructive is the case of James Kopp. On the night of October 23, 1998, Kopp fired a single round from an assault rifle at abortion doctor Barnett Slepian as he stood inside his kitchen in Amherst, New York, killing him. Kopp fled to Mexico, beginning a two-year run from the law. Later he traveled to London and then went underground in Dublin, Ireland, where Kopp may have received assistance from other anti-abortion activists. A break in the investigation came when Slepian's neighbor came forward with a description of an unusual vehicle seen in the area on the day of the assassination. Kopp was well-known to New York State Police for his anti-abortion protests; the vehicle seen in Amherst matched Kopp's vehicle, and the description of the driver matched Kopp. A tip from an informant later helped the FBI locate Kopp in Ireland. Yet Kopp fled Ireland before authorities could apprehend him. Traveling to Brittany, France, he was ultimately captured there without incident and extradited to the United States to stand trial.[45]

Lone wolves like James Kopp, James Earl Ray, Eric Rudolph, Joseph Paul Franklin, and Theodore Kaczynski were deadly criminals who possessed uncanny abilities to thwart massive law enforcement efforts to bring them to justice, abilities that have become part of a growing folklore about the lone wolf terrorist. But that talent seems to be a thing of the past.[46] Only one of the post-9/11 lone wolf terrorists eluded capture for more than a year—due not to the terrorist's ingenuity but to the fact that the FBI had focused on the wrong suspect. This was the case of Bruce Ivins, the government microbiologist responsible for the 2001 anthrax attacks that killed five and injured seventeen in the deadliest instance of biological terrorism in United States history to date.[47] Some in the FBI considered Ivins a suspect as early as 2002, but he did not become the main focus of investigation until late 2006. Up to that point, the FBI had been interested in another government scientist, Steven Hatfill, who was exonerated in early

2008 and subsequently awarded $5.8 million in damages. Once the FBI began questioning Bruce Ivins, he displayed signs of severe stress and went into treatment for depression and suicidal ideation. On March 19, 2008, police were called to Ivins's Maryland home, where they found him unconscious. Ivins was briefly hospitalized and in July investigators told Ivins that he was about to be prosecuted for the anthrax attacks. Ivins was committed to a hospital for psychiatric evaluation and released on July 24. Five days later he committed suicide without ever being arrested.[48]

Another sixteen of the post-9/11 lone wolves (24 percent) in our database were able to evade capture for a couple of weeks to a month or more. One of these cases, the Spokane bombing plot, suggests that future investigations of lone wolf terrorism will be successful when they concentrate on a suspect's affinity with online sympathizers. Online radicalization presents unique challenges for counterterrorism experts due to the anonymity afforded to users of online forums. Yet the Internet and social media have also led to a decentralization and fragmentation of real-world extremist movements, making it easier for counterterrorism experts to focus on the activities of specific individuals who express extremist views through the online culture of *oversharing*, which can involve the broadcasting of terrorist intent.

The Spokane Bombing Plot

On the morning of January 17, 2011, two sanitation workers in Spokane, Washington, noticed a backpack with visible wires sitting on a bench along the route for the city's annual Martin Luther King Day Unity parade.[49] The Spokane Police Department was called, and the bomb disposal unit neutralized the device before sending it to the FBI forensics lab in Quantico, Virginia. Analysts found that the bomb had been wrapped in two t-shirts with logos referencing Stevens County, which stretches north of Spokane toward the Canadian border. The bomb consisted of a steel pipe tube with one end welded shut, forming a "blast plate," and the other end open, like a mortar. The device was packed with 128 quarter-ounce fishing weights coated with rat poison, an anticoagulant. Duct-taped to the tube were 100 grams of black powder and a rocket igniter with a triggering device—a remote car starter—similar to those used against U.S. forces in the Middle East. The device was directional, meaning that it was designed to propel shrapnel out of the tube and into the crowd of marchers. The rat poison would cause anyone wounded by the blast to "bleed out." According to the FBI, the backpack contained "a deadly destructive device, likely capable of inflicting multiple casualties."[50]

Investigators zeroed in on the t-shirts referencing Stevens County. Canvassing area hardware stores, they found that an unusually large number of fishing weights identical to those found in the bomb had been sold the previous November at a Walmart in Colville, Washington. The weights had been purchased with a debit card belonging to one Kevin Harpham of Colville. A check revealed that the thirty-six-year-old Harpham had no prior criminal record and had previously served in the Army at Fort Lewis, Washington. A DNA sample from his Army records matched a sample found on the backpack's handle.

Within hours of identifying Harpham, FBI analysts matched him to someone named "Joe Snuffy" who posted on the Vanguard News Network, a popular neo-Nazi website. "Snuffy's" last posting was on January 15, two days before the backpack was discovered. One posting suggested that Harpham's radicalization was rooted in a personal grievance. "The older I get," he wrote, "[the] less I have to live for, and the less I have to live for, the less the laws of this country will be able to influence my actions."[51] In tracing Harpham's digital footprint, investigators discovered that he was a former member of the National Alliance, the organization founded by William Pierce. They also learned about Harpham's broadcasting of intent. Since 2004, Harpham had made more than a thousand postings to the Vanguard News Network, most of them diatribes against African Americans and Jews. But in a 2006 posting, Harpham wrote: *I can't wait till the day I snap.*[52] Investigators further discovered an enabler. Within Harpham's community of online sympathizers was the well-known racist Frazier Glenn Miller, former leader of the North Carolina–based White People's Party, a close personal friend of the imprisoned lone wolf celebrity Joseph Paul Franklin, and himself a lone wolf terrorist in waiting. (Miller would commit mass murder at the Jewish Community Center in Overland Park, Kansas, in 2014.) Harpham regularly communicated with Miller and had donated money to a Miller defense fund. This trove of investigative evidence was made possible entirely by Harpham's penchant for oversharing within a community of online sympathizers. Yet there was even more to be gained for the FBI.

Monitoring his online traffic, agents learned that Harpham was looking to buy a car, so they devised a plan to arrest him away from his home, fearing a repeat of the deadly 1992 siege at Randy Weaver's cabin in Ruby Ridge, Idaho—resulting in the killing of a U.S. Marshal and Weaver's wife and son—a decisive event in the radicalization of rightwing extremists throughout the Pacific Northwest.[53] Agents placed an online ad for a vehicle that was of interest to Harpham at a good price, and on March 9, Harpham left his house to check it out. As Harpham drove down the narrow mountain road leading to a small bridge at the bottom, FBI agents disguised as road workers stopped him. He was signaled onto the bridge and motioned to halt alongside a backhoe. The backhoe driver then slammed the steel bucket against the rear of Harpham's car, distracting Harpham's attention away from a dozen camouflaged agents there to arrest him. Harpham had remained at large for two months. He was later sentenced to thirty-two years in federal prison.

Kevin Harpham is, however, something of an anomaly among lone wolf terrorists of the post-9/11 era in our database. The vast majority of them (74 percent) were either arrested at the crime scene, hours after their attacks, killed by police, or committed suicide before they could be apprehended. As a group, they were just as violent as their predecessors, killing and wounding 258 people. Their political grievances were also varied, ranging from those of Islamists to those of anti-government extremists, anti-abortionists, and neo-Nazis. Ethnically diverse, they varied in age from fifteen to eighty-nine. They were typically single unemployed males with a criminal record. And also as before, they tended to broadcast their intent to commit terrorism, and their violence was usually precipitated by a triggering event. But there was a major difference: While the most infamous lone wolf terrorists of the pre-9/11 era survived as fugitives on the run, the most notorious lone wolves of the post-9/11 era chose a more fatal path whereby violence became a matter of human *performance* in the tradition of Eric Hoffer's true believer—"the man of fanatical faith who is ready to sacrifice his life for a holy cause."[54]

Going Out in a Blaze of Glory

Among them was Nidal Hasan. There is every reason to believe that Hasan intended to kill as many fellow soldiers at Fort Hood as he could until he was killed himself. In addition to the sophisticated semi-automatic weapon

Hasan used in the attack, he also carried a loaded Smith & Wesson .357 magnum revolver that he never got around to firing. The massacre ended only when a civilian policeman surprised Hasan with gunfire, striking Hasan five times in the back and severing his spinal cord.

Hasan had broadcasted his intent several times prior to the Fort Hood shooting. During his senior year of residency at Walter Reed Medical Hospital, Hasan set up a website where he condemned any Muslim who serves in "the armies of disbelievers and fights against the brothers."[55] Hasan also made a provocative PowerPoint presentation titled, "The Quranic World View as It Relates to Muslims in the U.S. Military." Hasan suggested that the Defense Department *"should allow Muslims* [sic] *Soldiers the option of being released as 'Conscientious objectors' to increase troop morale and decrease adverse events."*[56] He explained that the "adverse events" could include refusal to deploy, espionage, or the killing of fellow soldiers. On this final point, Hasan referred directly to Muslim American infantryman Hasan Akbar, who in 2003 killed or wounded sixteen fellow soldiers of the 101st Airborne in Iraq. In the months leading up to the Fort Hood attack, Nidal Hasan came to the FBI's attention not only for his e-mails to Anwar al-Awlaki (one read: "I can't wait to join you in the afterlife"), but also because of Internet postings Hasan had made about suicide bombings and his intention to join al-Qaeda. Put simply, Hasan had no business even being in the Army at this point. The FBI was aware of Hasan's attempt to contact al-Qaeda and that Hasan had "more unexplained connections to people being tracked by the FBI" than just al-Awlaki.[57] Two days before the shooting, Hasan gave away most of his belongings to a neighbor.[58] His attack was triggered by deployment orders for Afghanistan.

There is also every reason to believe that Jared Loughner meant to kill until he was killed. Loughner had no getaway plan, and during the attack carried only a small amount of cash, a 4-inch knife, and two additional 15-round magazines. The Tucson massacre ended only after a woman and two men tackled Loughner and wrestled his gun away as he attempted to reload the weapon. His broadcasting of intent was extensive, as discussed in chapter 7, and it was triggered by a routine activity of his primary victim.

Jim David Adkisson confessed that he intended to go on killing congregants inside the Knoxville Unitarian Church until police intervened and killed him. Not only did Adkisson broadcast his intent by posting a four-page online manifesto prior to the attack, he also mailed a hard copy to the Knoxville media. The shooting was triggered by Adkisson's inability to find "a good and decent job," a woman who could tolerate him, and his fear of becoming homeless.[59]

The only reason James von Brunn's attack on the Holocaust Museum ended is because he was shot in the head by a security guard. Prior to the shooting, von Brunn drew up a hit list of people he intended to kill (it was found in his car outside the museum). His family knew about the list but failed to notify police about his intentions. The shooting was triggered by von Brunn's recent loss of Social Security benefits and his son's decision to move from Washington, DC to Florida, which would have left von Brunn homeless.[60]

Byron Williams, a California career criminal facing life in prison as a three-strike offender, boldly attacked two highway patrolmen with high-powered firearms in the middle of a busy freeway—an obvious attempt at suicide by cop. While there was no broadcasting of intent, Williams's attack was triggered by the tirades of a stochastic terrorist.[61]

Keith Luke's grisly killing spree in Brockton, Massachusetts, likewise ended in a police shootout. Luke told police that he planned to "kill as many Jews, blacks, and Hispanics as humanly possible" before killing himself. During his three-year hospitalization for mental illness prior to the attack, Luke broadcasted his intent by telling medical staff that he harbored thoughts of raping, torturing, and killing.[62] The rejection of Luke's romantic overtures by a woman of color was the immediate triggering event. Yet there may have been another trigger: Twenty-four hours before Luke began his raping and killing, Barack Obama was inaugurated as the nation's first black president.

Also in an apparent attempt at suicide by cop, the only reason Paul Ciancia's massacre at the Los Angeles International Airport (chapter 6) ended is because he was shot four times by police, once in the face. His broadcasting came only hours before the attack.

In each of these cases, lone wolf terrorists did not surrender—they were stopped. Rather than surviving by their own wits as fugitives, they chose to stand their ground and murder like soldiers in pitched battle. Their intent was to go out in a blaze of glory, to die with great fanfare in a human performance similar to that of the suicide bombers of al-Qaeda and ISIS or the American assassins, none of whom had an escape plan, experts noted, and who "often assumed—or hoped—that they would be killed or captured after an attack."

Those post-9/11 lone wolves, who were killed by police at the crime scene, or committed suicide, shared important behavioral traits with the likes of Hasan, Luke, and Loughner. This is what a rigorous empirical analysis of lone wolf terrorism would hope to find. Those traits suggest a behavioral profile for the modern lone wolf terrorist, a profile that can be used to understand the atrocities at Tucson, Fort Hood, Oak Creek, Charleston, Orlando, and elsewhere: (1) Their goal is to commit mass murder with fire-arms (2) against those who symbolically represent state authority; (3) they are often socially alienated, have problems with depression and mental illness, and (4) are willing to die for their causes, no matter how eccentric or misunderstood those causes may seem to the public. Recently, lone wolf attacks have been preceded by conflicts with women. Indeed, recent research shows that more than half of the 110 mass shootings in the United States between 2009 and 2014 (overwhelmingly perpetrated by males) in-cluded the murder of a current or former spouse, an intimate partner, or a family member.[63] Along with Joshua Cartwright, Joseph Stack, and Omar Mateen (all women abusers), those post-9/11 lone wolf terrorists who died in a blaze of glory include the following.

• Joseph Ferguson, an eighteen-year-old white supremacist who went on a twenty-four-hour shooting spree in Sacramento, California, on Sep-tember 9, 2001, leaving five dead and two wounded. Ferguson's rampage was triggered by a breakup with his girlfriend. Midway through his attack, Fer-guson went to the home of a former work supervisor, killed him and made a suicide video in which he bragged of putting on "a hell of a show," adding, "I giveth and I taketh away, that's how it goes in fucking life." Ferguson blamed his problems on his mother who was in prison for molesting Fergu-son and another boy when they were children. After a high-speed pursuit in which Ferguson fired more than two hundred rounds at police, he crashed into a light pole and took his own life with a gunshot to the chin.[64]
• Jacob Robida, the eighteen-year-old neo-Nazi who embarked on a cross-country killing spree in February 2006. After entering a gay bar in New Bedford, Massachusetts, and cracking a customer in the head with a hatchet, Robida opened fire with a Ruger 9mm pistol, wounding three more customers. Robida then drove to Charleston, West Virginia, where he picked up a woman he once lived with. In Arkansas, Robida was pulled over by a highway patrolman. Robida killed him with a 9mm Smith & Wesson revolver. During a high-speed pursuit, Robida exchanged gunfire

with police and lost control of his vehicle, whereupon Robida killed his female companion and then killed himself with a gunshot to the head. On his Myspace page, Robida said that he suffered from anti-social personality disorder and described himself as "pure evil" and "absolutely terrifying."[65]

• Thirty-six-year-old John Bedell who used a 9mm Taurus pistol (bought in a Memphis police auction) to shoot two police officers at the main entrance of the Pentagon on March 4, 2010, before dying in an exchange of gunfire with the officers. Bedell embraced a grab bag of anti-government conspiracy theories about anarchism and the "truth" behind 9/11. He was a chronic marijuana user with a history of mental illness. Bedell's family first noticed mental disarray following the breakup of a long-term relationship with his girlfriend in 2002.[66]

• Wade Page, the forty-year-old neo-Nazi whose massacre at the Sikh temple was precipitated by a breakup with his girlfriend. He committed suicide with a Springfield 9mm revolver after being shot a dozen times by police.[67]

• Thirty-three-year-old ex-police officer Christopher Dorner's rampage against the Los Angeles Police Department, which ended with a self-inflicted gunshot wound to the head. Apropos of going out in a blaze of glory, Dorner titled his online manifesto, "The Last Resort." He had a history of problems with women. An ex-girlfriend once posted a warning about Dorner on a dating website saying, "If you value your sanity, stay away from this guy."[68]

• Twenty-six-year-old Christopher Harper-Mercer, who took his own life with a gunshot to the head after leaving eighteen college students dead and wounded in the Roseburg, Oregon, shooting of 2015. Harper-Mercer embraced eclectic beliefs involving opposition to organized religion and support for white supremacy. Known to have a history of learning difficulties and emotional problems related to his Asperger's Disorder, Harper-Mercer lived with an overprotective mother who encouraged his interest in gunplay and kept a large arsenal of loaded weaponry around the house— much like the mother of Adam Lanza, the twenty-year-old gunman who slaughtered children at Sandy Hook. Lanza also bonded with his mother through guns and suffered from Asperger's.[69] Like Nidal Hasan, Jared Loughner, Christopher Dorner, and Adam Lanza, Christopher Harper-Mercer *over-armed* himself for the Roseburg rampage. He carried six guns with him into the college, including a 9mm Glock, along with five magazines. In various Internet postings, Harper-Mercer expressed interests in mass murderers like Adam Lanza and complained of sexual frustration as a "beta boy" (a virgin).[70]

This is only a partial listing of the American lone wolf terrorists in the post-9/11 era who went out in a blaze of glory. Our data indicate that the frequency of this dangerous phenomenon has increased since 2012.

The Future of Lone Wolf Terrorism

Another defining characteristic of twenty-first-century American lone wolf terrorism is the targeting of uniformed police and military personnel. Of the 69 lone wolf cases identified between 2001 and mid-2016, 32 of them (46 percent) involved the use of firearms to attack police officers and soldiers, resulting in 101 being mortally wounded or injured. Nearly one-third of the victims killed or wounded by American lone wolf terrorists since 9/11 have been police or military officers. By and large, they were ambushed.

This trend is part of a global pattern of decentralized extremists targeting centralized authority by shooting police officers and soldiers. Attacks from 2014 through 2016 on uniformed officers in Canada, England, France, New York City, Philadelphia, San Bernardino, Dallas, and Baton Rouge, Louisiana, are part of the trend. Police and military are among the most visible symbols of state authority in Western societies, with police being especially vulnerable to attacks because they interact with local populations more closely than any other government body.[71] By attacking the uniform, extremists are attacking the validity of the state—an essential goal of terrorism.

In the United States, police fatalities occurring in conjunction with street crimes have decreased since 2010, yet the number of uniformed officers killed in ambushes has held steady; with the majority of these ambushes being perpetrated by individuals with radical rightwing or anti-government ideology.[72] Given the continued online spread of violent ideologies across the spectrum of extremist movements, it is likely that the United States and other Western nations will see a rise in police and military ambushes perpetrated by lone wolf terrorists in the years ahead. Evidence that this trend goes beyond the United States includes the recent lone wolf attacks against law enforcement in countries such as France, Belgium, Canada and Australia.[73]

The ability of law enforcement and intelligence agencies to prevent lone wolf terrorism will demand a clear understanding of the radicalization process that lone wolves go through prior to their attacks. This will not be easy. As the Israeli inquiry into the 1994 lone wolf attack at Hebron by Baruch Goldstein found: "The prospect of identifying this lone gunman in advance and finding out something about the time and place he intended to stage his attack is a near impossibility."[74] President Obama made a similar point in late 2015 when he drew a parallel between the challenges of preventing lone wolf terrorist attacks and the effort to prevent mass shootings (suggesting that lone wolf terrorism often manifests itself in a mass shooting). "It's not that different from us trying to detect the next mass shooter," Obama said of detecting lone wolf plots. "You don't always see it, they're not communicating publicly, and if you're not catching what they say publicly then it becomes a challenge."[75]

There is no silver bullet here, but insight into the radicalization of lone wolf terrorists may provide law enforcement with a rudimentary detection system of "signatures"—as minimal as they might appear—that an individual with a terrorist intent will demonstrate in preparing for an attack. According to our radicalization model, these signatures involve the integration of personal and political grievances; an affinity with online sympathizers and/or extremist groups; an interest in enablers who often operate as stochastic terrorists; the all-important broadcasting of terrorist intent; and a triggering event that oftentimes causes a dramatic change in behavior. To this list we can add a pattern of obsessive preparation centered on collecting an arsenal of weaponry; the shooter will often over-arm himself with far more weapons and ammunition than he actually uses.[76] Over-arming is extremely important because it indicates that an extremist has flipped from inspirational status to being fully operational. When fused with intelligence assembled by area specialists (criminologists, religious scholars, psychologists, communications experts, firearms specialists, and the like), some of these signatures may present early warning signs of a terrorist attack. Equally important, investigators must have an understanding of counterterrorism practices that have proven successful in the past, as well as the extent to which these successes have been derived from a working understanding of the radicalization process.

This research has shown that lone wolf radicalization is a deeply personal affair involving individual psychologies, interpersonal relations, and sociopolitical dynamics. Sometimes radicalization is inspired by militant Islam, sometimes by fundamentalist Christianity, neo-Nazism, or other forms of political nativism. And sometimes radicalization is so obscure and idiosyncratic that it defies understanding. It can only be known in full by the person undergoing the radicalization. Theodore Kaczynski once mapped out the motive for his bombing campaign in an elaborate formula that even the greatest mathematical minds at MIT could not figure out.

The process of radicalization is so complex that a coherent government policy to halt lone wolf terrorism has yet to emerge, despite heroic efforts to create one. Competing bureaucracies, changing managerial structures, and varying definitions of lone wolf terrorism have all compromised efforts to develop a consistent policy. Bureaucracies are not the problem, however, because bureaucracies are designed to solve complex problems. It was bureaucracies in Washington and Moscow that ultimately negotiated an end to the nuclear arms race in a campaign begun by President Dwight D. Eisenhower at the dawn of the Cold War. In 1952, to better understand the challenges ahead of him, Eisenhower read Eric Hoffer's *The True Believer* (1951), gave copies of *The True Believer* to friends, recommended it to others, and in 1956 called Eric Hoffer his "favorite author."[77]

Hoffer argued that faith in a political or religious cause is a substitute for the lost faith in ourselves and noted that the motivations for mass movements are interchangeable. Therefore, religious and nationalist movements—from Communism and Nazism to Protestantism and Islam—tend to attract the same type of followers, behave in the same way, and use the same tactics and rhetorical skills.

What is missing from modern security policy is this kind of all-encompassing intellectual framework for understanding the lone wolf terrorist's unique criminal thinking style and the specific circumstances that set these people on the pathway to extremism. Such a theory must also address the complex issues of misogyny, gun culture, and the effects of mental illness on radicalization. Criminology is well-suited for this task. Criminology is, after all, the study of crime, and today there is no crime perceived to be more threatening to Western societies than terrorism.

Criminological life-course theory—the idea that a person's crimes are caused by crucial turning points in life—can be used to identify the sequence of individual trajectories leading to terrorism and the extent to which those turning points are embedded in the commonalities of radicalization shared by most lone wolf terrorists (see figure 8.1). The theory can also be used to discern whether one commonality is more important than another. But life-course theory can tell us even more.

The emergence of a turning point in life opens up the possibility for a person to "knife off"—to completely amputate—the past from the present. "To ripen a person for self-sacrifice," argued Hoffer, "he must be stripped of his individual identity and distinctness."[78] Life-course theorists recognize the potential for major sociopolitical events like revolution and war to create an abrupt rupture in one's social relationships and identity.[79] Freed from personal history, the individual can invest in new relationships (real or virtual) that both provide social support for radicalization and encourage activities centered on violence. This transformation to radicalism is a highly emotional affair allowing for a confrontation with one's enemy—the "other"—and the circumvention of social and psychological barriers to violence. At this point, conditions exist for the individual to perform an identity transformation into an armed warrior.

In the following two chapters, we confront the challenge of applying life-course theory to lone wolf terrorism by drilling down on two paradigmatic cases of ambushing based on direct contact with the perpetrators who carried out the attacks.

CHAPTER 9

The Little Rock Military Shooting

Figure 9.1 Carlos Bledsoe, also known as Lil' Los, Abdulhakim Mujahid Muhammad, and Abdul Hakim Bledsoe. Source: www.defenddemocracy.org.

Carlos Leon Bledsoe was born to Melvin and Linda Bledsoe in Memphis, Tennessee, on July 9, 1985.[1] Like many children in the Memphis African American community, Carlos and his older sister, Monica, were raised in a home with strong middle-class values. Melvin, especially, taught his kids the importance of hard work, frugality, and family. Pets were part of the Bledsoe household, and they got their first dog when Carlos was five. An average student who attended the Baptist church, Carlos was only eight years old when he began working for the family tour bus business, River City Tours, where Melvin served as president and Linda as vice president. At age fifteen, he got a part-time job bussing tables at a Chuck-E-Cheese restaurant. Remembered as a gentle, happy-go-lucky teenager who loved playing basketball, telling jokes, swimming, dancing, and hip-hop music, Carlos also admired Martin Luther King, and he hung a picture of the great civil rights leader on his bedroom wall.

But then he drifted toward gang life. For Carlos, this change marked not only the beginning of an intense search for personal identity, but also unleashed a profound anger within him, the origins of which would later be attributed to a mental illness.

The Criminal Career

According to Memphis police reports, in 2002 Carlos Bledsoe joined a local street gang called MOB—Money Ova Bitches. Known on the streets as "Lil Los," Bledsoe was given several school suspensions for fighting, various street fights involving firearms and knives, and threats to commit murder. His most significant gang-related crime came months before his eighteenth birthday when Lil Los was arrested for possession of a chrome-plated set of brass knuckles which he had used to pulverize a woman's rear car window after she ran a stop sign and rammed into a vehicle Bledsoe was riding in. As Bledsoe smashed in the window, he yelled, "Bitch, I'm gonna kill you! Get out! I'm gonna kill you when I get your address!"[2] The case was processed out of court by juvenile authorities.

After graduating from Craigmont High School in 2003, Bledsoe left Memphis for Nashville, where he enrolled as a business administration student at Tennessee State University with the goal of one day taking over the family business and providing his parents with an early retirement. He moved into a campus dorm, where he developed a serious substance abuse problem, getting drunk four nights out of the week and smoking up to an ounce of marijuana a week. When Bledsoe moved into an off-campus apartment during his sophomore year, he got a dog for companionship, but the substance abuse continued, and he was involved in several altercations at nightclubs when he was drinking. He found part-time work as a bell-boy at Nashville's Opryland Hotel until he quit for temporary employment as a warehouse worker. Bledsoe's commitment to college began to wane, which only aggravated his criminality.

On Saturday night, February 21, 2004, Bledsoe was riding in the back-seat of a blue Mazda in Knoxville, Tennessee, when police pulled the car over for an equipment violation. The driver—an "unidentified black male" according to the police report—fled on foot leaving Bledsoe in the Mazda alongside a pound of marijuana, two shotguns, and a Russian-made SKS semi-automatic assault rifle with a chambered bullet. A pat down search revealed that Bledsoe carried a switchblade knife and a set of brass knuckles. He told police that he owned the weapons and had come to Knoxville to sell the shotguns on the streets. The SKS assault rifle he planned to keep. Bledsoe was jailed, arraigned in court, and released on bail. His weapons were confiscated, except for the assault rifle. Knoxville police allowed him to keep this gun. Facing a fourteen-year sentence on weapons charges, Bledsoe was given a plea arrangement in June whereby all but the switchblade violation was dropped in exchange for a year of probation. Curiously, the switchblade charge was dismissed, and Bledsoe was never assigned a probation officer. Even so, the experience frightened Bledsoe, and he set out to change his life.

The Pathway to Radicalization

He found new friends and embarked upon an intense study of religion. Questioning his Baptist faith, Bledsoe was initially drawn to Judaism. He visited a couple of Orthodox synagogues and was given some pamphlets to read, but was then turned away because, in Bledsoe's telling of it, he was black. After watching Spike Lee's acclaimed screen biography *Malcom X* and attending a TSU speech by Nation of Islam leader Louis Farrakhan, Bledsoe began attending the Islamic Center of Nashville (ICN), where he was emotionally stirred by the ritual of group prayer (*salah*). "It was amazing to watch about 50 to 75 people bowing and prostrating in a synchronized way," he recalled. "So I attempted to join."[3] In December 2004, when Bledsoe was nineteen years old, he converted to Islam at the Masjid Al-Salam Mosque in Memphis. "I was near a burning fire," he wrote of the conversion. "The Almighty seen me and guided me to Islam—the true religion—so all Praise to Allah."[4]

Bledsoe dropped out of Tennessee State in the fall of 2005, but stayed in Nashville and continued his involvement with the ICN, where he was further swayed by the sermons of Imam Abdulhakim Muhammad who preached from the Salafist tradition of Sunni Islam. Among the friends Bledsoe made at the ICN were several Somali immigrants tied to Nashville's Al Farooq Mosque, which catered to the city's growing Somali population. A Somali man moved into the apartment with Bledsoe and his dog. Meanwhile Bledsoe supported himself by bouncing from one low-wage job to another, his dream of taking over the family business now forgotten. When he went home to Memphis for Christmas in 2005, he got into a heated argument with Monica's husband over Islam, an event that would lead Melvin Bledsoe to say: "We saw another side of Carlos that we hadn't seen before." Around this time, the picture of Martin Luther King came down from his bedroom wall.

By 2006, Bledsoe had become an observant Muslim, foreswearing marijuana, alcohol, and hip-hop music. After being told that Muslims consider dogs to be unclean creatures, Bledsoe took his dog into the woods and abandoned it. He started wearing Arab-style clothing, and, like most Islamic converts, he chose a Muslim name to mark his symbolic birth into the religion. In honor of ICN's imam, Abdulhakim Muhammad, Bledsoe legally changed his name to Abdulhakim Mujahid Muhammad. The middle name, Mujahid, or "holy warrior," is uncommon among Muslims. The selection of this unusual name was the first observable indicator of Bledsoe's radicalization and represented the initial step toward an identity transformation that is a precondition for terrorism. His father witnessed the change. "At this point," Melvin recalled, "his culture was no longer important to him, only the Islamic culture mattered."

Locus of Radicalization, the Enabler, and Affinity with an Extremist Group

In September 2007, Bledsoe flew to Yemen, arriving on the sixth anniversary of the historic 9/11 attacks on America. While Melvin would maintain that the Somalis at the Al Farooq Mosque had arranged for Bledsoe's travel and a place for him to stay in Yemen, in his version of events, Bledsoe made the trip independently for religious reasons, claiming that his journey to Yemen was necessary for acquiring travel documents to Mecca. While there may be truth in both versions, the subjective effect of Bledsoe's experience in Yemen was nothing less than transformative.

"Yemen, it was beautiful," he recalled. "I mean from the moment I got off the plane on September 11, 2007. It was all love. The people treated me with so much respect, like those brothers I first met, so hospitable."[5] With a letter of recommendation from a former imam at the Al Farooq Mosque, Bledsoe secured a job teaching English language classes for $300 a month at a British school in the southern port city of Aden. He also enrolled at the City Institute in the capital city, Sana, where he studied Islamic law and Arabic to better understand the Koran. But most transformative of all, Bledsoe fell in love with a student named Reena Abdullah Ahmed Farag.

After selling his car in Memphis to raise money for a dowry, Bledsoe married Reena in a ceremony held in Aden in September 2008. In the eyes of the young man who once banged Money Ova Bitches, his new bride was "a great Muslim woman; the best I've met since I've been Muslim, no doubt."[6] He maintained e-mail contact with his family, and in the tradition of Malcolm X, who converted to Islam through the encouragement of his family, began proselytizing Monica about converting to the Muslim faith as well.

Bledsoe traveled a good bit while teaching in Yemen, thus widening his social network. In his travels he saw things that angered and upset him—child refugees from the war in Afghanistan, some of whom had missing arms and legs and others who were horribly disfigured; Afghan women who said they had been raped by American soldiers during the war. In early 2008, Bledsoe spent three months at a camp in the remote northwestern town of Dammaj near the Saudi Arabian border—home to one of the most important educational institutions in modern Islam, which is renowned for teaching Salafism. Visitors to the camp were required to wear ancient robes, memorize ancient texts, and learn the Islamic mysteries. Dammaj was, in essence, a known recruiting hub for al-Qaeda. (A year later, in 2009, Said Kouachi, one of the brothers involved in the Paris attack on *Charlie Hebdo* was also a visitor at Dammaj.[7]) According to Melvin, at the Dammaj camp Bledsoe was deprived of sleep for twenty-three hours a day and given hard-sell indoctrination into political Islam. Exactly whom Bledsoe met during his time in Yemen is unknown, but in a letter to the press, he discussed the influence of a terrorist network, stating that he was "asked many times to carry out a martyrdom operation in America, but I didn't have proper training in regards to explosives."[8]

As influential as they may have been, none of these personal experiences turned Carlos Bledsoe into a terrorist. That would happen through a specific locus of radicalization: the prison.

On November 14, 2008, two months after his marriage to Reena, Bledsoe was arrested at a roadside checkpoint in Sana for overstaying his visa. Found in his possession was a fake Somali passport, an explosives manual, a cell phone with numbers for terrorist fugitives in Saudi Arabia, and a computer jump drive containing literature from Anwar al-Awlaki, the Yemen-based American Islamic cleric, who was then having a major enabling influence on young English-speaking jihadists internationally. These included three of the four Islamists who had bombed three subway trains and a double-decker bus in London on July 7, 2005; underwear bomber Umar

Farouk Abdulmutallab; Najibullah Zazi, arrested in 2009 for plotting to blow up a New York subway; Roshonara Choudhry, who was convicted of stabbing British parliamentarian Stephen Timms in 2010; and the French terrorists Said Kouachi and Cherif Kouachi, perpetrators of the *Charlie Hebdo* attack in 2015. Al-Awlaki's recruiting success was built on the motivating power of religion combined with the universal quest of the young for identity.

Bledsoe later admitted that his plan was to travel to Somalia for training with Al-Qaeda in the Arabian Peninsula (AQAP) on how to build bombs, particularly car bombs. His lawyer would claim that Bledsoe simply found the phony Somali passport on a park bench and needed it because he had overstayed his visa; recently married, he had no intention of traveling to Somalia. Whatever the case, due to his arrest, Bledsoe was confined for two and a half months in Yemen's maximum-security political prison at Sana, known as the Political Security Organization, wherefrom some two dozen al-Qaeda operatives had recently escaped. Anwar al-Awlaki himself had recently been released from the Political Security Organization after serving eighteen months for his alleged involvement in an al-Qaeda plot to kidnap a U.S. military attaché (although he was never formally charged with a crime). Several weeks into his incarceration, Bledsoe was interviewed by FBI special agent Greg Thomason from the Nashville office who had been tracking Bledsoe since he left Tennessee a year earlier, likely as a result of Bledsoe's prior connections to Nashville's Al Farooq Mosque. Bledsoe was also interviewed by representatives of the U.S. Embassy. Back in Memphis, the Bledsoe family mounted a campaign to bring Bledsoe home by reaching out to the U.S. State Department, U.S. Representative Steve Cohen, the American Embassy in Sana, and agent Thomason, but their efforts were futile.

In prison, Bledsoe met fellow Muslim detainees from around the world—the Arabian Peninsula, the Middle East, and Europe—some of whom were reportedly tortured during interrogations. Others were beaten by guards and sodomized, leading Bledsoe to plead with the FBI to assist in his release, but again to no avail. Bledsoe also met members of al-Qaeda who told him that the American government had forsaken him and claimed that they were his "real brothers." Through these experiences, Bledsoe developed an affinity with an extremist group—al-Qaeda, then the world's most dangerous terrorist organization. He also developed a special empathy for four Cameroonian detainees who had been held without trial for nearly twelve years and who became a cause for Bledsoe. Upon his release he would smuggle a letter they wrote along with their names and finger-prints out of the prison and send it to international human rights organizations. Although Bledsoe was an Islamic militant before he went to prison, the experience amplified his radicalism and brought him to the most important turning point of his life. As he would later tell a psychiatrist, his time in the Yemeni political prison provoked him to launch a jihad against America.[9]

Personal and Political Grievances

At the urging of the American Embassy in Sana, the Yemeni government deported Bledsoe on January 29, 2009. He returned alone to the United States with a bitter hatred for the military over the ill-treatment of Muslims in the war on terrorism. This abhorrence for the military provided the political grievance to match his underlying personal rage. As he took on these intense beliefs and attitudes, Bledsoe experienced a severe constricting of his social networks.

After his family threw him a welcome home party, Bledsoe resettled with his parents in Memphis and began the difficult task of adjusting to life after prison. An old friend from the Nashville mosque saw Bledsoe, but saw nothing suspicious. More to the point of what happened later, however, Bledsoe was placed on the government's Terrorism Watch List and interviewed three more times by FBI agent Greg Thomason. The FBI also reopened a 2007 investigation into Bledsoe's involvement with a group of Somalis from Columbus, Ohio, who had attempted to travel to Somalia to wage jihad.

Despite these investigative efforts, the FBI did not place Bledsoe under surveillance once he returned home from Yemen, apparently believing that he did not pose a terrorist threat even though he was on the Watch List. "The FBI knew exactly what the hell was going on and they did nothing to stop it," howled Melvin Bledsoe on Fox News after the Little Rock shooting. The FBI missed another chance "to stop it" on March 18 when at the age of twenty-three, Bledsoe went to a Memphis notary public and recorded his last will and testament, stating that he wanted a Muslim burial and that any possessions he owned should be divided among the Tennessee mosques. With that, Carlos Bledsoe became a lone wolf in waiting.

Identity Transformation

In April, 2009, Melvin and Linda opened an office for River City Tours in Little Rock, Arkansas, to give Bledsoe a job so that he could afford to bring Reena to the United States. Melvin bought him a black 2003 Ford Explorer Sport Trac and Carlos settled in to a small apartment at 12201 Mara Lynn Road. Bledsoe has never discussed this part of his life, but what transpired inside the apartment is crucial to understanding his attack on the Army recruiting center. For it was here that Bledsoe completed his identity transformation into an armed warrior.

Other than the Koran, books held little appeal for Bledsoe. He did, however, spend hours on the Internet making Facebook postings and downloading such amateurish YouTube conspiracy videos as *Exposing Secrets of the CIA*, which resonated with his need to see government wrongdoing wherever he looked. Yet Bledsoe was old school. Rather than developing sympathy with any community of online "friends," he maintained his affinity for the jihadists he had personally known back in Yemen—the Salafist students at the Dammaj camp, the al-Qaeda brothers, and the longsuffering Cameroonians he had encountered in prison. (The only time that Bledsoe uses the word "love" in his writings is when he talks about the people he met in Yemen.) Their emotional appeals were far more important to him than anything he read over the Internet, and they would come to play a role in his subsequent transformation. But first he had to undergo an identity crisis. His old identity had to be completely amputated—"knifed off"—to make room for a new one.

As Bledsoe began his bus tours of Little Rock—servicing a Hilton Hotel where he was known by the name Hakim—it became apparent to his family that Bledsoe's post-prison reintegration was in jeopardy. He was relaxed one moment but highly anxious the next. Monica later said that her brother was distant and uneasy when he came back to America after being locked up in Yemen and that he angrily fumed whenever he saw news reports about the wars in Iraq and Afghanistan. "He was different," Monica recalled. "He was not Carlos." At that point, his social network dwindled to nothing. Bledsoe never attended the Islamic Center of Little Rock nor did he have any friends in the city. Alone and isolated in his apartment, he became a creature of his own criminal mentality.

On May 20, CNN reported the story of a foiled terrorist attack on a New York synagogue and military aircraft by four ex-convicts who had converted to Islam in prison. It was around this time that Bledsoe's plan for killing took shape. Using Google map searches, he researched Army facilities and Jewish organizations to attack in Little Rock. From there, he planned to wage similar attacks in Memphis and Nashville, in Florence, Kentucky, in Atlanta, Philadelphia, Baltimore, and finally, Washington, DC. However, Bledsoe was an inept criminal who was usually caught for his transgressions. Nowhere was this more apparent than in his failed attempt to travel to Somalia to acquire bomb-building skills from al-Qaeda in the Arabian Peninsula. Bledsoe would later admit that his subsequent terrorist plot in America "was foiled once I was arrested in Yemen."[10] Essentially, Bledsoe lacked any actual ability to carry out a coordinated series of terrorist attacks against the United States.

Yet Bledsoe had become obsessed with planning for the attacks and he began to over-arm himself. Even though he was on a limited budget, his apartment came to resemble an al-Qaeda sleeper cell of one, complete with an Islamic flag, Arabic CDs, maps of targets, stockpiled ammunition, material for assembling Molotov cocktails, and hardware equipment for making sawed-off shotguns. He purchased two guns on the streets for cash to avoid background checks and took target practice at a construction site. He also bought a .22-caliber Mossberg rifle with a scope and laser sight, and did so over the counter at a Walmart. Bledsoe would claim that the reason he made this purchase was to determine whether the FBI was following him. He had good reason to be suspicious, given that the FBI had placed him on the Terrorism Watch List. (However, as noted in chapter 8, suspects on the FBI Terrorism Watch List are not prohibited from buying firearms.) When Walmart did not put a hold on the firearm purchase, Bledsoe was free to pursue his plot. But he was ill-prepared for the task ahead of him. Despite his elaborate planning, in the cold light of day Bledsoe's attack would develop haphazardly.

Broadcasting Intent

Still wrestling with his identity at this late date, on May 23 Bledsoe filed a petition with the Pulaski County, Arkansas, clerk's office to legally change his name again, this time to Abdul Hakim Bledsoe, attributing the request to "religious reasons." Dropping the middle name Mujahid, or holy warrior, may have been an attempt by Bledsoe to cover his jihadist identity, or it might have been representative of a faltering resolve to carry out a jihadist attack. Nevertheless, around this time Bledsoe sat down at his computer and made a martyrdom video for Reena. He was dressed in all white Islamic attire, with his face wrapped in a white Arabic headdress; the SKS assault rifle was visible, as was the Islamic flag behind him. In a strong and determined voice, Bledsoe broadcasted his intent to commit terrorism by proclaiming that it was the duty of all Muslims to retaliate against "Zionists, Crusaders and slaves of the Cross and for what happened in Guantanamo Bay, Abu Ghraib, Bagram prisons, what's going on in Iraq, Afghanistan and Palestine and elsewhere."[11]

Triggering Event

Then, according to Bledsoe, on Sunday, May 31, he saw a news report about American troops who had urinated on a Koran in Afghanistan. This became the triggering event for Bledsoe. The event fused Bledsoe's personal proclivity for anger and violence together with his political grievance over the abuse of Muslims by U.S. military forces. Providing Bledsoe with the catalyst that would send him over the edge and into terrorism, it would also have the effect of resolving his identity crisis once and for all. Research suggests that mass shooters will often enter a tunnel of violence, or an altered state of consciousness, which is dream-like, frenzied, or out of themselves. "I just made up my mind to retaliate," Bledsoe said. "It's like I blacked out."[12]

The Attack

He began the jihad immediately. Predictably, it was a monumental failure, but not for want of weaponry. Bledsoe loaded his SUV with 562 rounds of ammunition, homemade silencers, a box of Molotov cocktails, the Mossberg rifle, a Lorcin L-380 semi-automatic handgun, a .22-caliber pistol, and his SKS assault rifle, granted to him courtesy of the Knoxville Police Department five years earlier. He also packed Arabic CDs, cellphones, binoculars, sweatshirts, caps, medicine, and some bottled water.

After a botched attempt against an unknown target in Little Rock, Bledsoe drove 350 miles north through Memphis to Nashville, where, under cover of night, he parked outside the home of a prominent Orthodox rabbi. Pulling a Molotov cocktail from the box, Bledsoe lit the explosive and threw it at a window but the device bounced off the glass, causing no damage. "Luckily, the terrorist didn't have his act together," said the rabbi. Undeterred, Bledsoe set off for Kentucky, where he planned to attack the Army recruiting center in Florence because it was near the I-71 freeway and thus would allow him easy egress. Bledsoe arrived in Florence only to abandon his plan at the last minute. After three failed attempts, he decided that it was time for him to go home and come up with a better plan.

He returned to Little Rock shortly after 10 A.M. on Monday, June 1, feeling emotionally frustrated by his bungled attempts at jihad, physically exhausted by the 1,200 mile round trip, and financially tapped out by gasoline prices of more than four dollars a gallon. But as he headed down Rodney Parham Road on the way to his apartment, Bledsoe came across a crime of opportunity that matched his end-of-the-road outlook on life: There stood two soldiers in fatigues smoking cigarettes near the entrance of the Army/Navy Recruiting Center—Private Andy Long, twenty-three, and Private Quinton Ezaegwula, eighteen.

Bledsoe drove around the corner and then headed back to the recruiting center. He pulled the SUV to a stop three feet from the soldiers, raised his SKS assault rifle, and fired seven shots at them, killing Long and critically wounding Ezaegwula.

Bledsoe sped away with his tailgate down spilling bottles of water onto the pavement. Intent on making the 150-mile drive to Memphis where he planned to switch cars, Bledsoe made a wrong turn into a construction zone and was stopped by a patrolman who identified Bledsoe's vehicle from eyewitness accounts of its open tailgate. Twelve minutes after the attack, Bledsoe stepped from the SUV with the .22 pistol shoved into his pants and a green ammo belt around his waist holding more than 150 rounds of ammunition and surrendered after warning the officer that he had a bomb in the vehicle (he did not). As Bledsoe was being transported to police headquarters, he told the officer: "It's a war going on against Muslims, and that's why I did it!" Bledsoe added that he "saw it on the news last night; *someone was pissing on the Koran!*"[13] Bledsoe said that his intent was to kill as many people in the Army as he could.

Copycats, Mental Illness, and the Terrorism
Research Quandary

The story went viral, reaching millions of Americans. Among them was Army Major Nidal Hasan who was about to be reassigned from his post at Walter Reed Medical Center in Bethesda, Maryland, to Fort Hood, Texas. A colonel who worked with Hasan after he arrived at Fort Hood in July recalled that news about the fatal shooting of an Army recruiter in Little Rock on June 1 greatly affected Hasan. It prompted him to make "outlandish" statements against the American military presence in Iraq and Afghanistan, such as declaring that "the Muslims should stand up and fight against the aggressor" and that "maybe we should have more of these [attacks]"[14] On August 1, Hasan went to the Guns Galore store in Killen, Texas, where he purchased the semi-automatic handgun used in the Fort Hood massacre three months later; and then, like Bledsoe, he began target practice. Based on this evidence, Bledsoe emerges as Hasan's indirect enabler and the inspiration for Hasan's copycat attack on Fort Hood. Bledsoe and Hasan were both lone jihadists who carried out mass shootings in 2009 with identical targets, ideological motives, and religious views. "Nidal Malik [Hasan] is the real Islamic warrior," Bledsoe declared, "and my plan . . . was on that scale."[15] Anwar al-Awlaki would confirm the lionization by posting on his website after Fort Hood: "Nidal Hassan [sic] is a hero . . . a man of conscience" who could not bear to take part in "leading the war against terrorism which in reality is a war against Islam. Nidal opened fire on soldiers who were on their way to be deployed to Iraq and Afghanistan."[16]

On January 2, 2010, with images of Hasan and his former e-mail correspondent al-Awlaki flashing on television screens across America, Bledsoe, unbeknownst to his attorneys, sent Pulaski County Circuit Judge Herb Wright a handwritten letter pleading guilty to one count of capital murder and fifteen counts of terrorist acts. Affirming that his sanity was intact, he stated: "I'm affiliated with Al-Qaeda in the Arabian Peninsula (al-Qaeda in Yemen). [I'm a] member of the Abu Basir's Army [a reference to the AQAP leader in Yemen at the time]. This was a Jihadi attack on infidel forces."[17] Months later, AQAP's *Inspire* announced the organization's strategic shift to lone wolf terrorism by encouraging American Muslims to "fight jihad on U.S. soil," rather than attempting to travel overseas for training. The article extolled the virtues of random killings and praised Nidal Hasan and Abdulhakim Mujahid Muhammad. With this public relations campaign waged by *Inspire*, Carlos Bledsoe and Nidal Hasan became the face of al-Qaeda in America.

Bledsoe's jihad did not end at the prison gate. While awaiting trial he was placed in administrative segregation at the Pulaski County Detention Facility after committing two jailhouse stabbings. One was against another inmate who had cursed Bledsoe's mother and Allah. In the other, Bledsoe shanked a guard who had recently returned from the Iraq War, yelling, "I got ya' white boy! You gonna die! Allah, Allah, Allah!" Bledsoe later justified the stabbing by claiming that the guard had "been bragging about killing sand niggers. So I decided to kill the motherfucker."[18] Further security restrictions were placed on Bledsoe after he was caught trying to radicalize other prisoners to the cause of jihad.

In the fall of 2010, an unknown assailant attacked five different military installations in the Washington, DC, area with gunfire; the attack included an October 19 assault on the Pentagon. That December, the FBI arrested a twenty-one-year-old Muslim convert named Antonio Martinez in connection with an attempted bombing of the Army recruiting center in Cantonsville, Maryland. Martinez admitted that he was influenced by Nidal Hasan's attack on Fort Hood. In early 2011, FBI agents in Lubbock, Texas, arrested twenty-year-old Saudi exchange student Khalid Aldawsari and charged him with the attempted use of a weapon of mass destruction in connection with an assassination attempt against former President George W. Bush and three former military guards at the Abu Ghraib prison in Iraq.

On March 10, 2011, Carlos Bledsoe was the subject of a congressional hearing on the domestic radicalization of Muslims. Melvin Bledsoe testified that his son had been brainwashed by extremists in the Nashville mosques who were responsible for "raping the minds of American citizens on American soil." He further noted that Carlos's experience in the Yemeni political prison was the "final stage of his radicalization."

On June 17, 2011, military police arrested twenty-two-year-old Marine Corps reservist Yonathan Melaku for the attempted bombing of Arlington National Cemetery. Found in his possession was a notebook containing the words "al Qaeda" and "Taliban rules." Upon further investigation, Melaku was also arrested on federal charges related to the Washington military shootings of 2010. Melaku told investigators that he was radicalized by the Iraq War, adding that his motive for the shootings was to make people "be afraid for supporting the war."

On July 11, 2011, the *Los Angeles Times* published an article questioning the Department of Justice decision not to prosecute Bledsoe on federal terrorism charges, but to defer to state prosecutors in Arkansas where he would stand trial under criminal statutes. Melvin Bledsoe told the reporter that he had learned of his son's incarceration in Yemen from a Tennessee FBI agent who had interviewed Bledsoe while he was locked up there, but that that was the last Melvin had heard from the FBI. He said that the FBI feared a federal trial because it would make them look bad—because they knew his son was a radicalized Muslim and yet did not watch him when he returned to the United States.

The article also excerpted part of another letter Bledsoe had written to Judge Wright, demanding a federal trial: "The facility where the shooting took place was a federal building. The army recruiters outside that federal building were federal employees. I was under federal investigation at the time of the shooting by the FBI. Why then is this a state case in a state court, [in]which the state seeks my execution? Injustice!"[19]

On July 22, 2011, a psychiatrist who examined Bledsoe on three occasions for the defense testified in court that he suffered from a delusional disorder at the time of the Little Rock shooting, adding that nothing in the record indicated that he was a member of a terrorist organization. Police investigators confirmed that Bledsoe acted alone without broader support. Bledsoe's claim of belonging to al-Qaeda was nothing more than grandiose thinking.

The psychiatrist determined that Bledsoe believed in conspiracy theories and assigned meaning to seemingly mundane things such as whether his spoon was in the right place on his food tray in jail or whether he was handcuffed with his hands in front of him or behind his back. "He clearly has a different version of reality than the rest of us," the psychiatrist concluded. Indicative of this "different version of reality" is an experience that we had with Bledsoe when arranging an interview for this research. Bledsoe said he would agree to the interview only if the National Institute of Justice guaranteed him a release from prison and extradition to a Third World country. Bledsoe's idea that he could somehow parlay his participation in a federal research project into a release from prison is revealing of the delusion thinking noted by the psychiatrist at his trial.

The event that had triggered Bledsoe's attack was the news report about American troops urinating on a Koran in Afghanistan. This defining event allowed Bledsoe to dehumanize his victims while elevating himself to a position of moral superiority whereby he became the holy warrior worthy of his chosen name, as conflicted as he may have been about that identity. "I saw it on the news last night," he would claim about May 31, 2009, "*someone was pissing on the Koran!*" The problem is—that never happened.

There is no evidence of a May 31, 2009, national news report about U.S. soldiers urinating on a Koran in Afghanistan. The major story that day came out of Wichita, Kansas, where abortion doctor George Tiller was shot and killed by the lone wolf terrorist Scott Roeder. It is unknown when Bledsoe's delusional disorder began, though experts contend that onset of the illness can occur as early as age eighteen and is often accompanied by negative emotions of depression, fear, or rage. This profile seems to fit with the onset of Bledsoe's criminal career, which occurred when he threatened to kill a woman in Memphis after a car accident. One form of the mental illness is grandiose delusional disorder that involves the individual's conviction of his or her importance and uniqueness and can present itself in a belief that the individual has a distinguished role to play in society. Suffice it to say that Bledsoe's delusional disorder influenced his radicalization at what was for him the most crucial stage of terrorist development: the triggering event.

Further complicating research into the Little Rock shooting is a 2010 letter to Judge Wright wherein Bledsoe claimed responsibility for killing a man in Nashville back in 2006. Bledsoe called the murder his first "jihad operation" and said that the victim was targeted because he "robbed and terrorized elderly Muslims and Muslim women at gunpoint."[20] Bledsoe stated that he shot the man several times with a Chinese-made AK-47 assault rifle. While this confession casts doubt on the theory that Bledsoe was radicalized in the Yemeni political prison, his letter did not include a victim's name or the date or exact location of the murder. Nor were Nashville police able to tie Bledsoe to any unsolved homicide. The confession only adds to the mounting evidence that Carlos Bledsoe is a fabulist, who thereby presents unsurmountable challenges to any researcher who engages in direct contact with him. Melvin would come to the conclusion that Carlos was simply "unable to process reality."

This presents a real quandary for qualitative research on lone wolf terrorism. If lone wolves are "unable to process reality," then how do we know when or whether their statements are factual? If lone wolves view the world through the distorted lenses of mental illness, then it is possible that everything they say is an inaccurate representation of the truth, in which case the only way to study a lone wolf terrorist is by observing his behavior. We are not alone in making this observation. After psychiatrists interviewed Anders Breivik on thirteen occasions, they concluded that he was motivated by "grandiose delusions about his own exceptional importance." The psychiatrists adopted the view that Breivik was psychotic while carrying out the Norway attacks and that he was still psychotic when they interviewed him.[21] Other researchers have documented the psychological barriers that have slowed progress in understanding the "terrorist mind," including the difficulties inherent in interviewing terrorists.[22]

On July 25, 2011, Bledsoe was sentenced to life in prison by the State of Arkansas. In an earlier acknowledgement of his criminal incompetence, Bledsoe told Little Rock police that he made two mistakes on the day of the shooting. He had mistakenly taken a wrong turn into the construction zone as he was fleeing the recruiting center; and he made the mistake of leaving the tailgate down on his SUV, which made his vehicle easy to identify. "I got myself caught," he admitted.[23]

Two days later, on July 27, 2011, a twenty-one-year-old AWOL soldier named Naser Jason Abdo walked into Guns Galore in Killen, Texas, and raised suspicions when he purchased bomb-making material. After finding Abdo in possession of other bomb-making ingredients and a copy of the *Inspire* article "Make a Bomb in the Kitchen of Your Mom," FBI agents arrested him for the attempted use of a weapon of mass destruction against military personnel at Fort Hood. While leaving his arraignment, Abdo declared his copycat intentions by shouting: "*Nidal Hasan—Fort Hood 2009!*"

Over the next three years the FBI would arrest other lone Islamic militants in attempted bombing plots against the U.S. military. Meanwhile federal prosecutors won cases against Antonio Martinez, Naser Jason Abdo, Khalid Aldawsari, and Yonathan Melaku and sent them to federal prison for terms ranging from twenty-five years to life. On September 30, 2011, Anwar al-Awlaki was killed by a U.S. predator drone strike in northern Yemen. Confined to a wheelchair and paralyzed from the neck down due to injuries sustained in the Fort Hood shooting, Nidal Hasan was sentenced to death on August 28, 2013. (Two months later, Omar Mateen would praise

Hasan when threatening to kill a sheriff's deputy in Florida.) Attacks against the military would continue.

In early March 2014, yet another disaffected soldier, Ivan Lopez, entered Guns Galore and bought a semi-automatic pistol. A month later, Lopez turned the weapon on fellow Fort Hood soldiers, killing three and wounding sixteen before taking his own life.

On July 16, 2015, twenty-six-year-old Muhammad Abdulazeez opened fire with an assault rifle on two military facilities in Chattanooga, Tennessee, killing four unarmed Marines and a naval officer and wounding a Marine recruiter and a patrolman before he was killed by police. Designated a "homegrown violent extremist" by the FBI, Abdulazeez had martyrdom videos by Anwar al-Awlaki on his computer.

Today Carlos Bledsoe is confined alone for twenty-three hours a day in an administrative segregation cell at the Varner Supermax in Grady, Arkansas. Essentially, he is being held in maximum-security confinement within a super maximum-security prison—a spot reserved only for the most dangerous inmates.

Carlos Bledsoe is no trifling figure in the age of lone wolf terrorism. He was the original—and to date, the only—fighter returning from a foreign land to commit violence on American soil, predating by half a decade the foreign fighter threat posed by ISIS. Understanding the sociopolitical context that shaped Bledsoe's radicalization offers rare insight into the new blended threat of terrorism facing the United States.

Bledsoe emerged at a time when lone wolf terrorism in the United States was undergoing dramatic changes in terms of race, ideology, and targets of attack. Not a single member of the U.S. armed forces was attacked by a lone wolf terrorist in the seventy years preceding Bledsoe's shooting in Little Rock. Since then, lone wolf terrorists have killed or wounded fifty soldiers and have tried to kill many more. While lone wolves of the post-9/11 era tend to be single white males around the age of thirty, those waging attacks against the military have been single minority males who are somewhat younger. All of them were Islamists angered by the wars in Iraq and Afghanistan. Bledsoe's shooting was the first attack in this new trend of lone wolf terrorism, and it became a paradigm for the attacks that followed.

The Bledsoe case also has relevance for understanding the evolving threat of terrorism in other Western nations. Bledsoe was, first and foremost, a violent criminal; his terrorism emerged from a distinct pattern of criminality. Violent criminals tend to wind up in prison, and that is where Bledsoe was radicalized to the cause of Salafi Jihad—in a Yemeni political prison while serving time for a visa violation in connection with his attempt to travel to Somalia for training with al-Qaeda. Once locked up in a U.S. prison, he attempted to radicalize other inmates to the cause. Similarly, of the thirty-one ISIS terrorists who attacked Paris and Brussels in 2015, fifteen of them were previously incarcerated for violent crimes, including their leaders who were radicalized behind bars.[24]

What these cases teach us, then, is that some of the most dangerous Western jihadi terrorists are criminals to begin with, a circumstance that highlights the importance of criminology for the contemporary study of terrorism.

CHAPTER 10

The Pittsburgh Police Shooting

Figure 10.1 Richard Poplawski, also known as RichP and Braced for Fate. Source: www.post-gazette.com.

R ichard Andrew Poplawski was born to Margaret and Richard Poplawski on September 12, 1986, in the Stanton Heights district on the East End of Pittsburgh, Pennsylvania.[1] The middle-class neighborhood had long been home to many of the city's police officers and firefighters. Officer Eric Kelly, one of the policemen killed by Richard Poplawski on April 4, 2009, lived just a few blocks from the Poplawski home on Fairfield Street.

His family life was troubled from the beginning. Richard's domineering grandfather, Charles Scott, had a history of alcoholism and violent behavior that left his children, including Richard's mother, Margaret, psychologically scarred. Scott kept a cache of guns, which he used to shoot animals and to play Russian roulette with his wife, Catherine Scott. He also liked to use his fists on his own family. Domestic disputes, some of which became violent, between Richard's own parents were a regular occurrence during his early years. His parents separated when Richard was a toddler. His father later explained in court that he got fed up by "too much bickering, too much fighting" in the household, so he left. The divorce was followed by fifteen years of sporadic court battles between the Poplawskis over unpaid child support. As a result, Richard basically grew up without a father. His attorney would later argue that Poplawski's turbulent family history had a major influence on his criminality, especially having a violent grandfather as his main male role model after his parents' divorce (until Scott fell ill when Richard was ten years old). "To say, 'Yes, he had a bad childhood,' is the biggest understatement I've heard in my life," the attorney stated at Poplawski's trial.[2]

Richard's relationship with his mother, Margaret, who worked as a nurse, was loveless and hostile. Margaret faced her own demons due to an abusive family upbringing. Over the years she would battle alcoholism and depression and make several suicide attempts. The most stable and loving influence in Richard's life was his maternal grandmother, Catherine Scott. During Poplawski's trial, the court heard that he wrote her family nickname ("Cuckie") in his own blood on a bedroom wall the day of the police murders.

Despite the upheaval at home, Poplawski was a bright and likeable child. He attended Immaculate Conception Catholic School in Bloomfield, Pennsylvania, where he scored 135 in an eighth-grade IQ test. Teachers considered him a gifted student, and he was well-liked by other students. As a teenager, Poplawski attended North Catholic High School but never graduated, having been expelled in his junior year for reasons that have not been fully disclosed. He later earned a high school equivalency degree.

A turning point in Poplawski's life came on December 13, 2004, when the eighteen year old enlisted in the U.S. Marine Corps. He entered boot camp at Parris Island, South Carolina, but was administratively discharged twenty-three days later for what a Marine Corps spokesman called a "psychological disorder" manifested in a fight with his drill sergeant during basic training. The experience of failing to become a Marine made Poplawski angry and laid the groundwork for a succession of searing personal grievances over the next five years.

After his discharge from the Marines, Poplawski returned to Pittsburgh and reunited with a girlfriend, Melissa Gladish, with whom he had a difficult relationship. Gladish soon filed for a domestic abuse protection order, alleging that Poplawski had grabbed her hair, threatened her, and spoken of a buried gun. Poplawski was never charged but was found in contempt of the protective order after he showed up at Melissa's workplace and proposed marriage. Then Margaret was found guilty of summary harassment for spitting on Gladish and ordered to pay a criminal fine.

The Pathway to Radicalization

In 2006, Poplawski left Pittsburgh to begin a new chapter in his life. He moved to Palm Beach County, Florida, where he took a rented room. His landlord and others who knew Poplawski in Florida remembered him as a polite and intelligent young man who spoke of plans to enroll in dental school.[3] Nothing came of dental school, though, and Poplawski went to work for a glass company, until his career ambitions shifted to computers. At that point Poplawski began to immerse himself in online discussions about American politics. More than any other factor in 2006, even more important than the contentious war in Iraq, was public outrage over government corruption. A prominent lobbyist with ties to the Republican administration, Jack Abramoff, was sentenced to prison for bribing members of the Bush administration and Congress. Eight other officials of the Bush White House were arrested in connection with public corruption scandals during the year.

Heeding this evolving political landscape, Poplawski took his discontent to the Internet and specifically to Stormfront.org, the most popular white supremacist website in the world, where he introduced himself by posting pictures of his tattoo, which he later described as a "deliberately Americanized version of the [Nazis'] iron eagle," along with writings about his favorite firearms.

Poplawski returned to Pittsburgh in late 2007, most likely for family reasons. From this point onward, he became increasingly engaged with extremist beliefs and paranoid politics. Unemployed much of the time, he began spending hours "lurking" on anti-government and white supremacy websites.

Locus of Radicalization, Enablers, and Affinity
with Online Sympathizers

Even though Poplawski would act alone in killing the Pittsburgh police officers, he was clearly not alone in his concern about the state of American society and politics. Never a joiner in the first place, Poplawski had no interest in becoming a member of any extremist organization; however, he did have friends with similar beliefs. Among them was a young hospital worker named Eddie Perkovic, who publicly self-identified as a white supremacist and anti-Semite.[4] Perkovic's digital footprint included the racist ranting of David Duke, a former Grand Wizard of the Ku Klux Klan, and excerpts from William Pierce's *The Turner Diaries*.[5]

The Internet was Poplawski's primary locus of radicalization. Some of his social media activity, such as his visits to StumbleUpon and Myspace sites, was relatively unremarkable, though they did reveal elements of the murderous ideology that led to his police ambush. Poplawski's postings on the StumpleUpon site, for example, included an article on stocking an emergency food pantry along with another titled "10 Extremely Useful Websites to Stop Big Brother from Snooping on You." It also referenced a website that collected and reposted suicide notes. Beginning in late 2007, his online postings became more frequent, and he began to share his beliefs and feelings more openly. Poplawski created a new Stormfront account with the screen name "RichP," which he used when posting racist comments. In both his correspondence with the authors of this study and his online postings, Poplawski often resorted to irony to make what was to him an obvious point. On Stormfront, for instance, Poplawski ascribed his antigovernment beliefs to his "solid upbringing" by his mother. And in another post Poplawski stated: "Don't mix your blood with dirt, son." After a number of such postings in 2007, Poplawski went silent, and it would be a year before he posted again on Stormfront. On that occasion, he confessed to being "a longtime lurker on Stormfront."[6]

Meanwhile, on the Pennsylvania Firearm Owners Association discussion forum, Poplawski inquired about "the best way to act if hassled [by police] which for some reason I anticipate happening," thereby revealing his increasingly hostile attitude toward law enforcement. In a November 24, 2007, posting, he openly broadcasted his belligerence toward the police:

> I don't care to bend at all from harassment from the police if I'm doing nothing more than exercising a right. If that means pissing a cop or two off, then so be it, if they are so ignorant as to try to trample my rights or inconvenience me in any way for no reason. I mean I'm not talking about DISRESPECTING any cops, just not bending for them in fear as so many people do.

While in the same post Poplawski assured readers that he was "not LOOK-ING for trouble," his writings concealed an increasingly combative attitude. His mother would later report that Poplawski only "liked police when they were not curtailing his constitutional rights, which he was determined to protect."[7]

Poplawski was indeed highly committed to his right to bear arms, like his grandfather before him. "There's going to be federal gun bans on the way. That's a *fact*," he posted on the Pittsburgh Penguins NHL Hockey site Letsgopens.[8] Along with his hording of canned goods and other surviv-alist material, Poplawski began stockpiling weapons and ammunition in anticipation of a forthcoming gun ban: Between 2007 and 2009, he acquired a rapid-fire AK-47 assault rifle, a .22-caliber shotgun, and at least two hand-guns, including a .357 Magnum revolver. All of these weapons were pur-chased legally. While most of the firearms, including the AK-47, were bought online, at least one of the weapons was sold to Poplawski at a gun store in Wilkinsburg, Pennsylvania—the same store where the .22 caliber revolver Ronald Taylor used in his 2000 shooting rampage was purchased. Poplawski regularly practiced his firearms skills at a primitive family-owned cabin in Clarion County, outside of Pittsburgh, which had a makeshift firing range featuring a discarded kitchen sink, a steel door, a metal wheel-barrow, and other junk.[9] His unfettered access to high-velocity firearms and ammunition meant that Poplawski had the criminal means to carry out his act of lone wolf terrorism. Poplawski's extremist views on the Sec-ond Amendment were enabled not only by his grandfather and his best friend, Eddie Perkovic, but also by virtue of his affinity with online sympa-thizers who routinely espoused conspiracy theories about government gun control and white supremacy ideology. Poplawski found validation and ex-pression for his beliefs in these online venues, none more important to him than Stormfront. Poplawski was also enabled by media commentators who warned that the government intended to confiscate citizens' guns and that "the world as we know it" was about to come to an abrupt end.

One of the places where Poplawski learned these conspiracy theories was Infowars, the website affiliated with Alex Jones. Poplawski visited Infowars multiple times between 2008 and 2009, shared links to it with others, and made three postings to the site. While he reveled in Jones's conspiracy the-ories, Poplawski also felt that Jones underestimated, at least in public, the extent to which the United States was controlled by "Zionist occupiers." In late March 2009, Poplawski reported that "My mind hasn't been made up on AJ [Alex Jones] 100%." He added: "For being such huge players in the endgame, too many 'infowarriors' are surprisingly unfamiliar with the Zionists. [This is] mainly [because] Alex refuses to call a spade a spade. Get me?"[10]

What increasingly appealed to Poplawski was the conspiracy theory about an imminent takeover of the citizenry by the Federal Emergency Management Agency (FEMA), which was believed to be running concentration camps across the country.[11] At one point, Poplawski posted a YouTube link on Stormfront featuring the conservative talk show host Glenn Beck warning viewers about the secret FEMA camps in an interview with Congressman and presidential candidate Ron Paul. After the Pittsburgh Steelers won Super Bowl XLIII, Poplawski used the local celebrations as an opportunity to showcase how the police were trying to control the cheering crowds in "an unrestful environment." He reported to fellow Stormfronters that at one time he yelled at a small group of white police officers on the streets: "HEY! WHEN THE SHIT REALLY HITS THE FAN, I HOPE YOU GUYS ARE ON OUR SIDE!" He also wrote: "It was just creepy seeing busses [*sic*] put into action by authorities, as if they were ready to transport busloads of Steeler fans to 645 FEMA drive if necessary."[12] Poplawski had done his homework. The number 645 referred to House Bill 645, the National Emergency Centers Establishment Act, which authorized the founding of national emergency centers on military bases across the country.

Personal and Political Grievances

Since returning to Pittsburgh in 2007, Poplawski had struggled to find employment. He rarely held a job for long and was always looking for opportunities to make money. Back in the days when Pittsburgh was America's steel capital, Poplawski might have been able to find a decent-paying job in the fire-belching mills, but "there was little or nothing for him or his kind in the handful of shiny glass offices that replaced them," as one commentator noted.[13] By 1986, the year Poplawski was born, the local steel industry was already in decline. Steel workers fell from as much as 10 percent of the workforce in 1980 to less than 1 percent by 2009.

In 2009, the *New York Times* described Pittsburgh as a success story of economic transition, evidenced by its low unemployment, growing wages, and rising home prices.[14] Entrepreneurship had bloomed in computer software and biotechnology, prominent companies were doing well, and commercial construction was still thriving. It took Pittsburgh some time to come to terms with the end of the steel era, but its economy was now "the envy of many recession-plagued communities," concluded the *Times*.[15] Several Stanton Heights men, including some unemployed steel workers, were able to take advantage of the economic development by securing jobs in sales and office occupations, service jobs, and construction and maintenance.[16] However, Poplawski, like many others with limited educational attainment, had failed to cash in on the city's economic rebirth and was growing increasingly pessimistic over his lack of employment opportunities in Pittsburgh. He had several career ideas but none of them panned out, and as his prospects of obtaining work went from dark to pitch-black, his personal grievance contributed to his growing conviction that the collapse of the economic and social order of the United States was at hand.

Poplawski's personal grievance resonated with his evolving political grievances. He found confirmation and validation of his political and racist views among his community of online sympathizers. Following the inauguration of President Obama in January 2009, Poplawski's tirades shifted to a focus on racial conspiracy theories, and he adopted the anti-Semitic theory that the United States was being controlled by "Zionist occupiers." In a 937-word tirade entitled "Decoding the Collapse," posted on Stormfront in late March 2009, Poplawski expressed his belief that "the federal government, mainstream media, and banking system in these United States are strongly under the influence of—if not completely controlled by—Zionist interest" and that "an economic collapse of the financial system is inevitable, bringing with it some degree of civil unrest if not outright balkanization of the continental US, civil/revolutionary/racial war, SHTF [Shit Hits The Fan] / TEOTWAKI [The End Of The World As We Know It] scenario etc." In a more measured tone he added:

> One can read the list of significant persons in government and in major corporations and see who is pulling the strings. One can observe the policies and final products and should walk away with little doubt there is Zionist occupation. I also don't think there is too much debate about the eventuality of a collapse of economic and social order in this country. All signs seem to point to a once great nation in the midst its last gasp.[17]

These anti-Semitic conspiracy theories only fueled Poplawski's paranoid political beliefs about gun control. Originally, he believed that the U.S. government was secretly plotting to restrict firearms ownership and impose gun bans, thus eroding his constitutional right to bear arms. Now, he believed that Jews were behind it all.

The election of President Obama heightened Poplawski's fear that the federal government would soon move to seize his growing arsenal of guns and ammunition. "What happens when the GOV [government] is the only entity with any real firepower? And they feel like trampling you. With what instruments will you fight the tyranny?" he asked.[18] All the while, Poplawski had been stockpiling firearms, ammunition, and food products such as rice, water, and sugar in anticipation of the impending economic and social collapse of the United States.

Identity Transformation

Starting in late 2008, Poplawski experienced a growing need to be confrontational. He increasingly embraced the warrior subculture proffered online by the radical Right and committed himself to the idea that he was not going to stand by and watch America collapse and have his constitutional rights be violated. Not without a fight, he wouldn't. On Stormfront, he issued what appears in retrospect to be a revolutionary call to arms for the far Right:

> It seems to me that our enemies would like nothing more than to see us retreat peaceably into the hills so that they could continue raping the remainder of the land without having to worry about "kooks" putting up a fight. So let's all migrate our way into taking back our nation. That will fix 'em. I'll subscribe to the camp that believes we are running out of time. A revolutionary is always regarded as a nutcase at first, their ideas dismissed as fantasy. (27)

Four weeks later he announced: "I see myself probably ramping up the activism in the near future." Poplawski had reached another turning point on his path to violent extremism. By now, he was prepared for some kind of confrontational action. Referring to a famous quotation by Thomas Jefferson and inscribed upon Timothy McVeigh's t-shirt when he bombed the Oklahoma City federal building in 1995 ("The tree of liberty must be refreshed from time to time with the blood of patriots and tyrants"), Poplawski wrote in one posting:

> Anybody that wants to be a sheep can be a sheep. The powers that be are happy they've converted you and even happier that you're willing to make things easy for them. You know what they say about the tree of liberty. (22)

He went on to argue like a warrior that "things get done because men fight and men die. Period. If you don't believe me, when TSHTF [The Shit Hits The Fan], step aside. But first, give me all your supplies." Poplawski could not contain himself:

> If a total collapse is what it takes to wake our brethren and guarantee future generations of white children walk this continent, if that is what it takes to restore our freedoms and recapture our land: let it begin this very second and not a moment later. Let comfort and convenience be damned, and I will welcome the hardship and embrace the pain secure in the knowledge that our people will rise above and overcome our darkest days. (8)

Reflecting this warrior stance, Poplawski changed his Stormfront screen name from "RichP" to "Braced for Fate." He last visited Stormfront in the early morning hours of April 4, 2009.[19]

Broadcasting Intent

Poplawski's online postings in the days leading up to the attack reveal his broadcasting of intent. The threat communicated in his postings, however, was relatively unspecific. He talked about "ZOG" (Zionist Occupation Government, an anti-Semitic conspiracy theory), about "our enemies," about "tyranny," and about "taking back our nation." He also bragged about his guns, told readers about the bulletproof vest he had recently purchased from an Army surplus store, and said that he would need these materials for the "outbreak of politico-racial violence" that he believed was inevitable. Some of his comments dealt directly with the Pittsburgh police, as for example when he stated that he would not "bend for them in fear as so many people do." Although these comments indicated a radical set of beliefs and feelings, they did not necessarily signal violent action.[20] Moreover, with some notable exceptions, they were voiced within an ideological environment of online sympathizers where such comments were not out of place and would barely have raised suspicion.[21]

The most specific broadcasting of intent occurred nearly two years before the attack. In May 2007, Poplawski, along with his racist friend Eddie Perkovic, recorded an Internet pirate radio broadcast called "The Eddie and P. O. Show." In this program, Poplawski praised the Virginia Tech massacre that had taken place on April 16 by saying:

> Pull the trigger. Pull the trigger. All I have to do is reach the trigger and, Pow! I plead not guilty. I plead not guilty. I plead not guilty. Thirty-three dead, I'm fairly impressed by that. Thirty-three people dead, I'm fairly impressed by that. Thirty-three people dead, I'm fairly impressed by that. This is fucking doomsday status.

Poplawski went on to list people whom he wanted to kill: "I want to kill my ex-girlfriend, her mother, her pets, my father, people I don't like, and *in a random measure a couple of members of the Pittsburgh police.*"[22] Twenty-three months later, Poplawski did exactly that.

Triggering Event

For months, twenty-two-year-old Richard Poplawski had been bracing himself for America's impending social and economic collapse. His anti-government beliefs had been further aggravated by the Obama election, which heightened his conviction that the government would soon move to introduce federal gun bans and seize his growing arsenal of weaponry. Poplawski's doomsday arrived on April 4, 2009—a day marking the forty-first anniversary of the assassination of Martin Luther King at the hands of James Earl Ray.

The immediate triggering event for the attack was a domestic dispute between Poplawski and his mother at their Stanton Heights home. Poplawski had taken to walking two pit bull mixes that the family had adopted from the Animal Rescue League. On the morning of April 4,

Poplawski's mother had woken up to discover dog urine on the floor. Fed up with her son's defiant attitude and lack of respect, she threatened to kick him out. At 7:03 A.M., she dialed 911 and asked police to come to the residence and remove her son, who had just returned home from a night of drinking. According to Poplawski, before passing out on the couch, he had taken some Xanax.

The Attack

Two Pittsburgh police officers responded to Margaret Poplawski's 911 call, which they interpreted as a typical domestic dispute. She met the officers at the front door and yelled, "Come and take his ass." It was not the first time police had been called to 1016 Fairfield Street for a domestic disturbance, and in the past officers had been able to defuse the situation peacefully. On this occasion, however, the officers were walking into an ambush.

Poplawski was infuriated by his mother's 911 call to the police. After hearing her call, he retreated to his bedroom and put on his bulletproof vest. The body armor was emblazoned with his nickname, "PO" (the letters "LICE" had been removed from the old vest). He armed himself to the teeth with his shotgun, his AK-47, and a handgun. He was suiting up for battle with the police, lying in wait for them. It had come to this: He would go out in a blaze of glory.

For the two policemen, Paul Sciullo II, thirty-six, and Stephen Mayhle, twenty-nine, Poplawski's violence came as a complete surprise. In her 911 call, Margaret Poplawski indicated that her son had weapons but that they were "all legal" and that he was not threatening her. In an astounding case of police miscommunication, information about the presence of weapons inside the Poplawski home was never relayed to officers Sciullo and Mayhle. Poplawski later said that his mother "was extremely stupid to call police knowing I had guns at the ready in the house."

When the officers entered the house, Poplawski aimed his shotgun at them and opened fire without warning. Sciullo was killed instantly. Poplawski turned on Mayhle and a shootout ensued. Seriously wounded, Mayhle ran from the house seeking cover as Poplawski followed firing three rounds at Mayhle from his AK-47 at point-blank range. Poplawski was so close he could read Mayhle's badge. A third officer, Eric Kelly, a fourteen-year veteran who had just ended his shift and was on his way home, arrived at the scene moments later. As he exited his police vehicle, Poplawski opened fire with the AK-47, striking Kelly multiple times. Officer Timothy McManaway, who arrived two minutes after Kelly and exchanged gunfire with Poplawski, pulled Kelly to cover behind a bullet-ridden SUV, where they remained until both were rescued by a SWAT team and attended to by medics. Kelly later died of his wounds. McManaway sustained injuries to his hand, while another officer broke his leg during the firefight.

Witnesses would later describe the scene as a war zone. So much gunfire was exchanged that the SWAT team ran out of ammunition and had to reload. Yet, in the course of the gunfire exchange, Poplawski managed to communicate on his cell phone. His friend Michael Bogert, the son of a Pittsburgh cop, called Poplawski after friends told him that news stations were reporting a shooting in Stanton Heights. "I got shot, I shot three cops. I'm probably going to bleed to death or go to jail for the rest of my life," Poplawski reportedly told him.[23] Poplawski also communicated with Perkovic explaining that he had been shot in the chest and leg, but that his bulletproof vest had shielded him. According to Perkovic, Poplawski told him in another cell phone call: "Eddie, I'm going to die today. Tell your family and friends I love them. This is probably the end."[24] At 9:45 A.M., Poplawski called 911 and said: "I'm lying in a pool of blood. I'm low on ammo but I promise I won't shoot anymore police officers. I'm going to jail for the rest of my life."

Mental Illness and Aftermath

"Crazy to me is letting each day slip past you," Poplawski once wrote on his Myspace page. "Crazy is being insignificant. Crazy is being obscure, pointless. Some could call me crazy; my answer would be that at least I insist to exist." Poplawski certainly was not "crazy" in a clinical sense. To the best of our knowledge, he has never been clinically diagnosed with a mental health problem. During his trial, Poplawski's attorney referred to "a mental illness component" but said it was not enough for an insanity defense.[25] Still, while in prison, Poplawski confessed that he had considered himself "mentally ill for as long as I can remember."[26] He was dismayed by his treatment in prison, where he was kept in administrative custody for twenty-three hours a day and took showers and meals alone. He said that he had "undergone psychological abuse, egregious verbal harassment and humiliation since the beginning of my incarceration."[27] He also claimed to have been denied a viable psychiatric treatment plan and access to religious and social services.

No longer "obscure," Richard Poplawski was charged in the worst police shooting in the modern history of Pittsburgh. He was tried, convicted of three counts of homicide, and sentenced to death by lethal injection in 2011. Yet Poplawski's defiance did not end at the prison gate. Not only has he appealed his sentence and requested a new trial, he also sent letters to the media in 2014 raising a number of "unanswered questions" about the shootings. That same year Poplawski filed a request under Pennsylvania's Right to Know Law, asking the Department of Corrections for information on "procedures and protocols for conducting executions, including types of drugs/chemicals, current inventory, expiration dates, and suppliers/providers."[28] His request was filed five days after Ohio executed death row inmate Dennis McGuire, who gasped and convulsed and took more than twenty-four minutes to die after officials injected him with a new combination of lethal chemicals. While the department denied Poplawski's initial request, the state's Office of Open Records, to which Poplawski appealed, ruled partly in his favor by stating that while the department met the legal burden to prove it did not have to disclose certain security procedures, it was required to disclose information regarding drugs used in the execution process.[29]

The Poplawski house on Fairfield Street was sold by mortgage-holder JP Morgan Chase to the city for $3,011.04. It was demolished in October 2011.

Copycats

Richard Poplawski's attack on law enforcement officers in Pittsburgh constitutes a paradigmatic case of anti-government and white supremacy–inspired lone wolf terrorism that has ballooned since the election of Barack Obama. The attack highlighted the emergence of "a new trend in right-wing extremism" in the United States.[30]

On April 25, 2009, Joshua Cartwright killed two Florida police officers who confronted him about a domestic abuse report from his wife. Cartwright believed that the U.S. government was conspiring against him. He had been severely disturbed that Obama had been elected president and was concerned about a federal crackdown on firearms.

On June 10, 2009, James von Brunn walked into the U.S. Holocaust Memorial Museum in Washington, DC, with a rifle at his side. He shot and killed the security guard at the front entrance before he was shot in the head by another guard. Von Brunn was known as a white supremacist who spun elaborate conspiracy theories about Jews and black people in leaflets, in books, and on his website.[31]

Byron Williams, the California career criminal, attacked two patrolmen with a firearm on a freeway on July 18, 2010. Williams was an antigovernment zealot with a profound hatred for President Obama. Williams was also alienated due to his inability to find employment because of his criminal record.

In November 2012 a rap video surfaced on YouTube praising Poplawski and threatening Pittsburgh police officers. The lyrics included the lines, "Let's kill these cops 'cause they don't do us no good. Pulling your Glock out 'cause I live in the hood."[32] The closing line was: "My momma told me not to put this on CD, but I'm gonna make this . . . city believe me."[33] The video also named specific officers who patrolled the area where Poplawski lived. The video was pulled from YouTube after police began investigating it. Two young male rappers from Pittsburgh's East End were later convicted of charges including witness intimidation and conspiracy in connection with the video. The officers referenced in the rap video had arrested the two men for firearm violations earlier in the year. The judge stated that the video "far exceeds what the First Amendment allows. . . . They did, in fact, attempt to intimidate and communicate a threat. The rap video, by its very nature, is a communication."[34] This type of broadcasting of violent intent ought to be taken very seriously, the judge argued.

Slain police officer Paul Sciullo II had wanted to make a difference and help his community. He had been serving with the Pittsburgh Police Department for a year and a half when he lost his life in the line of duty. On January 1, 2015, Sciullo was honored with a flora graph portrait on the Donate Life float in the 2015 Rose Parade in Pasadena, California, in recognition of his tissue donation.

Richard Poplawski remains on death row at the Pennsylvania State Correctional Institution at Graterford.

CHAPTER 11

Lone Wolf Sting Operations

The attacks by Carlos Bledsoe and Richard Poplawski represent paradigmatic lone wolf cases not only for their modus operandi and weaponry, but also for the challenges they present to law enforcement in identifying signs of radicalization. Even though Bledsoe was on the FBI's Terrorism Watch List and clearly broadcasted his intent to commit terrorism, his behavior leading up to the Little Rock military shooting apparently did not arouse suspicion among those in a position to intervene and alert authorities. Although Poplawski's broadcasting of intent indicated radical beliefs, they did not necessarily signal his attack on Pittsburg police and barely raised suspicions within his community of anonymous online sympathizers. Indeed, radicalization in opinion is different in important ways from radicalization in action.[1] And while Bledsoe and Poplawski were walking time bombs, their ambushes were triggered by the same unpredictable and mundane matter: urine. For Bledsoe it was his deluded belief that American soldiers had "pissed on the Koran" while the catalyst for Poplawski's attack was a pool of dog urine on the floor of his mother's home. How can law enforcement ever foresee such random events? One way—at least in theory—is through proactive police work, to get out in front of a possible lone wolf attack by mounting a law enforcement sting operation.

Since 9/11, the FBI has used extravagant ploys to entangle individuals into terrorist plots to attack America. In strictly academic terms, FBI sting operations are not authentic lone wolf cases because they fail to meet the standard definition of the crime. Lone wolf terrorism is political violence perpetrated by individuals who act alone. Stings are government-controlled law enforcement operations meant to simulate acts of terrorism carried out by multiple actors in a conspiracy. Lone wolf terrorists act without the direct influence of a leader or hierarchy. In stings, FBI agents and confidential informants portray themselves as members of a terrorist organization and assume leadership roles inside the conspiracies. Lone wolf terrorists wage their attacks without any direct outside command or direction. Sting targets conceive their tactics and methods with explicit direction from the FBI. While critics maintain that the United States is manufacturing terrorism cases by entrapping innocent people into the sting plots, U.S. courts have repeatedly rejected claims of entrapment, holding that sting defendants were predisposed to terrorism based upon their radical views.

These sting investigations begin when the FBI identifies a person who expresses interest in joining a terrorist group. Undercover FBI agents and confidential informants are then tasked with providing the necessary weapons, money, and transportation to carry out a terrorist attack. Almost always, these attacks involve the bombing of buildings, metros, or public gatherings. Once the sting target commits an overt criminal act in support of the bombing plot, he (they are mostly males) is arrested and prosecuted under federal "terrorism enhancement" provisions, which lead to draconian prison sentences. The FBI's rationale for the aggressive sting program is that by catching a lone wolf before he strikes, law enforcement can take him off the streets before he meets a real terrorist capable of helping him orchestrate another attack on the scale of 9/11.

Critics of the program maintain that those targeted in the stings lack the necessary skill to carry out an attack on their own and that no example exists of a lone wolf becoming operational through meeting an actual terrorist in the United States. Critics further contend that the would-be terrorists are usually uneducated, economically desperate, and vulnerable young men with mental health or drug problems.[2] Even FBI Director Comey has described lone wolf terrorists as "troubled souls who are seeking meaning in some misguided way."[3] Because the FBI's sting program concentrates its resources primarily in Muslim American communities, critics charge that the FBI has eroded community trust in those areas, instigated fear, and silenced dissent necessary for participatory democracy.[4] Moreover, say the critics, the United States is manufacturing terrorism by entrapping innocent Muslims.

In strictly pragmatic terms, FBI stings have become the nation's leading preemptive counterterrorism strategy. In February 2015, Director Comey announced that the bureau had investigations into "homegrown violent extremists" in all fifty states. Most of these cases were sting operations. The strategy has also been held up to international audiences as an effective means of combatting terrorism. Specifically, former United States Attorney General Eric Holder has implored European countries to adopt American-style sting tactics to prevent potential terrorists from traveling to Syria to join ISIS.

The FBI stings are therefore worthy of consideration in any research on lone wolf terrorism. Several important questions deserve our attention: In terms of background factors, how do those targeted in the stings differ from authentic lone wolf terrorists? Does the process of radicalization differ? Could those targeted in the stings have become would-be terrorists without the FBI's influence? Can knowledge of the stings be used to identify the next American ready to fly off to Syria and join the ranks of ISIS? And, even if stings are not considered legal entrapment, are they ethical? Answering these questions begins by placing the FBI sting program in historical context.

The FBI's sting program is often touted by government officials as successful because no one has ever been killed or wounded in the operations. That may be true, but it does not tell the whole story. One case from the pre-9/11 era demonstrates the potential danger of this counterterrorism strategy and clarifies why it has become so controversial in recent years. The danger came not from the target of an FBI sting, but from an undercover FBI informant who flipped sides and became a lone wolf terrorist of historical consequence.

Sara Jane Moore

In the wake of Patty Hearst's highly publicized kidnaping by the Symbionese Liberation Army in Berkeley, California, on February 4, 1974, Sara Jane Moore—a forty-five-year-old unemployed, five-time divorcee who had abandoned three of her four children and was about to lose her home—became the voluntary media liaison for the People in Need program established by newspaper magnate William Randolph Hearst to provide food for San Francisco's poor in response to SLA demands for the release of his daughter.[5] Consequently, Moore became a well-known figure in the Bay Area media. It was through her media contacts that Moore came to the attention of FBI agents assigned to the Hearst investigation and was recruited as a paid informant.

Beginning in April 1974, the FBI tasked Moore with providing surveillance on San Francisco's antiwar demonstrators and left-leaning political activists in an effort to discredit the dissidents. Moore's involvement with the FBI was part of COINTELPRO, the bureau's official program for disrupting radical organizations in the United States. Even though FBI Director J. Edgar Hoover officially ended the largely unconstitutional COINTELPRO (counter-intelligence programs) in 1971, offshoots of the program operated on an ad hoc basis into the mid-1970s.[6] Moore's connection with the FBI was well known to San Francisco's radical community. Indeed, she worked as a double agent, gathering information on bureau activities and sharing it with radical groups. In June 1975, Moore's duplicity caught up with her and the FBI dismissed Moore from her informant duties. Moore had extensive contacts in local law enforcement, however, and she began to operate as an ad hoc informant for the Bureau of Alcohol, Tobacco, and Firearms (ATF).

Following her termination from the FBI, Moore received an anonymous death threat. She bought a .44-caliber revolver for protection and— both to ensure her safety and to prove her commitment to the radical community—she aligned herself with one of the most dangerous elements of the Bay Area underground: the Maoist prison reform collective Tribal Thumb, which would later be designated a domestic terrorist group by the FBI. Through her affinity with Tribal Thumb, Moore came to believe that in order to jumpstart a revolution she had to kill President Gerald Ford, thereby making Vice President Nelson Rockefeller his successor. Neither of these men had been elected to office but had assumed their appointments following the resignation of Richard Nixon over the Watergate scandal. Moore reasoned that the multimillionaire Rockefeller would be unacceptable to the American public as its next president, and that this would provide the conditions necessary for a revolution.

On Saturday, September 20, 1975, the *San Francisco Chronicle* reported that President Ford would be visiting the city on September 22 to give a luncheon speech to the World Affairs Council at the St. Francis Hotel. Moore read the article, which provided the triggering event for turning her political grievances into terrorism. It also led to a broadcasting of her intent when later that day she phoned a San Francisco police detective she knew from her FBI work and asked him for advice regarding President Ford's visit to the Bay Area. The *Chronicle* stated that Ford would be dedicating a new law building at Stanford University on Sunday, September 21, and Moore wanted to drive to Palo Alto and inspect the president's security arrangements. Alarmed, the detective asked Moore if she owned a gun, to which Moore replied that she carried a .44-caliber for protection because of her death threat. The detective hung up and ordered officers to arrest Moore on Sunday morning and confiscate her weapon. Then the detective called the Secret Service and the FBI, warning agents that "We may have another Squeaky Fromme on our hands" (see chapter 6).[7]

However, the next morning—Sunday, September 21—Moore left home early to work with an ATF agent on an undercover sting involving illegal gun sales by a firearms dealer in Danville, California. This dealer had sold Moore the .44-caliber revolver, but for some reason the ATF agent did not arrest the dealer. As soon as Moore returned home, though, she was arrested by San Francisco police and charged with carrying a concealed weapon. Her .44 was confiscated, and Moore was released from custody at 4:00 P.M. Around 8:30 P.M., Moore was picked up at her home by the Secret Service and taken in for questioning, only to be released after agents determined that Moore presented no danger to the president.

On Monday morning, September 22, Moore placed calls to her contacts at the Secret Service, the FBI, and the San Francisco Police Department. None of them was in, however, as they were all preparing for Ford's speech at the St. Francis Hotel. Moore ended up leaving messages—perhaps she was reaching out for help—and then she set out to assassinate the president.

At 3:28 P.M., as Ford exited the St. Francis under what has been described as "heavy security," Moore fired a single shot at him with a .38-caliber Smith & Wesson revolver from forty feet away. The bullet ricocheted off the wall behind Ford as a bystander knocked Moore's arm down to prevent her from taking a second shot. As Secret Service agents pushed Ford into his limousine and sped away, police converged on Moore, twisted the gun from her grip, and slapped handcuffs on her wrists. It was later determined that Moore had bought the .38 in haste that same morning (from the Danville gun dealer who was supposed to have been arrested by the ATF the day before) and had failed to realize that the gun sights were six inches off the point-of-impact. Intelligence sharing among the various law-enforcement agencies had been abysmal. "The security was so stupid," Moore recalled of the shooting. "It was like an invitation."[8]

Years later Moore claimed that had the FBI not recruited her in 1974, she would never have gone any further inside dissident politics than the liberal edges. Once inside the radical community, Moore learned that the radicals were not the evil people they were portrayed to be by her FBI handlers, and she gained sympathy for them. The primary enabler of Moore's lone wolf terrorism, then, was the FBI. In this and other cases, the FBI seemed to create the very enemy it was hunting.

Lone Wolf Stings in the Post-9/11 Era

The first FBI sting designed to capture a lone wolf terrorist in the twenty-first century had nothing to do with the 9/11 attacks or Islamic extremism. Instead, as was the case for Eric Rudolph, Ronald Taylor, Richard Baumhammers, and others, the sting was enabled by the example set by Timothy McVeigh in Oklahoma City.

The target of the sting was a thirty-nine-year-old farmhand from Jackson, Tennessee, named Demetrius "Van" Crocker. Crocker, who had an IQ of 85 and a drug problem, was known to local law enforcement for his prior involvement with a neo-Nazi group.[9] In early 2004, Crocker came to the attention of the Tennessee Drug Task Force for dealing methamphetamine. In a later conversation with an undercover drug agent, Crocker remarked that Timothy McVeigh "did things right," adding that he wanted to follow McVeigh's example by killing the black population of Jackson with mustard gas. On September 16, 2004, the drug agent introduced Crocker to an undercover FBI agent posing as a fellow white supremacist and "security employee" at the weapons arsenal in Pine Bluff, Arkansas. Sensing a support system, Crocker upped his ante and told the agent that he wanted to use a radioactive bomb to attack the United States Capitol while the House and Senate were in session. Radioactive materials were off the table, but the agent offered to help Crocker obtain precursor materials to make sarin nerve gas. On October 25, after several more meetings in which Crocker was given an opportunity to back out of the plot, he paid the agent $500 for the sarin precursors, which, in turn, led to Crocker's arrest on terrorism charges.

After Crocker was sentenced to thirty years in federal prison, a U.S. Attorney described the sting as "one of the preeminent anti-terrorism cases of 2006 nationwide." Although the case received little national media attention, it is considered a model of anti-terrorism law enforcement. To this day, the Crocker case is featured on the FBI's website as an exemplar for combatting lone wolf terrorism. Crocker was investigated and prosecuted with strict adherence to the U.S. Constitution. There were no lingering ethical concerns that Crocker's arrest constituted entrapment, nor was community trust eroded during the investigation.

An equally uncontroversial case occurred in 2010, when FBI agents in Charlotte, North Carolina, were alerted by Planned Parenthood workers to threatening Facebook postings made by a twenty-six-year-old unemployed white Tea Party supporter named Justin Moose.[10] In one post, Moose described himself as "the Christian counterpart to Osama bin Laden." Agents obtained a search warrant and started reading Moose's private messages. In one he threatened a copycat of McVeigh's bombing in Oklahoma City. Based on these messages, the FBI began a sting operation against Moose, which started on September 3, 2010, when an informant phoned Moose and told him a story about his best friend's wife who was planning to have an abortion. Moose offered to help stop the procedure, and on September 4 Moose and the informant met in person. Moose described several bombs that the informant could make to destroy the clinic where the abortion was to be performed. The following day, Moose gave the informant detailed plans for making the bombs, and on September 13 Moose was arrested for distributing information pertaining to the use of an explosive. The arrest came with no media fanfare, and because he had no prior criminal record, Moose drew a light sentence and was released from prison in 2012.

There were at least thirteen other FBI lone wolf sting cases in the post-9/11 years, and these were not uncontentious. These cases demanded vast resources from the FBI, which was often operating under pressure from Congress and the White House to show that the bureau was winning the war on terrorism. The stings created enormous media coverage and editorializing, academic conferences and scholarly books, community meetings and protests, and elaborate trials with painful speeches by defendants before they were sentenced to federal prison for decades. The stings were based on the FBI's deliberate targeting of Muslim American communities.

FBI Stings and the War on Terrorism

A major legacy of Hoover's COINTELPRO was an FBI policy that prohibited agents from investigating a person without having credible information to believe that the person had committed a crime. In other words, a criminal predicate must exist to justify an investigation. That changed after 9/11 when the FBI's primary mission shifted from fighting organized crime to preventing another terrorist attack. In 2005, under a new set of guidelines known as the Domestic Investigations and Operations Guide, the FBI created the National Security Branch and empowered agents with the authority to gather intelligence on individuals who represented potential terrorist threats, even where there was no criminal predicate. Although the guide advised agents to refrain from profiling "solely" on the basis of race, ethnicity, or religion, agents were permitted to collect intelligence regarding "ethnic behaviors" associated with possible terrorist elements of an ethnic community.[11]

As a result of these revised guidelines, the FBI recruited an unprecedented number of informants who were tasked with infiltrating Muslim American communities across the country. An estimated fifteen thousand informants have been hired by the FBI since 9/11, which resulted in some fifty successful sting operations against more than one hundred Muslims in the United States (as of 2013).[12] Money is a common motivator for the informants, who can earn $100,000 or more on a single case.[13] The intended effect of the FBI's new program was two-fold. On one hand, it would act as a deterrent to terrorism by creating a hostile environment for actual al-Qaeda recruiters operating in such "radicalization incubators" as mosques, jails, cafes, taxi stands, barbershops, butcher shops, and hookah bars. On the other hand, it would provide FBI agents with intelligence necessary to develop detailed case histories of suspects, which could then be used to create threat assessments running along a radicalization spectrum from terrorist sympathizer to terrorist operator. Those designated as "operators" would become the target of FBI stings.

The FBI sting program required two essential elements: a naive suspect as the target and a convincing conman as the informant.[14] No informant would prove to be as convincing as the middle-aged Pakistani-born Shaheed Hussain (although that may not be his real name). His backstory is important for understanding the essential role played by informants in lone wolf stings.

A Muslim fluent in Arabic, Urdu, and Pashto as well as English, Hussain came to the FBI's attention in 2001 after he was arrested in upstate New York on federal fraud charges of helping immigrants illegally secure driver's licenses. Facing a possible prison term and deportation to Pakistan, Hussain pled guilty and, as part of his arrangement with the government, cooperated with the FBI by going undercover to secure evidence against his accomplices in the fraud. After that, Hussain was involved in some of the FBI's biggest terrorism stings in the United States and was assigned by the FBI to sting operations in London and Pakistan. For agents in the FBI's National Security Branch, Hussain became a super-informant capable of making cases that would stick in court. Playing the role of a wealthy, dapper member of a Pakistani terrorist group in the stings, Hussain was described by the FBI as an "important tool" in the war on terrorism. But for civil rights activists, defense attorneys, and those caught up in the stings, Hussain was an agent provocateur of the first degree, and one who would bend any rule to make a case.

At the 2012 sentencing of four impoverished black Muslims from Newburgh, New York, who were found guilty on terrorism charges related to a 2009 plot to bomb a synagogue in the Bronx, U.S. District Judge Colleen McMahon announced that during testimony involving his role as an informant in the case, Shaheed Hussain lied to the court about his finances, his immigration status, his residency, his business practices, and his income taxes. "I believe beyond a shadow of a doubt," declared McMahon about Hussain's influence on the Newburgh Four, "that there would have been no crime here except the government instigated it, planned it and brought it to fruition."[15] During the trial it was revealed that the FBI, working through Hussain, had offered the Newburgh Four $250,000 to commit the Bronx bombing. Instead of a payout, however, each of the four was sentenced to twenty-five years in federal prison. One observer called it "COINTELPRO all over again."[16]

The FBI's sting program against lone Muslims began in 2009 under the Obama administration. Each case involved plots that were conducted with the direct involvement of confidential informants in the tradition of Shaheed Hussain, including plots that were proposed or led by the informants.[17] They include:

- Michael Finton, convicted of the 2009 attempted bombing of the federal building in Springfield, Illinois. Sentence: twenty-eight years in federal prison.
- Hosam Smadi, convicted of the 2009 attempted bombing of the Wells Fargo Bank in Dallas, Texas. Sentence: twenty-four years in federal prison.
- Mohamed Mohamud, convicted of the 2010 attempted bombing of Courthouse Square in Portland, Oregon. Sentence: thirty years in federal prison.
- Antonio Martinez, convicted of the 2010 attempted bombing of an Army recruiting center in Cantonsville, Maryland. Sentence: twenty-five years in federal prison.
- Farooque Ahmed, convicted of the 2010 attempted bombing of the Washington, DC, metro. Sentence: twenty-three years in federal prison.
- Sami Hassoun, convicted of the 2010 attempted bombing of a Chicago nightclub. Sentence: twenty-three years in federal prison.
- Rezwan Ferdaus, convicted of the 2011 attempted bombing of the Pentagon and U.S. Capitol. Sentence: seventeen years in federal prison.
- Jose Pimentel, convicted of the 2011 attempted bombing of a New York City subway. Sentence: thirty-two years in the New York Department of Corrections.
- Sami Osmakac, convicted of the 2012 attempted bombing of a nightclub in Tampa, Florida. Sentence: forty years in federal prison.
- Amine el Khalifi, convicted of the 2012 attempted suicide bombing of the U.S. Capitol. Sentence: thirty years in federal prison.
- Adel Daoud, arrested for the 2012 attempted bombing of a Chicago nightclub. He is awaiting trial and faces life in prison.
- Quazi Nafis, convicted of the 2012 attempted bombing of the Federal Reserve Bank in New York. Sentence: thirty years in federal prison.
- Terry Loewen, arrested for the 2013 attempted bombing of the airport in Wichita, Kansas. He is awaiting trial.

Background Factors

Do these people differ from authentic lone wolf terrorists in terms of background factors? The following analysis is based on the fifteen sting cases presented above; they include thirteen Muslims along with the white supremacist Van Crocker and the anti-abortionist Justin Moose. The data, as drawn from cases in our database, indicate four differences.

First, those targeted in stings were younger. The average age for authentic lone wolf terrorists of the post-9/11 era was thirty-one years old; it was twenty-six for the sting cases. The youngest sting targets were Adel Daoud, an eighteen-year-old high school student at the time of his arrest; Hosam Smadi and Mohamed Mohamud, both nineteen at the time of their arrests; Antonio Martinez and Quazi Nafis, who were twenty-one; and Sami Hassoun, who was twenty-two.

Second, unlike authentic lone wolves, those targeted in stings were predominantly racial and ethnic minorities. While the majority of authentic lone wolf terrorists have been American-born Caucasians, the sting targets came from more diverse backgrounds, including North African, Kosovar, Bengali, Lebanese, Dominican, Asian, Arab American, and African American.

Third, sting targets were more likely than authentic lone wolves to hold a steady job. While most authentic lone wolf terrorists have been unemployed, the majority of those targeted in stings were working in occupations ranging from common laborer and retail sales clerk to technology specialist. At the time of their arrests, Farooque Ahmed was a computer network design contractor, and Terry Loewen was an avionics technician who held a government security clearance.

Fourth, sting targets were less likely to have a criminal record. The dissimilarities here are significant. While 60 percent of the authentic lone wolves had prior criminal histories, only 13 percent of the sting targets had a criminal background.

These, then, are the background differences between authentic lone wolf terrorists and those targeted by the FBI for sting operations: Authentic lone wolf terrorists are mainly unemployed white males with a criminal record, who on average are thirty-one years old; those arrested in sting operations are younger Muslim men from minority backgrounds with stable employment and no criminal past.

Additionally, there is the crucial issue of mental health to consider. Several of the sting targets suffered from severe mental illness. One was a schizophrenic who was incapable of caring for himself and who wore a diaper to hold his urine during the FBI sting. Another, struggling with a schizoaffective disorder causing nightmares, went missing from the sting and traveled to Saudi Arabia in the hopes of drinking holy water from Mecca to cure his hallucinations. Another was constantly intoxicated on alcohol, cocaine, marijuana, ecstasy, and heroin as the sting unfolded. Another, afflicted with schizophrenia and in anguish over the loss of a parent, believed that what was happening to him during the sting was a dream; it took agents and his lawyer days to convince him otherwise. And yet another man was so mentally ill that he tried to circumcise himself during the sting. However, sting targets are no different from authentic lone wolves in this regard. A total of 42 percent of the post-9/11 authentic lone wolves suffered from mental illness, while the rate of mental illness among the sting targets was 40 percent. Mental illness is common among loners, whether or not they have been recruited into an FBI sting.

The most articulate critic of the government's sting program is the journalist Trevor Aaronson, who argues:

> While the [sting] cases involve plots that sound dangerous—about bombing skyscrapers and synagogues and crowded public places—if you dig deeper, you see that many of the government's alleged terrorists seem hopeless; they are almost always young and down on their luck, penniless, without much promise in their lives, easily susceptible to a strong-willed informant's influence. They are blustery punks [who] would mature past their big-talking ways if left alone.[18]

The major question for research is: To what extent do personal problems contribute to a radicalization process that puts these "blustery punks" on the FBI's radar in the first place?

Radicalizing Sting Targets

Through our research we have developed a radicalization model that shows that lone wolf terrorism begins with personal and political grievances and moves to an affinity with either an extremist group or a community of online sympathizers (see chapter 8). Other phases involve an enabler, the broadcasting of intent, and, finally, a triggering event. How well does this model explain the radicalization of individuals targeted in the FBI stings?

Of the fifteen sting cases, only three (20 percent) evidenced both an identifiable personal vendetta and a political grievance.

Of the fifteen stings, fourteen (93 percent) displayed evidence of affinity with online sympathizers. Nearly all of these sympathizers were supporters of the Salafi Jihad.

In fully 100 percent of the cases there was evidence of an enabler: the FBI.

In 100 percent of the cases there was evidence of broadcasting. The broadcasting was directed solely toward FBI informants and undercover agents. Not once did the sting targets broadcast their intent to family, friends, or the media—a common feature of authentic lone wolf terrorism.

Of the fifteen sting cases, ten (67 percent) experienced a triggering event, most of which were political in nature. Rezwan Ferdaus is a good example. From the time of his first encounter with undercover FBI agents in early March 2011 until late April, Ferdaus produced "nothing tangible" to show them, as an agent reported. The event that triggered Ferdaus to radical action was the U.S. military killing of Osama bin Laden in Pakistan on May 1. Four days later, Ferdaus came up with something quite tangible. A graduate of Northeastern University with a degree in physics, Ferdaus gave his FBI handlers a comprehensive plan—complete with a written abstract, diagrams, and photographs—to attack the Pentagon and Capitol Hill with a bomb-laden remote-controlled aircraft.[19]

The model is therefore useful for understanding *how* FBI sting targets are radicalized, except for the aspect relating to personal and political grievances. The sting cases show considerable evidence of political grievances, but only a few were motivated by personal vendettas. As such, it seems that an FBI target is less likely to be a socially isolated Unabomber agonizing over his personal problems with women and the impending destruction of nature by corporate America than he is to be a Farooque Ahmed, a relatively well-grounded family man who was nonetheless culturally adrift in America, sympathetic to the Salafi Jihad, and angered by the wars in Iraq and Afghanistan.

The FBI has created a standard procedure for reaching out to individuals who fit this profile, providing them with the ideological support, material backing, and sense of belonging necessary for carrying out a terrorist attack. Similar to the much maligned "broken windows" theory of urban law enforcement, FBI agents and informants trawl cyber neighborhoods of the Internet looking for what they call "Kramer Jihadists" (after the bumbling *Seinfeld* character) who espouse violence against the United States. Even in the eyes of the FBI agents involved, these sting targets are not always the hard-core jihadists they are made out to be by the media. The FBI's lead investigator in the sting against the Kosovar immigrant Sami Osmakac, for example, described Osmakac as a "retarded fool" who did not have "a pot to piss in" and said that his terrorist ambitions were nothing more than a "pipe-dream scenario."[20] The FBI's mission is to lure people like this into conspiracies where agents can provide them with the tutelage, encouragement, and financial rewards necessary to turn ostensibly harmless people into would-be mass murderers—never once considering the ethical implications of this strategy and what that might mean for national security.

The FBI's Sting Strategy: "Create and Capture"

Could these people have become would-be terrorists without the FBI's assistance? Answering that question is difficult because it involves a counterfactual argument—that is, a theory about what might have happened, not a theory about what did happen. What *did* happen is that the FBI deliberately created networks of Islamic militants encouraging the radicalization of young Muslims and their involvement in conspiracies to commit what they thought were acts of terrorism. Once the FBI created the terrorists, they captured them.

One place *not* to look for answers to this question is in the criminal profiles of those targeted by the FBI. Like most young men who join the Salafi Jihad, few of the sting targets were criminals to begin with. But they became criminals of great magnitude due to the enabling influence of FBI informants and agents. The most compelling evidence for this is in the specific types of terrorist attacks that were planned for in the stings. And here there is unanimity: They were all bombings intended to kill innocent Americans. That those targeted in the stings were basically unskilled in bomb-building and weapons delivery is evidenced in the record of each specific case.

The Case of Quazi Nafis

A prime example of the FBI's "create and capture" strategy is the attempted bombing of the Federal Reserve Bank in New York City by Quazi Nafis in 2012.[21] Nafis (pronounced Na-*feece*) is the son of a banker, and that may

Figure 11.1 Quazi Nafis. Source: http://archive.thedailystar.net/newDesign/news-details
.php?nid=254519.

say something about his selection of the Federal Reserve Bank as a target
for violence. Born to a devout Muslim family in Dhaka, Bangladesh, in
1991, Nafis had a normal childhood until the age of nine, when he developed a stammer that set him apart from others. Nafis suffered beatings from
relatives and ridicule from his peers because of his stammer. "Growing up
as a child I did not have any real friends," he recalled. "My relationship
with my parents was not very friendly. I was afraid of them both."[22] Due to
an inability to concentrate on his studies, Nafis made poor grades in school,
disappointing his parents and leading him into profound depression. He
would later describe himself as a child who was always "tired, exhausted
and sad. . . . I hated myself. I felt like I was good for nothing."[23]

In 2009, eighteen-year-old Nafis enrolled at North South University in
Dhaka where he studied English and accounting with the goal of following his father into the banking business. At the same time, Nafis became
more religious and embarked upon a pious path to Islam. For young Nafis,
this created a personal conflict between the banking profession and Islam's
prohibition against lending money at interest, or usury, and, compounded
by his ongoing problems concentrating, his grades suffered. The year 2009
also marked the beginning of Nafis's involvement with Facebook, mainly
posting teenage jokes and photos of the rapper Eminem. Ultimately, Facebook would destroy his life.

Nafis spent two and a half years at North South University, making few
friends. His poor grades resulted in his being placed on academic probation and further disappointed his parents. He lived miles away from the
university and never learned to drive, so he spent hours traveling to classes

on miserably hot and overcrowded buses, which added to his depression. "My potential went down," he said, "draining my energy."[24] The only positive things in his life were a part-time job as a computer mentor for other students, and a new girlfriend. But he would eventually lose them both by dint of two major turning points occurring in his life during 2011.

The first involved a North South friend who had a cousin in the United States who was doing well at a university in Arkansas. Nafis and his friend wanted the same. With the support of their parents, the two visited a travel agency to explore educational opportunities in the United States and arrange student visas. It was through this travel agency that in July, 2011, Nafis and his friend were accepted as students at Southeast Missouri State University. The other turning point involved widespread media coverage of the CIA's killing of Anwar al-Awlaki in Yemen on September 30, 2011. Killed alongside al-Awlaki was the Pakistani American Samir Khan, founder and publisher of AQAP's *Inspire* and creator of "Make a Bomb in the Kitchen of Your Mom." Nafis was unfamiliar with both al-Awlaki and *Inspire* but he began studying al-Qaeda's call for violent jihad and the online sermons of al-Awlaki, including his 2009 "listicle" dubbed "44 Ways of Supporting Jihad." Although Nafis was certainly moving in an extremist direction, he had not yet committed himself to terrorism. In fact, he was far from it.

Nafis, his friend, and another student arrived at New York's JFK International Airport on January 13, 2012. Loretta Lynch, the New York federal attorney who would later prosecute Nafis (and go on to replace Eric Holder as U.S. Attorney General) argued in court that Nafis came to the United States not to further his studies but to advance the goals of jihad. Describing Nafis as one of the most dangerous terrorists the United States has faced since 9/11, Lynch told reporters that "he came here wanting to carry out a terrorist attack."[25] If that were the case, then Quazi Nafis would have stayed in New York when he arrived there on January 13 and begun his surveillance of the Federal Reserve Bank in Manhattan or some other high-value target. Instead, Nafis and his companions boarded connecting flights to Cape Girardeau, Missouri (population 37,941), home of Southeast Missouri State University (SEMO) where Nafis entered the most stable period of his life.

The three Bengali students moved into an off-campus apartment and joined the local Islamic Center. According to Nafis, he "made some good friends" at SEMO, where he took classes in computer science, math, and physics and worked as a volunteer advising new Muslim students on campus. Elected vice president of the Muslim Student Association,[26] he also did charity work for the Islamic Center, going door to door on Friday evenings with baskets of donated food for the poor. A classmate would later say that Nafis often remarked that true Muslims do not believe in violence. Another fellow student and member of the Islamic Center remembered that "Nafis was a good kid. He showed no traces of anti-Americanism or death to America, or anything like that. He was a trustworthy and honest kid."[27] Still another student, a fifty-four-year-old Iraq War vet who used to give Nafis a lift home after classes, would say "We talked quite a bit. . . . And this [the attempted Federal Reserve bombing] doesn't seem to be in character."[28] There is, then, no evidence indicating that Nafis came to the United States bent on committing jihadi terrorism.

The downfall of Quazi Nafis was likely due to a learning difficulty associated with attention deficit disorder. As the semester at SEMO went on, Nafis became buried under a mountain of homework and did not perform up to expectations due to his continuing inability to concentrate. "For some reason I cannot concentrate properly," recalled Nafis. "I just gaze at the book but not being able to memorize something I am trying to get by heart."[29] His biggest problem was computer science. When it became obvious that Nafis would fail the class, he scheduled an appointment with the college dean who offered a remedial course of study that would allow Nafis to work at his own pace. But then just as quickly, according to Nafis, the dean reneged on his promise, and Nafis was suspended from SEMO for poor grades.

In early June, 2012, Nafis moved to Albany, New York, where he was taken in by an uncle who helped him find temporary employment as a construction worker. But the work was sporadic, and Nafis became isolated in his uncle's apartment. Albany was the beginning of a downward spiral for Nafis. He had no friends, little money, and rarely left his bedroom. Battling depression, Nafis fell into the habit of sleeping well into the afternoon, praying, and then tethering himself to his laptop to surf the Internet and make Facebook postings until the sun came up. Over and over, day after day, he would repeat this behavior. In early July, Nafis's aunt complained about her nephew's idleness, and Nafis was asked to leave the apartment. But before he did, a new "friend" appeared on his Facebook page with the screen name Yaqueen. Unbeknownst to Nafis, "Yaqueen" was a thirty-six-year-old jobless felon from San Diego, California, named Howard Willie Carter II. When he sent Nafis a gruesome video of Muslims being slaughtered by Assad's barrel bombs in Syria, Nafis experienced a triggering event leading to his interest in retaliatory terrorism. "That video is what changed me," he said.[30]

Nafis located to a Bangladeshi community in Jamaica, Queens, New York, and moved in with four others at the apartment of a distant cousin. He found a job in a Manhattan pizza joint but quit because they served pork. Ever the pious Muslim, Nafis got jobs in a pet store and with a construction company making $80 a day, but quit them both because he refused to work on Friday. He also enrolled in classes at the ASA Institute of Business and Computer Technology in midtown Manhattan. But that did not last long because of his concentration problems. "I started to feel like someone who was physically and mentally disabled to be successful," Nafis later wrote to the magistrate who would sentence him to thirty years in prison, U.S. District Judge Carol Bagley Amon. "It is just like I could not cope up with the fast competitive world. I was falling into deep depression."[31] His life in Jamaica was fraught with problems—problems with the people he lived with, his employment, and his student visa, as well as ongoing problems with concentration, stammering, and depression. On top of that, Nafis learned that his girlfriend back in Bangladesh was cheating on him. That was the final straw. "I became overwhelmed," he said. "I became hopeless."[32]

Enter the life-after-death sermons of senior al-Qaeda recruiter and motivator Anwar al-Awlaki. Even though al-Awlaki had had no formal Islamic education, he had produced a massive, twenty-two-CD set of lectures entitled *The Hereafter*, in which he described the process human souls must travel through to reach either eternal life in paradise or hell. God's judgment depends on the soul's accountability to the requirements of the Koran. Those who pass the accountability test will be rewarded with paradise; otherwise, it's hell. Nafis became obsessed with this theory and believed that al-Awlaki was speaking directly to him. "Al-Awlaki put everything in a practical aspect," said Nafis.[33] Al-Awlaki preached that suicide is not allowed in Islam, but that self-sacrifice is different. By spending his nights alone listening to al-Awlaki's sermons about the hereafter, Nafis gained a sense of absolute certainty about his own death. "That way I justified my killing myself with a jihadist act," he wrote to Judge Amon.[34] Nafis can be added to the growing roster of young jihadists around the world who have been enabled by the sermons of Anwar al-Awlaki.

Nafis began broadcasting his jihadist intentions on Facebook. Among his friends were an Islamist in Bangladesh and a Bangladeshi Islamist in the United States, as well as Yaqueen, or Howard Willie Carter II. There is no evidence directly linking Carter to the FBI, nor has the FBI ever explained how Nafis came into contact with an undercover informant. However, shortly after meeting Carter on Facebook, Nafis was friended by someone with the screen name "Daoud," who was an FBI informant. This became the nucleus of the original Nafis cell to commit jihad in America: Nafis, the two Bengalis, Yaqueen, and the FBI informant, Daoud, with Yaqueen being the most provocative of the bunch. Nafis would never actually meet any of these people in face-to-face encounters. The cell existed entirely as a community of online sympathizers, with one minor exception.

On July 6, 2012, Nafis and Daoud spoke by cell phone. During the conversation (all conversations with Nafis were taped by the FBI), Nafis used the word *martyrdom*. This information was likely passed to Yaqueen because Yaqueen then began to inform Daoud of some ideas Nafis had for jihad. They included plans to kill President Obama and attack a military base in Baltimore. It is doubtful that any of this came from Nafis. He never expressed opinions against Obama, had never been to Baltimore, and knew nothing about a military base there. Yaqueen, though, was originally from Baltimore.

Casting further doubt on the credibility of statements made by Howard Willie Carter II is the fact that on July 14, Nafis told Daoud that he wanted to leave New York and return to Bangladesh so that he could patch things up with his girlfriend. That meant more to him than anything else at the time. Unlike many real lone wolf terrorists who tend to abuse and batter women before they attack, Nafis tried to win back the heart of a woman who could keep him from terrorism. Had Nafis been strong enough to think for himself and follow through with his trip back home (presuming he was not on the federal no-fly list), he might have avoided the hard road ahead of him. But he did not have that kind of strength, and the FBI intervened to claw Nafis back into the sting by connecting him to a member of al-Qaeda—not a faceless Facebook friend like the other conspirators, but a real person who would become his friend and mentor.

The Federal Reserve Plot

Quazi Nafis had never been to Central Park, so he was in exotic territory when he met the al-Qaeda brother there on the afternoon of July 24, 2012.

The meeting had been arranged by Daoud several days earlier. The brother presented himself as "Kareem" and said that he had connections for al-Qaeda resources and could make them available to Nafis. Unbeknownst to Nafis, Kareem was an undercover FBI agent, and all of their conversations would be recorded. Kareem was an "Arab guy," according to Nafis, about thirty-five years old. Nafis was much younger, having just turned twenty-one two weeks earlier. "He didn't look pious and acted more modern, he was dressed in jeans" said Nafis. "He wanted to help me and flashed astonishing money."[35] As a result of this Central Park meeting with the older, well-appointed al-Qaeda member, Nafis abandoned his plans for returning to Bangladesh.

A crucial date in the conspiracy was August 4, when Nafis unexpectedly confided to Kareem that he wanted to perform a suicide bombing at the Federal Reserve Bank on Liberty Street in New York's financial district. The FBI approved the plan, and on August 9, Nafis was covertly videotaped as he walked the financial district taking notes on how he would enter the fortress-like Federal Reserve building. There is no doubt that Nafis was emotionally ready to become a suicide bomber for al-Qaeda. On August 11, Nafis told brother Kareem that he wanted to strap on a suicide vest and pull its ripcord inside the Federal Reserve.

By now, Nafis had formed what he called a "strong bond" with the brother, telling Kareem that they would die together in the attack. Accordingly, Kareem drove Nafis back down to the financial district where Nafis took photos of the area. Meanwhile, FBI agents in San Diego placed Howard Willie Carter II under surveillance.

Yet there was growing friction among the plotters. On August 23, Kareem and Nafis met in a Queens hotel room where Nafis questioned Kareem's radical bona fides saying, "The thing that I want to ask you about is that, the thing that I'm doing, is it under al-Qaeda?"[36] Kareem said that he (Kareem) was indeed working for al-Qaeda but that al-Qaeda's leadership was unsure about Nafis's plan for suicide bombing. Instead, they were interested in a truck bomb like the ones used by al-Qaeda in the 1998 attacks on the U.S. embassies in Kenya and Tanzania. And they wanted Nafis to drive the truck. Nafis was opposed to the plan, not only because he could not drive, but because it did not conform to the conditions in Anwar al-Awlaki's fantastic dreams about the afterlife. Nafis wanted a suicide bombing and nothing less. "Can I ask you something?" Nafis further pressed Kareem, "Why aren't you [inaudible] to drive the car yourself? Why don't you want to be *shahid* [martyring yourself]?"[37] Court papers do not record Kareem's answer.

The Attack

A standard operating procedure in FBI stings is to offer the targeted person an opportunity to back out of a bombing plot by stressing the point that there are ways to do jihad nonviolently. Declining this opportunity shows a violent predisposition on the target's part and a firm commitment to political violence, both of which can help the government's case in court. The FBI bypassed this procedure with Nafis, however, and he was never given the chance to change his mind. One possible reason is that Nafis had, in fact, already changed his mind and was ambivalent about attacking the Federal Reserve with a truck bomb. If given an opportunity to decline a truck bombing, Nafis might have taken it. The FBI's sting operation was less than ironclad in other ways, too. Agents had nearly lost Nafis when he expressed interest in returning to Bangladesh back on July 14. Now they were about to lose him again.

On September 20, Nafis and Kareem met in a Queens hotel room where Nafis said that he wanted to return to Bangladesh to see his family one last time. This is not what the FBI had in mind because it did not conform to its "create and capture" strategy. To create their truck bomber, the FBI had to keep Nafis in the United States. And so Kareem told Nafis that he could not travel internationally if he truly intended to carry out his attack with al-Qaeda's assistance, although he also said that he would pass Nafis's travel request on to al-Qaeda leadership and get back to him. The answer came a week later when Kareem told Nafis that the al-Qaeda leaders could not wait for Nafis to return from Bangladesh and that he should proceed with the attack under Kareem's direction. Furthermore, they authorized Nafis to use a remote-controlled truck bomb rather than a suicide vest. After the truck bombing, Nafis could go home to Bangladesh. With this understanding, Nafis affirmed his commitment to al-Qaeda, and the plot resumed with Nafis fully on board. Predicting great things, Nafis told Kareem that their Federal Reserve bombing might even disrupt the upcoming presidential elections between Barack Obama and John McCain. Once again, the FBI had clawed Nafis back in.

The plot went operational in early October, when Kareem gave Nafis $200 and told him to buy some batteries and other electrical components that would be used to build the bomb. On October 4, Kareem and Nafis bought several large garbage bins to hold the explosives and then drove to a Queens warehouse where they stockpiled the materials in a rented storage unit. On October 12, the two offloaded twenty fifty-pound bags of (fake) explosive material into the storage unit along with a tarp Nafis bought with his own money. As they left, Nafis handed Kareem a thumb drive containing an article Nafis had written for *Inspire*. In the article, Nafis praises "Our beloved Sheikh Osama bin Laden" in justifying the fact that their bomb would likely kill women and children, adding: "I came to this conclusion that targeting America's economy is most efficient way to draw the path of obliteration of America as well as the path of establishment of Khiliapha [caliphate, or an Islamic State]. I decided to attack the Federal Reserve Bank of New York which is by far the largest (by assets), most active (by volume) and most influential of the 12 regional Federal Reserve Banks."[38] On October 15, Kareem called Nafis and told him that they would carry out the bombing in two days.

In the early morning hours of October 17, Kareem picked up Nafis in an FBI-rented van and set out for the warehouse. During the drive, Nafis told Kareem that he still wanted to become a martyr for al-Qaeda, saying that he had a "Plan B" to commit a suicide bombing if police were able to thwart their truck bombing. Every narrative about an FBI sting bears conflicting accounts, and the Nafis case is no exception. According to the FBI, Nafis singlehandedly assembled the bomb at the warehouse, mixing a thousand pounds of explosives in the trash bins, hoisting them into the van by himself, and then installing the detonator to coordinate with a cellphone signal. According to Nafis, "They [FBI agents] built the bomb," and Nafis had nothing to do with it.[39] What both agree on is that Nafis wanted to make a martyrdom video for release after the bombing.

The most amazing part of the story at this point is Nafis's jaw-dropping criminal and cultural naiveté. He and Kareem arrived at the financial district in the heart of New York City during the morning rush hour. Yet miraculously, there was a vacant parking space directly in front of the Federal Reserve Bank. "I didn't think anything of it," Nafis recalled. "There were cars parked over there [across the street] and on our side too."[40] Equally stunning, Nafis and Kareem exited the van, walked to the nearby four-star

Millennium Hotel, and went straight up to a $700-a-day guest room without checking in. This, too, Nafis thought nothing of.

Once inside the room, Kareem pointed a camcorder at Nafis, and he began his martyrdom statement. Covering his face with an Arabic scarf, wearing sunglasses and disguising his voice, Nafis proclaimed: "We will not stop until we attain victory or martyrdom."[41] Once the filming was done, Nafis sat on the bed and dialed a cellphone number intended to detonate the bomb at the Federal Reserve. The number did not work so Nafis dialed several more times before there was a knock on the door. Then FBI agents stormed into the room and arrested Nafis on terrorism charges.

Hours later, agents in San Diego arrested the man who likely delivered Nafis to the FBI in the first place, Howard Willie Carter II (Yaqeen), on federal charges of possessing child pornography.

Could Quazi Nafis have carried out this terrorist operation on his own, without the FBI's help? Most likely he could not, for two main reasons. First, he lacked the resources. Nafis could not drive; he had no vehicle of his own; and no money to buy the bomb-making components or to pay rent on the warehouse storage locker. The FBI supplied the money to make those purchases. Second, Nafis lacked the criminal skills necessary to build a bomb. Nafis did not have even rudimentary training in small-scale explosives. Moreover, explosive training requires considerable concentration, and Nafis had a deficit in that area. Nafis had no means to deliver the bomb to the Federal Reserve Bank. The FBI supplied the vehicle and an FBI agent drove it. Nafis likely did not build the bomb, and he certainly did not transfer it to the financial district. His primary responsibility was to detonate the bomb. An FBI agent taught him how to do this with a cell phone that Nafis had purchased at the FBI's direction. At the end of the day, Nafis was socialized into terrorism by the FBI and given tactical training for carrying out an attack against the United States. As the *New York Times* concluded about the Nafis sting: "The case appears to fit a model: in the process of flushing out people they believe present a risk of terrorism, federal law enforcement officials have played the role of enabler."[42]

That is precisely what happened. To say that Nafis *might* have received this level of terrorist training from al-Qaeda in Bangladesh or anywhere else, and that he *might* have returned to the United States as a committed terrorist, and that he *might* have then bombed an American target is to engage in a tangle of counterfactual speculation that is beyond resolution by social science.

Implications for Joining ISIS

Can the radicalization model be used to identify individuals with the potential for traveling to Syria and joining the jihad? There are two ways to answer this. One is by looking through the rearview mirror and analyzing a case in which the FBI failed to stop such an occurrence. The best known case is Moner Abu-Salha, the jihadist from Florida who in May 2014 became a suicide bomber for the al-Qaeda-affiliated al-Nusra Front in Syria (Abu-Salha was investigated by the FBI in 2014, along with the Orlando shooter Omar Mateen, after Mateen was himself targeted in a sting). The other way is to examine a case where the FBI successfully prevented an American from traveling to Syria and joining the Salafi Jihad. Such a case is presented next.

As will be seen, central to the FBI's success in this case was a recognition of the historical shift in lone wolf terrorism from an affinity with extremist groups to an affinity with online sympathizers—a transformation that has expanded the base of support for leaderless resistance to worldwide audiences. This is an international phenomenon confirmed by a pioneering British report on 125 Western foreign fighters affiliated with ISIS or al-Nusra in Syria. The study found that "a large number of foreign fighters receive their information about the conflict not from official channels provided by their fighting groups, but through so-called [online] disseminators—unaffiliated but broadly sympathetic individuals who sometimes appear to offer moral and intellectual support to jihadist opposition groups. The ability of jihadist groups to exert control over information has been significantly eroded, while private individuals, who are (mostly) based in the West and who may have never set foot inside Syria, possess significant influence over how the conflict is perceived by those who are actually involved."[43]

The Case of Nicholas Teausant

The case begins in 2012 when Nicholas Teausant, then a nineteen-year-old community college student and National Guard member from Lodi, California, was invited by a friend to attend services at the local mosque.[44] (After Teausant's arrest, journalists would refer to previous reports claiming that al-Qaeda leader Ayman Al-Zawahiri had been a visitor to the Lodi

Figure 11.2 Nicholas Teausant, also known as Ased Abdur-Raheem. Source: http://thisainthell.us/blog/?p=40416.

mosque in 1998 and 1999 as part of an international Islamic fund drive—a claim the FBI later found to be false.) Teausant converted to Islam, adopting the name Ased Abdur-Raheem, and began searching the Internet for information on his newfound faith. There is no evidence linking Teausant's radicalization to the Lodi mosque; instead, his extremism took shape after he discovered AQAP's *Inspire*. A classmate described Teausant as "nice but a little off in the head"—which might explain why he became a failed joiner: Shortly after converting to Islam, Teausant was dismissed from the National Guard because of poor grades at college. This dismissal became a personal grievance for Teausant and he set out to redress the injustice by becoming a Cyber Jihadist.

Writing as "Assad Teausant bigolsmurf" and attaching a personal photo, Teausant first expressed his grievances in a May 31, 2013, posting on Instagram. Teausant said that he was interested in the "down fall" of America, adding "I would love to join Allah's army but I don't even know how to start."[45] Teausant closed his message by asking if anyone could help him locate a link to the *Lone Mujahid Pocketbook*, a compilation of the first eleven issues of *Inspire*, described by the FBI as a "how-to guide for becoming a lone wolf terrorist."

Teausant continued his Internet searching and developed an affinity with online sympathizers over Facebook and other social networking venues. Through this anonymous online community, Teausant learned about ISIS and its fight against the Free Syrian Army in Syria's civil war. By this time the FBI was running thousands of informants, some being paid $100,000 or more on a case, plus "performance incentives" if a case resulted in a terrorism conviction. In July of 2013, one of these informants was trolling Ask.fm, a Latvia-based social networking site that encourages anonymous postings and has been linked to bullying and adolescent suicides. The informant spotted an opinionated user named "assadthelion" and after some preliminary questions the informant asked the user: "Are you a terrorist?"

"Lol as if I would tell the truth about That," came the reply; "haha wow and no I'm not." That could have been the end of it but the informant pressed on asking:

"Where do you want to fight?"

"I want to go to Syria."[46]

The informant conveyed this exchange to his FBI case agent, which led to the identification of Nicholas Teausant as the Ask.fm and Instagram poster through his Facebook page. And with that, Teausant was designated a terrorist operator, and the agent and the informant became Teausant's direct enablers.

The FBI informant first met with Teausant in Stockton, California, on October 5, 2013. Several meetings followed, and on October 20 Teausant told the informant that he wanted to go to Syria to fight but did not know how to get there. They began discussing the practicalities of such a trip, and on October 24 Teausant told the informant, "I'll be the pawn. You just figure out the brainy stuff." Four day later Teausant told the informant that his goal was to deliver a "maximum blow to the U.S. government" so that he could "watch it tumble and fall."[47]

But then Teausant changed his mind and began texting the informant about a plan to bomb the Los Angeles rail system. That came to no avail, however, and all grew silent until January 4, 2014, when Teausant sent a text to the informant saying that he wanted to renew his plans for traveling to Syria. When asked who he wanted to fight with, Teausant awkwardly broadcasted his intent by writing: "I like ISIS . . . Islamic State of um crap . . . I forget."[48] The informant advised Teausant to consider his options, and if he was still interested in joining ISIS, then there was a mentor who could facilitate the trip to Syria. Mention of a "mentor" widened the support network for Teausant, as well as providing him with the necessary triggering event for terrorism.

Between January 7 and February 10, 2014, Teausant and the informant made travel plans, and on February 22 Teausant bought a one-way railroad ticket to Vancouver, British Columbia, for March 15. From there he would fly to Syria with help from the mentor. On March 5, the informant took Teausant to a Stockton hotel room and introduced him to this mentor, an undercover FBI agent, and the agent advised Teausant on his plans for joining the jihad.

On March 15, Teausant boarded the Amtrak train in Lodi to begin his adventure in Syria, with FBI agents following close behind. At 11:40 P.M. on March 16, in Blaine, Washington, near the Canadian border, Teausant was removed from an Amtrak bus and arrested on charges of attempting to provide material support to a terrorist group.

Once in custody, Teausant was diagnosed as a paranoid schizophrenic and placed on medications. When asked by a reporter why he had made the decision to join ISIS, Teausant replied: "You've got to understand, at the time they were not doing the brutal stuff that they're doing now. I'm absolutely abhorred by that Foley [beheading]. I did not see that coming. ISIS was the informant's suggestion. At the time, ISIS was something small."[49] As of 2016, he was facing fifteen years in federal prison.

Ethical Implications of the FBI Sting Program

The FBI's sting program has generally proven to be an effective means of removing potential lone wolf terrorists from the streets and a safe method of law enforcement given that there have been no injuries or loss of life. But is it ethical to arrest, prosecute, and incarcerate a person who is incapable of planning and executing a terrorist attack by himself? The FBI has strict policies on both ethical behavior and lone wolf investigations. Far from secret, they are available on the FBI's website for all to see. Yet it is clear that these policies are being compromised by the results-driven culture of the "create and capture" sting program, which demands a steady stream of new lone wolf suspects necessary to justify funding for a perpetual war on terrorism.

The bureau defines a lone wolf terrorist as "a single individual driven to hateful attacks based on a particular set of beliefs without a larger group's knowledge or support."[50] In lone wolf sting cases, however, the FBI itself functions as "a larger group" that provides "knowledge and support" for an individual's "hateful attacks." The policy recognizes the primacy of preventing homegrown terrorism and states that it is only when "individuals cross the line into threats, the actual use of force or violence or other law-breaking activities that we can investigate." But in lone wolf stings, it is the FBI that actively encourages and provokes an individual to "cross the line" into violence.

The hallmark of ethical behavior for FBI agents is civility, defined as "treating others with respect."[51] Civility entails "considering the feelings of other persons, their positions, and their situations. It represents self-disciplined behavior and patience with those who may not deserve it." In lone wolf stings, the FBI makes a thorough assessment of "the feelings of other persons, their positions, and their situations," and then agents patiently employ that information against persons, even "those who may not deserve it," to effect their arrest, prosecution, and imprisonment. Along the way, the FBI exploits personal problems to push their targets in a new and dangerous direction. What remains to be understood is how these ethical abuses can be corrected to serve a broader counterterrorism purpose, or whether stings can actually prevent terrorism to begin with.

For instance, innovative counterterrorism approaches in Europe suggest that it may be possible for FBI agents to bring less harm to both the "troubled souls" who are arrested in lone wolf stings and the Muslim communities they come from—while still protecting public safety. Such an approach is not as far-fetched as it may sound. It is currently used in Denmark, where some one hundred returned Syrian foreign fighters—mostly males between the ages of fifteen and twenty-five—have been offered education, psychological counseling, and social services in lieu of jail time. The program does not try to change the fundamentalist beliefs of returning fighters—as long as they do not advocate violence.[52] The program has led to a sharp decline in jihadi traffic from Denmark to Syria. Whereas thirty Danes reportedly made the trip in 2013, only one did in 2014.[53] A similar program has been used with jihadists in foreign prisons where counter-radicalization policies share general premises with an extreme Islamic world-view including strident opposition to Western wars in Muslim lands, while differing from it on the essential issue of violence.[54] Other countries, such as Sweden and the Netherlands, have enlisted the help of former extremists to provide counseling and mentoring to young people at risk of radicalization. There is reason for optimism: As an FBI official told us, the bureau "is open" to these alternative approaches. This may be more than talk. According to open sources, between 2013 and 2015, at least fifty-one lone Muslims were arrested in FBI stings. Twenty of these operations involved

FBI-supported bombing plots. But in thirty-one of the stings, including the sting against Nicholas Teausant, the FBI used its vast resources to prevent a young Muslim from traveling to Syria with the intent of joining ISIS.[55] Because of this success, in 2015 the FBI initiated a Shared Responsibility Committee, which proposes to enlist local mental health professionals, religious leaders, teachers, local law enforcement, and social workers to develop strategies to counter violent extremism.[56]

The need for such a new direction in the FBI sting program is all too apparent in the final case study presented in this book.

CHAPTER 12

Lone Wolf Terrorism and FBI Mythmaking

Figure 12.1 Sami Hassoun. Source: www.dailyherald.com.

I f there is a showplace for America's experience with mass incarceration, it can be found along the banks of the Missouri River in a rural stretch of northeastern Kansas known locally as the "corrections center." Some ten thousand inmates are incarcerated there, a figure representing the total prison population of Syria. The center's success in the prison business is due mainly to cultural history.

The largest and oldest prison in the area, the Lansing Correctional Center (formerly the Kansas State Penitentiary in Lansing, Kansas), is the state's main maximum-security facility. Perry Smith and Richard Hickock, the subjects of Truman Capote's literary masterpiece *In Cold Blood*, were hung on the prison gallows there in 1965 for the murder of four members of the Herb Clutter family. Capote famously called the killers "brothers in the breed of Cain."[1] Lansing is also where Alvin "Creepy" Karpis met Fred Barker, and upon release they formed the Barker-Karpis gang, one of the most ruthless criminal enterprises of the Depression era, purportedly run by Fred's mother, "Ma Barker." In November 1934, after the bank robber "Baby Face Nelson" (Lester Gillis) was killed in an FBI shootout, Creepy

Karpis was named the new "Public Enemy Number 1" by J. Edgar Hoover. Today, the prison's most notable inmate is the lone wolf terrorist Scott Roeder, serving a "Hard 50" (life) for the assassination of Dr. George Tiller in Wichita.

Several miles up the road sit four other major prisons. The United States Disciplinary Barracks, the nation's only maximum-security military prison, is located on the grounds of Fort Leavenworth, recognized in U.S. history for its role as a key supply base for the settlement of the American West. Only military prisoners with extended sentences or those convicted of national security offenses are confined there. In recent years they have included Robert Bales, who killed sixteen Afghan civilians (including nine children) and wounded six others in Afghanistan during the Kandahar massacre of 2012; Charles Graner, who was convicted of prisoner abuse in connection with the Abu Ghraib torture scandal of 2004; and Chelsea Manning, who turned over hundreds of thousands of classified documents to the website WikiLeaks in 2010 while known as Bradley Manning. Historically called "The Castle" (portrayed in the 2001 film *The Last Castle*), the institution also houses the military's death row; twenty-one inmates have been executed there over the years, including fourteen German prisoners of war, who were hung in 1945. Today there are six prisoners on death row, including the lone wolf terrorists Hasan Akbar, who killed two military officers and wounded fourteen other soldiers while deployed to Camp Pennsylvania, Kuwait, on the eve of the 2003 invasion of Iraq, and the Fort Hood shooter Nidal Hasan.

Close by is the United States Penitentiary (USP), Leavenworth, operated by the Federal Bureau of Prisons (BOP). USP Leavenworth opened in 1903 and became the largest federal maximum-security prison in the United States.[2] Due to its lack of air-conditioning despite the sweltering Kansas summers, the prison was once dubbed the "Hot House" by a popular journalist, yet staff and inmates at Leavenworth typically use its old nickname: "The Big House."[3] A total of 1,400 inmates currently live behind its massive stone walls reaching 40 feet high, 40 feet below the surface, and 3,000 feet long, enclosing 23 acres and manned by armed guards in watchtowers. The most formidable feature of the prison, especially for one who encounters the massive institution for the first time, is the forty-two rock steps leading up to the entrance. It takes time and concentration to walk the steps, making one seriously think about where they are going. It is a brilliant work of prison architecture derived from the Auburn System—named after the Auburn Prison built in 1818 in upstate New York—which emphasized the transformative value for inmates of hard work, prayer, and contemplation. Hence, the forty-two steps at Leavenworth.

Leavenworth's list of notable convicts reads like a Who's Who of American crime. They include Prohibition-era gangsters George "Machine Gun" Kelly and George "Bugs" Moran; the "Birdman of Alcatraz," Robert Stroud, depicted by Burt Lancaster in a celebrated 1962 movie of the same name; Irish mob boss James "Whitey" Bulger; and James Earl Ray, locked up at USP Leavenworth for forgery in 1955 and released in 1958, ten years before he committed the historic assassination of Martin Luther King. And then there is Sami Hassoun.

The New Public Enemy Number 1

Sami Hassoun is serving a twenty-three-year sentence at USP Leavenworth—he will likely spend more time in the Big House than all the celebrity gangsters put together—for the *attempted* use of violence. That attempt was made with a fake bomb provided to him by undercover FBI agents. "Hassoun was an example of the so-called lone [wolf] offender," announced an FBI spokesman at Hassoun's sentencing. "He had no ties to organized terror groups, but he was clearly a terrorist—and potentially an extreme danger to the public."[4] Moreover, Sami Hassoun—along with all the other young Muslims who have been ensnared into terrorism by the government in recent years—has emerged as the FBI's new Public Enemy Number 1.

"Public Enemy Number 1" has been described by a noted historian of the FBI as "one of the most powerful, dangerous and ambiguously fascinating figures in American cultural history . . . used by J. Edgar Hoover to symbolize a perceived breakdown of law and order during the Prohibition era."[5] Drawing on this symbolization, Hoover created the most successful public relations campaign in law enforcement history. Operated out of the austere-sounding Crime Records Division, prior to World War II, this campaign involved FBI specialists producing such best-selling books as *G-Man* and *Ten Thousand Public Enemies*, along with movies, newspaper and magazine articles, radio shows, and later (1965–1974) a popular television program, *The FBI*, starring Efrem Zimbalist Jr.[6] "Public Enemy Number 1" was essentially a myth created by Hoover to enhance the FBI's image of invincibility.

The FBI's mythmaking apparatus was employed to devastating personal effect against suspected Communists during the Cold War, when Hoover's agents used electronic surveillance and surreptitious entries (home break-ins or "black bag jobs") to spy on tens of thousands of suspected subversives, often exaggerating the dangers they posed in stories planted in the news media.[7] In 1950, at the outbreak of the Korean War, Hoover sought to expand his powers to investigate Communists by submitting a top secret report to President Harry Truman warning of a terrorist holocaust at the hands of suicide bombers. He attributed his warnings to "ten substantial and highly reliable informants of the FBI."[8] Hoover's plan called for the detention of twelve thousand Americans suspected of disloyalty and a suspension of the writ of habeas corpus, but Truman did not act on the plan. Once out of office, Truman confided to a friend that J. Edgar Hoover should be trusted "as much as you would trust a rattlesnake with the silencer on its rattle."[9]

The mythmaking continued into the stormy 1960s and early 1970s, when Hoover used the authority of COINTELPRO (see chapter 11) to pursue radicals like Weather Underground leader Bernadine Dohrn. In an October 14, 1970, press release announcing Dohrn's placement on the FBI's Ten Most Wanted list following her indictment for inciting a riot at the 1969 Days of Rage antiwar protest in Chicago, Hoover called Dohrn "the most dangerous woman in America" and the "la Pasionara of the Lunatic Left."[10] Displayed in post offices from coast to coast, Dohrn's wanted poster—which quickly became an iconic image of sexual politics among American youth—described her as a "Communist revolutionary who advocates widespread terrorist bombings." Hoover mounted a vigorous campaign to capture Dohrn, leading FBI agents in New York and New Jersey to initiate a range of illegal activities against suspected Weather Underground members. Warrantless wiretaps, black bag jobs, and mail intercepts were used in a vain attempt to find Dohrn.[11]

The FBI's Number Two man at the time, Mark Felt (later revealed as "Deep Throat" in the *Washington Post* investigation of Watergate), went so far as to float the idea that agents should kidnap the infant son of Jennifer Dohrn, Bernadine's sister, as a way of pressuring Bernadine into surrendering.[12] Animated by the sexual mythology of Bernadine Dohrn's wanted poster, agents who broke into Jennifer's New York apartment subsequently presented their boss with a pair of her panties, which they had enclosed in a glass case.[13] Absent any legal evidence linking Bernadine Dohrn to terrorism, the fugitive warrant on her eventually expired, and in early 1982 she turned herself in. "The most dangerous woman in America" received three years' probation and walked away to start a new life as a law school professor. Mark Felt did not fare so well. He was convicted of crimes associated with the Dohrn investigation and faced ten years in federal prison until Felt was granted a pardon by President Reagan in late 1981, days before Dohrn's surrender to the FBI.[14]

Mythmaking—especially at this level—requires a powerful source of misinformation.[15] This is an old tactic of espionage, one that informed Hoover's machinations: When spies obtain knowledge but not secrets, they tend to dress up mere information to make it look like intelligence; and when they do not have solid information, they sometimes fabricate it.[16] The tactic was on full display during operation NEWKILL, the joint FBI–New York Police Department investigation of the domestic terrorist group known as the Black Liberation Army (BLA), thought to be responsible for the killing of ten police officers across the United States between 1971 and 1974. During the investigation, opinion on the BLA was divided between those agents and officers who saw the group as a serious threat and those who thought the BLA was merely a fabrication of 1960s radicalism in its twilight and that the group did not really exist. The former position held sway and focused on a twenty-five-year-old BLA member named Joanne Chesimard (Assata Shakur), whose face—surrounded by an Afro and wearing a Dashiki—appeared on FBI wanted posters in New York City, San Francisco, and Atlanta in connection with scores of crimes and police ambushes. An NYPD official described her as "the final wanted fugitive, the soul of the gang, the mother hen who kept them together, kept them moving, kept them straight."[17] Yet there was little evidence to back up these claims, and all the charges for which Chesimard was originally hunted by the FBI were either dismissed or ended in acquittal at her trial.[18] Like the case against Bernadine Dohrn, the case against Joanne Chersimard was poisoned by the fruit of FBI mythmaking.

In 2013, author Bryan Burrough interviewed one of the original investigators in the BLA case. "Chesimard is no fucking saint," he said, "but was she the heart and soul of the BLA? Hell, no. The guys back then demonized her because, unlike the others [in the BLA], she was educated. She was young and pretty. I can point to at least two other women in the BLA who were more important than Joanne Chesimard ever was. We created that myth. The cops did."[19]

More than forty years later, the FBI has created a similar myth around Muslim Americans arrested in lone wolf sting operations. Sami Hassoun, as will be seen, represents a paradigmatic case of FBI mythmaking in the post-9/11 era.

Sami Hassoun

Between July and September 2014, we exchanged a series of letters with Hassoun followed by a two-day interview with him at USP Leavenworth. The following narrative is based upon those interactions, combined with extensive information in federal court records. However, as will also be seen, by his own admission Sami Hassoun is an inveterate liar. There is no other way to say this. Not only does Hassoun's dishonesty pose a challenge for understanding his case; it was his lying that put him in prison. The narrative attempts to resolve this dilemma by using collaborative sources to back up what Hassoun said in the interviews, or by simply ignoring his most apparent lies.

Background

Siham Hassoun was only fifteen years old when she gave birth to Sami Samir in Beirut, Lebanon, on January 20, 1988.[20] Siham brought her baby home to the West African city of Abidjan, Ivory Coast, where her Lebanese husband, Samir, had settled during Lebanon's civil war of 1975. Since then, with the help of a Jewish friend and business partner, Samir had established a thriving electronics firm serving the urban business districts of West Africa and was therefore able to provide a comfortable life for his family by the time Sami came along. Due also to the economic stability of Ivory Coast at the time, the Hassouns lived in an upscale condominium where Sami grew up surrounded by his paternal grandparents, several cousins, and friends, most of whom were also foreigners (30 percent of Abidjan's three million citizens were émigrés). A photograph from the period shows Sami as the picture of good health and happiness, stylishly dressed in high-end soccer gear and encircled by friends. "We had a very beautiful and good life, living with Sami's grandparents," recalled Siham. "Sami loved them a lot." Samir traveled constantly for his business, and Sami was raised primarily by his mother. Yet Samir was a devoted father who showered his son with gifts whenever he returned home. "I was a very spoiled only child," Sami recalled, "and I had everything a boy my age would dream to have and most kids wanted to hang out with me. We would go to school together and then after school hang out and play soccer. I was the first one [in the group] with a computer, which made up for my dad being away so much."[21] But Sami's privileged existence came crashing down when he was eleven years old. Little did he know, but Sami Hassoun was about to experience the most important turning point of his life.

At 3:00 A.M. on December 23, 1999, six disgruntled soldiers took up firearms and rebelled against Ivory Coast President Henri Konan Bedie, kidnaping his wife and accusing Bedie of failing to make good on back payments due to military personnel. The insurgency resonated throughout the ranks, and Bedie was overthrown in a coup d'état the next day. After rebel soldiers dissolved the nation's government, parliament, and courts, they took control of the Abidjan airport and key bridges, set up checkpoints, and opened prison gates to release political prisoners and other inmates. The soldiers commandeered vehicles and set about the streets of Abidjan firing automatic rifles in the air. Renegade mobs of young men—many wearing bandanas with their faces covered in black soot—took advantage of the power vacuum to use hand grenades to blow open downtown stores, hijack cars, and mug commuters. "It was so terrible," recalled Sami's mother. "They were killing people including women and children. Sami would watch from [the] balcony, he would see people with machetes running, stopping cars, taking people out of cars and killing them, people waving machetes and dancing around after the killing, lots of blood on the street and horrible screaming. We were living in fear that any time they would break the lock for the main gate for our building and get in to kill us. Sami saw everything from our balcony."

The mayhem continued for two long weeks, and its most devastating effects were felt by immigrants like the Hassouns. Along with the killing and dismembering he saw from the balcony, Sami also witnessed the rape of "a woman dressed in white" as he would recall. "A car pulled up and someone inside grabbed her and pulled her in. The car remained stopped for a long time and I could hear horrible screams. I was only eleven years old and did not understand what was really happening."[22] Confirming that such atrocities were occurring in the Ivory Coast uprising, Human Rights Watch reported: "During home attacks, husbands are tied up and forced to watch as wives, daughters, and other female family members are being raped. The worst treatment is almost always reserved for the immigrant populations."

On January 13, 2000, French military forces secured the Abidjan airport, and a momentary truce was declared with the rebels, allowing for the evacuation of women and children only. The American Embassy in Abidjan provided emergency visas to those who were eligible. Because Siham had a brother in Wilmette, Illinois, she was able to secure U.S. visas for herself and Sami. They left immediately on a flight bound for Chicago. Sami was forced to leave everyone behind—his father, his grandparents, his cousins, and friends—without a word of goodbye.

They arrived in the United States a week before Sami's twelfth birthday and moved in with his uncle, Dr. Michael Maitar, in Wilmette. Unlike previous birthdays when his father spoiled him with gifts, there were no presents in 2000, and no father or grandparents. Sami was enrolled in the Marie Murphy Middle School but since he spoke only French, his adjustment was difficult from the start. In fact, he spoke little at all, not even to his mother. He worried constantly about his father and feared that he might never see him again. Clearly showing signs of post-traumatic stress, Sami experienced sleeplessness and nightmares and was unable to defend himself when bullied by classmates because he was different. But more importantly, he was physically ill. "I had awful stomach problems," Sami remembered. "There were days when I was in constant pain and threw up bile. I lost a lot of weight and became very thin."[23] Siham would also recall that Sami "experienced fever, stomach pains, weight loss, chills, shaking, shivering. They were always calling us from school and saying your son threw up a lot. . . . The pain was so bad that he could not walk sometimes." Dr. Maitar examined Sami and concluded that his stomach problems were caused by stress from the Ivory Coast ordeal—although in fact the source of his pain lay in something far more serious that would go undiagnosed for years to come. Then suddenly, in June 2000, Sami's father was able to escape Abidjan and resettle in Lebanon. Six months later, Sami and his mother left on a plane bound for Beirut. As Siham would tell it, awaiting them was "a new hard life for my son Sami."

The year had not been kind to Sami's father. Samir's electronics business had been demolished by the looters in Abidjan, and his entire inventory was lost. Siham and Sami found him living in an impoverished village near Beirut, struggling to get by. But it was Sami's health that concerned his parents the most. Nearing his thirteenth birthday, Sami stood five-five and weighed only sixty pounds. "I saw a lot of changes in my son's health," recalled Samir. "He lost weight and he was always sick and had stomach pains." Complicating matters was the cultural shock of adjusting to life in another a new country. "In Lebanon was also tough days," continued Samir. "Life there is quite different. You must declare your religion, Muslim or Christian, and if Muslim you have to say Sunni or Shiite. It was so tough for Sami especially as he didn't speak Arabic at that time and had no idea what they were talking about. He tried to fit in but he couldn't." Sami's parents were born into Shiite families, but they were not religious and did not attend mosque, so Sami did not know the difference between Sunnis and Shias and could not communicate with others even if he did.

Samir scraped up the money to enroll Sami in an American school in Saida, Lebanon, a city of 160,000 located on the Mediterranean coast about twenty-five miles south of Beirut. (Sami would learn both Arabic and English there.) But again he experienced cultural dislocation. Most of the students at the school came from wealthy families, and Sami's comparative poverty set him apart from his peers and made him feel like a social outcast. "I felt shame, and I felt I had to lie about my family and who I was in order to get accepted by them," Sami recalled.[24] This lying about his social status set in motion a behavioral trait that Sami's lawyers would later call the first of his many efforts to be a "psychological and social chameleon." Essentially, Sami developed the capacity to "become whatever his current situation demanded in order to fit in and escape attack."

In 2002, the Hassouns moved to a Sunni neighborhood in Beirut, where Sami's ability for being a chameleon was put to the test. To fit into the religious scheme of the neighborhood, Sami lied about being a Sunni when he was around Sunnis and about being a Shia when he was in the company of Shiites. And in order to fit into the economic scheme of things, he turned to crime, beginning with theft and drug dealing, and eventually his life "spun out of control."[25]

Sami was still attending school in Saida, making the two-hour round trip commute from Beirut each day by bus, where he was introduced to the trappings of a criminal subculture. He became obsessed with the mob movies *Scarface* and *The Godfather* and began dressing like a Western gangster with flashy shirts and pointed Italian shoes. Sami may have been a poor kid who had to take the bus to school instead of driving his own car like the other students, but at least now he stood out—like broken glass on a beach, just the way he wanted it. Reminiscent of his early life in Ivory Coast, Sami became popular—but within a clique of other troublemakers—and he started a teenage romance with "the most beautiful girl in school," as he would describe her.[26]

Around this time his behavior underwent a noticeable change due mainly to his commitment to family and the gangster lifestyle. The entire Hassoun clan would witness the transformation. During this period, one of Sami's many uncles was involved in a real estate scam leading to the loss of some property held by the Hassoun family and further adding to Samir Hassoun's financial woes. Sami decided to take matters into his own hands. At a gathering of more than a hundred family members, Sami pulled a pistol on the uncle and threatened to kill him. After he calmed down, another uncle took Sami aside and gave him a stern warning that if he was not careful, he was "going to crash." But there was a bright spot on the horizon. Siham was pregnant again, and in 2003 she gave birth to a son, Adnan, giving Sami a little brother to care for.

But physically, he was a wreck. Sami's stomach attacks continued, starting with a fast build-up of symptoms: high-grade fever and unendurable abdominal pain causing him to walk bent over and rendering him bedridden, followed by a spontaneous remission, until the next attack occurred. Twice he was admitted to the American University of Beirut Medical Center, where doctors evaluated him. On January 23, 2003, when Sami was fourteen years old, he was finally diagnosed as suffering from Familial Mediterranean Fever (FMF), a hereditary disease affecting people of Sephardic Jewish, Arabic, Turkish, and Armenian ancestry. FMF presents as severe stomach and chest pains, fever, and neurological manifestations that can lead to impairment of social development. The disease is known to be exacerbated by stress. FMF cannot be cured, but it can be managed with daily doses of the prescription drug colchicine, which sold on the Lebanese pharmaceutical market for the U.S. equivalent of $4.85 per tablet. Sami began taking colchicine when his family could afford it. When they could not, he went without and endured the pain, sometimes relying on another kind of medicine—heroin.

War and Identity Transformation

On February 14, 2005, former Lebanese Prime Minister Rafic Hariri was killed along with twenty-one others when a massive TNT bomb exploded as his motorcade drove near the St. George Hotel in Beirut. Lebanese security forces later found compelling evidence that the assassination was carried out by Hezbollah. The assassination set off religious conflicts and days of protests and riots. "The memories of Abidjan all came back," Sami recalled. "I was living in fear and now I had a baby brother . . . who I was worried about. I didn't want him to have to witness and see all this, to have to live my past through all this chaos."[27]

There seemed to be no end to the chaos. By 2006, the Hassouns had relocated to Saida where they took up residence in an inner-city apartment building next to a power plant. On July 12, 2006, Hezbollah fired rockets at Israeli border towns and attacked two armored Humvees patrolling the Israeli side of the border, leaving three dead soldiers. Hezbollah kidnaped two Israeli soldiers and took them to Lebanon, demanding the release of Lebanese prisoners held by Israel. Israel refused, and over the next thirty-four days Israeli fighter jets pounded Lebanon with airstrikes; targets included civilian infrastructure. Buildings in Beirut and Saida were destroyed, and smoke filled the sky. Roads and bridges were closed, and homes were bombed. As entire neighborhoods were flattened, the International Committee of the Red Cross expressed "serious concern about the humanitarian consequences of the current conflict on the people of Lebanon." Before it was over, the Israelis would kill some 1,300 Lebanese, one third of them children, and displace approximately one million. At the height of the war, a child psychologist told the Associated Press that her clients were showing a variety of disturbing symptoms, ranging from depression and hypertension to withdrawal.

Sami Hassoun was likewise affected; the war damaged him both mentally and physically. Saida was hit hard by the bombing, leaving the city a cauldron of suffering and despair. "I saw people with their hands and legs blown off in hospitals," said Sami, who lost relatives and friends to the violence and watched as children lay dying in the streets. Amid these events, the Israelis bombed the power plant next to the Hassoun apartment, shaking the building's foundation, shattering all of its windows, and causing Sami to go momentarily deaf. "It took years from my life that day," recalled Siham. "We ran almost naked to the basement. Sami had awful stomach pains and fever from the stress of the bombings and the war. He was so sick at that time, but all he wanted is to protect his little brother."

As the war wore on, against the advice of his parents, Sami felt compelled to help with the national relief effort by volunteering through a charity organization. Sami recalled that "Saida was like a zoo, with people sleeping in the streets and in schools. People were constantly being rushed to the hospitals, and I saw bodies cut in half and people with their brains out in front of my eyes." The charity organization later issued a statement saying that Sami was "among the few volunteers who kept working . . . who risked their lives . . . to help the displaced people to receive aid during those times. Lives were saved because of people like Sami Samir Hassoun."

The war had a profound effect on Sami's worldview, and it elicited a fundamental aspect of his character: unfailing kindness for those in need. "I used to fear death," he would later say about his service during the war, "but then I didn't care anymore. I said to myself, 'I'll be dead or alive, whatever.'" Sami also did volunteer work at a home for elderly people, where he was recognized by the head administrator for having an "affectionate heart that radiates warmth to the elderly." He bought sandwiches for some homeless teenagers on the streets and gave away his jacket and umbrella to a homeless man.

The Israel-Hezbollah War of 2006 unleashed a rampant criminality upon the streets of Saida and Beirut. This also had a profound effect on Sami, and it hardened his identity as a budding gangster. "I saw people doing whatever it took to survive," he said. "Young girls were prostituting, crime went up, there was raping." This was not a world of Islamic militias trying to conquer the Middle East, but of straight up criminals. Sami explained his identity transformation like this:

After we survived [the war], a great shift in my life happened. I became a person that's not me. I wanted money in any way. I wanted to run the street life. I became so cold; I wanted to be part of the underworld. If we had money and were rich we would be safe and we could leave [Lebanon]. Money was a big issue in my life. I'm going to make money at any cost. I was such a good liar. I would believe in my own lies. Reality and lying became one in my head. Lying made me feel smarter than anyone else. I could do and be anything or anyone by lying.[28]

When the war ended, Sami befriended a street hustler named Amir—"kind of slow in the head"—and the two began boosting clothing and pulling off minor crimes until they had a falling out, at which point Amir warned Sami, "One day, you're going to crash."[29] Sami also met some refugees from southern Lebanon who were running a prostitution ring in Saida, and they formed a short-lived gang. Some were Hezbollah but Sami wanted nothing to do with their politics. He was interested only in making money. The gang gathered to discuss plans in the bombed-out rubble of a hospital. Lying next to them was a pile of dead bodies. "They had their heads blown off, arms blown off," said Sami." He organized a human smuggling operation within the gang yet nothing came of it. "I thought I might turn a buck on the deal," said Sami, but the gang was ill-suited to the complex criminal skills required for human smuggling. By this time, Sami was eighteen years old and living in his parents' apartment with no electricity, running water, or food. He was broke, stressed out, and often in physical pain.

His parents did all they could. In the fall of 2006, they paid for Sami's tuition at the prestigious American University of Beirut (AUB). He moved into a dorm and took classes in archeology, chemistry, geology, and calculus, but he was haunted by the trauma of war and had trouble concentrating on his studies. After breaking up with his girlfriend, and breaking his arm in a fight with her brother over the affair, Sami fell into a depression. But he still needed to make money, so he did what a gangster does. Upon meeting a group of wealthy Saudi students on the AUB campus, he began robbing them of their cash and credit cards. "I made lots of money off those Saudi kids," he confessed about the muggings. Essentially, Sami was unprepared for college at this point in his life. "I didn't want to study," he said, "just make money."[30] While his grades fell, Sami turned more and more to drug dealing. Among his customers was an attractive AUB English professor who took Sami to her bed, improving his self-image and proving a definite adjunct to the gangster lifestyle. After three semesters of poor performance, Sami dropped out of school and returned to his family in Saida. He continued his criminal career, though, and became further hooked into a subculture that would eventually lead to Sami's calamitous encounter with an FBI informant.

The Chicago Sting

In the spring of 2009, police in Chicago arrested an Arab drug dealer known only as Nadim on charges of distributing marijuana. Upon being questioned, Nadim said that he had recently sold some pot to a young foreigner who worked at a Lebanese bakery and that the kid was interested in moving product for the Assyrian Mafia, a powerful drug smuggling gang based in Turkey. With Nadim facing stiff jail time, detectives were able to flip him and turn him over to the FBI, where agents recognized his potential as a Confidential Informant (CI) in the domestic war on terrorism. Nadim was assigned to meet and befriend the young man at the bakery. He soon came back with essentials: The suspect's name was Sami Hassoun, and he lived at 4720 N. Kedzie Avenue, Chicago and drove a gold Honda with Illinois plates. "He was like a father figure to me," said Sami of Nadim, "and he had a lot of influence on me."[31]

The Hassoun family had begun making plans to move to the United States following the war in Lebanon. Sami's parents wanted to get away from the political turmoil of the Middle East and provide their sons with educational opportunities in America. After months of waiting, their U.S. visas were approved and in July 2008, together with the family of one of Sami's uncles, the Hassouns arrived at O'Hare International Airport hoping to find a good life in the Promised Land and recoup their losses from the Ivory Coast disaster. They would rely on relatives for financial support until something came along. They found a four-bedroom upper apartment on Kedzie Avenue, a major north–south Chicago artery featuring a number of Mediterranean restaurants. After buying some used furniture for the apartment, Sami set out to find a job, enthused by his prospects. "Back in Lebanon it's a dream for people to come to America," he said, "and they make you believe 'you could pick up money with a shovel' from how much money you could make."[32] It would not be that easy: 2008 was the midpoint of the Great Recession when U.S. unemployment rates inched toward 10 percent. After beating the streets of Chicago for weeks, Sami landed a job as a baker's manager at Nazareth Sweets, known for their freshly baked baklava, located down the street from the apartment at 4806 Kedzie. He was offered $500 a week and expected to work long hours. That was it: Sami was now the breadwinner for a family of four.

Shortly after he began working at the bakery, Sami took notice of several customers who "had something going on," he said, "big stacks of money. Some of them were Latin Kings and Assyrian Mafia with nice cars. Greed started to hit me."[33] Ever the gangster and wanting to get started in this scene, Sami looked around for a weed connection and met "an Arab guy" who was selling primo buds for $1,000 an ounce. This was Nadim, a member of the Assyrian Mafia. Nadim offered Sami a deal on some pot and began to advise him on how to do things in the Windy City. "Nadim filled an empty spot for me," recalled Sami, "and I started making $500 here and there."[34] But then Nadim got busted, and the calculus changed. When Sami told Nadim (after the bust) that he had a source in Detroit for some fake Viagra, Nadim was all in, "wanting to know everything," said Sami. "And I trusted him as a protector. I started selling the Viagra to win Nadim's attention."[35]

Given his obsession with pleasing people, Sami was a perfect foil for Nadim's informant work. Nadim was a lot older than Sami. He wore a beard, spoke fluid Arabic, and had the best reefer on Kedzie Ave. He also spoke the language of jihad and had been a paid informant for the FBI on a previous sting investigation. Moreover, after his drug arrest Nadim was paid by the FBI to engage Sami Hassoun in an act of domestic terrorism over the course of the next year—perhaps earning as much as $100,000 and also requesting immigration benefits for his services. All of this was granted by the FBI in the name of counteracting violent extremism in the post-9/11 era.

Nadim and Sami began meeting several times a week and developed a friendship. To impress Nadim with his gangster bona fides, Sami began to fabricate stories about his criminal exploits in Chicago, saying that he had already sold heroin, robbed a stash house run by the Latin Kings, and in just two-weeks' time had slung over ten kilos of cocaine at $25,000 a package. It was all talk on Sami's part; he was playing his role as a social and psychological chameleon.

In the fall of 2009, a young white girl from Evansville, Indiana, known only as Anne, walked into the bakery and struck up a conversation with Sami. The two flirted, and soon Sami had his first American girlfriend. According to Sami, Anne "had needs" she couldn't satisfy. She did not like the car she drove, hated her job, had a mound of debt, and was in a bad

relationship with a dentist. Anne also had a backstory that Sami was unaware of. She too had been busted for drugs and flipped by the government into the role of a CI. Sami now had not one but two FBI informants
on his trail.

Just as the FBI sting was getting underway, on the bitterly cold night of
December 14, 2009, a nineteen-year-old Syrian American psychology student from Kansas named Duaa Albadawi stumbled into Nazareth Sweets
by mistake and asked Sami for directions to a restaurant where she was
meeting friends for dinner. It was love at first sight. After making small
talk, they exchanged digits, and soon their romance was off and running.
"Sami was a number of things," Duaa recalled: "charming, intelligent, and
ambitious. We would stay up all night talking on the phone. . . . Sami was
my soul-mate."

At this crucial juncture in his life, according to Sami, Nadim "began
fishing. Saying we should do something in Chicago. I played along because
I'm a compulsive liar."[36] It was not yet clear what that "something" might
be, but around this time Sami saw a television program alleging corruption in the administration of Chicago Mayor Richard M. Daley. Sami had
never heard of Mayor Daley and knew nothing about his administration.
Nevertheless, Sami's interest in Mayor Daley planted the seed for a terrorist attack organized by the FBI.

Sami turned twenty-two on January 20, 2010. He had packed a lifetime
into two decades. Most remarkably, he had endured civil strife and war.
But his parents had never sought psychological counseling for the trauma
he went through. "I feel so bad I never took Sami to a psychologist," reflected his mother. "He never received any kind of mental health treatment, none after [the] Ivory Coast coup or after [the] Lebanon war. I didn't
know he needed help." But he needed a lot of help. A later BOP medical
evaluation would reveal that at this time Sami was not only suffering from
recurring bouts of fever and stomach pains from his Familial Mediterranean Fever, but also experiencing sharp pains in his upper back, which
caused him to writhe in agony and give a look of extreme distress. He also
had chronic dental problems from grinding his teeth to the pulp, conjunc-
tivitis (pink eye), acute constipation, and gastritis. And he had a severe substance abuse problem. "After my twenty-second birthday," he recalled, "I
would start drinking in the morning and continue drinking throughout
the day. By two or three months before my crime [September 2010], I was

drinking all day, every day. I was at the point where I would open a bottle of Johnnie Walker Black in the morning and finish it by evening, while also drinking vodka and beer. I used drugs, too, to deal with the thoughts that were eating away at me. I smoked marijuana two to three times daily. . . . I was using cocaine and ecstasy multiple times per week, and even tried heroin."[37]

Many things were eating away at him. First, as always, was the money problem. He was barely getting by on his salary from Nazareth Sweets and had recently become involved in a counterfeiting scam with someone in Kansas, which further contributed to the FBI's interest in him. He was also showing signs of stress at home. His mother noticed that Sami was growing nervous and moody. He stayed out late every night and was prone to fits of crying. He had a seven-year-old brother to worry about and now, a fiancé. He and Duaa Albadawi were engaged to be married, but this also caused Sami stress because Duaa came from a wealthy Kansas City family, and Sami feared that he would lose her because he did not make enough money at the bakery. Sami calculated that "to be with her needs a million dollars."[38] "I didn't want to lose her—at any cost. I wanted to impress her because I thought she would love me more when I had money."[39]

The solution to this problem, and the source of his greatest stress, was to so impress Nadim that he would connect Sami to the Assyrian Mafia and its pot of drug gold. Nadim was aggressively grooming Sami for this role, knowing full well that his weak spot was money. But it was a long shot for both Sami and the FBI. Nadim was himself an unpredictable figure, and this became acutely obvious to the FBI when, a week after Sami's birthday (while still working on the Hassoun case), Nadim was again arrested on a federal drug charge, leading the FBI to admonish him and question his suitability for the sting. The FBI would deal with this problem by first allowing Nadim to ensnare his target into the sting, and then cutting him loose as soon as possible.

Concocting the Threat of Lone Wolf Terrorism

While Nadim had been working Sami for about six months at this point, he was not close to turning Sami into a terrorist. That would take more time, patience, and a gradual approach, which began with a plan to set up Sami as a major heroin dealer in Chicago. This would not be difficult since

Sami would sell whatever drug made him money, or do whatever Nadim told him. A psychologist who later examined Sami would argue that his untreated war trauma compromised Sami's ability to resist the antisocial influences of the government's CI. Yet when Nadim proposed the heroin trafficking idea to his FBI handlers in March 2010, he was again admonished, this time for skirting the legal boundaries of entrapment.

It would be Sami himself, always the grandiose talker, who provided the first breakthrough, when on May 13 he made a comment to Nadim about the Times Square bombing attempt in New York by Faisal Shahzad. In another effort to impress Nadim, Sami made the outlandish claim that he could build such a bomb from nothing more than baking soda, explaining that he had received bomb training in Africa and Beirut four years ago. While that was another bold-faced lie, this was the first time that the subject of a bomb came up in their discussions, and Nadim adopted a new strategy as a result: He would let Sami talk all he wanted, and eventually he would talk himself into handcuffs. Such a strategy is consistent with Hassoun's character. "I'm a storyteller," said Sami.[40]

By now Sami had lost his job at Nazareth Sweets but had found employment as a cashier at a Lebanese grocery store on Kedzie Avenue called Sanabel Bakery where he was expected to work six and a half days each week and do what he was told. His employer later said that Sami "worked tirelessly . . . taking on even the most difficult work assignments . . . to help his family buy groceries and pay rent." To impress Nadim, Sami made up a story that the grocery store and a neighboring school were run by al-Qaeda. This was the first mention of al-Qaeda, and it led Nadim to up the ante with Sami at a June 2 meeting at the Hookah Lounge on Kedzie, where Nadim said that he had connections to "two friends" who were capable of committing an act of terrorism in the United States. They would pay Sami to help if he was in. Sami knew little about terrorism, but mention of the "two friends" and their money provided him with a wider set of enablers beyond the CI. Nadim sensed another opening when Sami said that he wanted to start "a revolution" and had recently done an Internet search on Mayor Daley, trying to find a weak spot in his daily schedule. Sami bragged about multiple file folders he was keeping on the mayor, which were aimed at determining when and where to get him. What he planned to do to Daley, said Sami, depended on how much money he could get from the highest bidder. Then he brainstormed some ideas: placing a bomb in downtown Chicago for $20,000; poisoning the city's water supply, or unleashing a biological weapon, which would cost more. He knew not a thing about bombs, poison, or biological weaponry. As his attorney later said, Sami was simply "an incompetent who talked too much."

A crucial date in the conspiracy was June 4, when Sami and Nadim met at an undisclosed Chicago hotel for what was essentially a dry run for a future meeting with Nadim's "two friends." Nadim was wearing a wire, and his plan was to let Sami talk all he wanted about whatever he wanted to talk about. Sami was a storyteller and a serious substance abuser, which may explain the bizarre plot that unfolded.

At the meeting, Sami introduced the harebrained idea that they could somehow overthrow the City of Chicago in a gangster coup. He proposed that they set off a bomb near Wrigley Field, home of the Chicago Cubs, in order to embarrass Mayor Daley and force his resignation, thereby paving the way for a replacement mayoral candidate whom Sami and Nadim could buy off and manage. Thus they would take over the City of Chicago and its billion dollar economy, become rich beyond measure, and have all their problems solved. After the bombing, they could distance themselves from their actions by sending a video to the media claiming responsibility in the name of either al-Qaeda or a fictitious Islamist group. "Call it, 'the jihad in U.S.,'" said Sami. "Just make something up . . . . So all the heat is transferred to them."[41] The following exchange illustrates the patience and interviewing skills that made Nadim a top-notch informant:

CI: How long you been thinkin' about this?

HASSOUN: About a year, man.

CI: What, when did you . . .

HASSOUN: Every time I feel like uh, strangled, you know, American stuff.

CI: Yeah.

HASSOUN: Sit myself down, ideas come.

CI: What, what started this? Why, why didn't, what prompted this change?

HASSOUN: You know like, like, when I started working I see, like, how it's, it's like back home here. You have the money and the power, you do anything you wanna do. You know. . . . It's like I see police buying, bought off in front of me.

HASSOUN: And, there's no jobs out there. That's what pisses me off. Because of, because of Daley.[42]

This recorded conversation about criminal motive, and the very mention of jihad and al-Qaeda, was exactly what Nadim's FBI supervisors were looking for. It provided the grist for creating a myth that Sami Hassoun was an Islamic terrorist, even though he had never read the Koran, had never set foot inside a mosque, and could not explain the difference between a Sunni and a Shiite. Most lone wolf terrorists combine personal frustrations with wider political grievances. Sami had his share of the former but none of the latter. His motive was making money, not influencing the government for political reasons. Nor did anything in his criminal history suggest that he had the skills necessary to bomb Wrigley Field, let alone take over Chicago. Yet, Nadim enabled the ludicrous plot by saying that he had Assyrian Mafia brothers in California who were willing to put "green on the table" if Sami would help them commit the bombing. Predictably, Sami said that he had already been on his laptop researching ways to make a bomb like the one used by McVeigh in Oklahoma City. Digging himself an even deeper hole, Sami also made a threat against the dentist involved with Anne around this time. All of this highly incriminating evidence was thrown into the FBI's mythmaking machine.

Between June 7 and June 9, Nadim made three calls to Sami attempting to arrange a meeting at a Starbucks coffee shop where they could discuss possible targets around Wrigley Field, encouraging Sami to come up with specific suggestions and to write down a list of bomb-making components they would need. The next crucial meeting took place at an undisclosed location on June 14. Sami showed up in an anxious mood, saying that he had been with Anne at a bar over the weekend and was in an altercation with a guy over Anne's needs. Sami said that he had a lot on his mind. Although it took longer than expected, Sami had produced the list of bomb-making ingredients consistent with the Oklahoma City bombing— Tovex sausages, blasting caps, detonators, a timer, and dynamite; Nadim said that he had delivered it to the brothers and that they were making plans to meet Sami. Instead of a lethal bomb, though, Sami proposed that the plot should involve a fake bomb that would merely cause public hysteria, assuming that no one would be injured. Sami was specific as to how this would happen. He would intentionally leave one wire disconnected so the bomb would not explode. Sami indicated that he had been thinking about placing the fake bomb at the upcoming Arabian Festival held at the Daley Center. Then maybe they could do the same thing around Wrigley Field. Fake bombs were not what the CI had in mind, so another meeting was scheduled for June 22. In a further effort to ingratiate himself to Nadim at this meeting, Sami said that he had recently received a bomb-making manual from relatives in Lebanon. It contained instructions for making non-traceable explosives (another lie). "Little by little, I'm building it up," boasted Sami. "I will fuck Chicago."[43]

A turning point in the conspiracy came on July 8. Driving a vehicle provided by the FBI, Nadim picked up Sami around noon and headed to an Embassy Suites Hotel on North Columbus Drive to meet one of the Assyrian Mafia brothers from California. During the ride, Nadim asked Sami if he was ready to meet the brother, and Sami replied that he was ready to impress him and that he had been waiting for this day. The Assyrian Mafia brother (the first of Nadim's "two friends") was an undercover FBI agent, and all conversations would be taped.

Once inside room 838, Nadim got the ball rolling by asking Sami to tell the brother about his plans for revolution. Sami told a long and mostly fictitious story about his upbringing before launching into a tirade about the Chicago police force, saying that they had "been undermined by [Mayor Daley] reducing it by 40 percent" and followed up with the idea that they should "take advantage of [the situation] to replace the Mayor." Sami was again clear that he did not want to use real bombs, but said that if they planted some fake bombs, "the people will blame the security and the police officers" and then "will start blaming Daley."[44] At the close of the meeting, Nadim set the hook in Sami by saying: "The people in California are very interested in your genius ideas and you will make millions of dollars." Those words sealed the fate of Sami Hassoun and provided the triggering event for his involvement in a terrorist conspiracy. He was not strong enough to extricate himself from a hustle to make "millions of dollars." Essentially, the FBI had its sting target, and Sami was all in, at any cost.

At 2:40 P.M., July 21, Sami knocked on the door of room 3088 at the Hilton O'Hare Hotel where he was greeted by the undercover FBI agent who introduced him to a second undercover agent. His work on the case now complete, Nadim was not present. It was time for the conspiracy to move on to practical matters. Sami began with explaining his plan to create chaos in Chicago and erode trust in the city's leadership, saying that the attacks should be designed solely to create fear using fake bombs that would "ignite but don't blow." Together, the three drove to Wrigley Field, where they discussed places to plant such a device, and then on to Daley Plaza.

When one agent asked Sami precisely how they would parlay their attack into political control of the city (by forcing Mayor Daley out and replacing him with one of their own), Sami replied: "I have no clue." (This was characteristic of Hassoun's criminal profile dating back to his failed attempt to run a human smuggling operation in Lebanon. Now, in the Chicago sting, he would repeatedly tell agents that he had no way of executing his fantasies.) The agent told Sami that there would be no shame in backing out of the plot at this point, but Sami was intransigent, saying "to make a change, you have to sacrifice people."[45] This was obviously another attempt to please the agent since Sami was interested only in fake bombs. Sami grew impatient, saying that so far he had been the only one to advance the plot forward, so he chastised the agents, demanding "a more serious" commitment from them and adding that he was barely surviving on his baker's salary.

He was clearly feeling the stress of the situation, and as before, it triggered his FMF attacks, sending Sami into life-threatening substance abuse. So days later, to placate Sami and keep him in the mix, the agents put Hassoun on the FBI payroll, ultimately paying him roughly $3,000, most of which he gave to his parents. Sami was at least able to quit his boring job at Sanabel Bakery and free to work full time for the FBI on a case that was expressly designed to put him behind bars for decades.

This far down the line in most cases of lone wolf terrorism, there will be a broadcasting of intent, usually to family members or online sympathizers. While Sami's recorded conversations with the FBI are replete with statements about his intent to take over Chicago, there is no evidence that he announced his intent to anyone beyond the conspirators. There is not a sliver of evidence in Sami's Facebook postings about Chicago politics, Mayor Daley, or jihad. He said nothing about these things to his family or co-workers; nor did he mention them to Duaa Albadawi, his soul mate, who never heard Sami say a word about Mayor Daley. That was entirely the product of Sami's imaginative naivety and the FBI's exploitation of his personal vulnerabilities. Most likely, Sami did not broadcast his intent to others because he was told to keep his mouth shut by the government agents inside the conspiracy. He would get his money, but only if he kept quiet. His silence was essential for FBI mythmaking.

Sami may have been all in with the conspiracy but he was not yet committed to killing. He had been clear about this in the July 8 meeting when he told an agent that he was not planning to kill anybody but to plant several fake bombs. He repeated this on July 21, saying that the devices would "ignite but don't explode." But fake bombs do not make a myth unless they are planted under FBI supervision. Everything changed after an August 16 meeting with both agents inside room 248 at the Residence Inn Hotel in Rosemont, Illinois, where one of the agents informed Sami:

> I talked to my brothers over there [in California] and we were talking and I just, okay, it is going to be a lot easier to get, probably, explosives than what we were talking about, what you would prefer.[46]

In other words, it was the FBI who made the final determination that the bomb would be real, not Sami Hassoun. He "preferred" fake bombs. Sami considered the FBI agents to be the supervisors of the plot, which they were, and saw himself as their employee, which he was. Sami would later tell agents, "I do what I'm asked to do." So, in reply to the agent's talk about live explosives Sami responded: "If you want, you can bring me whatever you want and I will plant it. . . . You bring me a bag and I, I will plant it."[47] The meeting ended with Sami being given a new laptop computer to replace his old laptop bought by his father in Ivory Coast back in 1996. He was also given a new camcorder and $1,000 in cash. All of this pleased Sami, and he doubled his commitment to the plot.

Because Sami was totally inexperienced with bomb building, he was told by agents that "the brothers" would construct the device. On the day of the attack, they would set the timer and activate the bomb's arming mechanism. The purpose of all of this was not to prevent an imminent threat of violence by Sami Hassoun, but for the FBI to gain credit for thwarting another terrorist attack on American soil.

By late August, at the FBI's insistence, Sami (intoxicated on whiskey and any number of other substances and accompanied once by an unknown "friend from Lebanon") had conducted three surveillance runs to the Wrigley Field area, which he filmed with his camcorder. When he was debriefed by agents on the evening of August 14, Sami was once again told that he could back out of the plot and that he would "still be friends" with the brothers, but Sami insisted "I can do it."[48] Using cash given to him by the FBI in July, he had also purchased a backpack and batteries and handed them over to one of the agents—still thinking that he was working for the Assyrian Mafia in a "genius" plan to make millions of dollars.

On September 9, experts at the FBI crime lab in Quantico were ordered to construct "an inert device using the back pack and batteries HASSOUN brought to the 08/31/2010 meeting." The device was to be made of six inert blocks of C4 explosive, ball bearings, an inert blasting cap, and a digital timer. Back in Chicago, agents decided that the delivery method for the explosives would be a backpack bomb and set a time and date for the attack. It would come down at midnight, September 18, following a concert by the Dave Matthews Band at Wrigley Field, when the neighborhood bars would be crowded. Sami was unfamiliar with the Dave Matthews Band and had no concept of the jam band culture surrounding Wrigley Field in the summertime. That was the FBI's touch of mythmaking. Not only would the concert provide a dramatic news story about the sting, but because most of these bars served beer made outside the state of Illinois, this violation of interstate commerce laws would contribute to the federal charges against their sting target. Sami agreed to carry the backpack bomb and was told that it would contain enough shrapnel and C-4 explosive to destroy half a city block.

While Sami may not have broadcasted his intent to commit this act of state-sponsored terrorism, he clearly experienced great agony in the days leading up to the attack. Duaa Albadawi later recalled that in September 2010, "I began to notice some strange behavior that Sami had never displayed before. He would call me at times panting, stuttering his words, asking me to stay on the phone with him until he fell asleep. . . . During that period, he would call me every single hour of the day." On the day before the attack, Sami kept Duaa on the line for five hours, never saying what was bothering him. Sami's father also saw the despair. "I noticed changes," he said. "Sami was lying to us and stayed out till late, coming home very moody and his sickness increased." On the morning of the attack, Samir found Sami crying in bed. "I asked him why, but he always said nothing." In our conversation at Leavenworth years later, Sami was asked what he did when he rose from bed that morning. "I started drinking," he said.

So came Saturday night, September 18, 2010. Around eleven o'clock, Sami met the agents at a Rosemont hotel, where they discussed his plans to flee Chicago after the bombing. The agents told Sami to lay low for several days and then catch a flight to California where the brothers would meet him and provide safe housing. To tide him over until his plane left, an agent peeled five $100 bills from his roll and gave them to Sami. He slid into the passenger's seat of a white FBI-rented van, and it departed for Wrigley Field. On the way, an agent set the bomb's timer switch for thirty minutes but

Sami complained (in Arabic) that thirty minutes was too long, so the agent reset the timer to twenty minutes. Capturing it all was a concealed camcorder on the dashboard. The agents dropped Sami off near the ballpark just past midnight. Three sheets to the wind by now, Sami walked up the crowded sidewalk wearing a black hoodie and carrying a gray shopping bag containing the backpack. To complete the concoction of this sordid scenario, another FBI agent stood down the street secretly filming the scene, which would soon be introduced as evidence in federal court and then posted on YouTube. The film shows Sami dropping the bag into a trash receptacle outside Slugger's Lounge and walking away at a brisk pace. He was instantly arrested for the attempted use of a weapon of mass destruction and branded a lone wolf terrorist by the FBI.

Sami Hassoun was no saint, but neither was he a terrorist. Terrorism requires a political motive, and prosecutors acknowledged that Sami was not inspired by ideological extremism, religious fanaticism, or any other firmly held conviction. He displayed none of the characteristics common to the radicalization of lone wolf terrorists. There was no integration of a personal vendetta with a political grievance, no affinity with online sympathizers who encouraged extremism, no broadcasting of terrorist intent to family or friends, and no identity transformation into an armed warrior. He was driven solely by an immature desire to fit in and impress people within a criminal subculture that had been deliberately created by the FBI. Hassoun's preposterous plan to stage a gangster coup against the city of Chicago would have never gone beyond the talking stages were it not for the FBI's direct enabling. Not only did FBI agents provide Sami with a fake bomb and the training and transportation to use it, but they gave him a sense of purpose and belonging. Nadim was especially devious in this regard, at one point telling Sami that if he convinced the agents of his violent predisposition—the necessary legal requirement for the FBI to avoid entrapment—they would take Sami "into their family." And if he followed their directions, they would provide him with "a house and a nice car." On top of that, the Assyrian Mafia promised Sami millions of dollars if he detonated the bomb outside Slugger's Lounge, a promise that ultimately triggered his crime.

This is what FBI stings look like from the inside. "Over time," says a prominent legal scholar on FBI sting operations, "the suspect's acts turn out to be more and more remote from acts of violence themselves, and more like potential beginning steps in a direction that might or might not someday take the suspect in the direction of jihadi violence."[49] Stings are designed to push suspects in the direction of jihadi violence, rather than push them toward a means for addressing personal problems that can be at the heart of a violent tendency. Massive resources are being spent on this program. The FBI budget for 2016 exceeds $8.4 billion, and most is going to countering violent extremism. Much of the FBI's intelligence in this area involves informant provocateurs working in Muslim communities. It is estimated that ten times as many FBI informants are on the streets today as there were during the COINTELPRO program under J. Edgar Hoover.[50] To keep this enormous bureaucracy afloat, the FBI must continue to show the White House and Congress that violent extremism is an imminent threat to national security. This demands that agents amplify the threat of Islamic terrorism by producing compelling narratives of deadly attacks that they have foiled. Sami Hassoun is a paradigmatic case in this regard: Without the deceitful FBI informant and a deliberate FBI mythmaking campaign that ultimately (and ironically) did more to romanticize the jihadi life than anything else, there would be no case against him. According to our research, the same can be said for the other stings against Muslim Americans since 9/11. Every one of them involved an exaggerated threat of terrorism and an overeager informant who exploited the vulnerabilities of easily susceptible men on the margins of society. Alas, FBI agents and informants have themselves been *radicalized* by the policy of countering violent extremism.

Conclusion

Countering Lone Wolf Terrorism

T he United States can play an important role in countering the international threat of lone wolf terrorism. Indeed, America has more experience with this particular form of political violence than any other nation. Research indicates that the United States leads the world in lone wolf terrorism; an estimated 40 percent of the world's lone wolf terrorism attacks have occurred in the United States.[1] This may be due to any number of reasons, be it America's tradition of individualism, its gun culture, or its foreign policies, the echoes of slavery, the appeal of conspiracy theories, celebrity worship, or what Richard Hofstadter famously called the "paranoid style" in American politics. "The distinguishing thing about the paranoid style," Hofstadter wrote about the American radical Right in 1964 though he could have been describing today's antigovernment extremists and jihadists as well, "is that the paranoid spokesman sees the fate of conspiracy in apocalyptic terms—he traffics in the birth and death of whole worlds, whole political orders, and whole systems of human values. He is always manning the barricades of civilization. He constantly lives at a turning point."[2]

Lone wolf terrorism is a complex crime that will present enormous challenges for security agencies in the years ahead. Given its familiarity with the phenomenon, America's efforts to prevent lone wolf terrorism may provide the kind of information that authorities in other countries can either use in their prevention strategies, or avoid because they have proven ineffective.

The United States has a three-pronged approach for combatting lone wolf terrorism and each has its complications. The first is digital diplomacy designed primarily to prevent terrorist attacks from abroad. Since 9/11, the U.S. State Department and the National Security Staff at the White House have tried a range of approaches for engaging youth of the Middle East— from slick Madison Avenue public relation campaigns to student exchange programs and visitation initiatives—but they have shown little promise in curbing radicalization. Nonetheless, since the emergence of ISIS in 2013 and its growth to approximately 38,000 foreign fighters in Syria alone, the government has redoubled its efforts to engage young people online with the hope of reaching potential jihadists across the globe. Realizing that ISIS has achieved wider resonance than al-Qaeda ever did due to its mass use of social media, the State Department currently operates websites in Muslim-majority countries, where it posts a stream of anti-ISIS messages including information on the group's battlefield losses and moral failings, which are in turn reposted numerous times each day on Facebook, You-Tube, Twitter, or Ask.fm using the hashtag #Think Again Turn Away. The campaign's slogan is "Contest the Space"—a concept introduced by President Obama in a September 24, 2014, speech before the United Nations in which he said that the fight against extremism demands "contesting the space that terrorists occupy—including the Internet and social media."[3]

Yet the program has many critics. Some contend that the government's digital workforce is vastly outnumbered by ISIS's multilingual online supporters (an estimated fifty thousand "fan boys" and "fan girls" around the world) who encourage allegiance to the group through what the UN Security Council describes as a "cosmopolitan" embrace of social media platforms, which have displaced the "long and turgid messaging" from al-Qaeda.[4] Of special concern to the FBI is the recent switch by ISIS supporters to encrypted communication via the dark web, which makes online monitoring almost impossible and has led FBI Director Comey to confess that the radicalization problem may be too difficult to fix.[5] Other critics argue that America's digital diplomacy is seen by young Muslims as a blatant attempt at manipulating their perceptions and that the program of "tweeting at terrorists" actually worsens attitudes toward the West. In short, the counter-narrative has no brand. It represents an anemic attempt at neutralizing the urbane recruitment efforts of ISIS. ISIS's spectacular online beheading videos, in particular, are largely intended to serve as a recruiting tool for Western youth by projecting courage and power through what terrorism scholars call "jihadi cool" whereby "it is fashionable to emulate terrorists."[6] From a Syrian battlefield in August of 2014, for instance, Abdel Bary, a twenty-three-year-old British rapper, uploaded to Twitter a picture of himself holding up a severed head. The caption read: "Chillin' with my homie or what's left of him."[7]

Some scholars argue that such profound brutality is religiously sanctioned in the DNA of Sharia law.[8] Others maintain that ISIS's program of torturing, raping, kidnaping, and beheading will eventually lead to the group's downfall.[9] ISIS is betting the opposite—that through its highly stylized online performance of political violence, ISIS will accumulate charismatic capital around the world and thereby entice a large audience of viewers and a steady stream of new recruits into its ranks. From this perspective, ISIS is seen not as a religiously motivated terrorist organization with regional interests, but as the political vanguard of an Arab Sunni revivalism intended to end nation-states as they currently exist from the Middle East to Africa and then across the European Continent. In this doomsday scenario, ISIS will not stop its murderous campaign until a black flag hovers over the White House. As the anthropologist Scott Atran warned the UN Security Council in 2015, ISIS represents "a thrilling cause that promises glory and esteem. Jihad is an egalitarian, equal-opportunity employer: fraternal, fast-breaking, glorious, cool—and persuasive."[10] It is for this very reason that the governments of Canada, France, and the United Kingdom have enacted sweeping counterterrorism reforms allowing officials to remove online postings by ISIS supporters.

The second U.S. approach to countering lone wolf terrorism is a joint FBI–Homeland Security program to forge ties with Muslim community leaders who are positioned to detect potential militants in their midst and disrupt their radicalization.[11] The program provides training to help state and local law enforcement in identifying and countering the terrorism threat, including indicators of violent extremism and lone wolf attacks.[12] Critics of the government's community-based initiatives (centered in the large Muslim populations of Boston, Minneapolis, and Los Angeles) maintain that these programs are potentially ineffective because "leaders" per se are not easily identifiable in modern Muslim communities, especially those who may have influence with the young. Support for this criticism is found in an Oxford University study which found that only one in twenty

ISIS foreign fighters was radicalized in mosques.[13] Either way, young Muslims first have to be convinced that the U.S. government is not engaged in a war against Islam. Other critics of the community-based program maintain that the government singles out specific ethnic or minority groups for scrutiny while majority communities are overlooked. Meanwhile, the most vocal critics maintain that the government's community-based program has become a smokescreen for police departments to conduct criminal investigations and collect intelligence on Muslim youth who display highly questionable indicators of extremism. The irony here is that a program ostensibly designed to prevent radicalization in Muslim communities may actually create an atmosphere of uncertainty and fear in those communities and make it more likely that some will end up supporting terrorism.[14]

The third approach is the FBI sting program, America's leading strategy for preventing lone wolf terrorism, which was described in detail in the preceding two chapters. Despite billions of dollars and thousands of informants, however, the FBI has prevented few acts of lone wolf terrorism in the United States. Even when the FBI had such a truly dangerous loner as Omar Mateen in the crosshairs, a sting operation did not prevent him from committing the greatest act of terrorism witnessed in America since 9/11. The Jared Loughners of the world, the Carlos Bledsoes, the Richard Poplawskis, and the Dylann Roofs still go unnoticed, free to wantonly slaughter people in churches, classrooms, movie theaters, shopping centers, and other public spaces. The FBI's lone wolf sting program has not aided the government's ability to stop this violence. On the contrary, it has impaired that ability by diverting essential resources away from the real problem.

What can be done about this problem? First, the FBI can focus its attention on behavioral patterns that are proven to be common among most authentic lone wolf terrorists. The most important of these behaviors are the broadcasting of terrorist intent and a noticeable affinity with online sympathizers who encourage violent extremism. These behaviors—often accompanied by "oversharing" and "over-arming" with firearms and bullets—can be observed by family members, friends, and associates, who can then act upon their observations by alerting authorities. Doing so can actually prevent a lone wolf attack as we have seen in such critical cases as the Mad Bomber, the Unabomber, and the would-be presidential assassins Richard Pavlick and James Cummings. Most warning signs are ignored, but this study has also suggested a new way of thinking about the "by-stander effect" by stressing relationships *among* bystanders, rather than *between* bystanders and the terrorist. In other words, focusing on what family members, friends, teachers, counselors, gun store clerks, and police say to one another about the radicalization of a potential terrorist in their midst may be more important than what a terrorist says to the bystanders.[15] This may be especially so when mental illness is involved.

Second, the FBI can scale back its practice of creating crimes to solve crimes so that the bureau can claim victory in its fight against terrorism. This will require a reassessment of the results-driven culture of the FBI sting program. Trevor Aaronson makes a vital point here by reasoning that "if the FBI's top priority is to find and stop lone wolves and [if] these lone wolves are found only through FBI stings . . . then how will the Bureau ever know when terrorism is no longer a threat, and the time has come to shift priorities?"[16] Such a reassessment also speaks to the matter of ethics, calling into question the FBI's practice of persuading, provoking, and even paying people to cross the line into terrorism. In the Sami Hassoun sting, FBI agents went the extra mile by collaborating with an organized crime network, the Assyrian Mafia. The sting against Hassoun was successful for the FBI because Sami was a joiner by nature and he was given something he needed—a sense of belonging, trust, and financial reward—which is why he fell for the government's scheme to commit the bombing in Chicago.

Omar Mateen, on the other hand, was not a joiner. He was a loner by nature, and Mateen needed nothing from the FBI—not their trust, their money, or their "brotherhood"—which is why the sting against him failed. Unlike the "Kramer Jihadists" routinely targeted in FBI stings, not only was Mateen a true lone wolf who slipped under the radar, he was a "known wolf" who had undergone two extensive FBI investigations and still became a terrorist, who committed a historically lethal attack.

The ramifications of the FBI's failed sting against Mateen will not be known until a full and impartial investigation of the Orlando attack is complete. As of this writing, it has just begun. Yet there are only two possible conclusions for the inquiry. The first is that the failed sting had no effect on Mateen: He would have carried out the Orlando massacre anyway based upon his own personal and political grievances, which were sparked to violent action by a triggering event, most likely ISIS's call for jihad against U.S. civilian targets during the month of Ramadan 2016.

The other conclusion is more complex. It suggests that the experience of being coerced into a phony plot to commit terrorism by an undercover FBI informant, combined with three interrogations by FBI agents, created in Mateen a powerful anger against the government, which accelerated his already formidable inclination toward jihadi violence and moved him on the road toward Orlando. Was it a coincidence, for example, that Mateen's suspected involvement with three jihadi terrorists who brought him to the FBI's attention in 2013 and 2014—the Tsarnaev brothers and Moner Abu-Selha—were the same three terrorists he name-checked during his rampage at the Pulse nightclub in 2016? Moreover, the sting against Mateen may have backfired, with devastating consequences.

Whatever the conclusion, at the end of the day we are left with the same reality: If the FBI sting program works only with marginal criminals, and not with the real threats like Mateen, then the policy only inflates the FBI's prosecution numbers without making us safer.

To effectively fight lone wolf terrorism, the FBI should review its full range of options. If a hammer is the only tool the FBI has for this fight, then the whole world begins to look like a nail. Here again, the ethics of the sting program matter. That is, there comes a point in each sting when FBI agents might have called on a family member, a psychologist, or a member of the clergy to provide counseling in a secure setting, instead of encouraging a person to kill innocent Americans with a bomb. There were numerous opportunities for such an intervention with Sami Hassoun. Many loved him. We can only wonder what might have happened if FBI agents had given Omar Mateen an off-ramp to his radicalization when they had a chance to do so. The outcome of the stings would have been the same (no one was hurt in the operations), except that those targeted in the stings would have received help for their problems rather than severe punishment. Muslim communities might have been spared the fear of wondering whether their family members would be the next ones rounded up in a sting and hauled off to federal prison for decades. By reconsidering options available for lone wolf investigations, the FBI could convert costly methods of wrecking lives into soft-power approaches to save them. Ultimately, that may be the only way to stop lone wolf terrorism.

Appendix

List of Cases: Pre-9/11

YEAR	NAME	TERRORIST EVENT	SOURCE
1) 1940–56	George Metesky	New York City bombings	Spaaij
2) 1958	Izola Curry	King assassination attempt	Hamm
3) 1960	Richard Pavlick	J. F. Kennedy assassination attempt	Hamm
4) 1963	Floyd Simpson	Alabama civil rights murder	Hewitt
5) 1963	Byron de la Beckwith	Evers assassination	Hewitt/Spaaij
6) 1968	James Earl Ray	King assassination	Hewitt
7) 1968	Valorie Solanas	Warhol assassination attempt	Hamm
8) 1968	Sirhan Sirhan	R. Kennedy assassination	Spaaij/Hewitt
9) 1970–75	Neal Long	Dayton, OH, murder spree	Spaaij/Hewitt
10) 1972–73	Mark Essex	New Orleans police killings	Spaaij/Hewitt
11) 1973–74	Muharem Kurbegovic	Los Angeles airport killings, nerve gas threat	Spaaij
12) 1974	Samuel Byck	Nixon assassination attempt	Hamm
13) 1975	Lynnette Fromme	Ford assassination attempt	Hamm
14) 1975	Sara Jane Moore	Ford assassination attempt	Hamm
15) 1977–80	Joseph Paul Franklin	Murder, bombing spree	Spaaij/Hewitt
16) 1978–95	Theodore Kaczynski	Bombing campaign	Spaaij

17) 1978	Dan White	Moscone and Milk assassinations	Hamm
18) 1980	Joseph Christopher	Buffalo, NY, killing spree	Spaaij/Hewitt
19) 1981	Claude Dallas	Idaho game warden killings	Hamm
20) 1982	Frank Spisak	Cleveland, OH, killing spree	Spaaij/Hewitt
21) 1982	Norman Mayer	Washington, DC, bomb plot	Spaaij
22) 1983	Hussein Kholya	Texas plane hijacking	Spaaij
23) 1989	Leroy Moody	Southeastern mail bombings	Spaaij/Hewitt
24) 1992–93	Rachelle Shannon	Western abortion attacks	Spaaij
25) 1993	Mir Aimal Kansi	CIA shootings	Spaaij/Hewitt
26) 1993	Michael Griffin	Pensacola, FL, abortion killing	Spaaij/Hewitt
27) 1993	Colin Ferguson	Long Island, NY, train shootings	Spaaij
28) 1993	Jonathan Haynes	Chicago and San Francisco killings	Pitcavage
29) 1994	Rashid Baz	New York City shooting	Spaaij
30) 1994	Paul Hill	Pensacola, FL, abortion killing	Spaaij/Hewitt
31) 1994	John Salvi	Boston abortion killing	Spaaij/Hewitt
32) 1996	Larry Shoemake	Mississippi shootings	Spaaij
33) 1996–98	Eric Rudolph	Southern bombing spree	Spaaij/Hewitt
34) 1997	Ali Abu Kamal	New York City shooting	Spaaij
35) 1998	James Kopp	Amherst, NY, abortion killing	Spaaij
36) 1999	Benjamin Smith	Midwestern killing spree	Hewitt
37) 1999	Buford Furrow	Los Angeles shootings	Spaaij/Hewitt
38) 2000	Ronald Taylor	Pennsylvania shootings	Spaaij
39) 2000	Rich Baumhammers	Pittsburgh, PA, killing spree	Spaaij

List of Cases: Post-9/11

YEAR	NAME	TERRORIST EVENT	SOURCE
40) 2001	Richard Bracklow	California police killings	Pitcavage
41) 2001	Joseph Ferguson	California killing spree	Pitcavage
42) 2001	Bruce Ivins	Anthrax attacks	Hamm
43) 2001	Clayton Waagner	Anthrax hoaxes	Spaaij
44) 2002	Andrew Mickel	California police killing	Pitcavage

45) 2002	Luke Helder	Midwestern mail bombings	Spaaij
46) 2002	Hesham Hadayet	Los Angeles airport shooting	Spaaij
47) 2002	Steve Kim	United Nations shooting	Spaaij
48) 2002	Charles Bishop	Florida plane attack	Spaaij
49) 2003	Dwight Watson	Lincoln Memorial bomb plot	Spaaij
50) 2003	George Davis	Montana shooting	Pitcavage
51) 2004	Van Crocker★	Tennessee ricin plot	Hamm
52) 2006	M. Taheri-azar	Chapel Hill, NC, auto attack	Spaaij
53) 2006	Naveed Haq	Seattle shootings	Spaaij
54) 2006	Jacob Robida	Eastern and southern killing spree	Pitcavage
55) 2007	Paul Evans	Austin, TX, abortion bombing	Spaaij
56) 2008	Marc Ramsey	McCain anthrax hoax	Hamm
57) 2008	Jim David Adkisson	Knoxville, TN, church shootings	Hamm
58) 2008	James Cummings	Maine dirty bomb plot	Drake
59) 2009	Scott Roeder	Wichita, KS, abortion killing	Spaaij
60) 2009	Carlos Bledsoe	Little Rock, AK, military shooting	Spaaij/Hamm
61) 2009	Michael Finton★	Springfield, IL, bomb plot	Hamm
62) 2009	Nidal Hasan	Fort Hood shooting	Spaaij
63) 2009	Richard Poplawski	Pittsburgh, PA, police shooting	Hamm
64) 2009	Joshua Cartwright	Florida police killings	Hamm
65) 2009	James von Brunn	Washington, DC, Holocaust Memorial killing	Hamm
66) 2009	Keith Luke	Massachusetts killing spree	Hamm
67) 2009	Hosam Smadi★	Dallas bomb plot	Hamm
68) 2009	Christopher Monfort	Seattle police shootings	Pitcavage
69) 2010	Joseph Stack	Austin, TX, IRS plane attack	Spaaij
70) 2010	M. Mohamud★	Portland bomb plot	Hamm
71) 2010	James Lee	Washington, DC, Discovery Channel attack	Drake
72) 2010	Yonathan Melaku	North Virginia military shooting	Drake
73) 2010	Sandlin Smith	Florida mosque bombing	Hamm
74) 2010	Justin Moose★	North Carolina abortion bombing	Hamm

75) 2010	Byron Williams	California police shootout	Hamm
76) 2010	John Bedell	Pentagon police shooting	Hamm
77) 2010	Casey Brezik	Missouri assassination attempt	Hamm
78) 2010	Antonio Martinez★	Maryland military bomb plot	Hamm
79) 2010	Farooque Ahmed★	Washington metro bomb plot	Spaaij
80) 2010	Sami Hassoun★	Chicago bomb plot	Hamm
81) 2011	Khalid Aldawsari	Bush bomb plot	Hamm
82) 2011	Rezwan Ferdaus★	Pentagon bomb plot	Hamm
83) 2011	Jared Loughner	Tucson, AZ, Gabrielle Giffords shootings	Hamm
84) 2011	Kevin Harpham	Spokane, WA, MLK parade bombing	Hamm
85) 2011	Jose Pimentel★	New York subway bomb plot	Hamm
86) 2011	Ralph Lang	Wisconsin abortion clinic attack	Hamm
87) 2011	Naser Jason Abdo	Fort Hood bomb plot	Hamm
88) 2011	O.R.O-Hernandez	Obama assassination plot	Drake
89) 2012	Sami Osmakac★	Tampa, FL, bomb plot	Spaaij
90) 2012	Amine el Khalifi★	Capitol suicide bomb plot	Hamm
91) 2012	Wade Page	Milwaukee Sikh shootings	Hamm
92) 2012	Thomas Caffall	Texas A&M shootings	Hamm
93) 2012	Floyd Corkins	Washington, DC, shooting	Hamm
94) 2012	Adel Daoud★	Chicago bomb plot	Hamm
95) 2012	Francis Grady	Wisconsin abortion clinic arson	Hamm
96) 2012	Gregory Weiler	Oklahoma church bomb plot	Hamm
97) 2012	Quazi Nafis★	Federal Reserve bomb plot	Hamm
98) 2012	Raulie Casteel	Michigan highway shootings	Hamm
99) 2013	Derek Shrout	Alabama school bomb plot	Hamm
100) 2013	Jimmy Lee Dykes	Alabama kidnaping	Hamm
101) 2013	Christopher Dorner	Los Angeles shootings	Hamm
102) 2013	Matthew Buquet	Spokane, MA, ricin plot	Hamm
103) 2013	Jason Woodring	Arkansas power grid attack	Hamm
104) 2013	Paul Ciancia	Los Angeles airport shooting	Hamm
105) 2013	Terry Loewen★	Wichita, KS, bomb plot	Hamm
106) 2014	Frazier Glenn Miller	Kansas shooting	Hamm
107) 2014	Eric Frein	Pennsylvania Police shooting	Hamm
108) 2014	Alton Nolen	Oklahoma beheading	Hamm
109) 2014	Zale Thompson	Queens, NY, police ambush	Hamm

110) 2014	Ali Brown	Seattle, WA, killings	Hamm
111) 2014	Larry McQuilliams	Austin, TX, court attack	Hamm
112) 2015	Craig Hicks	Chapel Hill, NC, killings	Hamm
113) 2015	Dylann Roof	Charleston, SC, massacre	Hamm
114) 2015	John Houser	Louisiana movie shooting	Hamm
115) 2015	M. Abdulazeez	Chattanooga, TN, military attack	Hamm
116) 2015	Shannon Miles	Texas police killing	Hamm
117) 2015	Jason Smith	New York City bomb threat	Hamm
118) 2015	Unidentified	Phoenix, AZ, freeway shootings	Hamm
119) 2015	Christopher Mercer	Oregon college shooting	Hamm
120) 2015	Faisal Mohammad	California college stabbings	Hamm
121) 2015	Robert Dear	Colorado Planned Parenthood shooting	Hamm
122) 2016	Edward Archer	Philadelphia police shooting	Hamm
123) 2016	Omar Mateen	Orlando, FL, mass murder	Hamm

* FBI sting operation (except for Jose Pimentel, case 85, NYPD sting)

Summary

123 cases

39 pre-9/11 cases (all authentic lone wolf cases)

84 post-9/11 cases

15 post-9/11 stings (not included in authentic lone wolf cases)

69 authentic lone wolf post-9/11 cases

Sources

Caleb Drake: research assistant for Mark S. Hamm and Ramon Spaaij, *American Lone Wolf Terrorism: Using Knowledge of Radicalization Pathways to Forge Prevention Strategies* (Washington, DC: National Institute of Justice, 2015).

Mark S. Hamm: research for Mark S. Hamm and Ramon Spaaij, *American Lone Wolf Terrorism: Using Knowledge of Radicalization Pathways to Forge Prevention Strategies* (Washington, DC: National Institute of Justice, 2015); Mark S. Hamm, *The Spectacular Few: Prisoner Radicalization and the Evolving Terrorist Threat* (New York: New York University Press, 2013); Mark S. Hamm, *Terrorism as Crime: From Oklahoma City to Al-Qaeda and Beyond* (New York: New York University Press, 2007).

Christopher Hewitt, *Understanding Terrorism in America: From the Klan to Al-Qaeda* (New York: Routledge, 2003).

Mark Pitcavage, "Cerberus Unleashed: The Three Faces of Lone Wolf Terrorism," *American Behavioral Scientist*, June 3, 2015, 1555–1680.

Ramon Spaaij: research for Mark S. Hamm and Ramon Spaaij, *American Lone Wolf Terrorism: Using Knowledge of Radicalization Pathways to Forge Prevention Strategies* (Washington, DC: National Institute of Justice, 2015).

Ramon Spaaij, *Understanding Lone Wolf Terrorism: Global Patterns, Motivations and Prevention* (New York: Springer, 2012).

Notes

Introduction

1. "Obama: 'Lone Wolf' Terror Attack More Likely than Major Coordinated Effort," Associated Press (AP), August 16, 2011.
2. "James Foley Killing Was a Terrorist Attack," *NBC News*, August 22, 2014.
3. "A Necessary Response to ISIS," *New York Times*, August 25, 2014.
4. "NYPD: Threat to U.S. 'Growing Exponentially with ISIS,'" *CBS News*, September 11, 2014.
5. "FBI Director Says Agency Focused on Terrorism," *Arizona Republic*, September 10, 2014.
6. "State of the Union," CNN, October 26, 2014.
7. "Latest Terrorism in N.Y., Canada Could Be Inspired by ISIS," *Detroit Free Press*, October 29, 2014. See also "Excerpts from 'Indeed Your Lord Is Ever Watchful,'" *Dabiq*, no. 4 (September 2014): 6–9.
8. Liz Alvarez and Richard Perez-Pena, "Praising ISIS, Gunman Attacks Gay Nightclub, Leaving 50 Dead in Worst Shooting on U.S. Soil," *New York Times*, June 13, 2016.
9. "State of the Union."
10. "Threat of American ISIS Fighters 'Not Even Close to Being Under Control,' Top FBI Official Says," *World News*, February 11, 2015.
11. Statement of James R. Clapper, Director of National Intelligence, Worldwide Threat Assessment of the U.S. Intelligence Community, Senate Armed Services Committee, February 9, 2016.

12. Homeland Security Committee, *#Terror Gone Viral: Overview of the 75 ISIS-Linked Plots Against the West, 2014–2016*, March 2016.

13. Peter Bergen, *United States of Jihad: Investigating America's Homegrown Terrorists* (New York: Crown, 2016), 261.

14. "Gunman in Orlando Posted to Facebook During Nightclub Attack, Lawmaker Says," *New York Times*, June 17, 2016.

15. "FBI Chief: Radicalization by ISIS Is a Top Concern of Agency," Reuters, July 8, 2015.

16. "New DOJ Pilot Program Aims to Deter Americans from Joining Terrorist Groups," *Homeland Security News Wire*, September 26, 2014; Statement of James R. Clapper.

17. Fred Burton and Scott Stewart, "The 'Lone Wolf' Disconnect," STRATFOR Global Intelligence, 2008, http://www.stratfor.com/weekly/lone_wolf_disconnect.

18. Bruce Hoffman, *Inside Terrorism* (New York: Columbia University Press, 2006).

19. Ibid., 42.

20. Jonathan R. White, *Terrorism: An Introduction* (Belmont, CA: Wadsworth, 2003), 43.

21. Brian Michael Jenkins, *Stray Dogs and Virtual Armies: Radicalization and Recruitment to Jihadist Terrorism in the United States since 9/11* (Santa Monica, CA: RAND, 2011), 21.

22. Carolyn Turpin-Petrosino, *Understanding Hate Crime: Acts, Motives, Offenders, Victims, and Justice* (New York: Routledge, 2015). The boundaries between hate crime and terrorism are not always ironclad. Omar Mateen, for example, may have attacked patrons of the Orlando gay nightclub due to ISIS's well-known history of brutal and relentless persecution of those perceived to deviate from mainstream sexuality and his own personal hatred of homosexuals.

23. Jeffrey D. Simon, *Lone Wolf Terrorism: Understanding the Growing Threat* (Amherst, NY: Prometheus Books, 2013), 67, 266.

24. Paul Gill, *Lone-Actor Terrorism: A Behavioral Analysis* (New York: Routledge, 2015).

25. Christopher Hewitt, *Understanding Terrorism in America: From the Klan to Al-Qaeda* (New York: Routledge, 2003).

26. Bruce Hoffman, *Inside Terrorism* (New York: Columbia University Press, 1998), 42–43.

27. Bruce Hoffman, *Al Qaeda, Trends in Terrorism, and Future Potentialities: An Assessment* (Santa Monica, CA: RAND, 2003).

28. Bruce Hoffman, Interview on KCFW Radio *To the Point*, June 13, 2016.

29. Ramon Spaaij, *Understanding Lone Wolf Terrorism: Global Patterns, Motivations and Prevention* (New York: Springer, 2012).

30. Mark S. Hamm, *In Bad Company: America's Terrorist Underground* (Boston: Northeastern University Press, 2002).

31. Hoffman, *Inside Terrorism* (2006), 40.

32. "New DOJ Pilot Program."

33. A summary of findings can be found in Mark S. Hamm and Ramon Spaaij, *American Lone Wolf Terrorism: Using Knowledge of Radicalization Pathways to Forge Prevention Strategies* (Washington, DC: National Institute of Justice, 2015).The views expressed in this research are the authors' and do not necessarily reflect those of NIJ.

34. We recognize that some scholars trace lone wolf terrorism in America to at least the assassination of President William McKinley in 1901. Yet we also recognize the difficulty both of confirming that earlier cases were lone wolf attacks and of gathering historical data worthy of inclusion in a database. For instance, McKinley's assassin, Leon Czolgosz, admitted to his association with other prominent New York City anarchists at the time, including Emma Goldman (who was briefly jailed for her suspected involvement in the assassination). On the other hand, several definitive studies, presented in chapter 1, identify George Metesky as the original American lone wolf terrorist. His first bombing occurred in 1940. It is for these reasons, then, that we select 1940 as our starting point for the database.

35. Andrew Silke, "Research on Terrorism: A Review of the Impact of 9/11 and the Global War on Terrorism," in *Terrorism Infomatics: Knowledge Management and Data Mining for Homeland Security*, ed. H. Chen, E. Reid, J. Sinai, A. Silke, and B. Ganor, 27–49 (New York: Springer, 2008); Andrew Silke, e-mail to Mark Hamm, May 4, 2014.

1. Identifying Commonalities Among Lone Wolf Terrorists

1. Data accessed at http://opencrs.com/.

2. Department of Homeland Security, *Rightwing Extremism: Current Economic and Political Climate Fueling Resurgence in Radicalization and Recruitment* (Washington, DC: DHS, 2009).

3. Edwin Bakker and Beatrice de Graaf, "Lone Wolves: How to Prevent This Seemingly New Phenomenon" (The Hague: International Centre for Counter-Terrorism, 2010).

4. Jeffrey D. Simon, *Lone Wolf Terrorism: Understanding the Growing Threat* (Amherst, NY: Prometheus Books, 2013).

5. Christopher Hewitt, *Understanding Terrorism in America: From the Klan to Al-Qaeda* (New York: Routledge, 2003), 78.

6. Jeffrey Kaplan, "Leaderless Resistance," *Terrorism and Political Violence* 9 (1997): 80–95.

7. Federal Bureau of Investigation Press Release, November 10, 2000.

8. Hewitt, *Understanding Terrorism in America*, 78.

9. Ramón Spaaij and Mark S. Hamm, "Key Issues and Research Agendas in Lone Wolf Terrorism," *Studies in Conflict & Terrorism* 38 (2015): 167–78.

10. COT Institute for Safety, Security and Crisis Management, *Lone Wolf Terrorism*, Report for the European Commission Sixth Framework Program Transnational Terrorism, Security, and the Rule of Law (The Hague: COT Institute for Safety, Security and Crisis Management, 2007), in authors' possession; Ramón Spaaij, "The Enigma of Lone Wolf Terrorism: An Assessment," *Studies in Conflict & Terrorism* 33 (2010): 854–70; Ramon Spaaij, *Understanding Lone Wolf Terrorism: Global Patterns, Motivations and Prevention* (New York: Springer, 2012).

11. Andrew Gumbel and Roger Charles, *Oklahoma City: What the Investigation Missed and Why It Still Matters* (New York: William Marrow, 2012); Stuart A. Wright, *Patriots, Politics, and the Oklahoma City Bombing* (New York: Cambridge University Press, 2007).

12. See James Swanson, *Manhunt: The 12-Day Chase for Lincoln's Killer* (New York: Harper Collins, 2006).

13. See Philip Shenon, *A Cruel and Shocking Act: The Secret History of the Kennedy Assassination* (New York: Henry Holt, 2013).

14. This definition thus excludes the "criminal lone wolf" that features in Jeffrey D. Simon's typology of lone wolf terrorism. Simon, *Lone Wolf Terrorism*.

15. Brian J. Phillips, "Deadlier in the U.S.? On Lone Wolves, Terrorist Groups, and Attack Lethality," *Terrorism and Political Violence*, May 2015, http://www.tandfonline.com/doi/abs/10.1080/09546553.2015.1054927?journalCode=ftpv20.

16. Spaaij, *Understanding Lone Wolf Terrorism*, 32.

17. COT Report, 88.

18. Randy Borum, "Radicalization into Violent Extremism I: A Review of Social Science Theories," *Journal of Strategic Security* 4 (2011): 7–36; Clark McCauley and Sophia Moskalenko, "Mechanisms of Political Radicalization: Pathways Toward Terrorism," *Terrorism and Political Violence* 20 (2008): 415–33.

19. See also Jessica Stern, *Terror in the Name of God: Why Religious Militants Kill* (New York: Ecco, 2003).

20. Ariel Merari, *Driven to Death: Psychological and Social Aspects of Suicide Terrorism* (New York: Oxford University Press, 2010); John Horgan, *The Psychology of Terrorism* (New York: Routledge, 2005); Andrew Silke, "Courage in Dark Places: Reflections on Terrorist Psychology," *Social Research* 71 (2004): 177–98; Marc Sageman, *Leaderless Jihad: Terror Networks in the Twenty-First Century* (Philadelphia: University of Pennsylvania Press, 2008).

21. Paul Gill, *Lone-Actor Terrorists: A Behavioural Analysis* (New York: Routledge, 2015); Paul Gill, John Horgan, and Paige Deckert, "Bombing Alone: Tracing the Motivations and Antecedent Behaviors of Lone-Actor Terrorism," *Journal of Forensic Sciences* 59 (2014): 425–35.

22. See Randy Borum, "Lone Wolf Terrorism," in *The SAGE Encyclopedia of Terrorism*, ed. Gus Martin, 361–62 (London: SAGE, 2011).

23. Jerrold M. Post, "Terrorist Psycho-Logic: Terrorist Behavior as a Product of Psychological Forces," in *Origins of Terrorism*, ed. Walter Reich, 25–41 (Washington, DC: Woodrow Wilson Center Press, 1988).

24. See Gerry Gable and Paul Jackson, *Lone Wolves: Myth or Reality?* (Ilford, UK: Searchlight, 2011); Matthew Feldman, "Comparative Lone Wolf Terrorism: Toward a Heuristic Definition," *Democracy and Security* 9 (2013): 270–86.

25. Bakker and de Graaf, "Lone Wolves."

26. Mark S. Hamm, "Lone Wolves on the Rise: The New Threat of Lone Wolf Terrorism, from the Unabomber to the Standalone Jihadist," (The Hague: International Centre for Counter-Terrorism, 2010).

27. Ibid.

28. Ibid.

29. Quoted in Spaaij, *Understanding Lone Wolf Terrorism*, 3.

30. See Gill, Horgan, and Deckert, "*Bombing Alone.*"

31. Rafaello Pantucci, *A Typology of Lone Wolves: Preliminary Analysis of Lone Islamist Terrorists* London: International Centre for the Study of Radicalization and Political Violence, 2011).

32. Ibid., 19.

33. Ibid., 20.

34. Jarret Brachman, *Global Jihadism: Theory and Practice* (New York: Routledge, 2008).

35. Sageman, *Leaderless Jihad*.

36. Brian Michael Jenkins, "Foreword," in Jeffrey D. Simon, *Lone Wolf Terrorism: Understanding the Growing Threat* (Amherst, NY: Prometheus Books, 2013).

37. "Fort Hood Killer: Terrified . . . or Terrorist?" *Time*, November 11, 2009.

38. Jonathan R. White, *Terrorism and Homeland Security*. Belmont, CA: Wadsworth, 2014), 5.

39. Jenkins, "Foreword," 9.

2. Old Wine in New Skin

1. Ramon Spaaij, *Understanding Lone Wolf Terrorism: Global Patterns, Motivations and Prevention* (New York: Springer, 2012).

2. All "known cases" does not imply that we have identified all cases. For example, little is known of airplane hijackers. Between 1961 and 1972, 159 commercial flights were hijacked in the United States, yet many of the hijackers' names have been lost to history. See Brendan I. Koerner, *The Skies*

Belong to Us: Love and Terror in the Golden Age of Hijacking (New York: Crown, 2013).

3. Kevin J. Strom, *Building on Clues: Examining Successes and Failures in Detecting U.S. Terrorist Plots, 1999–2009* (Durham, NC: Institute for Homeland Security Solutions, 2010). For a discussion of why this may be the case, see for example: Spaaij, *Understanding Lone Wolf Terrorism*; George Michael, *Lone Wolf Terror and the Rise of Leaderless Resistance* (Nashville, TN: Vanderbilt University Press, 2012); Fred Burton and Scott Stewart, "The 'Lone Wolf' Disconnect," STRATFOR Global Intelligence, 2008, http://www.stratfor.com /weekly/lone_wolf_disconnect. These authors all stress the typically limited capability of lone wolf terrorists in comparison with their group-based counterparts.

4. Cited in Jeffrey D. Simon, *Lone Wolf Terrorism: Understanding the Growing Threat* (Amherst, NY: Prometheus Books, 2013), 184.

5. *The Plot to Kill Nixon*, directed by Patrick Taulere, The History Channel, 2007.

6. Spencer Heinz, "Praying with Fire: The Genesis of Shelly Shannon," *Oregonian*, November 14, 1993.

7. Jonathan R. White, *Terrorism: An Introduction* (Belmont, CA: Wadsworth, 2003), 43.

8. Paul Gill, John Horgan, and Paige Deckert, "Bombing Alone: Tracing the Motivations and Antecedent Behaviors of Lone-Actor Terrorists," *Journal of Forensic Sciences* 59 (2013): 425–35.

9. Hampton Sides, *Hellhound on His Trail: The Stalking of Martin Luther King, Jr., and the International Hunt for His Assassin* (New York: Doubleday, 2010).

10. "ISIS' Online 'Training Manual' Teaches Sympathizers How to Disguise Themselves as Westerners and Build Bombs to Carry Out Attacks," *Christian Post*, March 18, 2015.

11. Masha Geeson, *The Brothers: The Road to An American Tragedy* (New York: Riverhead, 2015).

12. "Both San Bernardino Attackers Pledged Allegiance to ISIS, Official Says," *Washington Post*, December 8, 2015.

13. Jerry Mitchell, "National Alliance Founder William Pierce's Writing Inspires Slaughter," *Intelligence Report*, Southern Poverty Law Center (Winter 1999): 93.

14. One source used in the investigation was Mark S. Hamm, *In Bad Company: America's Terrorist Underground* (Boston: Northeastern University Press, 2002).

15. Marc Sageman, *Leaderless Jihad: Terror Networks in the Twenty-First Century* (Philadelphia: University of Pennsylvania Press, 2008); Marc Sageman, *Understanding Terror Networks* (Philadelphia: University of Pennsylvania Press, 2004).

16. Edwin Bakker, *Jihadi Terrorists in Europe: Their Characteristics and the Circumstances in Which They Joined the Jihad: An Exploratory Study* (The Hague: Clingendael Institute, 2007).

17. Mark S. Hamm, *The Spectacular Few: Prisoner Radicalization and the Evolving Terrorist Threat* (New York: New York University Press, 2013); Mark S. Hamm, *American Skinheads: The Criminology and Control of Hate Crime* (Westport, CT: Praeger, 1993); Pete Simi and Robert Futrell, *American Swastika: Inside the White Power Movement's Hidden Spaces of Hate* (Lanham, MD: Rowman & Littlefield, 2010); Brent L. Smith, *Terrorism in America: Pipe Bombs and Pipe Dreams* (Albany: State University of New York Press, 1994).

18. See Randy Borum, "Radicalization into Violent Extremism I: A Review of Social Science Theories," *Journal of Strategic Security* 4 (2011): 7–36.

19. These cases are not among the five originally analyzed in Spaaij, *Understanding Lone Wolf Terrorism*.

20. George Pavlich, "Paradigmatic Cases," in *Encyclopedia of Case Study Research*, ed. A. Mills, G. Durepos, and E. Wieber, 646–48 (Thousand Oaks, CA: Sage, 2010).

21. Michel Wieviorka, "Case Studies: History or Sociology?," in *What is a Case? Exploring the Foundations of Social Inquiry*, ed. C. C. Ragin and H. S. Becker, 159–72 (New York: Cambridge University Press, 1992).

22. Michael Kenney, "Learning from the 'Dark Side'—Identifying, Accessing and Interviewing Illicit Non-State Actors" in *Conducting Terrorism Field Research: A Guide*, ed. Adam Dolnik, 26–45 (New York: Routledge, 2013).

23. John H. Laub and Robert J. Sampson, "Turning Points in the Life Course: Why Change Matters to the Study of Crime," *Criminology* 31 (1993): 301–25.

24. Hamm, *The Spectacular Few*.

25. Ibid.

26. This does not mean that there are no challenges or limitations to interviewing terrorists in prison, of course. An instructive discussion of the methodological and ethical challenges involved in interviewing terrorist inmates is offered in Mark S. Hamm and Ramón Spaaij, "Paradigmatic Case Studies and Prison Ethnography: New Directions in Terrorism Research," in *Handbook on the Criminology of Terrorism*, ed. Joshua Freilich and Gary LaFree (New York: Wiley, 2016).

3. The American Lone Wolf Terrorist

1. Michael Becker, "Explaining Lone Wolf Target Selection in the United States," *Studies in Conflict & Terrorism* 37, no. 11 (2014): 959–78; Jeffrey D. Simon, *Lone Wolf Terrorism: Understanding the Growing Threat* (Amherst, NY: Prometheus Books, 2013).

2. Ramon Spaaij, *Understanding Lone Wolf Terrorism: Global Patterns, Motivations and Prevention* (New York: Springer, 2012), 28.

3. Jeff Gruenewald, Steven Chermak, and Joshua D. Freilich, "Distinguishing 'Loner' Attacks from Other Domestic Extremist Violence," *Criminology & Public Policy* 12 (2013): 83.

4. Simon, *Lone Wolf Terrorism*, p. 239.

5. Fifteen lone wolf cases after 9/11 were law-enforcement sting operations involving confidential informants and undercover agents; they do not qualify in our view as *authentic* lone wolf cases, since more than one individual was involved. The sting cases were nevertheless included in the database because stings against standalone extremists have become an important counterterrorism strategy since 9/11. (In the list of cases in the appendix, stings are marked with an asterisk.) The fifteen sting cases will be considered in a separate part of the study. The increase in the number of authentic cases after 9/11 reflects a greater number of plots as compared to the pre-9/11 era, as well as the effects of modern computer technology, which allows for greater searching capacity for cases.

6. Simon, *Lone Wolf Terrorism*.

7. Breanne Fahs, *Valerie Solanas: The Defiant Life of the Woman Who Wrote SCUM (and Shot Andy Warhol)* (New York: Feminist Press, 2014). SCUM was a "society" of one: Solanas.

8. Jess Bravin, *Squeaky: The Life and Times of Lynette Alice Fromme* (New York: St. Martin's, 1997).

9. For evidence that there seems to be little or no effect on crime of license-to-carry laws, see Wolfgang Stroebe, "Firearm Possession and Violent Death: A Critical Review," *Aggression and Violent Behavior* 18 (2013): 709–21.

10. Marc Sageman, *Leaderless Jihad: Terror Networks in the Twenty-First Century* (Philadelphia: University of Pennsylvania Press, 2008), 139.

11. Study of Terrorism and Responses to Terrorism (START), *Understanding Lone-Actor Terrorism: A Comparative Analysis with Violent Hate Crimes and Group-Based Terrorism*, Report to the Resilient Systems Division, Science and Technology Directorate, U.S. Department of Homeland Security, 2013, 8–11.

12. E-mail from START authors to Mark Hamm, October 24, 2013.

13. The cases are also discussed in Simon, *Lone Wolf Terrorism*; Spaaij, *Understanding Lone Wolf Terrorism*; Kevin J. Strom, *Building on Clues: Examining Successes and Failures in Detecting U.S. Terrorist Plots, 1999–2009* (Chapel Hill, NC: Institute for Homeland Security Solutions, 2010). Curiously, all of these studies were indeed based on the Global Terrorism Database (GTD).

14. Bryan Burrough, *Days of Rage: America's Radical Underground, the FBI, and the Forgotten Age of Revolutionary Violence* (New York: Penguin, 2015).

15. Becker argues that bombings define the post-9/11 lone wolf in America. However, Becker bases this conclusion almost entirely on the FBI stings, not authentic lone wolf cases. Becker, "Explaining Lone Wolf Target Selection in the United States."

16. E-mail from Task Force member to Mark Hamm, June 14, 2013.

17. See Pamela Haag, *The Gunning of America: Business and the Making of American Gun Culture* (New York: Basic Books, 2016).

18. Mark S. Hamm, *In Bad Company: America's Terrorist Underground* (Boston: Northeastern University Press, 2002).

19. Andrew Gumbel, "Seeds of Terror in Norway," *Los Angeles Times*, July 28, 2011.

20. *United States of America v. Jason Woodring*, Criminal Complaint, October 12, 2013.

21. "Assault on California Power Station Raises Alarm on Potential for Terrorism," *Wall Street Journal*, February 5, 2014.

22. Loren Coleman, *The Copycat Effect: How the Media and Popular Culture Trigger the Mayhem in Tomorrow's Headlines* (New York: Simon and Schuster, 2004). For a recent reflection on the copycat effect, see also Malcolm Gladwell, "Thresholds of Violence," *New Yorker*, October 19, 2015, http://www.newyorker.com /magazine/2015/10/19/thresholds-of-violence.

23. Elliott Leyton, *Hunting Humans: The Rise of the Modern Multiple Murderer* (New York: Carroll & Graf, 2001), 27, 322, 360.

24. Terry D. Turchie and Kathleen M. Puckett, *Hunting the American Terrorist: The FBI's War on Homegrown Terror* (New York: History Publishing, 2007); Jelle Van Buuren, "Performative Violence? The Multitude of Lone Wolf Terrorism," *Terrorism: An Electronic Journal and Knowledge Base* 1 (2012): 1–23.

25. Edwin Bakker and Beatrice de Graaf, "Preventing Lone Wolf Terrorism: Some CT Approaches Addressed," *Perspectives on Terrorism* 5, no. 5/6 (2011), http:// www.terrorismanalysts.com/pt/index.php/pot/article/view/preventing-lone -wolf.

26. Aborted attacks differ from foiled plots due to intent. In the first instance, intent has been abandoned, and in the second, it has not.

27. Edwin Bakker, *Jihadi Terrorists in Europe: Their Characteristics and the Circumstances in Which They Joined the Jihad; An Exploratory Study* (The Hague: Clingendael Institute, 2007).

28. Marc Sageman, *Understanding Terror Networks* (Philadelphia: University of Pennsylvania Press, 2004).

29. Gruenewald, Chermak, and Freilich, "Distinguishing 'Loner' Attacks from Other Domestic Extremist Violence"; Mark S. Hamm, *American Skinheads: The Criminology and Control of Hate Crime* (Westport, CT: Praeger, 1993); Brent L. Smith, *Terrorism in America: Pipe Bombs and Pipe Dreams* (Albany: State University of New York Press, 1994).

30. The database does not contain a category for education. However, education levels were estimated from employment histories and other biographical information on the lone wolves.

31. Alston Chase, *Harvard and the Unabomber: The Education of an American Terrorist* (New York: Norton, 2003).

32. Gruenewald, Chermak, and Freilich, "Distinguishing 'Loner' Attacks from Other Domestic Extremist Violence."

33. Bakker, *Jihadi Terrorists in Europe.*

34. Sageman *Understanding Terror Networks.*

35. Ibid., 78.

36. Ibid., 98.

37. Robert Pape, *Dying to Win: The Strategic Logic of Suicide Terrorism* (New York: Random House, 2005).

38. Jonathan R. White, *Terrorism: An Introduction* (Belmont, CA: Wadsworth, 2003), 43.

39. Jerrold M. Post, *The Mind of the Terrorist: The Psychology of Terrorism from the IRA to Al-Qaeda* (New York: Palgrave Macmillan, 2007).

40. Mark S. Hamm, *Terrorism as Crime: From Oklahoma City to Al-Qaeda and Beyond* (New York: New York University Press, 2007).

41. James William Gibson, *Warrior Dreams: Violence and Manhood in Post-Vietnam America* (New York: Hill and Wang, 1994).

42. Mark S. Hamm, *Apocalypse in Oklahoma: Waco and Ruby Ridge Revenged* (Boston: Northeastern University Press, 1997).

43. Sageman, *Leaderless Jihad.*

44. Ibid; Bakker, *Jihadi Terrorists in Europe*; White, *Terrorism.*

45. "Izola Ware Curry, Who Stabbed King in 1958, Dies at 98," *New York Times*, March 21, 2015.

46. This is consistent with Simon's research indicating that there have been no U.S. female lone wolves in the post-9/11 period. However, Simon does not include among his pre-9/11 cases Curry, Solanas, Fromme, or Moore. There have been few female lone wolves but there are more than Simon documents. Simon, *Lone Wolf Terrorism.*

47. Ibid., chapter 4.

48. Sageman, *Understanding Terror Networks*; Bakker, *Jihadi Terrorists in Europe.* See also John Horgan, *The Psychology of Terrorism* (New York: Routledge, 2005), among others.

49. For documentation of mental illness we are primarily relying on court documents, psychiatric evaluations, and news coverage. In some cases mental health problems were not clinically diagnosed. We have not had the resources to commission an independent analysis of mental health status using the Diagnostic and Statistical Manual of Mental Disorders (DSM-5) classification and indicators. This needs to be kept in mind when interpreting the research findings.

50. National Institute of Mental Health, "Any Mental Illness (AMI) Among U.S. Adults," 2014, http://www.nimh.nih.gov/health/statistics/prevalence/any-mental-illness-ami-among-us-adults.shtml. AMI includes a broad spectrum ranging from mild to serious mental illness.

51. Doris J. James and Lauren E. Glaze, "Mental Health Problems of Prison and Jail Inmates," Bureau of Justice Statistics, Special Report, September 2006.

52. Robert A. Fein and Bryan Vossekuil, "Assassination in the United States: An Operational Study of Recent Assassins, Attackers, and Near-Lethal Approachers," *Journal of Forensic Science* 44 (1999): 321–33.

53. Christopher Hewitt, *Understanding Terrorism in America: From the Klan to Al-Qaeda* (New York: Routledge, 2003).

54. Emily Corner and Paul Gill, "A False Dichotomy? Mental Illness and Lone-Actor Terrorism," *Law and Human Behavior* 39 (2015): 23–34.

55. Jeanine de Roy Van Zuijdewijn and Edwin Bakker, *Lone-Actor Terrorism: Policy Paper 1: Personal Characteristics of Lone-Actor Terrorists* (The Hague: International Centre for Counter-Terrorism, 2016).

56. Hamm, *In Bad Company*; Sageman, *Understanding Terror Networks*; Alexandre S. Wilner and Claire-Jehanne Dubouloz, "Transformative Radicalization: Applying Learning Theory to Islamist Radicalization," *Studies in Conflict and Terrorism* 34 (2011): 418–38.

57. E-mail from Task Force member to Mark Hamm, October 24, 2013.

58. Martha Crenshaw, "The Psychology of Terrorism: An Agenda for the 21st Century," *Political Psychology* 21 (2000): 405–20; Horgan, *The Psychology of Terrorism*; Sageman, *Understanding Terror Networks*.

59. D. Weathersone and J. Moran, "Terrorism and Mental Illness: Is There a Relationship?" *International Journal of Offender Therapy and Comparative Criminology* 47 (2003): 698–713.

60. Bakker, *Jihadi Terrorists in Europe*.

61. Robert H. Busch, *The Wolf Almanac: A Celebration of Wolves and Their World* (Guilford, CT: Lyons Press, 2007), 54.

62. Michael Kimmel, *Angry White Men: American Masculinity and the End of an Era* (New York: Nation Books, 2015).

63. Burrough, *Days of Rage*.

64. Jack Hoffman and Daniel Simon, *Run Run Run: The Lives of Abbie Hoffman* (New York: Putnam, 1994), 224.

65. Fathali M. Moghaddam, "The Staircase to Terrorism: A Psychological Exploration" *American Psychologist* 60 (2005): 161–69.

66. Masha Gessen, *The Brothers: The Road to An American Tragedy* (New York: Riverhead, 2015).

67. Fiore Geelhoed, *Purification & Resistance: Global Meanings of Islamic Fundamentalism in the Netherlands* (Rotterdam: Erasmus University Press, 2012); Hamm, *In Bad Company*; Mark S. Hamm, *The Spectacular Few: Prisoner Radicalization and the Evolving Terrorist Threat* (New York: New York University Press, 2013); Jessica Stern, *Terror in the Name of God: Why Religious Militants Kill* (New York: Ecco, 2003).

4. The Roots of Radicalization

1. On self-radicalization, see Clark McCauley and Sophia Moskalenko, "Mechanisms of Political Radicalization: Pathways Toward Terrorism," *Terrorism and Political Violence* 20 (2008): 415–33; Susan Curie Sivek, "Packaging Inspiration: Al-Qaeda's Digital Magazine *Inspire* in the Self-Radicalization Process," *International Journal of Communication* 7 (2013): 584–606.

2. Mary Stanton, *Freedom Walk: Mississippi or Bust* (Jackson: University Press of Mississippi, 2003).

3. Reed Massengill, *Portrait of a Racist: The Man Who Killed Medgar Evers?* (New York: St. Martin's, 1994).

4. Peter Hernon, *A Terrible Thunder: The Story of the New Orleans Sniper* (New Orleans: Garrett County Press, 2010).

5. Maryanne Vollers, *Lone Wolf: Eric Rudolph and the Legacy of American Terror* (New York: Harper Perennial, 2006).

6. Hampton Sides, *Hellhound on His Trail: The Stalking of Martin Luther King, Jr., and the International Hunt for His Assassin* (New York: Doubleday, 2010).

7. Mel Ayton, *Dark Soul of the South: The Life and Crimes of Racist Killer Joseph Paul Franklin* (Washington, DC: Potomac Books, 2011).

8. Jerrold M. Post, *The Mind of the Terrorist: The Psychology of Terrorism from the IRA to Al-Qaeda* (New York: Palgrave Macmillan, 2007).

9. Louise Richardson, *What Terrorists Want: Understanding the Enemy, Containing the Threat* (New York: Random House, 2006).

10. Mariah Blake, "Internal Documents Reveal How the FBI Blew Ft. Hood," *Mother Jones*, August 27, 2013; *Final Report of the William H. Webster Commission on the FBI, Counterterrorism Intelligence on the Events at Fort Hood, Texas, on November 5, 2009* (n.d.) (Webster Report); Scott Shane, *Objective Troy: A Terrorist, a President, and the Rise of the Drone* (New York: Tim Duggan Books, 2015).

11. Rick Romell, "Shooter's Behavior Did Not Go Unnoticed," *Journal Sentinel*, August 7, 2012; Pete Simi, "Exclusive: Interview with Professor Who Extensively Studied Alleged Wisconsin Mass Killer," *Huffington Post*, August 8, 2012; Pete Simi, interview with Mark Hamm, February 1, 2014.

12. Jessica Stern, *Terror in the Name of God: Why Religious Militants Kill* (New York: Ecco, 2003), 172.

13. Marc Sageman, *Understanding Terror Networks* (Philadelphia: University of Pennsylvania Press, 2004), 97.

14. John J. Goldman and Rebecca Trounson, "Empire Rampage Linked to Financial Setback," *Los Angeles Times*, February 25, 1997; Matthew Purdy, "The Gunman Premeditated the Attack, Officials Say," *New York Times*, February 25, 1997.

15. James A. Aho, *The Politics of Righteousness: Idaho Christian Patriotism* (Seattle: University of Washington Press, 1990); Joe Guillen, "Frank Spisak Executed

for 1982 Slayings of Three People at Cleveland State University," *Plain Dealer*, February 17, 2011.

16. Mike Weiss, *Double Play: The Hidden Passions Behind the Double Assassination of George Moscone and Harvey Milk* (San Francisco: Vince Emory Productions, 2010).

17. Lois Presser, "Getting on Top through Mass Murder: Narrative, Metaphor, and Violence," *Crime, Media, Culture* 8 (2012): 3–21; Bob Fowler, "Friends: Suspect had Two Sides; Court Records Detail Troubled Marriage, DUI," *Knoxville News Sentinel*, July 29, 2008, https://en.wikipedia.org/wiki/Knoxville_News _Sentinel.

18. Carlin D. Miller, "Joe Stack Plane Crash Austin Aftermath: 13 Injured, Two Critically," *CBS News*, February 18, 2010.

19. Alston Chase, *Harvard and the Unabomber: The Education of an American Terrorist* (New York: Norton, 2003).

20. Jeffrey Manning, Statement by Judge Manning in Baumhammers' Sentencing, Allegheny County Common Pleas Court, September 6, 2001; Andres Martinez, "Richard Baumhammers' Latvian Universe," *Post-Gazette*, May 14, 2000; Barbara Perry, *Hate Crime: Issues and Perspectives* (Westport, CT: Praeger, 2009); Dennis B. Roddy, "History of Mental Illness and Racist Politics Weigh on Baumhammers' Murder Trial," *Post-Gazette*, April 27, 2001.

21. David Holthouse, "Was Alleged Massachusetts Spree Killer a Neo-Nazi? Keith Luke Makes It Official," Southern Poverty Law Center, May 11, 2009.

22. Anne Aly, "Radicalization and the Lone Wolf: What We Do and Do Not Know," *Homeland Security News Wire*, December 19, 2014.

23. Rick Price and Passmate are used as pseudonyms for security reasons.

24. Department of Homeland Security, *Rightwing Extremism: Current Economic and Political Climate Fueling Resurgence in Radicalization and Recruitment* (Washington, DC: Department of Homeland Security, 2009).

25. "Supremacists Extend Reach with the Web," *New York Times*, July 6, 2015.

26. Mark Potok, "Carnage in Charleston," *Southern Poverty Law Center Intelligence Report*, Winter 2015: 20–24.

27. Mark S. Hamm, *American Skinheads: The Criminology and Control of Hate Crime* (Westport, CT: Praeger, 1993).

5. The Enablers

1. Ramon Spaaij, *Understanding Lone Wolf Terrorism: Global Patterns, Motivations and Prevention* (New York: Springer, 2012).

2. Peter Applebome, "Shadowy Bombing Case Is Focusing on Reclusive and Enigmatic Figure," *New York Times*, July 20, 1990; Ray Jenkins, *Blind Vengeance:*

The Roy Moody Mail Bomb Murders (Athens: University of Georgia Press, 1997); Mark Winne, *Priority Mail: The Investigation and Trial of a Mail Bomber Obsessed with Destroying Our Justice System* (New York: Scribner, 1995).

3. Maryanne Vollers, *Lone Wolf: Eric Rudolph and the Legacy of American Terror* (New York: Harper Perennial, 2006).

4. Brandon Stickney, *"All-American Monster": The Unauthorized Biography of Timothy McVeigh* (Amherst, NY: Prometheus, 1996).

5. Quoted in Mark S. Hamm, *Apocalypse in Oklahoma: Waco and Ruby Ridge Revenged* (Boston: Northeastern University Press, 1997), 179.

6. "Alex Jones Profile," Southern Poverty Law Center, https://www.splcenter.org /fighting-hate/extremist-files/individual/alex-jones.

7. John Hamilton, "Progressive Hunter," *Media Matters*, October 2010, http:// mediamatters.org/research/2010/10/11/progressive-hunter/171471.

8. Affidavit of Special Agent Garrett Nabors, August 16, 2012, in authors' possession; "DC Shooter Wanted to Kill as Many as Possible, Prosecutors Say," CNN, February 7, 2013, http://www.cnn.com/2013/02/06/justice/dc-family-research -council-shooting/.

9. Juan Ignacio Blanco, "Ronald Taylor," *Murderpedia*, n.d., http://murderpedia .org/male.T/t/taylor-ronald.htm

10. Walter Griffin, "Report: 'Dirty Bomb' Parts Found in Slain Man's Home," *Bangor Daily News*, February 10, 2009.

6. Broadcasting Intent

1. Louise Richardson, *What Terrorists Want: Understanding the Enemy, Containing the Threat* (New York: Random House, 2006), 103.

2. E-mail from U.S. Marshals Lone Wolf Terrorism Task Force member to Mark Hamm.

3. Michael M. Greenburg, *The Mad Bomber of New York: The Extraordinary Story of the Manhunt that Paralyzed a City* (New York: Union Square Press, 2011).

4. Ibid., 45.

5. Ibid., 128.

6. "Police From All Over Gather in NYC to Formulate Plan to Stop 'Lone Wolf' Terrorists," *CBS New York*, November 6, 2014.

7. Phillip Kerr, "JFK: The Assassin Who Failed," *New Statesman*, November 27, 2000; Dan Lewis, "The Kennedy Assassin Who Failed," Smithsonian.com, December 6, 2012.

8. Peter Hernon, *A Terrible Thunder: The Story of the New Orleans Sniper* (New Orleans: Garrett County Press, 2010).

9. Ibid., 52.

10. Bryan Burrough, *Days of Rage: America's Radical Underground, the FBI, and the Forgotten Age of Revolutionary Violence* (New York: Penguin, 2015).

11. Ibid., 92. Italics added.

12. Ibid., 92.

13. Quoted in ibid., 243. See also Christopher Hewitt, *Political Violence and Terrorism in Modern America: A Chronology* (Westport, CT: Praeger, 2005).

14. Jess Bravin, *Squeaky: The Life and Times of Lynette Alice Fromme* (New York: St. Martin's, 1997).

15. Ibid., 228.

16. Rev. 9:4 (English Standard Version).

17. Bravin, *Squeaky*, 121.

18. Ibid., 199. Italics added.

19. Mel Ayton, *Dark Soul of the South: The Life and Crimes of Racist Killer Joseph Paul Franklin* (Washington, DC: Potomac Books, 2011).

20. Maryanne Vollers, *Lone Wolf: Eric Rudolph and the Legacy of American Terror* (New York: Harper Perennial, 2006).

21. Ibid., 23. Italics added.

22. The exchange appears verbatim in ibid., 23.

23. On the Atlanta bombing investigation and the FBI's and media's treatment of Jewell, see Terry D. Turchie and Kathleen M. Puckett, *Hunting the American Terrorist: The FBI's War on Homegrown Terror* (New York: History, 2007).

24. Ramón Spaaij, "The Enigma of Lone Wolf Terrorism: An Assessment," *Studies in Conflict & Terrorism* 33 (2010): 854–70.

25. Asne Seierstad, *One of Us: The Story of a Massacre in Norway—and Its Aftermath*, trans. Sarah Death (New York: Farrar, Straus and Giroux, 2015), 284–87.

26. Paul Duggan, "Oscar Ramiro Ortega-Hernandez Charged with Attempt to Assassinate Obama," *Washington Post*, November 17, 2011; U.S. Attorney's Office, District of Columbia, Press Release, "Idaho Man Pleads Guilty to Terrorism and Weapons Offenses in Connection with November 2011 Shooting at the White House," September 18, 2013.

27. U.S. Attorney's Office, District of Columbia, Press Release, "Idaho Man Pleads Guilty to Terrorism and Weapons Offenses in Connection with November 2011 Shooting at the White House," September 18, 2013.

28. Duggan, "Oscar Ramiro Ortega-Hernandez Charged with Attempt to Assassinate Obama."

29. "Oscar Ramiro Ortega-Hernandez Declares He Is Jesus Christ," YouTube, May 16, 2012, https://www.youtube.com/watch?v=W2Cv5hZfOmk.

30. Ibid.

31. Duggan, "Oscar Ramiro Ortega-Hernandez Charged with Attempt to Assassinate Obama."

32. Los Angeles World Airport, *Active Shooter Incident and Resulting Airport Disruption* (Los Angeles: Los Angeles World Airport, 2014), https://www.lawa.org/uploadedFiles/LAX/LAWA%20T3%20After%20Action%20Report%20March%2018%202014.pdf; "Shooting at LA Airport," *Washington Post*, November 1, 2013.

33. Brian Michael Jenkins, "Outside Experts View," preface to Daveed Gartenstein-Ross and Laura Grossman, *Terrorists in the U.S. and U.K.: An Empirical Examination of the Radicalization Process* (Washington, DC: FDD's Center for Terrorism Research, 2009).

34. Eric Hoffer, *The True Believer: Thoughts on the Nature of Mass Movements* (New York: Harper Perennial Modern Classics, 2002).

35. Randy Borum, "Understanding Terrorist Psychology," in *The Psychology of Counter-Terrorism*, ed. Andrew Silke, 19–33 (London: Routledge, 2010).

36. John Horgan, "From Profiles to Pathways and Roots to Routes: Perspectives from Psychology on Radicalization into Terrorism," *Annals of the American Academy of Political and Social Science* 618 (2008): 80–94.

37. Clark McCauley and Sophia Moskalenko, "Mechanisms of Political Radicalization: Pathways Toward Terrorism," *Terrorism and Political Violence* 20 (2008): 415–33.

38. Jonathan R. White, *Terrorism: An Introduction* (Belmont, CA: Wadsworth, 2003), 43.

39. National Counterterrorism Center, https://www.nctc.gov/.

40. "Gunman in Orlando Posted to Facebook During Nightclub Attack, Lawmaker Says," *New York Times*, June 16, 2016.

41. "Security Firm Gunman Worked For Has Received Black Eyes Worldwide," *New York Times*, June 18, 2016.

42. "Gunman in Orlando Massacre Excelled in Tests at Firing Range, Records Show," *New York Times*, June 23, 2016.

43. "F.B.I. Studied Shooter Years Before Attack," *New York Times*, June 13, 2016.

44. Ibid.

45. FBI Press Release, remarks by James D. Comey, Director, June 13, 2016.

46. Max Blumenthal and Sarah Lazare, "Before Omar Mateen Committed Mass Murder, the FBI Tried to Lure Him into a Terror Plot," *AlterNet*, June 16, 2016.

47. Ibid.; "Violence and Contradictions on the Path to a Gay Nightclub," *New York Times*, June 14, 2016.

48. "Police Defend Actions as the Clock Ticked," *New York Times*, June 21, 2016.

49. "Orlando Shooter Called Boston Marathon Bombers His 'Homeboys,'" *CBS News*, June 13, 2016.

50. "Orlando Gunman's Wife Gave No Warning to Cops Before Attack," *ABC News*, June 14, 2016.

51. "Omar Mateen: Angry, Violent 'Bigot' Who Pledged Allegiance to ISIS," CNN, June 14, 2016.

52. "'Always Agitated': Mateen's Path from Troubled Child to Aggrieved Killer," *New York Times*, June 19, 2016.

53. "'Suspicious': Gun Store Turned Away Orlando Shooter," *ABC News*, June 16, 2016.

54. "FBI Chief Stakes Out High-Profile Role," *USA Today*, June 20, 2016.

55. "ISIS Calls For More Attacks on West During Ramadan," CNN, May 22, 2016.

56. Eric Lichtblau, "'94 Assault Weapons Ban Shadows Gun Control Bid," *New York Times*, June 20, 2016.

57. On his shaved head, see "Mateen Altered Looks, Researched Anti-Psychotic Drugs Before Attack," Reuters, June 23, 2016.

58. "Orlando Shooter on Facebook: Now 'Taste' ISIS Vengeance," *ABC News*, June 15, 2016.

59. FBI Press Release, "Investigative Update Regarding Pulse Nightclub Shooting," June 20, 2016; "Orlando Shooter Called Boston Marathon Bombers His 'Homeboys.'"

60. FBI Press Release, "Investigative Update Regarding Pulse Nightclub Shooting."

61. "Local Orlando News Station Says Mateen Called During Shooting," *CBS News*, June 15, 2016.

62. "Gunman in Orlando Posted to Facebook During Nightclub Attack, Lawmaker Says."

63. Katherine S. Newman, Cybelle Fox, David J. Harding, Jal Mehta, and Wendy Roth, *Rampage: The Social Roots of School Shootings* (New York: Basic Books, 2004), 251.

7. Triggering Events

1. Jeff Long, *Outlaw: The True Story of Claude Dallas* (New York: William Morrow, 1985); Dan Popkey, "How Did Notorious Idaho Outlaw, Claude Dallas, Escape?," *Idaho Statesman*, March 23, 2008.

2. Ibid., 130.

3. Ibid., 29.

4. Ibid., 31.

5. William Klaber and Philip H. Melanson, *Shadow Play: The Murder of Robert F. Kennedy, the Trial of Sirhan Sirhan, and the Failure of American Justice* (New York: St. Martin's, 1997); "Sirhan Says Liquor, Anger Led Him to Killing," Associated Press, September 27, 1980.

6. Klaber and Melanson, *Shadow Play*, 183.

7. "Sirhan Says Liquor, Anger Led Him to Killing."

8. See Evan Thomas, *Robert Kennedy: His Life* (New York: Simon & Schuster, 2000).

9. Jacob Soboroff, "Robert F. Kennedy Discussed Gun Control in Roseburg 50 Years Ago," MSNBC, October 7, 2015, http://jacobsoboroff.com/post/130684140905/in-1968-robert-f-kennedy-called-for-gun-control.

10. See Pamela Shifman and Salamishah Tillet, "To Stop Violence, Start at Home." *New York Times*, February 3, 2015.

11. Walter DeKeseredy and Martin Schwartz, *Dangerous Exits: Escaping Abusive Relationships in Rural America* (New Brunswick, NJ: Rutgers University Press, 2009).

12. Quoted in Asne Seierstad, *One of Us: The Story of a Massacre in Norway—and Its Aftermath*, trans. Sarah Death (New York: Farrar, Straus and Giroux, 2015), 166, 196.

13. Robbyn Brooks and Tom McLaughlin, "FDLE Releases Report Detailing Shooting of Two Deputies," *Northwest Florida Daily News*, October 9, 2009.

14. Ibid.

15. "Charges Filed In 'Heinous, Tragic Hate Crime,'" KIRO TV, August 2, 2006; Josh Felt and Brendan Kiley, "Waiting Period: Jewish Federation Shooting Suspect Naveed Haq's Lost Summer," *Stranger*, August 3–9, 2006; "Incidents Clash with Image Suspect Conveyed in School," *Seattle Times*, July 7, 2006; "Naveed Haq," *Murderpedia*, http://murderpedia.org/male.H/h/haq-naveed.htm.

16. "Incidents Clash with Image Suspect Conveyed in School."

17. Felt and Kiley, "Waiting Period."

18. Ibid.

19. Ibid.

20. Ibid., this quote and the preceding.

21. "Charges Filed In 'Heinous, Tragic Hate Crime.'"

22. Ibid.

23. "A Sampling of Jared Loughner's Social Media Postings," CNN, January 11, 2011; "About Rep. Gabrielle Giffords," *K. F. Stone Weekly*, January 10, 2011; "A Look Back: October 20, 1997–March 8, 1998," *Tucson Business*, October 20, 1997; Leo W. Banks, "The Krentz Bonfire: Will the Murder of a Respected Cochise County Rancher Change Anything on Our Border?," *Tucson Weekly*, April 29, 2010; Dan Barry, "Looking Behind the Mug-Shot Grin," *New York Times*, January 15, 2011; Nick Baumann, "Exclusive: Loughner Friend Explains Alleged Gunman's Grudge Against Giffords," *Mother Jones*, January 10, 2010; Rhonda Bodfield, "Threats Lead Grijalva to Close Tucson, Yuma Offices," *Arizona Daily Star*, April 24, 2010; Cindy Carcamo and Michael Mello, "Reports

Detail Jared Loughner's Behavior Before Tucson Shooting," *Los Angeles Times*, March 27, 2013; "Congresswoman Gabrielle Giffords Talks Palin Cross Hairs," MSNBC, March 25, 2010; Gabrielle Giffords and Mark Kelly, with Jeffrey Zaslow, *Gabby: A Story of Courage, Love, and Resilience* (New York: Scribner, 2011); "Gabrielle Giffords Shooting in Tucson: Did it Stem from State of Political Discourse?," *Washington Post*, January 9, 2011; "Loughner's Dad Feared He Was 'Out of Control,' Neighbor Says," CNN, January 13, 2011; Suzy Khimm, "After Giffords' Shooting, Rep. Grijalva Blames Rage-Fueled Political Climate," *Mother Jones*, January 8, 2011; Adam Klawonn, "What Motivated Giffords' Shooter?" *Time*, January 9, 2011; Richard A. Serrano and Michael Muskal, "Chronology Shows Jared Laughner in Hours Before Shooting Rampage," *Los Angeles Times*, January 15, 2011; "Shooting Throws Spotlight on U.S. Political Rhetoric," CNN, January 10, 2011; "The Great CD8 Debate," *Tucson Weekly*, September 18, 2008; "Tucson: Descent Into Madness," *60 Minutes*, January 16, 2011; Kurt F. Stone, *The Jews of Capital Hill: A Compendium of Jewish Members of Congress* (Lanham, MD: Scarecrow Press, 2011); "Obama to Send More Troops to Southwest Border Region," CNN, March 25, 2010; "Tucson Gunman Before Rampage: 'I'll See You on National T.v.,'" *CBS News*, April 11, 2014.

24. "About Rep. Gabrielle Giffords."
25. "A Look Back."
26. Baumann, "Exclusive."
27. "Loughner's Dad Feared He Was 'Out of Control,' Neighbor Says."
28. Baumann, "Exclusive."
29. Richard Hofstadter "The Paranoid Style in American Politics," *Harper's Magazine*, November 1964, 77–86.
30. "Tucson: Descent into Madness."
31. Baumann, "Exclusive."
32. Ibid.
33. Klawonn, "What Motivated Giffords' Shooter?"
34. "The Great CD8 Debate."
35. Bodfield, "Threats Lead Grijalva to Close Tucson, Yuma Offices."
36. "Congresswoman Gabrielle Giffords Talks Palin Cross Hairs."
37. Ibid.
38. Giffords and Kelly, *Gabby*, 11.
39. "Obama to Send More Troops to Southwest Border Region."
40. See Banks, "The Krentz Bonfire."
41. Baumann, "Exclusive."
42. James A. Aho, *The Politics of Righteousness: Idaho Christian Patriotism* (Seattle: University of Washington Press, 1990).
43. Carcamo and Mello, "Reports Detail Jared Loughner's Behavior Before Tucson Shooting."

44. "Tucson: Descent into Madness."
45. "Loughner's Dad Feared He Was 'Out of Control,' Neighbor Says."
46. "Tucson Gunman Before Rampage."
47. Ibid.
48. "A Sampling of Jared Loughner's Social Media Postings."
49. "Tucson Gunman Before Rampage."
50. Giffords and Kelly, *Gabby*, 164.
51. Baumann, "Exclusive."
52. Serrano and Muskal, "Chronology Shows Jared Laughner in Hours Before Shooting Rampage."
53. "Tucson Gunman Before Rampage."
54. Barry, "Looking Behind the Mug-Shot Grin."
55. "Shooting Throws Spotlight on U.S. Political Rhetoric."
56. "Gabrielle Giffords Shooting in Tucson."
57. Khimm, "After Giffords' Shooting, Rep. Grijalva Blames Rage-Fueled Political Climate."
58. "Congresswoman Gabrielle Giffords Talks Palin Cross Hairs."
59. "Remarks by the President at a Memorial Service for the Victims of the Shooting in Tucson, Arizona," White House, Office of the Press Secretary, January 12, 2011, http://www.whitehouse.gov/the-press-office/2011/01/12/remarks -president-barack-obama-memorial-service-victims-shooting-tucson.

8. The Radicalization Model of Lone Wolf Terrorism

1. Ramón Spaaij, "The Enigma of Lone Wolf Terrorism: An Assessment," *Studies in Conflict & Terrorism* 33 (2010): 854–70.
2. Dan Ephron, *Killing a King: The Assassination of Yitzhak Rabin and the Making of Israel* (New York: Norton, 2015).
3. Asne Seierstad, *One of Us: The Story of a Massacre in Norway—and Its Aftermath*, trans. Sarah Death (New York: Farrar, Straus and Giroux, 2015).
4. Marc Sageman, *Understanding Terror Networks* (Philadelphia: University of Pennsylvania Press, 2004).
5. Ariel Merari, *Driven to Death: Psychological and Social Aspects of Suicide Terrorism* (New York: Oxford University Press, 2010), 96.
6. Robert A. Fein and Bryan Vossekuil, "Assassination in the United States: An Operational Study of Recent Assassins, Attackers, and Near-Lethal Approachers," *Journal of Forensic Science* 44 (1999): 321–33.
7. Leena Malkki, "Political Elements in Post-Columbine School Shootings in Europe and North America," *Terrorism and Political Violence* 26 (2014): 185–210.

8. Peter Bergen, *United States of Jihad: Investigating America's Homegrown Terrorists* (New York: Crown, 2016), 43.

9. Bruce Hoffman, ed., *The Radicalization of Diasporas and Terrorism, Conference Proceedings* (Santa Monica, CA: RAND, 2007).

10. Paul Gill, *Lone-Actor Terrorism: A Behavioral Analysis* (New York: Routledge, 2015).

11. Clark McCauley and Sophia Moskalenko, "Toward a Profile of Lone Wolf Terrorists: What Moves Individuals from Radical Opinion to Radical Action," *Terrorism and Political Violence* 26 (2014): 83.

12. Brian J. Phillips, "Deadlier in the U.S.? On Lone Wolves, Terrorist Groups, and Attack Lethality," *Terrorism and Political Violence*, May 2015; Ramon Spaaij, *Understanding Lone Wolf Terrorism: Global Patterns, Motivations and Prevention* (New York: Springer, 2012).

13. "Al Qaeda Video Resurfaces Claiming How Easy It Is to Buy Guns in U.S.," CNN, April 12, 2013.

14. Christopher Ingraham, "From 2004 to 2014, Over 2,000 Terrorist Suspects Legally Purchased Guns in the United States," *Washington Post*, November 16, 2015.

15. Pamela Haag, *The Gunning of America: Business and the Making of American Gun Culture* (New York: Basic Books, 2016), 185.

16. Douglas Weibe, "Homicide and Geographic Access to Gun Dealers in the United States," *BMC Public Health* 9 (June 2009), http://bmcpublichealth .biomedcentral.com/articles/10.1186/1471-2458-9-199.

17. See Richard B. Felson and Henry J. Steadman, "Situational Factors in Disputes Leading to Criminal Violence," *Criminology* 21 (1983): 59–74.

18. Ephron, *Killing a King*.

19. Seierstad, *One of Us*.

20. Merari, *Driven to Death*.

21. Diego Gambetta, ed., *Making Sense of Suicide Missions* (Oxford: Oxford University Press, 2006).

22. Masha Gessen, *The Brothers: The Road to An American Tragedy* (New York: Riverhead, 2015), 128.

23. Fein and Vossekuil, "Assassination in the United States."

24. United States Secret Service, *The Final Report and Findings of the Safe School Initiative* (Washington, DC: U.S. Secret Service, 2002). See also Katherine S. Newman, Cybelle Fox, David J. Harding, Jal Mehta, and Wendy Roth, *Rampage: The Social Roots of School Shootings* (New York: Basic Books, 2004).

25. Seierstad, *One of Us*.

26. Spaaij, *Understanding Lone Wolf Terrorism*.

27. Louise Richardson, *What Terrorists Want: Understanding the Enemy, Containing the Threat* (New York: Random House, 2006), 103.

28. Anthony Summers and Robbyn Swan, *The Eleventh Day: The Full Story of 9/11 and Osama Bin Laden* (New York: Ballantine, 2011).

29. Mina Al-Lami, *Studies of Radicalization: State of the Field Report* (London: Royal Holloway University of London, 2009).

30. Ken Ballen, *Terrorists in Love: True Life Stories of Islamic Radicals* (New York: Free Press, 2011); Farhad Khosrokhavar, *Suicide Bombers: Allah's New Martyrs* (London: Pluto Press, 2005).

31. Jerrold Post, Keven Ruby, and Eric Shaw, "The Radical Group in Context: 1. An Integrated Framework for the Analysis of Group Risk for Terrorism," *Studies in Conflict and Terrorism* 25 (2002): 97.

32. Mark S. Hamm, *Apocalypse in Oklahoma: Waco and Ruby Ridge Revenged* (Boston: Northeastern University Press, 1997).

33. Sari Horwitz and Michael E. Ruane, *Sniper: Inside the Hunt for the Killers Who Terrorized the Nation* (New York: Random House, 2003).

34. United States Secret Service, *The Final Report and Findings of the Safe School Initiative*.

35. George Michael, *Lone Wolf Terror and the Rise of Leaderless Resistance* (Nashville, TN: Vanderbilt University Press, 2012); Jeffrey D. Simon, *Lone Wolf Terrorism: Understanding the Growing Threat* (Amherst, NY: Prometheus Books, 2013); Gabriel Weimann, "Lone Wolves in Cyberspace," *Journal of Terrorism Research* 3 (2012): 75–90.

36. Sageman, *Leaderless Jihad*, 109.

37. E-mail from Task Force member to Mark Hamm, June 14, 2013.

38. McCauley and Moskalenko propose two profiles of lone wolf terrorists and relate these profiles to pathways to participating in a terrorist group ("radicalization pyramids"), but they do not develop a model for lone wolf terrorism. McCauley and Moskalenko, "Toward a Profile of Lone Wolf Terrorists."

39. See Sageman, *Leaderless Jihad*; Mitchell D. Silber and Arvin Ghatt, *Radicalization in the West: The Homegrown Threat* (New York: New York Police Department, 2007); Robert Pape, *Dying to Win: The Strategic Logic of Suicide Terrorism* (New York: Random House, 2005).

40. Silber and Ghatt, *Radicalization in the West*

41. Peter R. Neumann, "The Trouble with Radicalization," *International Affairs*, 89 (2013): 873–93.

42. The model has been peer-reviewed by the National Institute of Justice, as well as various editors and external reviewers of journals and edited volumes where we have published results based on the database. Altogether, approximately twenty terrorism researchers and experts have reviewed the model. A number

of radicalization models created by other researchers appear as online working papers that have not been through the peer-review process.

43. Likewise, Sageman argues that his four-stage model is neither a linear nor a progressive model with easily identifiable boundaries. Sageman, *Leaderless Jihad*.

44. Hampton Sides, *Hellhound on His Trail: The Stalking of Martin Luther King, Jr., and the International Hunt for His Assassin* (New York: Doubleday, 2010).

45. John Wells, *Sniper: The True Story of Anti-Abortion Killer James Kopp* (New York: Harper Collins, 2013).

46. One exception is the self-styled survivalist Eric Frein, who was the subject of a forty-eight-day manhunt though the Pocono Mountains after gunning down two Pennsylvania state troopers on September 12, 2014.

47. David Willman, *The Mirage Man: Bruce Ivins, the Anthrax Attacks, and America's Rush to War* (New York: Bantam, 2011); Jeanne Guillemin, *American Anthrax* (New York: Henry Holt, 2011); Department of Justice, *Amerithrax Investigative Summary* (Washington, DC: U.S. Department of Justice, 2010).

48. Expert Behavioral Analysis Panel, *Amerithrax Case: Report of the Expert Behavioral Analysis Panel* (Vienna, VA: Research Strategies Network, 2011).

49. Bill Morlin, "The Spokane Bomb Attempt: Who is Kevin William Harpham?" *Hatewatch*, March 10, 2011.

50. Morlin, "The Spokane Bombing Attempt."

51. Ibid.

52. Ibid. Italics added.

53. Hamm, *Apocalypse in Oklahoma*.

54. Eric Hoffer, *The True Believer: Thoughts on the Nature of Mass Movements* (New York: Harper Perennial Modern Classics, 2002), xii.

55. Scott Shane and James Dao, "Tangle of Clues About Suspect at Fort Hood," *New York Times*, November 14, 2009.

56. Dana Priest, "Fort Hood Suspect Warned of Threats Within the Ranks," *Washington Post*, November 10, 2009.

57. Martha Raddatz, Brian Ross, and Mary-Rose Abraham, "Senior Official: More Hasan Ties to People Under Investigation by FBI," *ABC News*, November 10, 2009.

58. Mariah Blake, "Internal Documents Reveal How the FBI Blew Ft. Hood," *Mother Jones*, August 27, 2013; *Final Report of the William H. Webster Commission on the Federal Bureau of Investigation, Counterterrorism Intelligence, and the Events at Fort Hood, Texas, on November 5, 2009*, 2013, https://archive.org/details/final-report-of-the-william-h.-webster-commission.

59. Lois Presser, "Getting on Top Through Mass Murder: Narrative, Metaphor, and Violence," *Crime, Media, Culture* 8 (2012): 3–21.

60. Erik von Brunn, "Statement by Erik von Brunn," *ABC News*, June 12, 2009.

61. John Hamilton, "Progressive Hunter," *Media Matters*, October 11, 2010, http://mediamatters.org/research/2010/10/11/progressive-hunter/171471.

62. Anti-Defamation League (ADL), "White Supremacist Shooting Spree Leaves Blood Trial," *Combatting Hate*, January 22, 2009.

63. Everytown for Gun Safety, *Guns and Violence Against Women*, 2015, http://everytown.org/article/guns-and-violence-against-women/.

64. "Joseph Ferguson," *Murderpedia*, http://murderpedia.org/male.F/f/ferguson-joseph.htm.

65. John Gonzales, "Darkness Falls," *Boston Magazine*, May 2006.

66. Ian Shapira, "Pentagon Shooter's Spiral from Early Promise to Madness," *Washington Post*, March 7, 2010.

67. Rick Romell, "Shooter's Behavior Did Not Go Unnoticed," *Journal Sentinel*, August 7, 2012.

68. Christopher Goffard, Joel Rubin, and Kurt Streeter, "The Manhunt for Christopher Dorner," *Los Angeles Times*, December 3, 2013.

69. Matthew Lysiak, *Newtown: An American Tragedy* (New York: Gallery Books, 2013).

70. Ruben Vives, "Oregon Shooter Was Anxious and Liked Guns and Target Shooting," *Los Angeles Times*, October 2, 2015.

71. See The Soufan Group, "Targeting the Uniform," *TSG IntelBrief*, December 22, 2014, http://soufangroup.com/tsg-intelbrief-targeting-the-uniform/.

72. Ibid.

73. "Man Held in France in Attack on Soldier," *New York Times*, May 30, 2013; "Gunman's Attack on Parliament Shakes Ottawa," *New York Times*, October 23, 2014; "Melbourne Shooting: Man Being Investigated over Terrorism Shot Dead after Stabbing Police Officers Outside Endeavour Hills Police Station," *ABC News*, September 24, 2014.

74. Quoted in Ephron, *Killing a King*, 92.

75. "Obama: Fighting Lone Wolf Terrorism Is Like Trying to Stop Mass Shootings," *Hill*, December 18, 2015.

76. See also Randall Collins, *Violence: A Micro-Sociological Theory* (Princeton: Princeton University Press, 2008).

77. Max Blumenthal, "Ike's Other Warning," *New York Times*, September 2, 2009.

78. Hoffer, *The True Believer*, 62.

79. Robert J. Sampson and John R. Laub, "Socioeconomic Achievements in the Life Course of Disadvantaged Men: Military Service as a Turning Point," *American Sociological Review* 61 (1996): 340–57. The Iraq War served as a recruiting tool for al-Qaeda, increasing by one-third the number of fatal attacks by jihadists around the globe. See J. M. Berger, *Jihadi Joe: Americans Who Go to War in the Name of Islam* (Washington, DC: Potomac Books, 2011).

9. The Little Rock Military Shooting

1. The following composite is drawn from Abdulhakim Muhammad's letters to *Memphis Commercial Appeal* reporter Kristina Goetz, May 18, September 1, and September 30, 2010; Randall Collins, "Entering and Leaving the Tunnel of Violence: Micro-Sociological Dynamics of Emotional Entrainment in Violent Interactions," *Current Sociology*, 6 (2012): 132–51; Competency Evaluation for Abdulhakim Mujahid Muhammad, Arkansas Department of Human Services, Arkansas State Hospital, Forensic Report, July 20, 2010; James Dao, "A Muslim Son, a Murder Trial and Many Questions." *New York Times*, February 10, 2010; Daveed Gartenstein-Ross, "Lone Wolf Islamic Terrorism: Abdulhakim Mujahid Muhammad (Carlos Bledsoe) Case Study," *Terrorism and Political Violence* 26 (2014): 110–28; Kristina Goetz, "Muslim Who Shot Soldier in Arkansas Says He Wanted to Cause More Death," *Memphis Commercial Appeal*, November 13, 2010; Kristina Goetz, "When Carlos Bledsoe Became Abdulhakim Mujahid Muhammad," *Memphis Commercial Appeal*, November 14, 2010; Kristina Goetz, "Muhammad Admits on Interrogation Video that Killing Was Retribution," *Memphis Commercial Appeal*, July 22, 2011; Kristina Goetz, "Delusion Guided Accused Shooter of Soldiers at Little Rock Recruiting Center," *Memphis Commercial Appeal*, July 23, 2011; Little Rock Police Department, Affidavit for Search & Seizure Warrant and Search Warrant Inventory, June 2, 2009; Americans for Peace & Tolerance, *Losing Our Sons*, 2012 (DVD); NPR, *All Things Considered*, June 8, 2009; Richard A. Serrano, "Federal Government Isn't Touching Arkansas Terrorism Case," *Los Angeles Times*, July 11, 2011; Scott Shane, *Objective Troy: A Terrorist, A President, and the Rise of the Drone* (New York: Tim Duggan Books, 2015); Statement of Melvin Bledsoe, "The Extent of Radicalization in the American Muslim Community and that Community's Response," Committee on Homeland Security, U.S House of Representatives, March 10, 2011; Jeff Tang, "Man Confesses to 'Jihad Operation' Murder in Nashville," NewsChannel5.com, April 13, 2011. Correspondence from Bledsoe to Mark Hamm is used only to confirm media reports due to the fact that Bledsoe refused to sign an informed consent statement. References for specific quotations by Bledsoe are provided in the notes following.
2. Goetz, "Muslim Who Shot Soldier in Arkansas Says He Wanted to Cause More Death."
3. Letter from Muhammad to Goetz, May 18, 2010.
4. Ibid.
5. Letter from Muhammad to Goetz, September 1, 2010.
6. Letter from Muhammad to Goetz, May 18, 2010.

7. "Al Qaeda in Yemen Claims Responsibility for Charlie Hebdo Attack," *Wall Street Journal*, January 14, 2015.

8. Goetz, "Muslim Who Shot Soldier in Arkansas Says He Wanted to Cause More Death."

9. Bledsoe's father, his attorney, and the FBI would all agree that Bledsoe was radicalized in the prison.

10. Goetz, "Muslim Who Shot Soldier in Arkansas Says He Wanted to Cause More Death."

11. Letter from Muhammad to Goetz, September 30, 2010.

12. Goetz, "Muhammad Admits on Interrogation Video that Killing Was Retaliation."

13. Competency Evaluation for Abdulhakim Mujahid Muhammad.

14. Terry Lee, "Was Madman Nidal Hasan Part of a Sleeper Cell?" Fox News Interview with Colonel Terry Lee, November 6, 2009.

15. Goetz, "Muslim Who Shot Soldier in Arkansas Says He Wanted to Cause More Death."

16. Shane, *Objective Troy*, 11.

17. Competency Evaluation for Abdulhakim Mujahid Muhammad.

18. Ibid.

19. Serrano, "Federal Government Isn't Touching Arkansas Terrorism Case."

20. Tang, "Man Confesses to 'Jihad Operation' Murder in Nashville."

21. Asne Seierstad, *One of Us: The Story of a Massacre in Norway—and Its Aftermath*, trans. Sarah Death (New York: Farrar, Straus and Giroux, 2015), 421.

22. Jessica Stern, *Terror in the Name of God: Why Religious Militants Kill* (New York: Ecco, 2003); Jeff Victoroff, "The Mind of the Terrorist: A Review and Critique of Psychological Approaches," *Journal of Conflict Resolution* 49 (2005): 3–42.

23. Competency Evaluation for Abdulhakim Mujahid Muhammad.

24. Alissa Rubin, "Radicalization of a Promising Student Turned Bomb-Maker in Brussels." *New York Times*, April 8, 2016.

10. The Pittsburgh Police Shooting

1. The ensuing composite is drawn from the following sources: Commonwealth of Pennsylvania, "Police Criminal Complaint, Commonwealth of Pennsylvania v. Richard Andrew Poplawski," April 4, 2009; Judge A. J. Manning, "Commonwealth of Pennsylvania v. Richard Andrew Poplawski, No. CC 200905652, In the Court of Common Pleas of Allegheny County, Pennsylvania, Criminal Division," *Pittsburgh Legal Journal* 161, no. 8 (2013): 145–61; Rich Lord and Paula Reed Ward, "A Portrait of Contrasts Emerges from Those Who Knew Poplawski." *Pittsburgh Post-Gazette*, April 12, 2009; Carl Prine,

"Poplawski's Teen Trouble Deepens into Alienation, Anger," *Pittsburgh Tribune-Review*, April 8, 2009; Dennis B. Roddy, "Suspect in Officers' Shooting Was into Conspiracy Theories," *Pittsburgh Post-Gazette*, April 5, 2009; Associated Press, "Dispute Led to Shootings in Pittsburgh," *New York Times*, April 6, 2009, A13; Dennis B. Roddy, "Richard Poplawski: Two Profiles Emerge," *Pittsburgh Post-Gazette*, April 4, 2009; Joe Mandak, "Jury Sentences Convicted Killer to Death for Murdering 3 Pittsburgh Police Officers in 2009," Associated Press, June 29, 2011; Joe Mandak, "Pennsylvania Man Found Guilty in Killing of 3 Pittsburgh Police Officers in 2009," Associated Press, June 26, 2011; Joe Mandak, "Jury Hears of Suspect Describing Pittsburgh Police Shooting in Phone Calls During Standoff," Associated Press, June 22, 2011; Liz Robbins and Sean D. Hamill, "Gunman Kills 3 Police Officers in Pittsburgh," *New York Times*, April 5, 2009, A19; Sean D. Hamill, "Man Accused in Pittsburgh Killings Voiced Racist Views Online," *New York Times*, April 7, 2009, A19; Jill King Greenwood and Jeremy Boren, "Poplawski's Statement, Police Reports Detail Stanton Heights Shootout," *Pittsburgh Tribune-Review*, April 8, 2009; Dennis B. Roddy, "Poplawski Was 'Braced for Fate' in Days Leading to Attack," *Pittsburgh Post-Gazette*, April 6, 2009; Dennis B. Roddy, "Poplawski's Web Postings Warned of 'Enemies,'" *Pittsburgh Post-Gazette*, April 7, 2009; Anti-Defamation League, "Richard Poplawski: The Making of a Lone Wolf," April 8, 2009, http://archive.adl.org/learn/extremism_in_the_news/white_supremacy /poplawski%20report.html#.V-1ag9QrL4Y; Anti-Defamation League, "Richard Poplawski: Selected On-Line Postings, 2007–2009," http://archive.adl.org /extremism/richard-poplawski-comments-categorized.pdf; Will Bunch, *The Backlash: Right-Wing Radicals, Hi-Def Hucksters, and Paranoid Politics in the Age of Obama* (New York: Harper, 2010); Daryl Johnson, *Right-Wing Resurgence: How a Domestic Terrorist Threat Is Being Ignored* (Lanham, MD: Rowman & Littlefield, 2012). Correspondence from Richard Poplawski to the authors is used only to corroborate media reports due to the fact that he refused to sign an informed consent statement. Poplawski further provided the authors with a one-page public statement regarding his case, which marked the fifth anniversary of his April 4, 2009, attack. Sources for specific quotations of Poplawski and his significant others are provided in the following notes.

2. Timothy McNulty, Paula Reed Ward, and Sadie Gurman, "Jury Decides Poplawski Should Die for Killing 3 Officers," *Pittsburgh Post-Gazette*, June 28, 2011.

3. Lord and Reed Ward, "A Portrait of Contrasts Emerges from Those Who Knew Poplawski."

4. Bunch, *The Backlash*.

5. "Pittsburgh: On Richard Poplawski, Edward Perkovic and Right-Wing White Supremacy," *Common Struggle*, April 9, 2009.

6. Anti-Defamation League, "Richard Poplawski," 5.

7. Commonwealth of Pennsylvania, "Police Criminal Complaint, Commonwealth of Pennsylvania v. Richard Andrew Poplawski."

8. Anti-Defamation League, "Richard Poplawski," 30.

9. Johnson, *Right-Wing Resurgence*, 268–69.

10. Anti-Defamation League, "Richard Poplawski," 16.

11. Bunch, *The Backlash*.

12. Anti-Defamation League, "Richard Poplawski," 14–15.

13. Bunch, *The Backlash*, 277.

14. David Streitfeld, "For Pittsburgh, There's Life after Steel," *New York Times*, January 8, 2009, A1.

15. Ibid.

16. "Stanton Heights Neighborhood in Pittsburgh, Pennsylvania (PA), Detailed Profile," http://www.city-data.com/neighborhood/Stanton-Heights-Pittsburgh-PA.html.

17. Anti-Defamation League, "Richard Poplawski," 6–8.

18. Ibid., 13.

19. Hamill, "Man Accused in Pittsburgh Killings Voiced Racist Views Online."

20. McCauley and Moskalenko rightly argue that there is an important difference between radicalization in opinion and radicalization in action. McCauley and Moskalenko, "Toward a Profile of Lone Wolf Terrorists: What Moves Individuals from Radical Opinion to Radical Action," *Terrorism and Political Violence* 26 (2014).

21. One such exception is Poplawski's conspiracy theory postings on Letsgopens, the Pittsburgh Penguins fan site, to which a fellow poster replied: "Life must be pretty rough in your paranoid, dark world."

22. Bunch, *The Backlash*; Will Bunch, "The Pittsburgh Cop Killer, the Radio 'Hit List,' and the Right-Wing Media," Philly.com, August 31, 2010, http://www.philly.com/philly/blogs/attytood/Poplawski.html. Italics added.

23. Mandak, "Jury Hears of Suspect Describing Pittsburgh Police Shooting."

24. Robbins and Hamill, "Gunman Kills 3 Police Officers in Pittsburgh."

25. "Poplawski Trial: Day 6," *Pittsburgh Post-Gazette*, June 25, 2011; "No Insanity Defense in Pittsburgh Police Deaths," Associated Press, April 19, 2011.

26. Sadie Gurman, "Poplawski Ends Silence from his Jail Cell," *Pittsburgh Post-Gazette*, June 16, 2009.

27. Ibid.

28. Pennsylvania Office of Open Records, "Final Determination in the Matter of Richard Poplawski v. Pennsylvania Department of Corrections," March 12, 2014, 2.

29. Ibid.; "Pa. Inmate Asks for Info on Drugs for Execution," *Legal Monitor Worldwide*, May 13, 2014.

30. Johnson, *Right-Wing Resurgence*, 273.

31. Michael E. Ruane and Madonna Lebling, "Von Brunn, White Supremacist Holocaust Museum Shooter, Dies," *Washington Post*, January 7, 2010.

32. "Online YouTube Rap Video Praises Triple Pittsburgh Cop-Killer, Urges Killing Other Officers," Associated Press, November 17, 2012.

33. Liz Navratil, "2 Rappers Sought for Video Threats on Police," *Pittsburgh Post-Gazette*, November 17, 2012.

34. Ibid.; "2 Men Convicted in Western Pa. in Online Rap Video Targeting Pittsburgh Police," Associated Press, November 22, 2013.

11. Lone Wolf Sting Operations

1. Clark McCauley and Sophia Moskalenko, "Toward a Profile of Lone Wolf Terrorists: What Moves Individuals from Radical Opinion to Radical Action," *Terrorism and Political Violence* 26 (2014): 415–33.

2. Trevor Aaronson, *The Terror Factory: Inside the FBI's Manufactured War on Terrorism* (Brooklyn, NY: ig, 2013); Human Rights Watch, *Illusion of Justice: Human Rights Abuse in US Terrorism Prosecutions* (New York: Columbia Law School Human Rights Institute, 2014).

3. "FBI Director on Threat of ISIS, Cybersecurity," *60 Minutes*, October 5, 2014.

4. Arun Kundnani, *The Muslims Are Coming! Islamophobia, Extremism, and the Domestic War on Terror* (New York: Verso, 2014).

5. Geri Spieler, *Taking Aim at the President: The Remarkable Story of the Woman Who Shot at Gerald Ford* (New York: Palgrave Macmillan, 2009).

6. Betty Medsger, *The Burglary: The Discovery of J. Edgar Hoover's Secret FBI* (New York: Knopf, 2014).

7. Spieler, *Taking Aim at the President*, 148.

8. Ibid., 155.

9. Mark S. Hamm, *Terrorism as Crime: From Oklahoma City to Al-Qaeda and Beyond* (New York: New York University Press, 2007).

10. Source: various news reports.

11. Kundnani, *The Muslims Are Coming!*

12. Human Rights Watch, *Illusion of Justice.*

13. Trevor Aaronson, "The Sting: How the FBI Created a Terrorist," *Intercept*, March 16, 2015, https://firstlook.org/theintercept/2015/03/16/howthefbicreate daterrorist/.

14. Tim Weiner, *Enemies: A History of the FBI* (New York: Random House, 2012).

15. Peter Finn, "Documents Provide Rare Insight into FBI's Terrorism Stings," *Washington Post*, April 13, 2012.

16. Kate Davis and David Heilbrover, *The Newburgh Sting*, HBO documentary, 2014.

17. An estimated 50 percent of the more than 500 federal counterterrorism convictions since 9/11 have resulted from informant-based cases (see Aaronson, *The Terror Factory*).

18. Aaronson, *The Terror Factory*, 55.

19. Affidavit of Special Agent Gary S. Cacace, September 28, 2011, http://www .investigativeproject.org/documents/case_docs/1690.pdf.

20. Aaronson, "The Sting."

21. Hamm, letters and interview with Quazi Nafis, Federal Prison Camp, Edgefield, SC, August 4 and 5, 2015; Collen Long, "Obama Was Allegedly Considered as a Target in Terrorism Plot," *Huffington Post*, October 18, 2012; Quazi Nafis, Letter to Judge Carol Bagley Amon, July 31, 2013; Dean Nelson, "New York Fed Bomb Plot: How Quazi Nafis Became Radicalized," *Telegraph*, October 18, 2012; Mosi Secret, "Man Is Charged with Plotting to Bomb Federal Reserve Bank in Manhattan," *New York Times*, October 17, 2012; Mosi Secret, "F.B.I. Arrests Second Suspect in Bomb Plot Against Bank," *New York Times*, October 18, 2012; "SEMO Classmate Is Shocked at Terror Subject's Arrest," *St. Louis Post-Dispatch*, October 19, 2012; Scott Shane, *Objective Troy: A Terrorist, a President, and the Rise of the Drone* (New York: Tim Duggan Books, 2015); *USA v. Quazi Mohammed Rezwanul Ahsan Nafis*, Criminal Complaint (undated).

22. Nafis letter to Hamm, April 8, 2015.

23. Ibid.

24. Ibid.

25. U.S. Attorney's Office, Eastern District of New York, Press Release, February 7, 2013.

26. Hamm interview with Nafis.

27. Long, "Obama Was Allegedly Considered."

28. "SEMO Classmate Is Shocked at Terror Subject's Arrest."

29. Nafis letter to Hamm.

30. Hamm interview with Nafis.

31. Nafis letter to Judge Amon.

32. Hamm interview with Nafis.

33. Ibid.

34. Nafis letter to Judge Amon.

35. Hamm interview with Nafis.

36. *USA v. Nafis*, 10.

37. Ibid., 11.

38. Ibid., 16–17.

39. Hamm interview with Nafis.

40. Ibid.

41. *USA v. Nafis*, 19.

42. Secret, "Man Is Charged with Plotting to Bomb Federal Reserve Bank in Manhattan."

43. Joseph A. Carter, Shiraz Maher, and Peter R. Neumann, *Greenbirds: Measuring Importance and Influence in Syrian Foreign Fighter Networks* (International Centre for the Study of Radicalisation and Political Violence: King's College London, 2014).

44. Sam Stanton and Denny Walsh, "Lodi-Area Terror Suspect Says He Would Not Have Acted Against His Own Country," *Sacramento Bee*, August 16, 2014; *USA v. Nicholas Michael Teausant*, Criminal Complaint, March 17, 2014. The case is not in the database because it occurred after 2013.

45. *USA v. Teausant*, 3.

46. Ibid., 6.

47. Ibid, 9.

48. Ibid., 12.

49. Stanton and Walsh, "Lodi-Area Terror Suspect Says He Would Not Have Acted Against His Own Country."

50. FBI, "Domestic Terrorism in the Post-9/11 Era," 2015, http://www.fbi.gov /news/stories/2009/september/domterror_090709.

51. Andrew Borrello, "Focus on Ethics: The Power of Police Civility," *FBI Law Enforcement Bulletin*, August 2012, http://leb.fbi.gov/2012/august/focus-on-ethics -%20the-power-of-police-civility.

52. "Denmark Offers Some Foreign Fighters Rehab Without Jail Time—But Will It Work?" CNN, October 28, 2014.

53. David Von Drehle, "The European Front," *Time*, January 26, 2015.

54. Mark S. Hamm, *The Spectacular Few: Prisoner Radicalization and the Evolving Terrorist Threat* (New York: New York University Press, 2013).

55. See for example "U.S. Steps Up Fight to Stem Flow of Volunteers to the Islamic State," *New York Times*, October 9, 2014. Other information comes from the authors' ongoing collection of terrorism cases in the United States.

56. Seamus Hughes, "Islamic State Is Successfully Radicalizing Americans. How Do We Stop Them?," *Los Angeles Times*, May 18, 2016.

12. Lone Wolf Terrorism and FBI Mythmaking

1. Truman Capote, *In Cold Blood: A True Account of a Multiple Murder and Its Consequences* (New York: Random House, 1993), 260. See also Travis Linnemann, "Capote's Ghosts: Violence, Media and the Spectre of Suspicion," *British Journal of Criminology* 55 (2015): 514–33.

2. The prison held this distinction until 2005, when it was downgraded to a medium-security facility.

3. Pete Earley, *The Hot House: Life Inside Leavenworth Prison* (New York: Bantam, 1992).

4. FBI Press Release, "Act of Terror Averted: Would-Be Bomber Sentenced in Chicago," May 31, 2013.

5. Athan G. Theoharis, ed., *The FBI: A Comprehensive Reference Guide* (Phoenix: Oryx Press, 1999), 266.

6. Ronald Kessler, *The FBI* (New York: Pocket Books, 1993).

7. Betty Medsger, *The Burglary: The Discovery of J. Edgar Hoover's Secret FBI* (New York: Knopf, 2014).

8. Tim Weiner, *Enemies: A History of the FBI* (New York: Random House, 2012), 171.

9. David McCullough, *Truman* (New York: Simon & Schuster, 1992), 972.

10. La Pasionara or "the Passion Flower" was a name given to the Spanish Civil War Communist leader Isidora Dolores Ibarruri Gomez.

11. Neil J. Welch and David W. Marston, *Inside Hoover's FBI: The Top Field Chief Reports* (New York: Doubleday, 1984).

12. Medsger, *The Burglary*.

13. Interview with Jennifer Dohrn, *Democracy Now!*, June 2, 2005, http://www.democracynow.org/2005/6/2/exclusive_jennifer_dohrn.

14. Dan Berger, *Outlaws of America: The Weather Underground and the Politics of Solidarity* (Oakland, CA: AK Press, 2006). Although the FBI accused the Weather Underground of some forty bombings from 1970 to 1978, many were in fact committed by imitators. The group took responsibility for twelve bombings. Dorhn was directly involved in one nonfatal attack: the March 2, 1971 bombing of the ladies restroom at the U.S. Senate. Susan Braudy, *Family Circle: The Boudins and the Aristocracy of the Left* (New York: Knopf, 2003).

15. Victor E. Kappeler and Gary W. Potter, *The Mythology of Crime and Criminal Justice* (Long Grove, IL: Waveland, 2004).

16. Ben Macintyre, *A Spy Among Friends: Kim Philby and the Great Betrayal* (New York: Crown, 2014).

17. T. J. English, *The Savage City: Race, Murder, and a Generation on the Edge* (New York: William Morrow, 2011), 381.

18. Chesimard was later convicted as an accomplice to the 1973 BLA murder of a policeman on the New Jersey Turnpike. She escaped from jail in 1979 and fled to Cuba, where she reportedly lives to this day.

19. Bryan Burrough, *Days of Rage: America's Radical Underground, the FBI, and the Forgotten Age of Revolutionary Violence* (New York: Penguin, 2015), 239.

20. Peter N. Bouckaert, "Bouckaert: Both Israel and Hezbollah Committing 'War Crimes,'" Council on Foreign Relations, August 7, 2006; Richard Cornwell,

"Africa Watch: Cote d'Ivoire; Asking for It," *African Security Review* 9 (2000): 80–93; Scheherezade Faramarzi, "Trauma of War Is Scarring Lebanese Children," *St. Louis Post Dispatch*, July 30, 2006; Human Rights Watch, *Afraid and Forgotten: Lawlessness, Rape, and Impunity in Western Côte d'Ivoire*, October 2010; Hamm letters and interviews with Sami Hassoun, August 11, September 30, and October 1, 2014; Avi Livneh and Pnina Langevitz, "Diagnostic and Treatment Concerns in Familial Mediterranean Fever," *Bailliere's Clinical Rheumatology* 14 (2000): 477–98; Donald G. McNeil, "Ivory Coast Coup Draws French Reply," *New York Times*, December 26, 1999; *USA v. Sami Samir Hassoun*, Criminal Complaint, September 20, 2010. Direct quotations from Hassoun are referenced separately.

21. Letter from Sami Hassoun to Mark Hamm, August 11, 2014.
22. Sami Hassoun letter to Judge Robert W. Gettleman, October 12, 2012.
23. Ibid.
24. Ibid.
25. Hassoun interview with Hamm, September 30, 2014.
26. Ibid.
27. Hassoun letter to Judge Gettleman.
28. Ibid., this quote and the preceding.
29. Hassoun interview with Hamm, September 30, 2014.
30. Ibid., this quote and the preceding.
31. Hassoun letter to Hamm, August 11, 2014.
32. Ibid.
33. Hassoun interview with Hamm, October 1, 2014.
34. Ibid.
35. Ibid.
36. Ibid.
37. Hassoun letter to Judge Gettleman.
38. Hassoun interview with Hamm, October 1, 2014.
39. *USA v. Sami Hassoun.*
40. Hassoun interview with Hamm, October 1, 2014.
41. *USA v. Sami Hassoun.*
42. Ibid., Government's Sentencing Memorandum, 6–7.
43. *USA v. Sami Hassoun.*
44. Ibid., this quote and the preceding.
45. Ibid., this quote and the preceding.
46. *USA v. Sami Hassoun*, Defense Memorandum, 20.
47. Quotes from *USA v. Sami Hassoun.*
48. Ibid.
49. Karen Greenberg quoted in "Center Data Used in Study of Accused Terrorist Sting Operation," MSNBC.com, March 25, 2014.

50. Trevor Aaronson, *The Terror Factory: Inside the FBI's Manufactured War on Terrorism* (Brooklyn, NY: ig, 2013).

Conclusion

1. Ramon Spaaij, *Understanding Lone Wolf Terrorism: Global Patterns, Motivations and Prevention* (New York: Springer, 2012).
2. Richard Hofstadter, "The Paranoid Style in American Politics," *Harper's Magazine*, November 1964, 92.
3. "To Rebut ISIS Propaganda, U.S. Posts Anti-Militant Message on Arab Social Media," *New York Times*, September 27, 2014.
4. "Foreigners from 80 Countries Are Joining ISIS on 'Unprecedented Scale,'" *Homeland Security News Wire*, October 31, 2014.
5. "July 4 Terror Plots Foiled, F.B.I. Chief Says," *New York Times*, July 10, 2015.
6. Marc Sageman, *Leaderless Jihad: Terror Networks in the Twenty-First Century* (Philadelphia: University of Pennsylvania Press, 2008), 159–60.
7. Simon Cottee, "The Challenge of Jihadi Cool," *Atlantic*, December 2015.
8. Michael Weiss and Hassan Hassan, *ISIS: Inside the Army of Terror* (New York: Regan Arts, 2015).
9. Jessica Stern and J. M. Berger, *ISIS* (New York: Ecco, 2015). Indeed, press reports indicate that Abdel Bary later defected from ISIS due to his disenchantment with the group.
10. Scott Atran, "The Youth Needs Values and Dreams." Testimony before the UN Security Council, April 23, 2015.
11. The program is similar to the well-known PREVENT initiative in the U.K.
12. "U.S. Trying to Fight Lure of ISIS for Young Muslims," *New York Times*, October 5, 2014.
13. Atran, "The Youth Needs Values and Dreams."
14. Arun Kundnani, *The Muslims Are Coming! Islamophobia, Extremism, and the Domestic War on Terror* (New York: Verso, 2014).
15. This is confirmed by research suggesting that the degree to which an individual identifies with an extremist may restrict his or her willingness to recognize that person's behavior as extreme. See Michael J. Williams, John G. Horgan, and William P. Evans, "The Critical Role of Friends in Networks for Countering Violent Extremism: Toward a Theory of Vicarious Help-Seeking," *Behavioral Sciences of Terrorism and Political Aggression*, 8 (2016): 45–65.
16. Trevor Aaronson, *The Terror Factory: Inside the FBI's Manufactured War on Terrorism* (Brooklyn, NY: ig, 2013), 226.

Index

Essex, Mark, 43, 45, 47, 62, 97–99, 156, 157
ethnography, 33
Europe: counterterrorism in, 233; lone wolf terrorism in, 17
Evans, Paul, 47
Evers, Medgar, 27–28, 38
executions, 204
extremist groups: affinity with, 26, 74–80, 150, 156–57, 158; identification with, 18–19
extremists, Islamic, 63
extremists, online contact with, 20
extremists, rightwing, 15, 51; and leaderless resistance, 17; radicalization of, 63; revival of, 52. *See also* white supremacists
Ezaegwula, Quinton, 184

Facebook, 142, 220, 222, 223
Familial Mediterranean Fever (FMF), 244, 256
family, as locus of radicalization, 63
Family Research Council (FRC) attack, 86–88
Farag, Reena Abdullah Ahmed, 177–78, 181
Farook, Syed Rizwan, 27, 66, 152
Fatah, al-, 151
FBI: COINTELPRO, 97, 209, 213, 214, 238, 259, 260; as enablers, 211, 218, 219, 228, 231; investigation of Abdo, 189; investigation of Bledsoe, 180, 187; investigation of Mateen, 118–19; mythmaking by, 238–40, 254, 256, 257, 258, 260; NEWKILL, 239; policies of, 232–33; public relations campaign, 237–38; and Pulse massacre, 119
FBI sting operations, 11–12; create and capture strategy, 219, 265; criticism

of, 207, 217; Crocker, 211–12, 216; described, 207; ethical implications of, 232–34; ethics of, 266; focus on Muslim Americans, 207, 212, 213, 260; Hassoun, 32–33, 250–59, 265, 266; implications of, 219; informants, 213–14; Mateen, 118, 229, 264, 265–66; Nafis, 219–28; need for new direction in, 234; Newburgh Four, 214; in post-9/11 era, 211–59; potential danger of, 208, 211; in pre-9/11 era, 208–11; radicalizing targets, 217–19; Smadi, 46, 215, 216; suggestions for, 264–65; targets, 215–19; Teausant, 229–32
Federal Emergency Management Agency (FEMA), 197
Federal Reserve Bank, attempted bombing of, 219, 225, 226–27
Federal Reserve System, 139
Feinstein, Dianne, 3, 4, 70
Felt, Mark, 238, 239
Ferdaus, Rezwan, 215, 218
Ferguson, Joseph, 168
Finton, Michael, 215
Finucane, Patrick, 155
firearms, 37, 43–44, 51–52, 120, 140, 153, 189, 190, 196. *See also* weaponry
First Amendment, 205
FISA (Foreign Intelligence Surveillance Act), 13, 70
Florida police shootings, 129–30
Flynt, Larry, 103, 105
Ford, Gerald, 38, 45, 99–102, 209–11
Foreign Intelligence Surveillance Act (FISA), 13, 70
Fort Hood, 21–22, 41, 46, 190. *See also* Hasan, Nidal
Fox News, 86, 133